藤崎 竜 (hi)

Here's *Hoshin Engi* volume 1.
Dakki, who's hugely popular, appears a lot in this volume. Nothing would make me, as the creator of *Hoshin Engi*, happier than for you to thoroughly enjoy this series on multiple levels! Plus, if you like it, it will give me the power to write on.

Ryu Fujisaki

Ryu Fujisaki's *Worlds* came in second place for the prestigious 40th Tezuka Award. His *Psycho +, Wāqwāq* and *Hoshin Engi* have all run in *Weekly Shonen Jump* magazine, and *Hoshin Engi* anime is available on DVD in Japan and North America. A lover of science fiction, literature and history, Fujisaki has made *Hoshin Engi* a mix of genres that truly showcases his amazing art and imagination.

HOSHIN ENGI VOL. 1
The SHONEN JUMP Manga Edition

STORY AND ART BY RYU FUJISAKI
Based on the novel *Hoshin Engi*, translated by Tsutomu Ano,
published by Kodansha Bunko

Translation & English Adaptation/Tomo Kimura
Touch-up Art & Lettering/Rina Mapa
Additional Touch-up/Josh Simpson
Design/Sean Lee
Editor/Joel Enos

Editor in Chief, Books/Alvin Lu
Editor in Chief, Magazines/Marc Weidenbaum
VP of Publishing Licensing/Rika Inouye
VP of Sales/Gonzalo Ferreyra
Sr. VP of Marketing/Liza Coppola
Publisher/Hyoe Narita

Printed in the U.S.A.

Published by VIZ Media, LLC
P.O. Box 77010
San Francisco, CA 94107

SHONEN JUMP Manga Edition
10 9 8 7 6 5 4 3 2 1
First printing, June 2007

THE WORLD'S
MOST POPULAR MANGA
www.viz.com
www.shonenjump.com

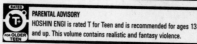

HOSHIN ENGI™

VOL. 1
BEGINNINGS

STORY AND ART BY
RYU FUJISAKI

VOL. 1
BEGINNINGS

CONTENTS

Hoshin Engi...

...is based on *The Creation of the Gods*, by Xu Zonglin, one of China's four classic fantasy novels.

CHAPTER 1: THE HOSHIN LIST

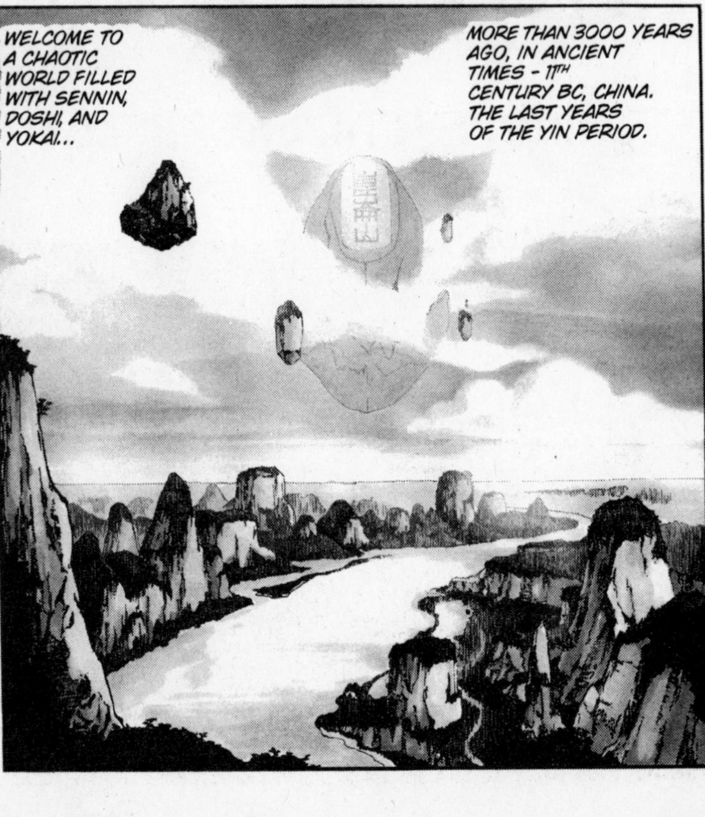
MORE THAN 3000 YEARS AGO, IN ANCIENT TIMES - 11TH CENTURY BC, CHINA. THE LAST YEARS OF THE YIN PERIOD.
WELCOME TO A CHAOTIC WORLD FILLED WITH SENNIN, DOSHI, AND YOKAI...

HOSHIN ENGI

Chapter 1: The Hoshin List

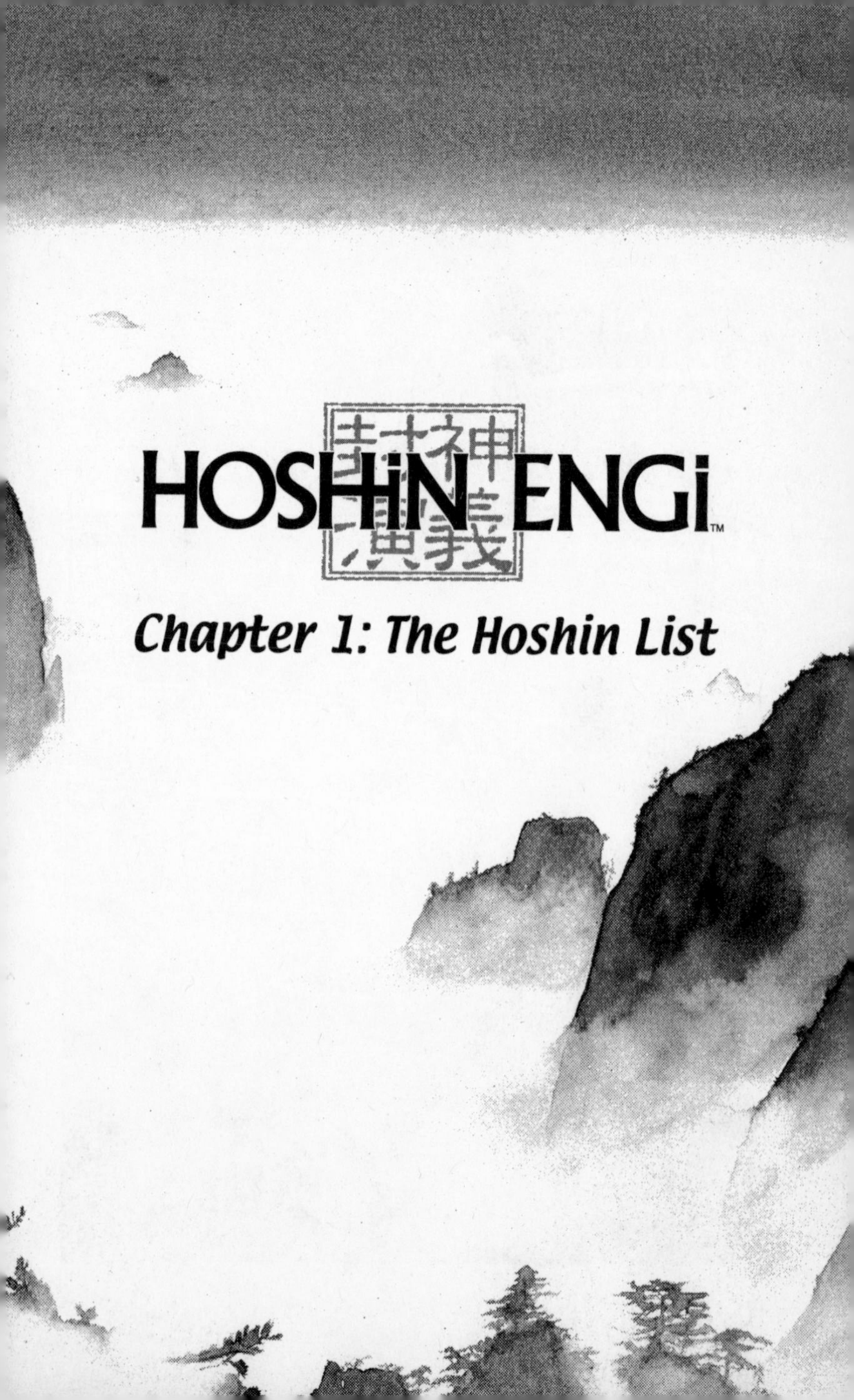

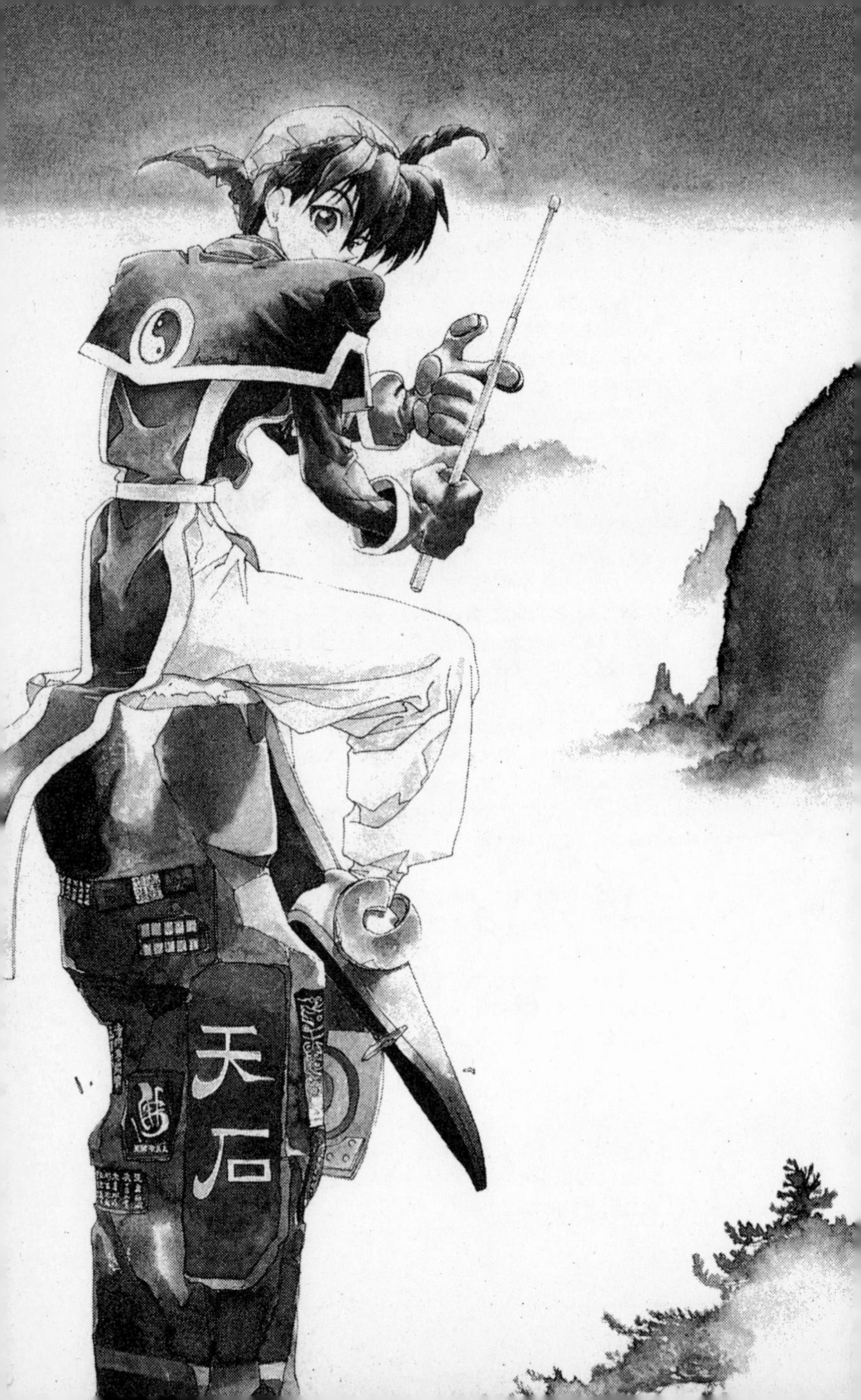
天石

You don't have to read it, but since there's a blank page:

Side Notes • I'm a self-professed sci-fi mangaka (yes, self-professed) originally, so I didn't think that I would be drawing a historical fantasy like this.
• I like science, psychology, and literature.
• Regarding history, I love ancient Rome — that was about it. I only knew about Chinese history from books written by Mr. Masamitsu Miyagitani, for example.
• So when it was decided that I would draw *Hoshin Engi*, I was a little worried. I read *Saiyuki (Journey to the West)* by Cheng'en Wu and *Suikoden*, based on *Shui Hu Zhuan (Outlaws of the Marsh)*, by Shi Nai'an. I even read specialized books like *The Mystery of the Fall of Ancient Chinese Dynasties*. And, I really got into Chinese history...

• Surprisingly, people of widely different ages seem to be reading this manga, from grade schoolers to dads and moms. I'm very happy. I was aiming to draw such a manga, so this gives me power. I'll do my best.

• And, I always write this: Thank you very much for lots of letters.
• I read them when I'm feeling "I don't want to work anymore!!" They strengthen my heart, and I feel that "No, I've got to do it!!" Letters are energy drinks for my soul!!

• To finish this off...
• In this manga, I made Taikobo's real name "Ryobo." This is because I read the works of the great Rohan Koda sensei and found them very influential.

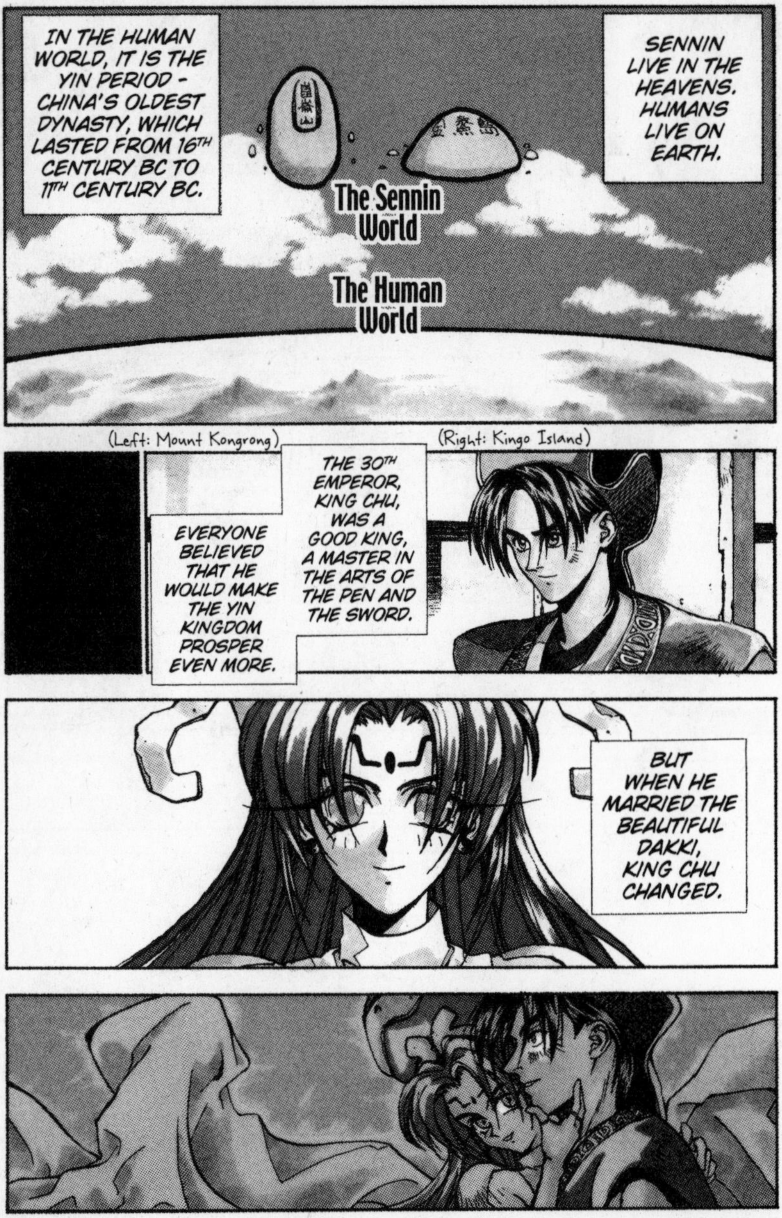
SENNIN LIVE IN THE HEAVENS. HUMANS LIVE ON EARTH.
IN THE HUMAN WORLD, IT IS THE YIN PERIOD - CHINA'S OLDEST DYNASTY, WHICH LASTED FROM 16TH CENTURY BC TO 11TH CENTURY BC.
The Sennin World
The Human World
(Right: Kingo Island)
(Left: Mount Kongrong)
THE 30TH EMPEROR, KING CHU, WAS A GOOD KING, A MASTER IN THE ARTS OF THE PEN AND THE SWORD.
EVERYONE BELIEVED THAT HE WOULD MAKE THE YIN KINGDOM PROSPER EVEN MORE.
BUT WHEN HE MARRIED THE BEAUTIFUL DAKKI, KING CHU CHANGED.

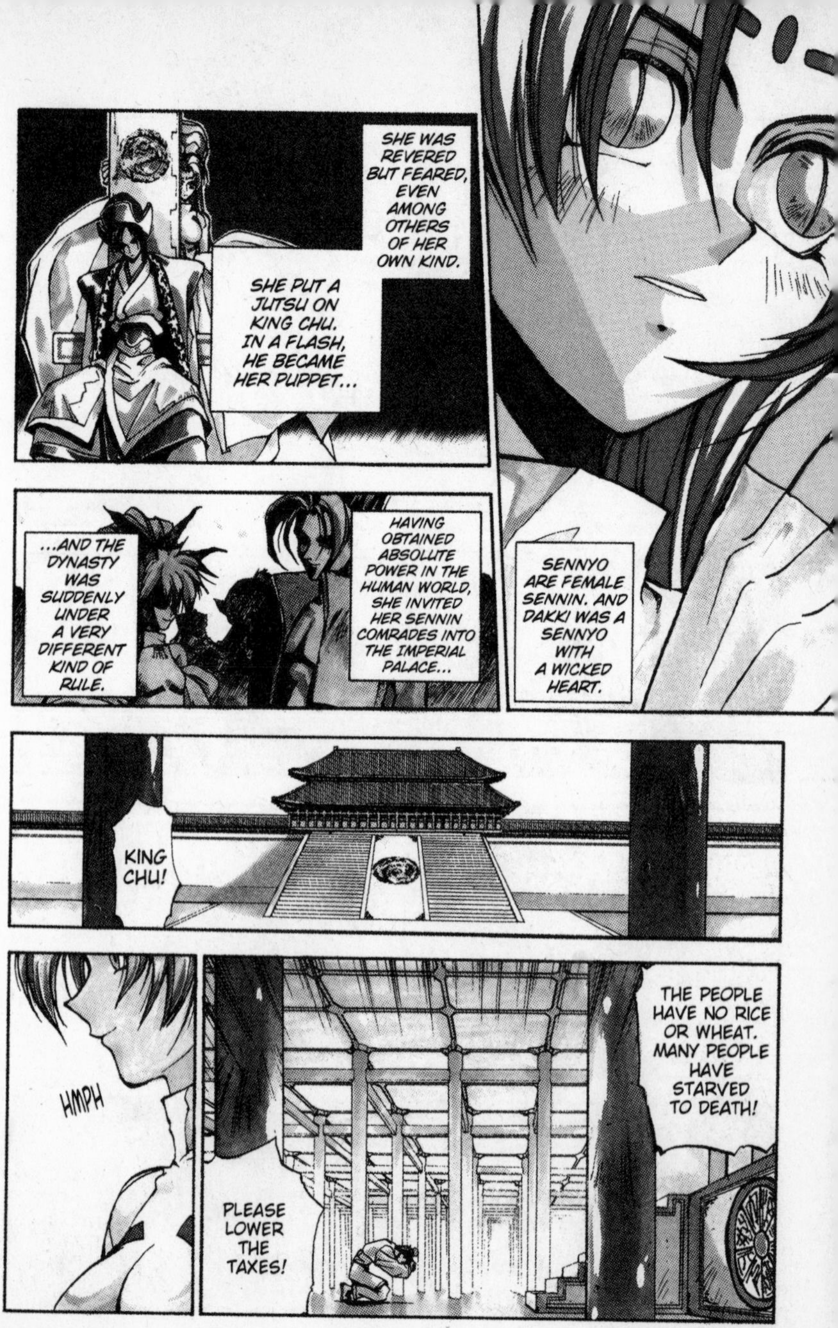

SENNYO ARE FEMALE SENNIN. AND DAKKI WAS A SENNYO WITH A WICKED HEART.
SHE WAS REVERED BUT FEARED, EVEN AMONG OTHERS OF HER OWN KIND.
SHE PUT A JUTSU ON KING CHU. IN A FLASH, HE BECAME HER PUPPET...
HAVING OBTAINED ABSOLUTE POWER IN THE HUMAN WORLD, SHE INVITED HER SENNIN COMRADES INTO THE IMPERIAL PALACE...
...AND THE DYNASTY WAS SUDDENLY UNDER A VERY DIFFERENT KIND OF RULE.
KING CHU!
THE PEOPLE HAVE NO RICE OR WHEAT. MANY PEOPLE HAVE STARVED TO DEATH!
PLEASE LOWER THE TAXES!
HMPH

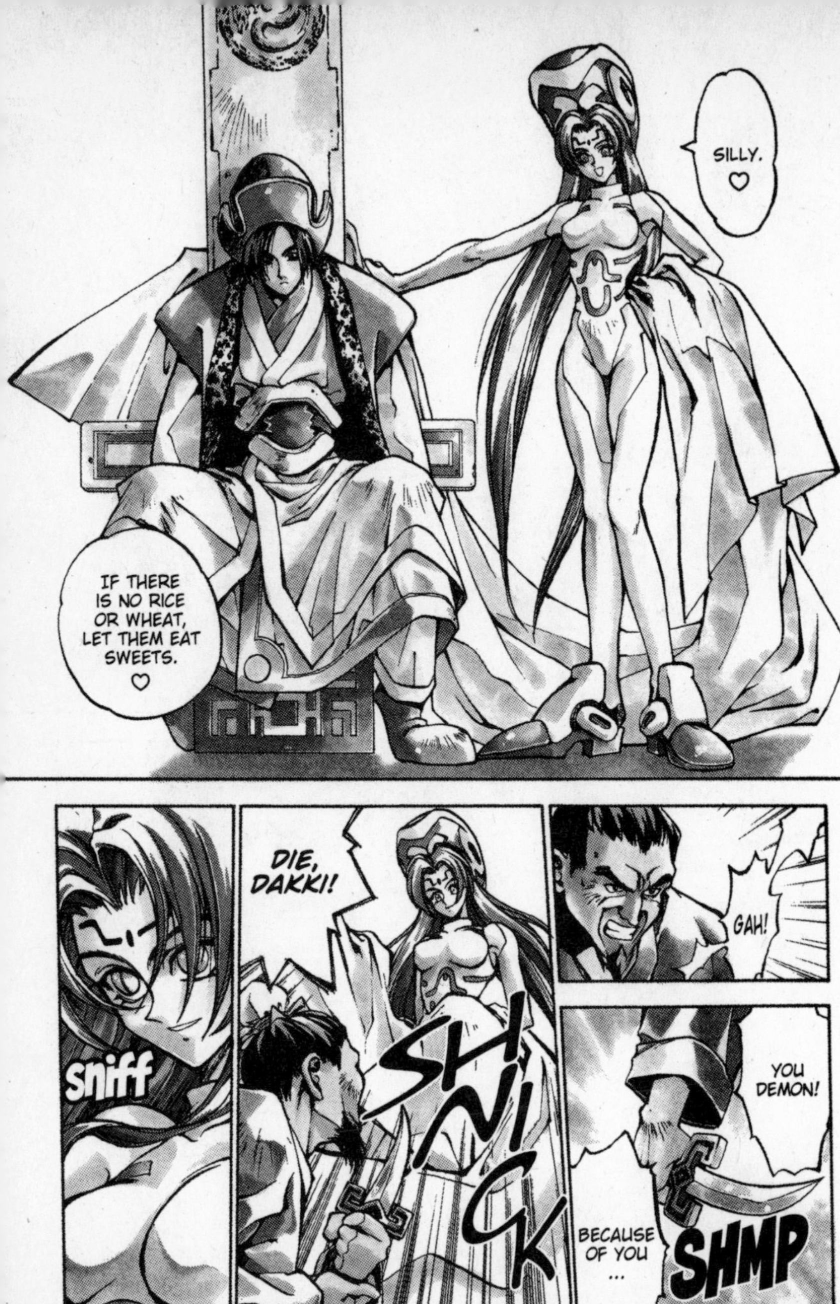
SILLY. ♡
IF THERE IS NO RICE OR WHEAT, LET THEM EAT SWEETS. ♡
GAH!
YOU DEMON!
BECAUSE OF YOU ...
SHMP
DIE, DAKKI!
SHNICK
sniff

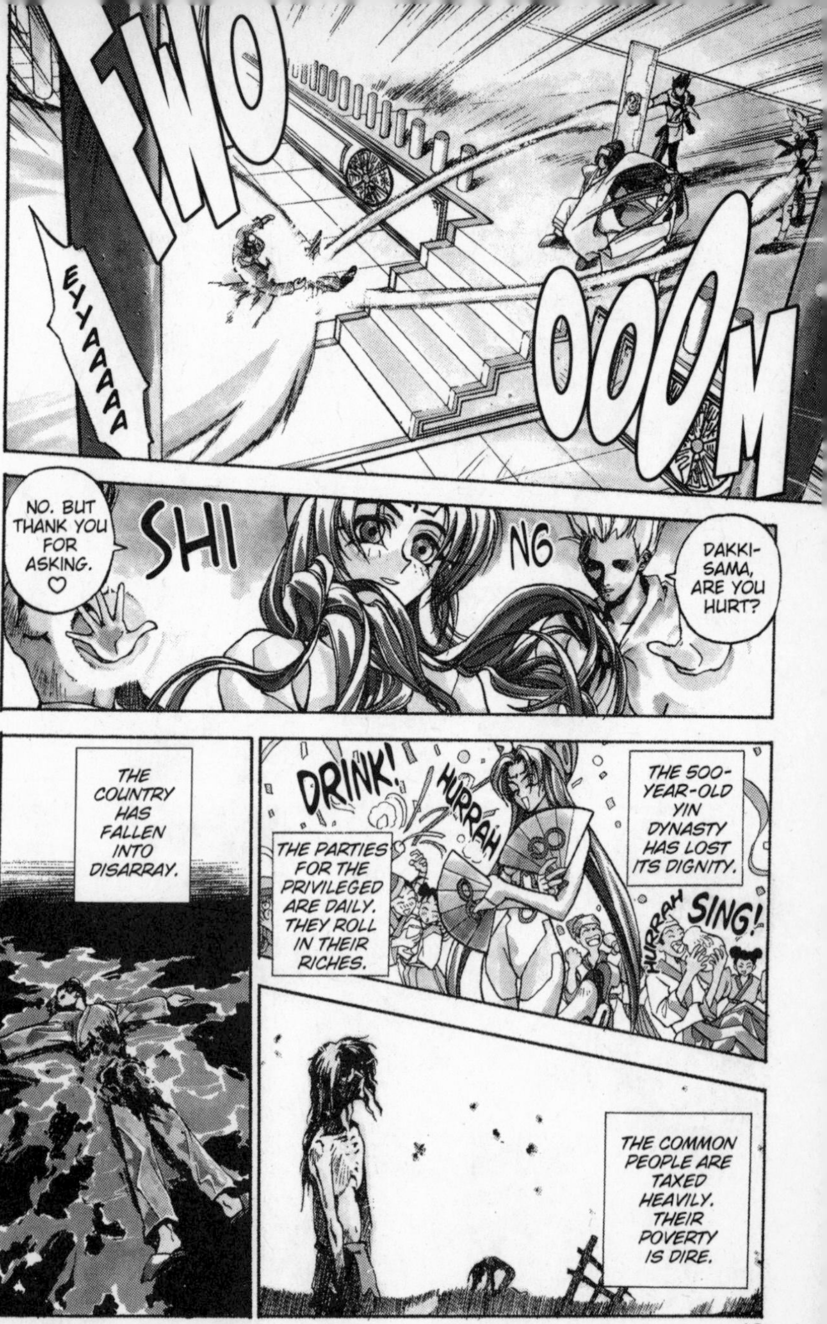
TWO
OOOOM
EYYAAAAAA
DAKKI-SAMA, ARE YOU HURT?
SHING
NO. BUT THANK YOU FOR ASKING. ♡
THE 500-YEAR-OLD YIN DYNASTY HAS LOST ITS DIGNITY.
SING!
HURRAH
HURRAH
DRINK!
THE PARTIES FOR THE PRIVILEGED ARE DAILY. THEY ROLL IN THEIR RICHES.
THE COMMON PEOPLE ARE TAXED HEAVILY. THEIR POVERTY IS DIRE.
THE COUNTRY HAS FALLEN INTO DISARRAY.

READ THIS WAY

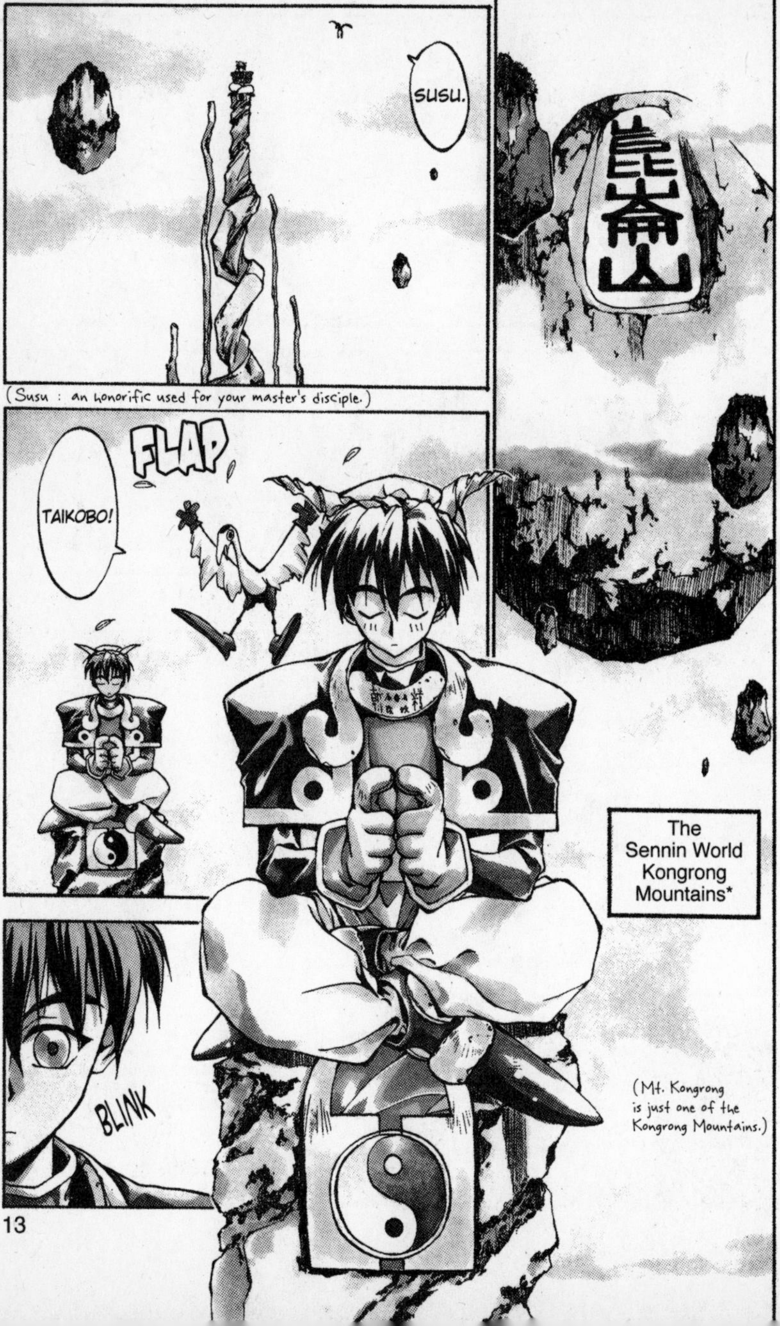
崑崙山
The Sennin World Kongrong Mountains*
(Mt. Kongrong is just one of the Kongrong Mountains.)
SUSU.
(Susu : an honorific used for your master's disciple.)
FLAP
TAIKOBO!
BLINK

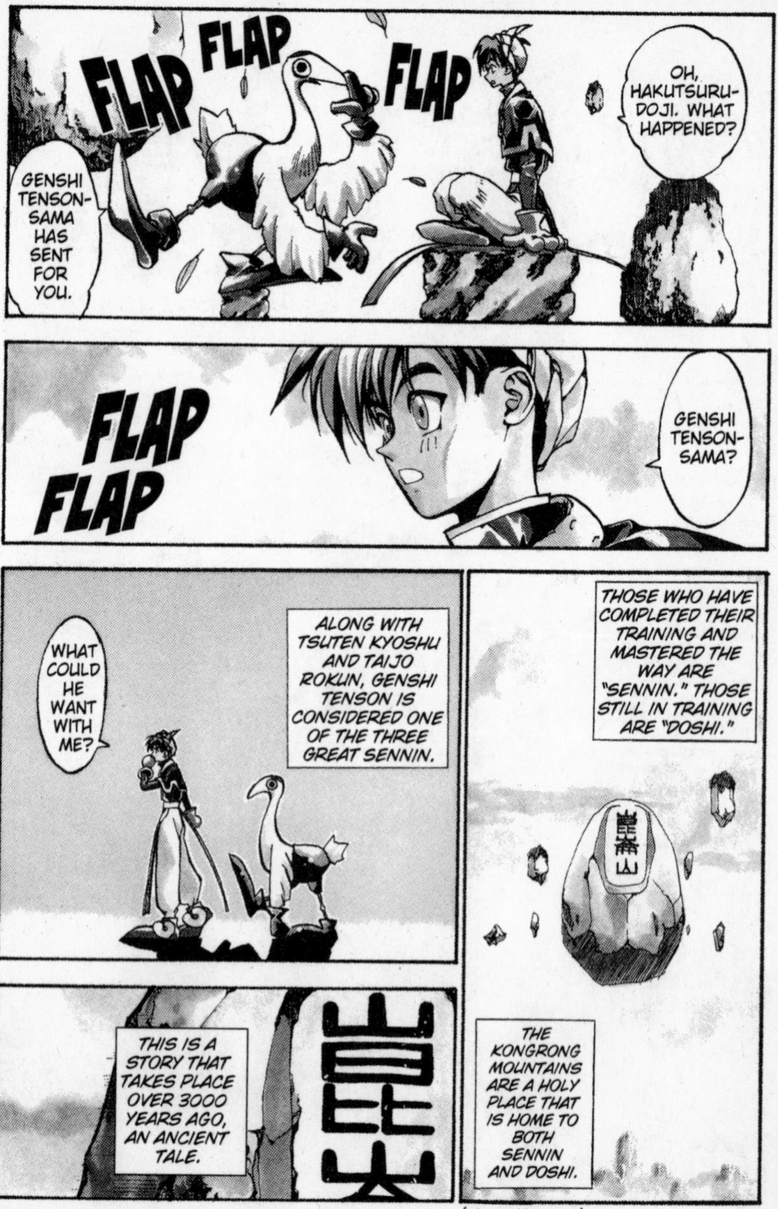
OH, HAKUTSURU-DOJI. WHAT HAPPENED?
FLAP
FLAP
FLAP
GENSHI TENSON-SAMA HAS SENT FOR YOU.
GENSHI TENSON-SAMA?
FLAP FLAP
THOSE WHO HAVE COMPLETED THEIR TRAINING AND MASTERED THE WAY ARE "SENNIN." THOSE STILL IN TRAINING ARE "DOSHI."
THE KONGRONG MOUNTAINS ARE A HOLY PLACE THAT IS HOME TO BOTH SENNIN AND DOSHI.
ALONG WITH TSUTEN KYOSHU AND TAIJO ROKUN, GENSHI TENSON IS CONSIDERED ONE OF THE THREE GREAT SENNIN.
WHAT COULD HE WANT WITH ME?
THIS IS A STORY THAT TAKES PLACE OVER 3000 YEARS AGO, AN ANCIENT TALE.

(Mount Kongrong)

READ THIS WAY

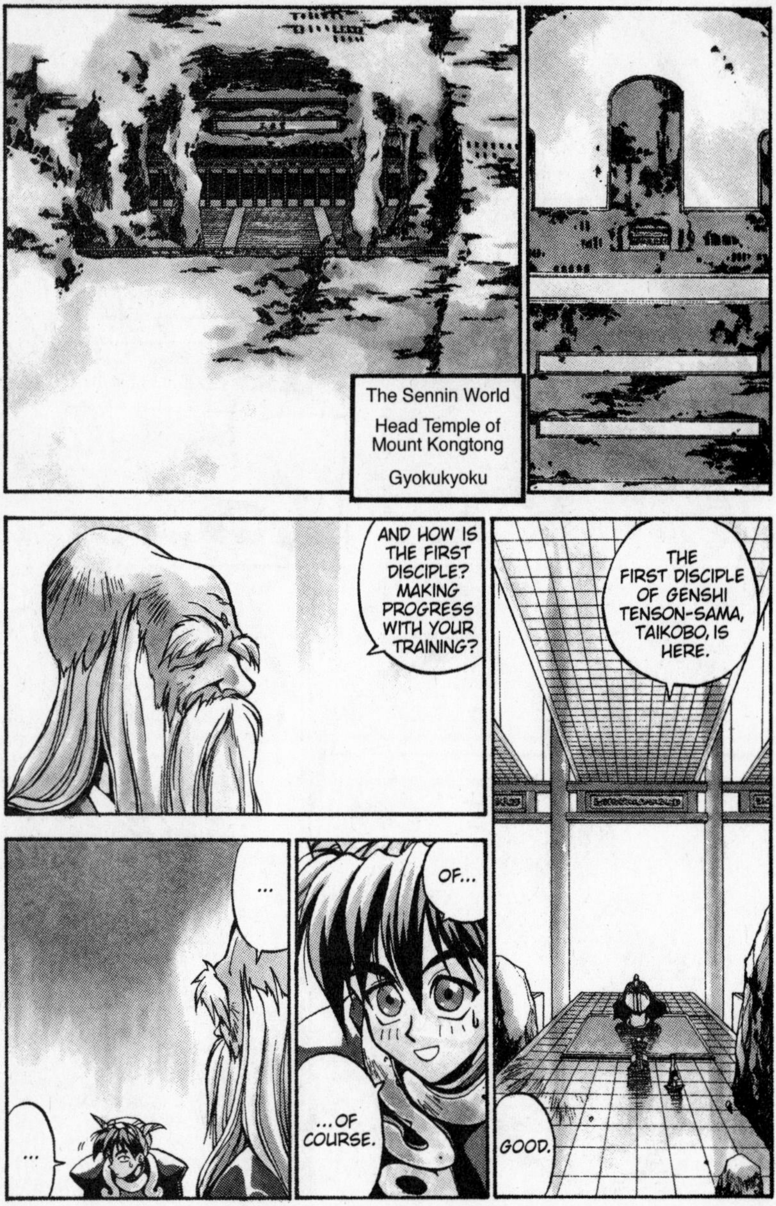

The Sennin World
Head Temple of Mount Kongtong
Gyokukyoku
THE FIRST DISCIPLE OF GENSHI TENSON-SAMA, TAIKOBO, IS HERE.
GOOD.
AND HOW IS THE FIRST DISCIPLE? MAKING PROGRESS WITH YOUR TRAINING?
OF...
...OF COURSE.
...
...

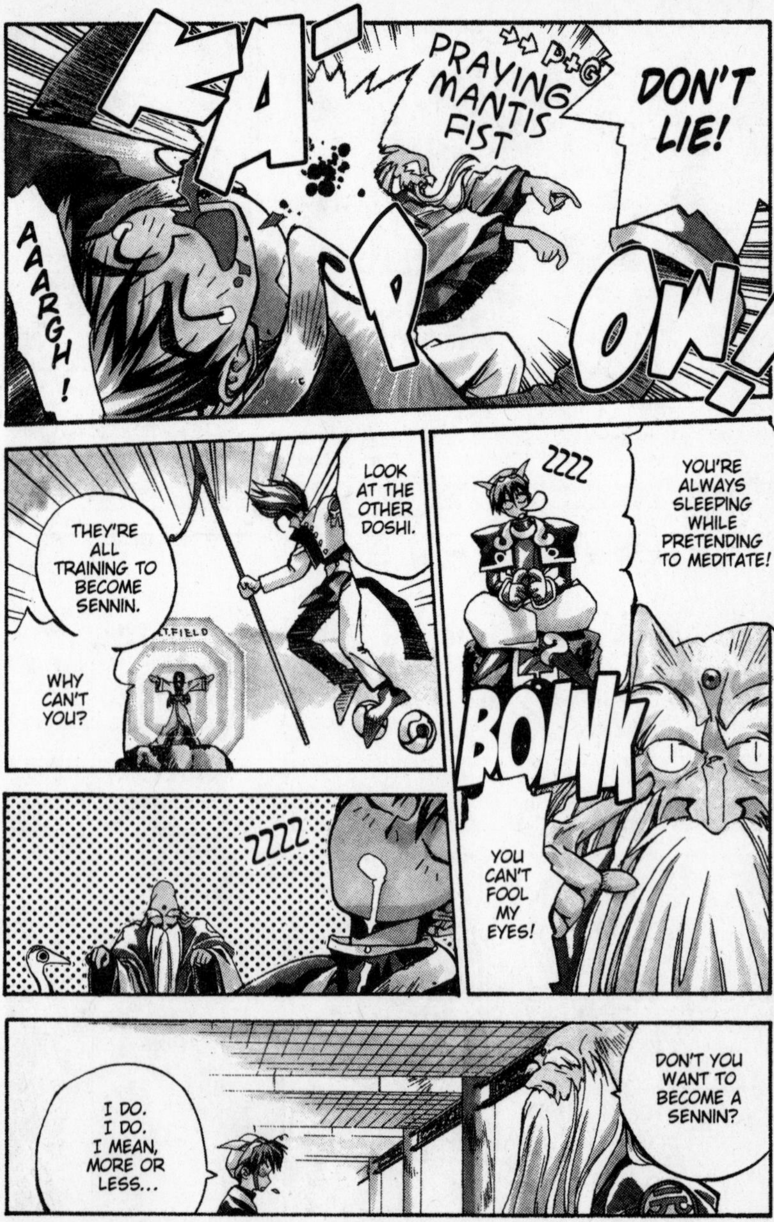
DON'T LIE!
P+G
PRAYING MANTIS FIST
KA-POW!
AAARGH!
YOU'RE ALWAYS SLEEPING WHILE PRETENDING TO MEDITATE!
ZZZZ
BOINK
YOU CAN'T FOOL MY EYES!
LOOK AT THE OTHER DOSHI.
THEY'RE ALL TRAINING TO BECOME SENNIN.
WHY CAN'T YOU?
ZZZZ
DON'T YOU WANT TO BECOME A SENNIN?
I DO. I DO. I MEAN, MORE OR LESS...

READ THIS WAY

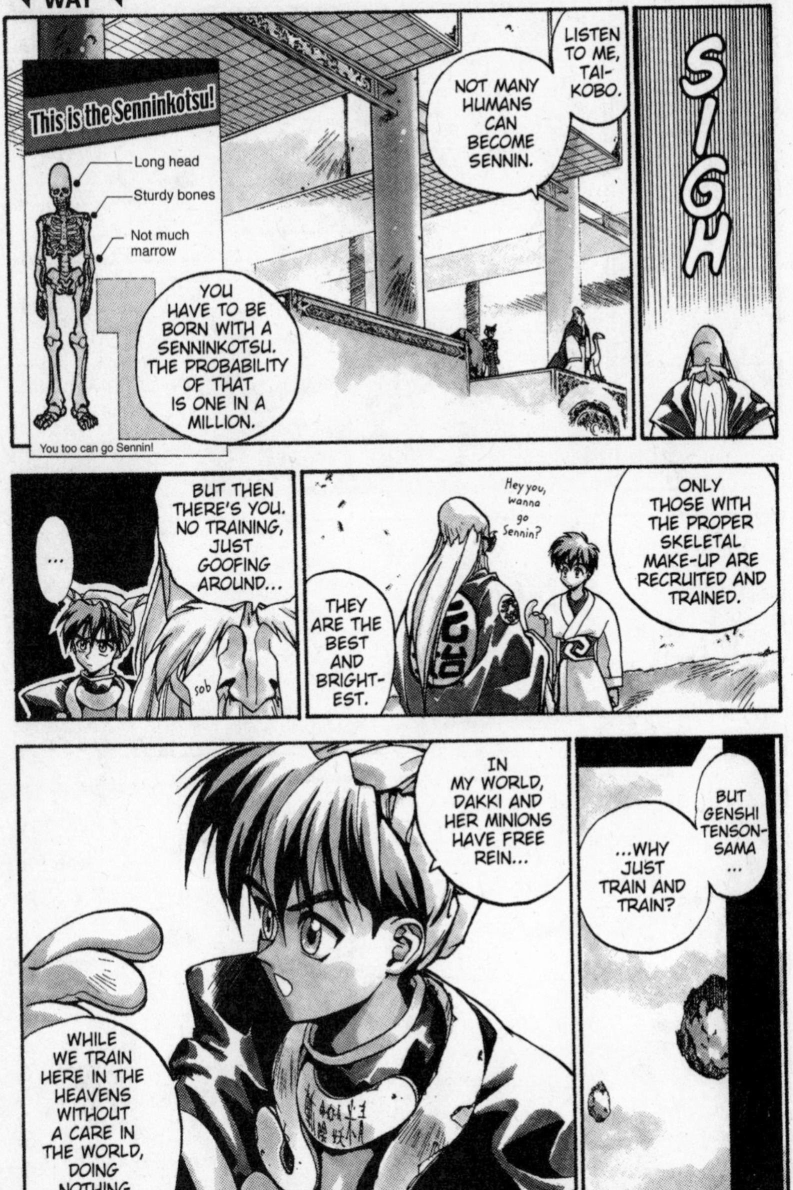
SIGH
LISTEN TO ME, TAI-KOBO.
NOT MANY HUMANS CAN BECOME SENNIN.
YOU HAVE TO BE BORN WITH A SENNINKOTSU. THE PROBABILITY OF THAT IS ONE IN A MILLION.
This is the Senninkotsu!
Long head
Sturdy bones
Not much marrow
You too can go Sennin!
ONLY THOSE WITH THE PROPER SKELETAL MAKE-UP ARE RECRUITED AND TRAINED.
Hey you, wanna go Sennin?
THEY ARE THE BEST AND BRIGHT-EST.
BUT THEN THERE'S YOU. NO TRAINING, JUST GOOFING AROUND...
...
sob
BUT GENSHI TENSON-SAMA...
...WHY JUST TRAIN AND TRAIN?
IN MY WORLD, DAKKI AND HER MINIONS HAVE FREE REIN...
WHILE WE TRAIN HERE IN THE HEAVENS WITHOUT A CARE IN THE WORLD, DOING NOTHING.

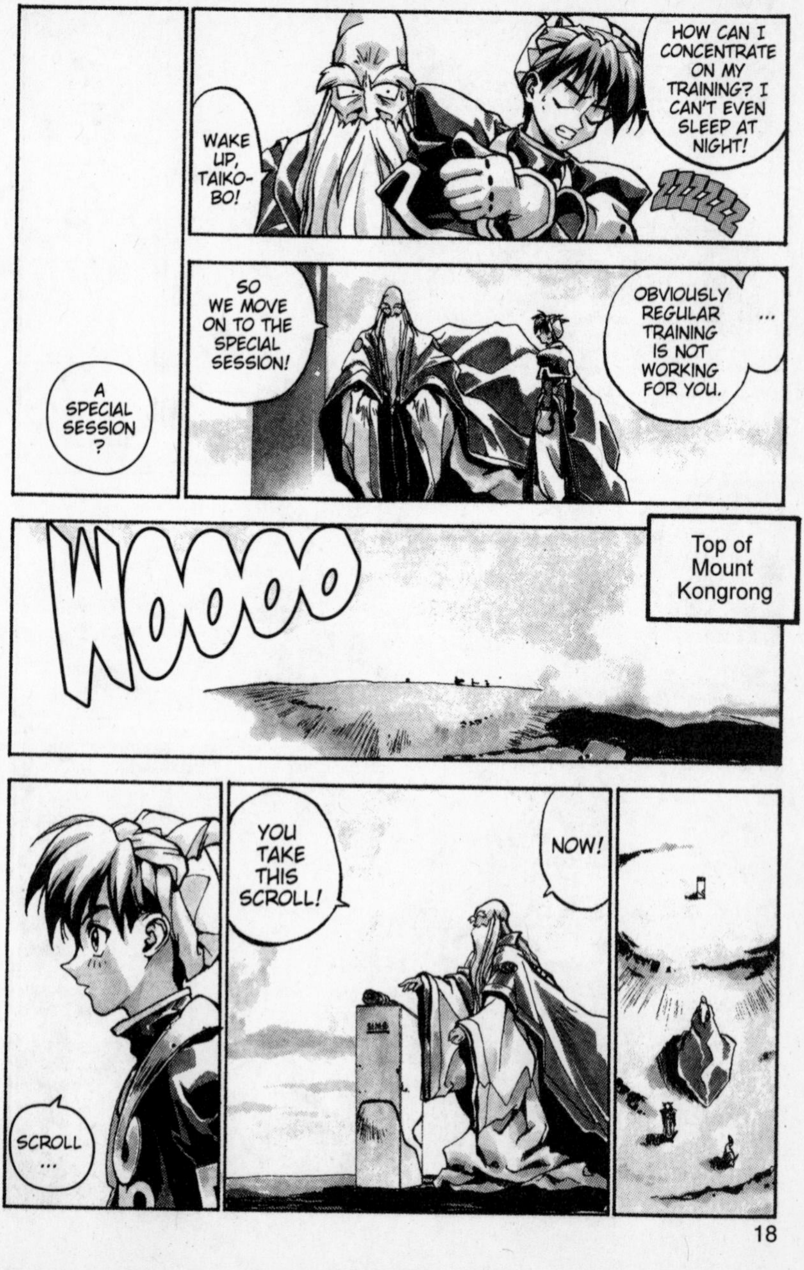
HOW CAN I CONCENTRATE ON MY TRAINING? I CAN'T EVEN SLEEP AT NIGHT!
ZZZZZZ
WAKE UP, TAIKO-BO!
...
OBVIOUSLY REGULAR TRAINING IS NOT WORKING FOR YOU.
SO WE MOVE ON TO THE SPECIAL SESSION!
A SPECIAL SESSION?
Top of Mount Kongrong
WOOOO
NOW!
YOU TAKE THIS SCROLL!
SCROLL...

READ THIS WAY

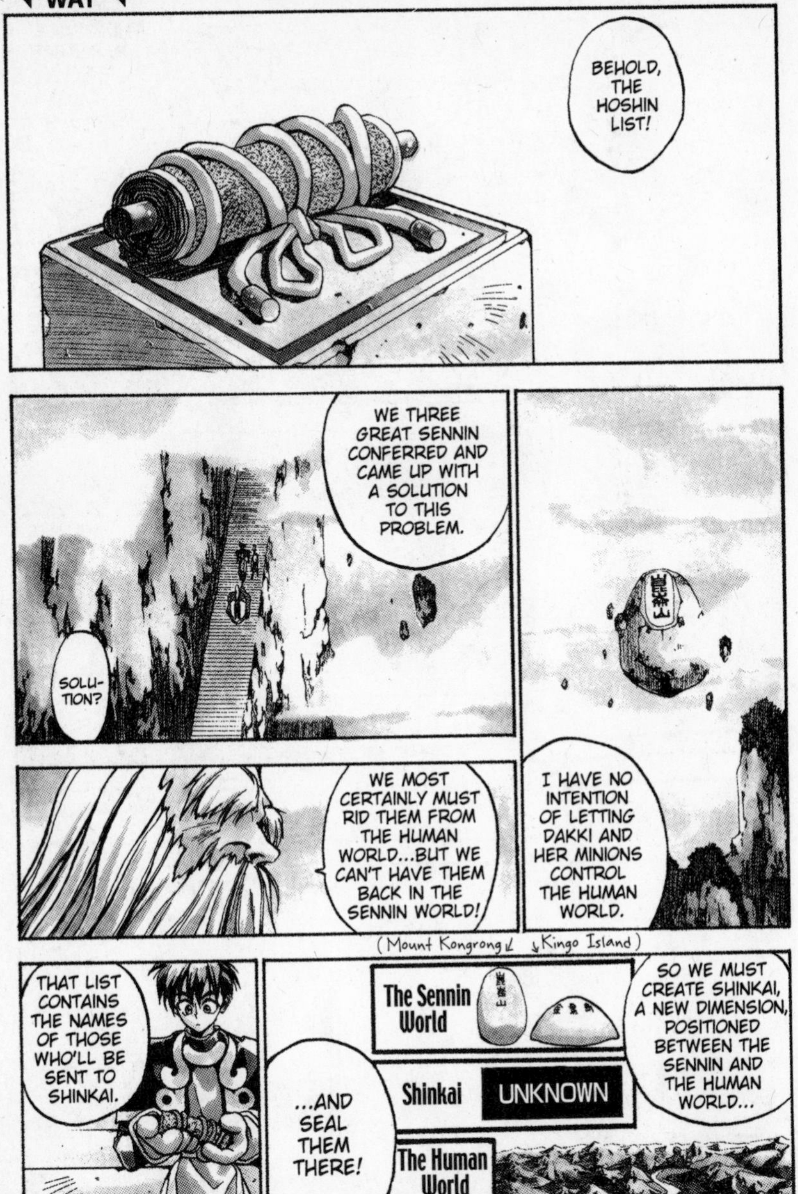
BEHOLD, THE HOSHIN LIST!
I HAVE NO INTENTION OF LETTING DAKKI AND HER MINIONS CONTROL THE HUMAN WORLD.
WE THREE GREAT SENNIN CONFERRED AND CAME UP WITH A SOLUTION TO THIS PROBLEM.
SOLU-TION?
WE MOST CERTAINLY MUST RID THEM FROM THE HUMAN WORLD...BUT WE CAN'T HAVE THEM BACK IN THE SENNIN WORLD!
(Mount Kongrong ↙ ↓Kingo Island)
SO WE MUST CREATE SHINKAI, A NEW DIMENSION, POSITIONED BETWEEN THE SENNIN AND THE HUMAN WORLD...
The Sennin World
Shinkai
UNKNOWN
The Human World
...AND SEAL THEM THERE!
THAT LIST CONTAINS THE NAMES OF THOSE WHO'LL BE SENT TO SHINKAI.

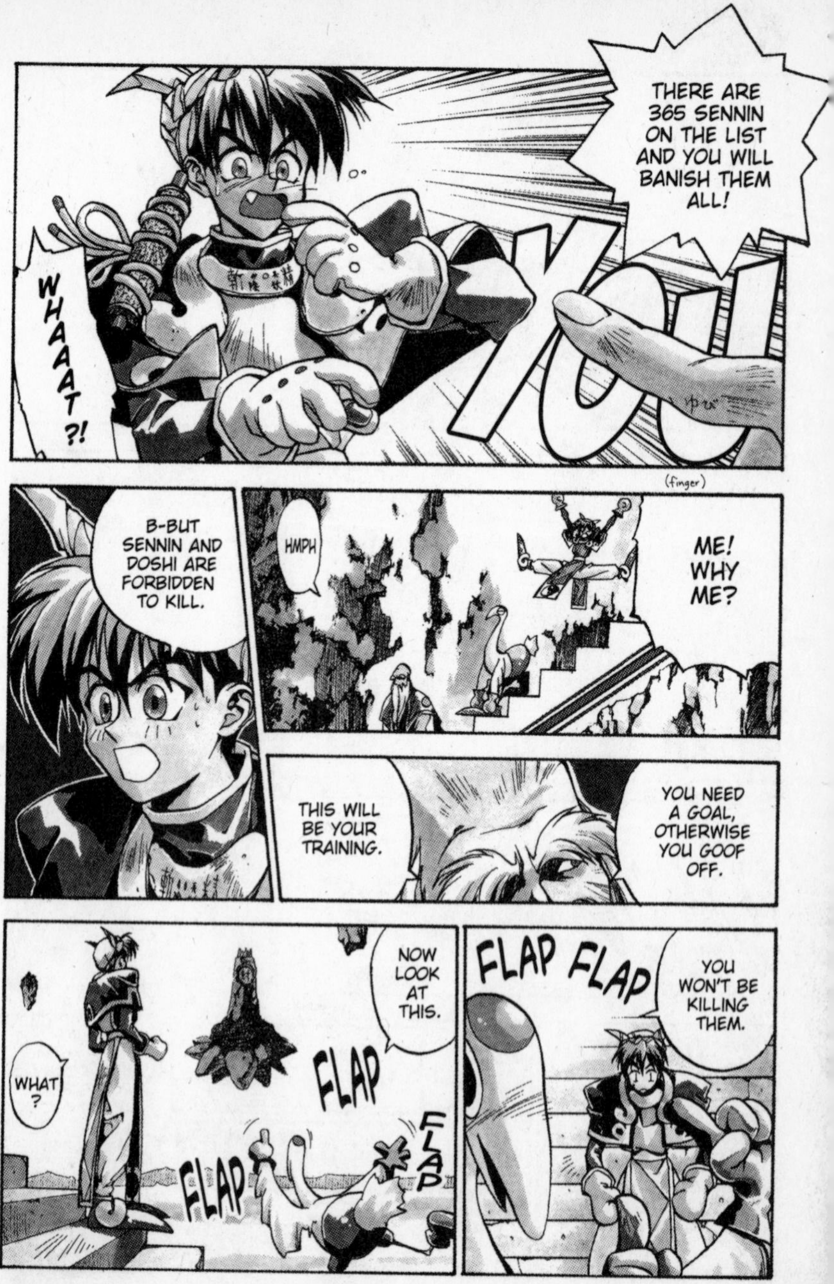
THERE ARE 365 SENNIN ON THE LIST AND YOU WILL BANISH THEM ALL!
YOU
WHAAAAT?!
(finger)
ME! WHY ME?
HMPH
YOU NEED A GOAL, OTHERWISE YOU GOOF OFF.
THIS WILL BE YOUR TRAINING.
B-BUT SENNIN AND DOSHI ARE FORBIDDEN TO KILL.
YOU WON'T BE KILLING THEM.
FLAP FLAP
NOW LOOK AT THIS.
FLAP
FLAP
FLAP
WHAT?

READ THIS WAY

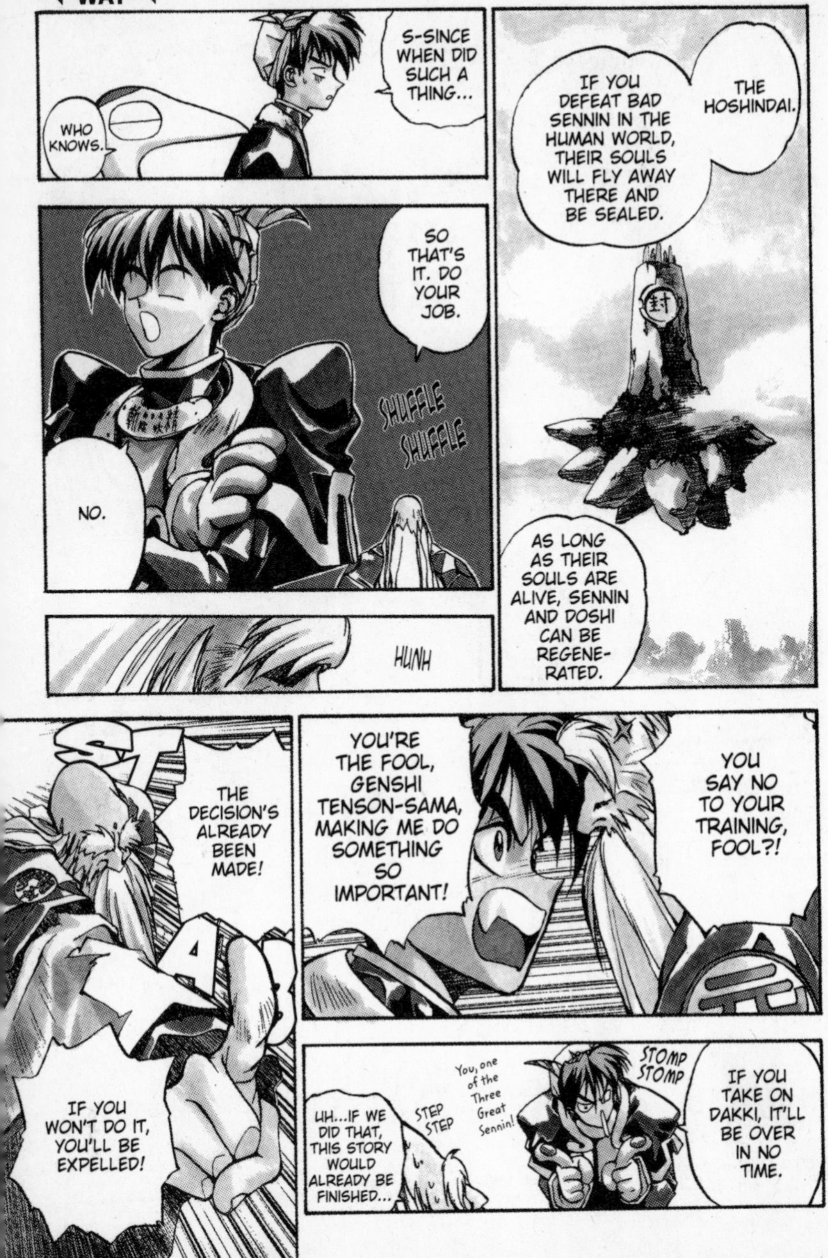
THE HOSHINDAI.
IF YOU DEFEAT BAD SENNIN IN THE HUMAN WORLD, THEIR SOULS WILL FLY AWAY THERE AND BE SEALED.
AS LONG AS THEIR SOULS ARE ALIVE, SENNIN AND DOSHI CAN BE REGENERATED.
S-SINCE WHEN DID SUCH A THING...
WHO KNOWS.
SO THAT'S IT. DO YOUR JOB.
SHUFFLE SHUFFLE
NO.
HUNH
YOU SAY NO TO YOUR TRAINING, FOOL?!
YOU'RE THE FOOL, GENSHI TENSON-SAMA, MAKING ME DO SOMETHING SO IMPORTANT!
IF YOU TAKE ON DAKKI, IT'LL BE OVER IN NO TIME.
STOMP STOMP
You, one of the Three Great Sennin!
STEP STEP
UH...IF WE DID THAT, THIS STORY WOULD ALREADY BE FINISHED...
ST
THE DECISION'S ALREADY BEEN MADE!
A
IF YOU WON'T DO IT, YOU'LL BE EXPELLED!

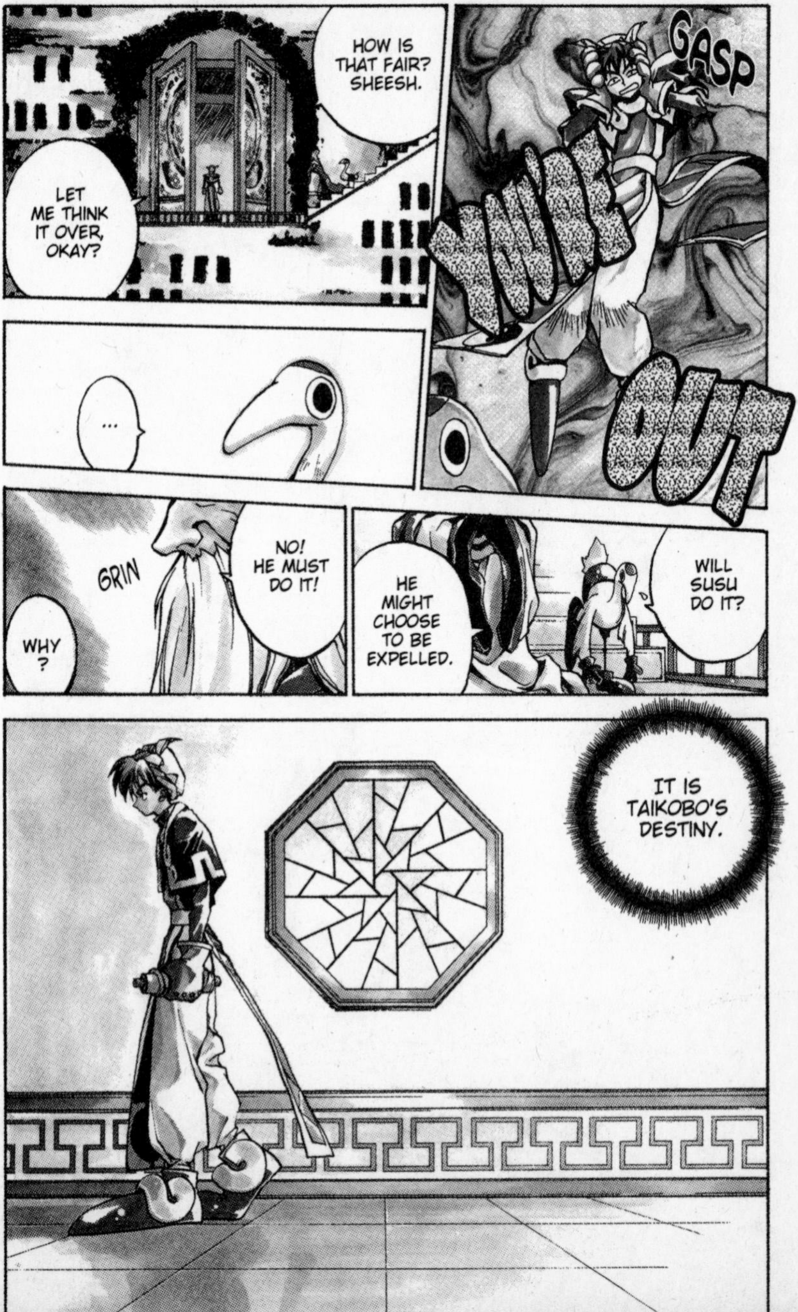
GASP
YOU'RE OUT
HOW IS THAT FAIR? SHEESH.
LET ME THINK IT OVER, OKAY?
...
WILL SUSU DO IT?
HE MIGHT CHOOSE TO BE EXPELLED.
NO! HE MUST DO IT!
GRIN
WHY?
IT IS TAIKOBO'S DESTINY.

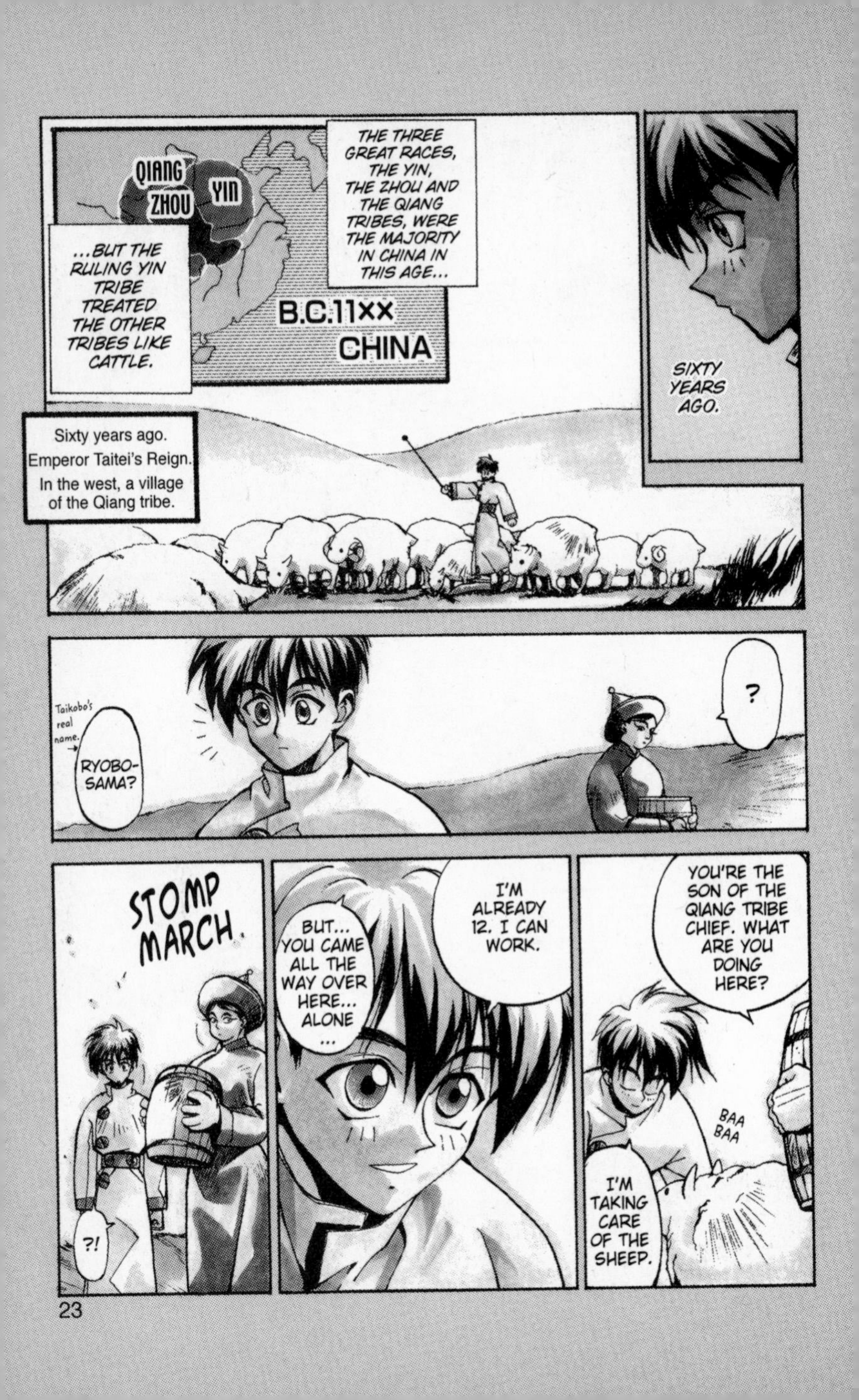
SIXTY YEARS AGO.
THE THREE GREAT RACES, THE YIN, THE ZHOU AND THE QIANG TRIBES, WERE THE MAJORITY IN CHINA IN THIS AGE...
QIANG
ZHOU
YIN
B.C.11××
CHINA
...BUT THE RULING YIN TRIBE TREATED THE OTHER TRIBES LIKE CATTLE.
Sixty years ago.
Emperor Taitei's Reign.
In the west, a village of the Qiang tribe.
?
Taikobo's real name.
RYOBO-SAMA?
YOU'RE THE SON OF THE QIANG TRIBE CHIEF. WHAT ARE YOU DOING HERE?
BAA BAA
I'M TAKING CARE OF THE SHEEP.
I'M ALREADY 12. I CAN WORK.
BUT... YOU CAME ALL THE WAY OVER HERE... ALONE ...
STOMP
MARCH
?!

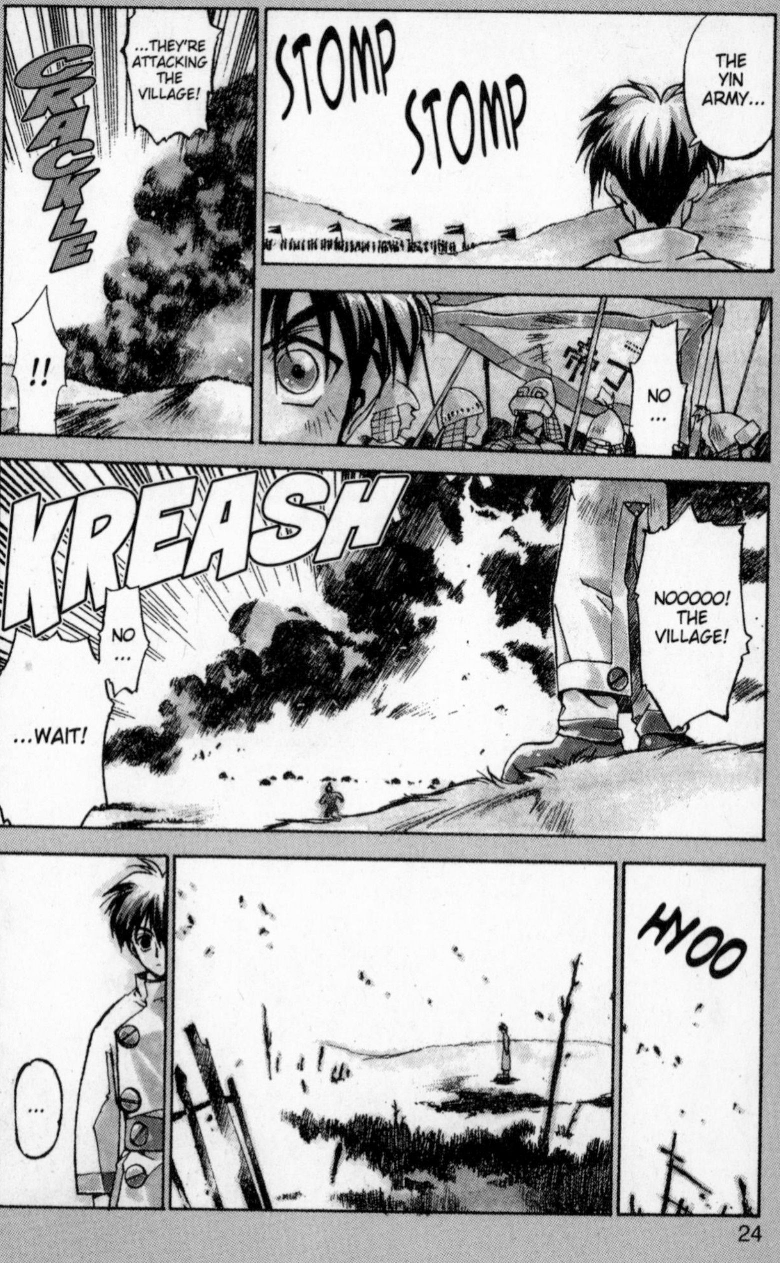
THE YIN ARMY...
STOMP
STOMP
NO ...
...THEY'RE ATTACKING THE VILLAGE!
CRACKLE
!!
NOOOOO! THE VILLAGE!
KREASH
NO ...
...WAIT!
HYOO
...

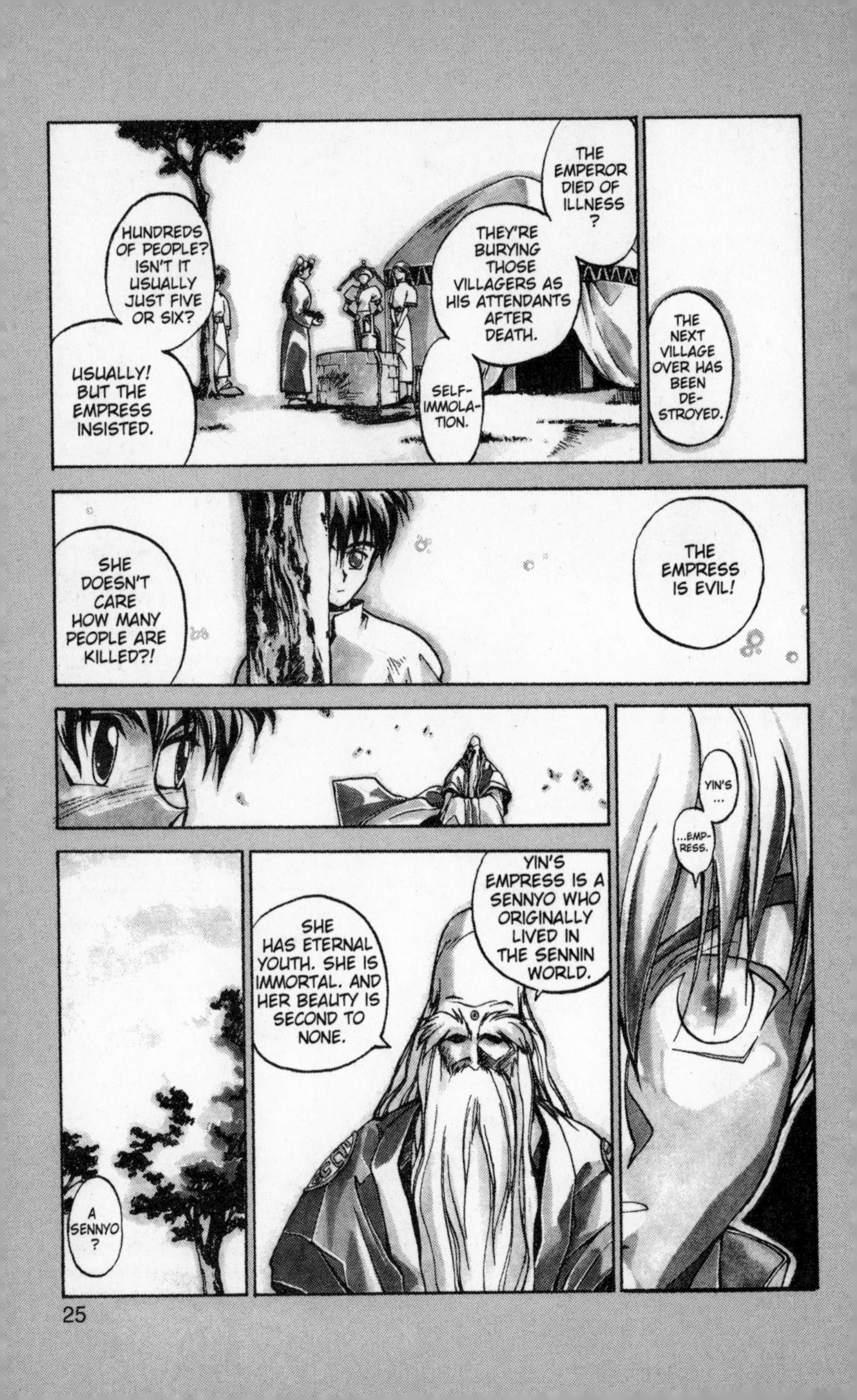
THE NEXT VILLAGE OVER HAS BEEN DE-STROYED.
THE EMPEROR DIED OF ILLNESS?
THEY'RE BURYING THOSE VILLAGERS AS HIS ATTENDANTS AFTER DEATH.
SELF-IMMOLA-TION.
HUNDREDS OF PEOPLE? ISN'T IT USUALLY JUST FIVE OR SIX?
USUALLY! BUT THE EMPRESS INSISTED.
THE EMPRESS IS EVIL!
SHE DOESN'T CARE HOW MANY PEOPLE ARE KILLED?!
YIN'S...
...EMP-RESS.
YIN'S EMPRESS IS A SENNYO WHO ORIGINALLY LIVED IN THE SENNIN WORLD.
SHE HAS ETERNAL YOUTH. SHE IS IMMORTAL. AND HER BEAUTY IS SECOND TO NONE.
A SENNYO?

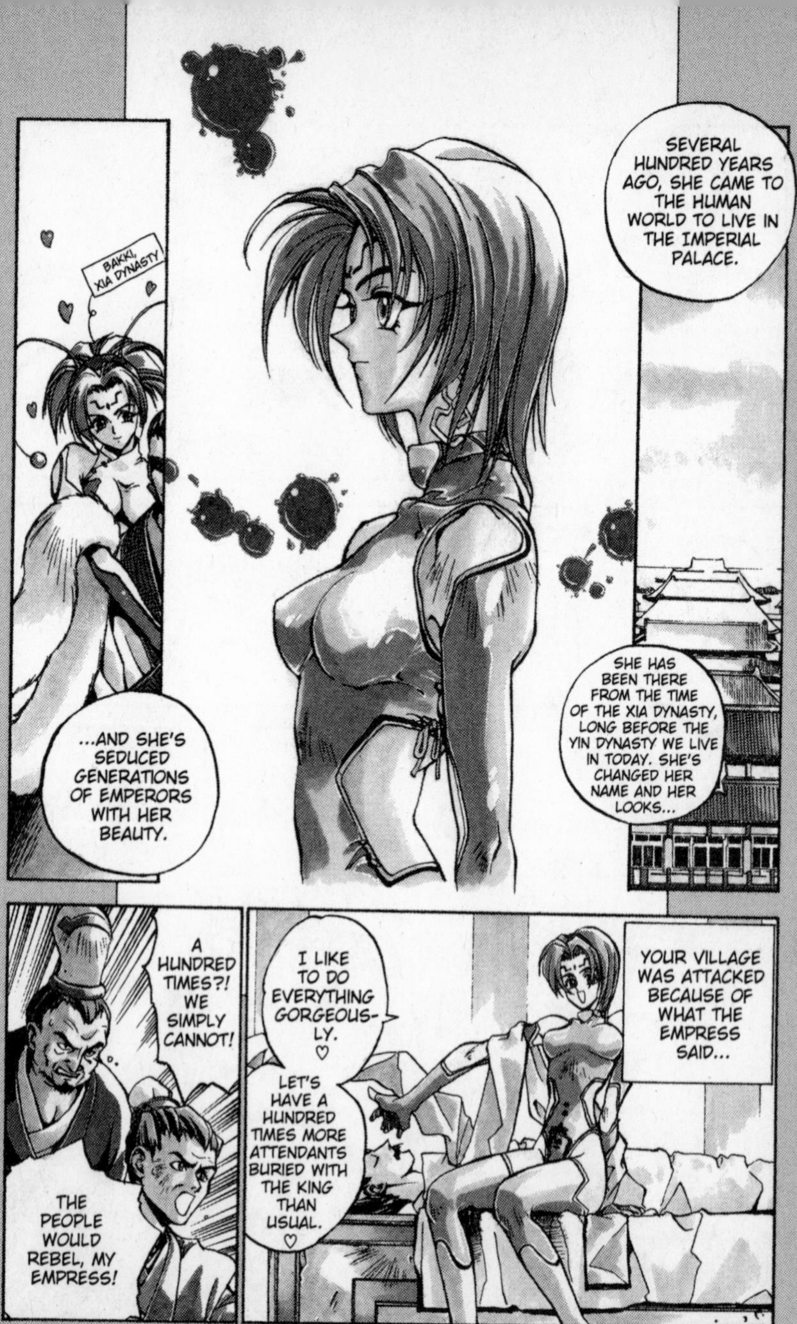

SEVERAL HUNDRED YEARS AGO, SHE CAME TO THE HUMAN WORLD TO LIVE IN THE IMPERIAL PALACE.
SHE HAS BEEN THERE FROM THE TIME OF THE XIA DYNASTY, LONG BEFORE THE YIN DYNASTY WE LIVE IN TODAY. SHE'S CHANGED HER NAME AND HER LOOKS...
BAKKI, XIA DYNASTY
...AND SHE'S SEDUCED GENERATIONS OF EMPERORS WITH HER BEAUTY.
YOUR VILLAGE WAS ATTACKED BECAUSE OF WHAT THE EMPRESS SAID...
I LIKE TO DO EVERYTHING GORGEOUS-LY. ♡
LET'S HAVE A HUNDRED TIMES MORE ATTENDANTS BURIED WITH THE KING THAN USUAL. ♡
A HUNDRED TIMES?! WE SIMPLY CANNOT!
THE PEOPLE WOULD REBEL, MY EMPRESS!

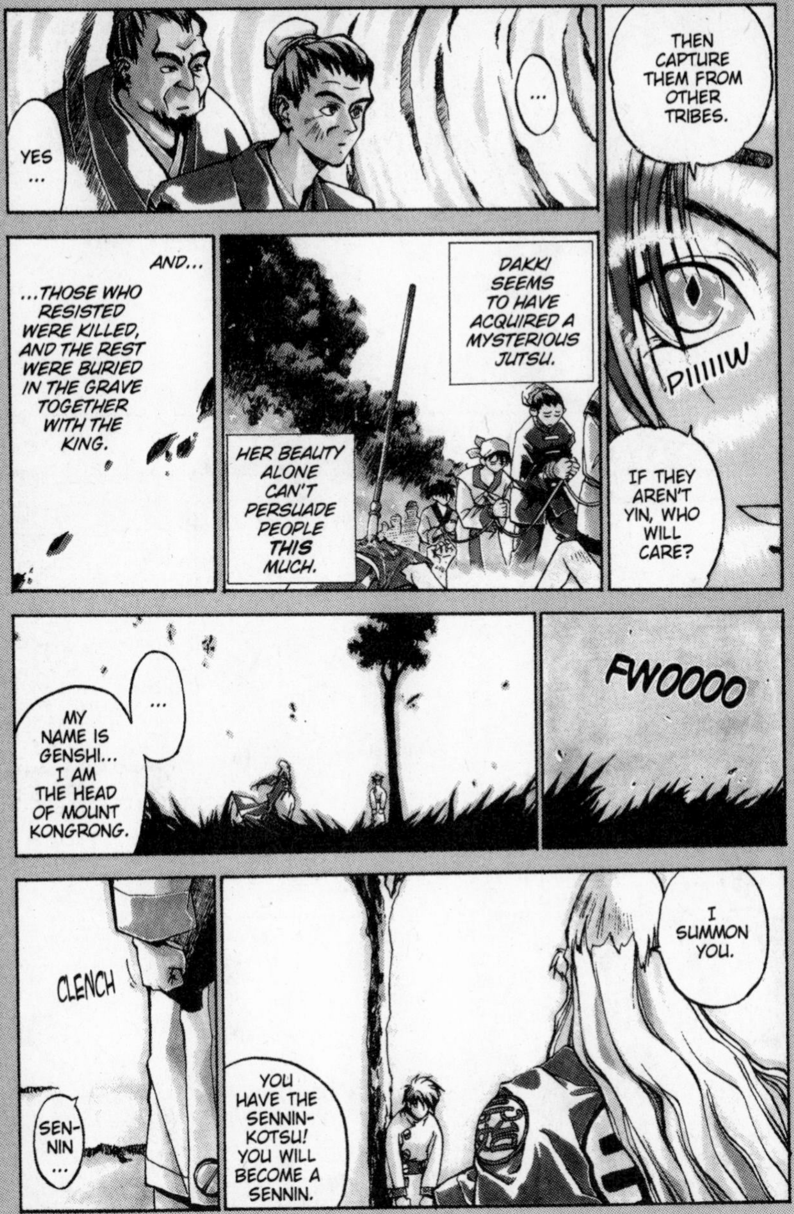
THEN CAPTURE THEM FROM OTHER TRIBES.
PIIIIIW
IF THEY AREN'T YIN, WHO WILL CARE?
...
YES ...
DAKKI SEEMS TO HAVE ACQUIRED A MYSTERIOUS JUTSU.
HER BEAUTY ALONE CAN'T PERSUADE PEOPLE THIS MUCH.
AND...
...THOSE WHO RESISTED WERE KILLED, AND THE REST WERE BURIED IN THE GRAVE TOGETHER WITH THE KING.
FWOOOO
...
MY NAME IS GENSHI... I AM THE HEAD OF MOUNT KONGRONG.
I SUMMON YOU.
YOU HAVE THE SENNIN-KOTSU! YOU WILL BECOME A SENNIN.
CLENCH
SEN-NIN ...

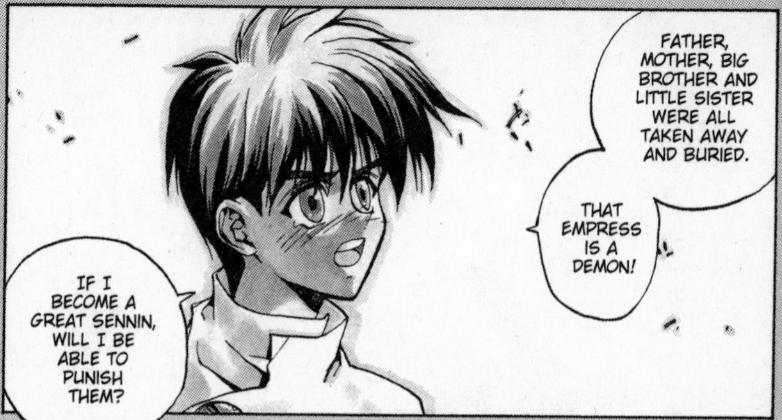
FATHER, MOTHER, BIG BROTHER AND LITTLE SISTER WERE ALL TAKEN AWAY AND BURIED.
THAT EMPRESS IS A DEMON!
IF I BECOME A GREAT SENNIN, WILL I BE ABLE TO PUNISH THEM?

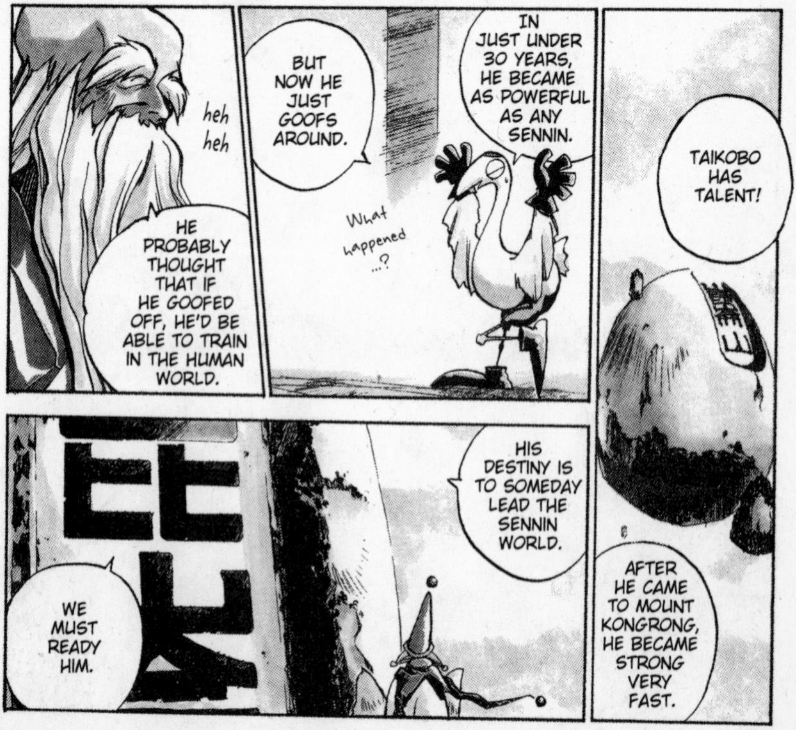
TAIKOBO HAS TALENT!
AFTER HE CAME TO MOUNT KONGRONG, HE BECAME STRONG VERY FAST.
IN JUST UNDER 30 YEARS, HE BECAME AS POWERFUL AS ANY SENNIN.
BUT NOW HE JUST GOOFS AROUND.
What happened ...?
heh heh
HE PROBABLY THOUGHT THAT IF HE GOOFED OFF, HE'D BE ABLE TO TRAIN IN THE HUMAN WORLD.
HIS DESTINY IS TO SOMEDAY LEAD THE SENNIN WORLD.
WE MUST READY HIM.

READ THIS WAY

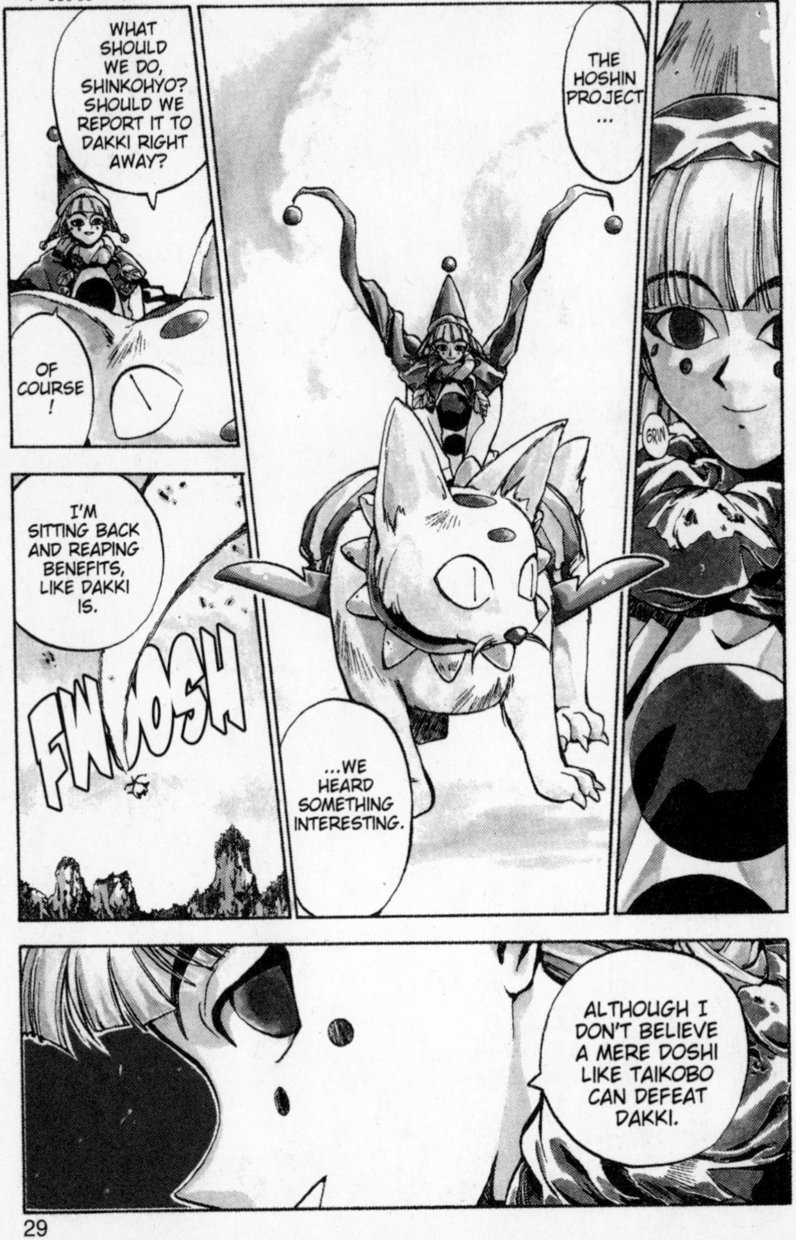
GRIN
THE HOSHIN PROJECT ...
...WE HEARD SOMETHING INTERESTING.
WHAT SHOULD WE DO, SHINKOHYO? SHOULD WE REPORT IT TO DAKKI RIGHT AWAY?
OF COURSE!
I'M SITTING BACK AND REAPING BENEFITS, LIKE DAKKI IS.
FWOOSH
ALTHOUGH I DON'T BELIEVE A MERE DOSHI LIKE TAIKOBO CAN DEFEAT DAKKI.

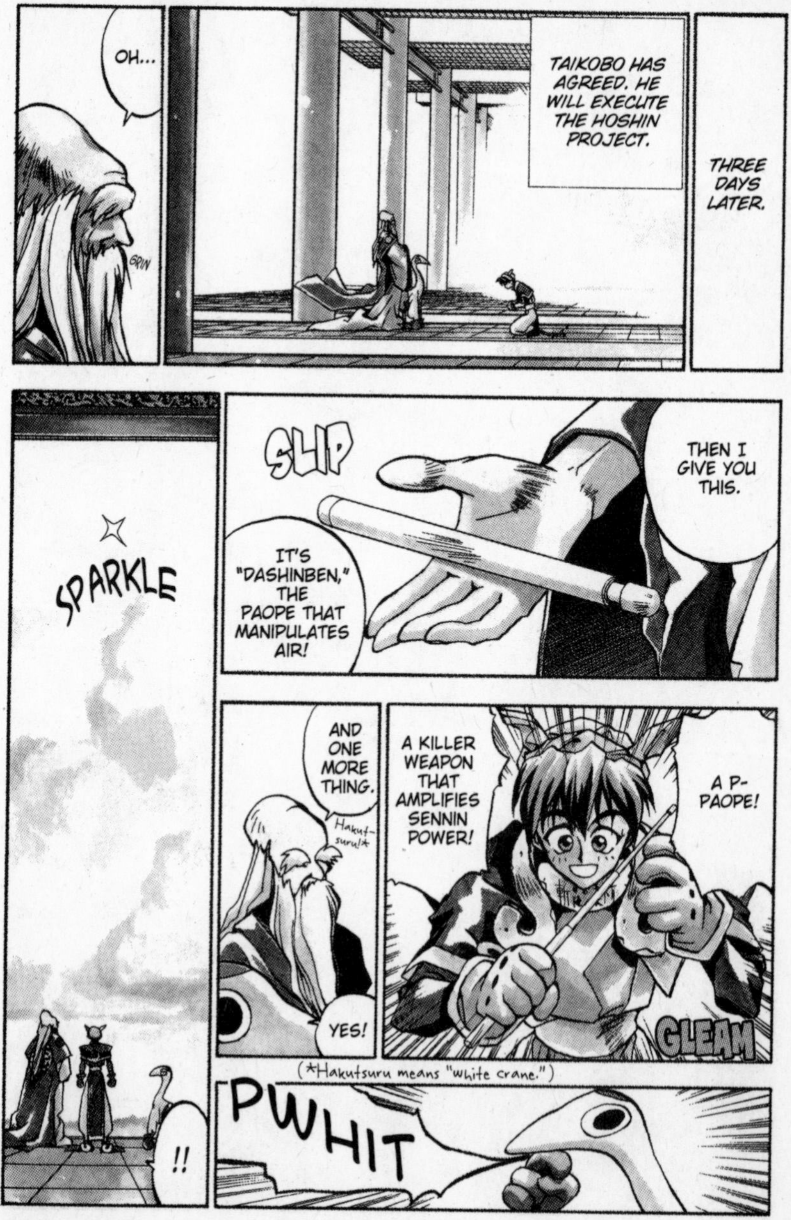
THREE DAYS LATER.
TAIKOBO HAS AGREED. HE WILL EXECUTE THE HOSHIN PROJECT.
OH...
GRIN
THEN I GIVE YOU THIS.
SLIP
IT'S "DASHINBEN," THE PAOPE THAT MANIPULATES AIR!
A P-PAOPE!
A KILLER WEAPON THAT AMPLIFIES SENNIN POWER!
GLEAM
AND ONE MORE THING.
Hakutsuru!*
YES!
(*Hakutsuru means "white crane.")
PWHIT
SPARKLE
!!

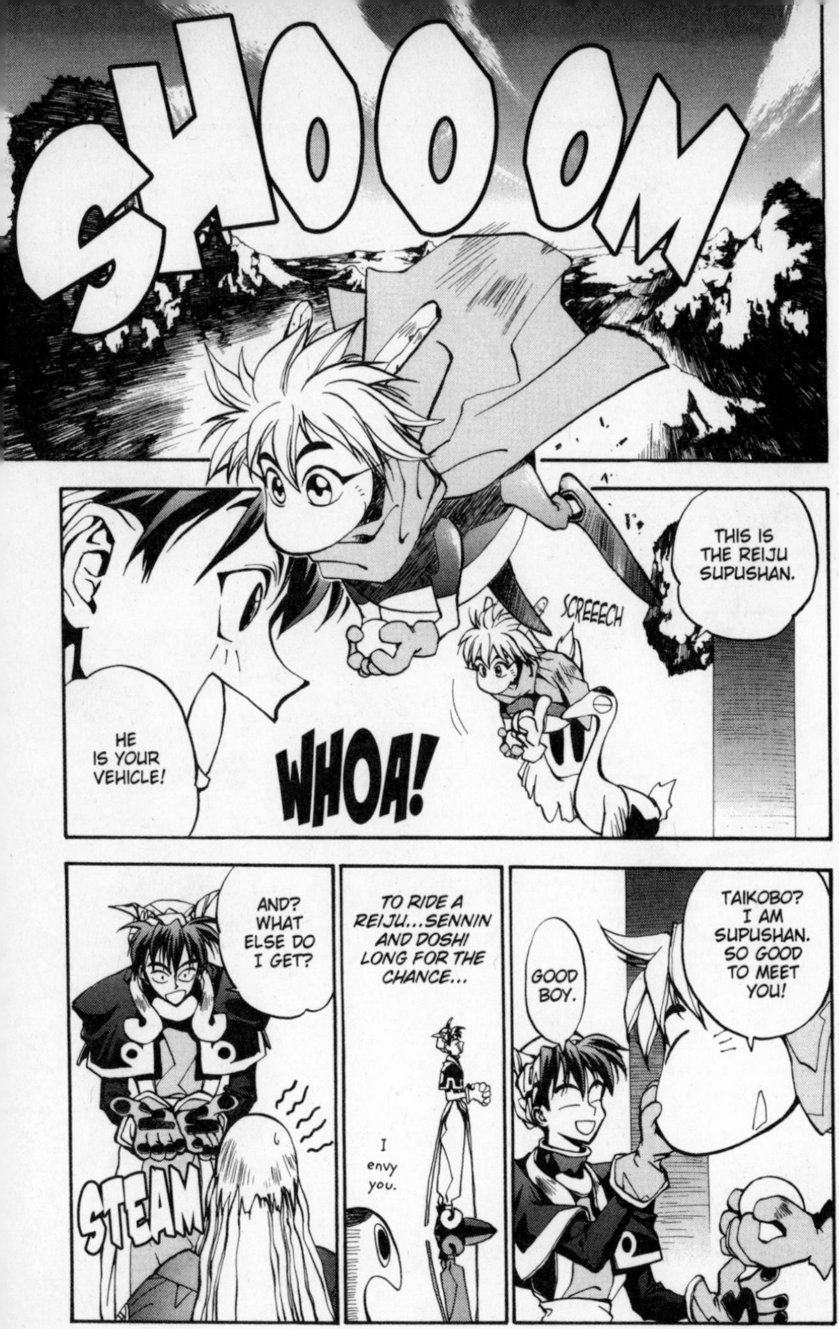
SHOOOM
THIS IS THE REIJU SUPUSHAN.
SCREEECH
WHOA!
HE IS YOUR VEHICLE!
TAIKOBO? I AM SUPUSHAN. SO GOOD TO MEET YOU!
GOOD BOY.
TO RIDE A REIJU...SENNIN AND DOSHI LONG FOR THE CHANCE...
I envy you.
AND? WHAT ELSE DO I GET?
STEAM

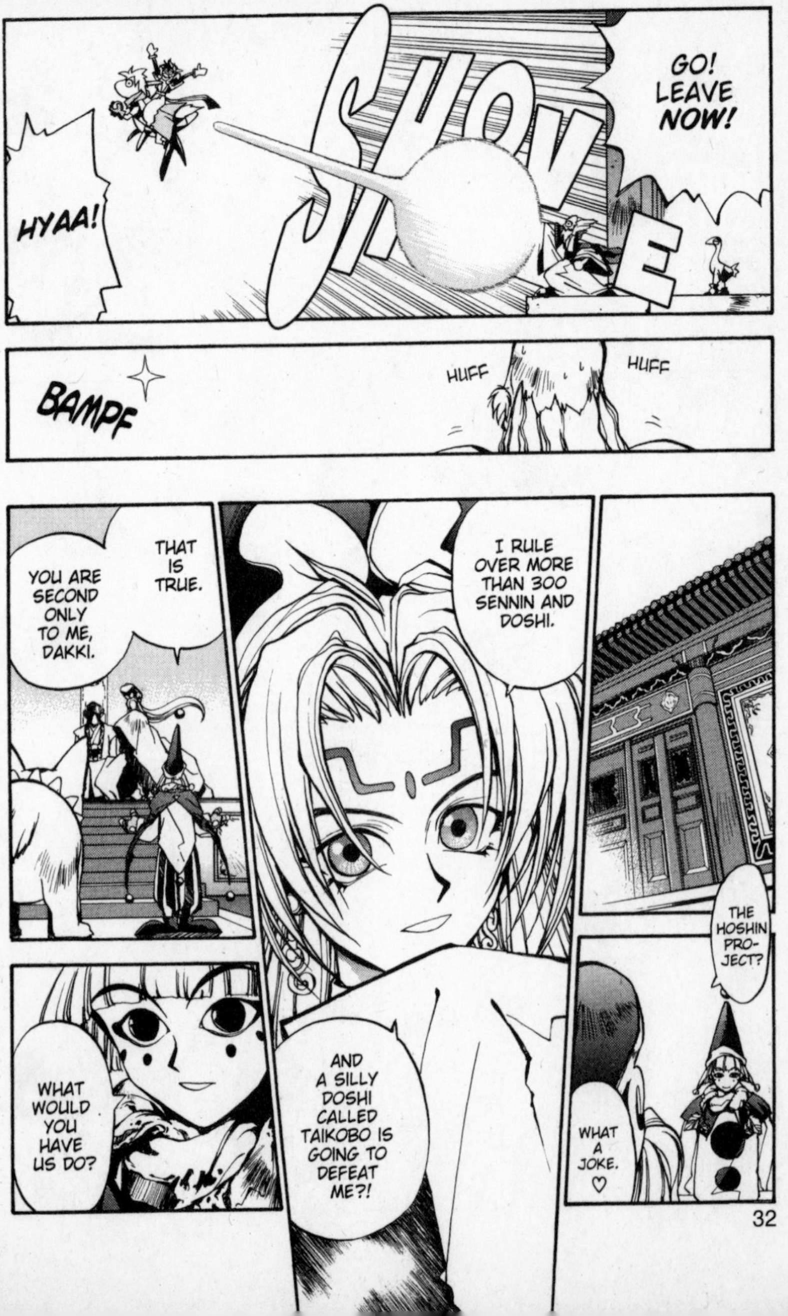
GO! LEAVE NOW!
SHOVE
HYAA!
HUFF
HUFF
BAMPF
THE HOSHIN PROJECT?
WHAT A JOKE. ♡
I RULE OVER MORE THAN 300 SENNIN AND DOSHI.
AND A SILLY DOSHI CALLED TAIKOBO IS GOING TO DEFEAT ME?!
THAT IS TRUE.
YOU ARE SECOND ONLY TO ME, DAKKI.
WHAT WOULD YOU HAVE US DO?

READ THIS WAY

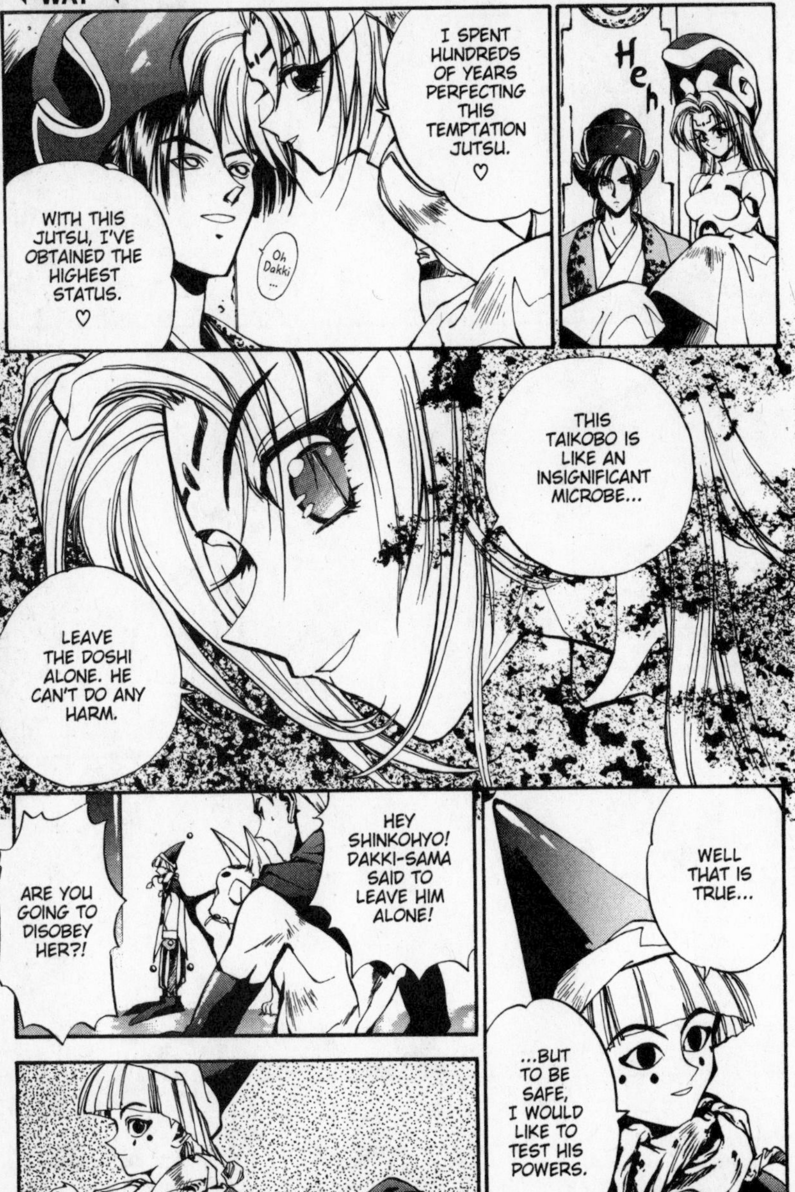
Heh
I SPENT HUNDREDS OF YEARS PERFECTING THIS TEMPTATION JUTSU. ♡
Oh Dakki...
WITH THIS JUTSU, I'VE OBTAINED THE HIGHEST STATUS. ♡
THIS TAIKOBO IS LIKE AN INSIGNIFICANT MICROBE...
LEAVE THE DOSHI ALONE. HE CAN'T DO ANY HARM.
WELL THAT IS TRUE...
...BUT TO BE SAFE, I WOULD LIKE TO TEST HIS POWERS.
HEY SHINKOHYO! DAKKI-SAMA SAID TO LEAVE HIM ALONE!
ARE YOU GOING TO DISOBEY HER?!

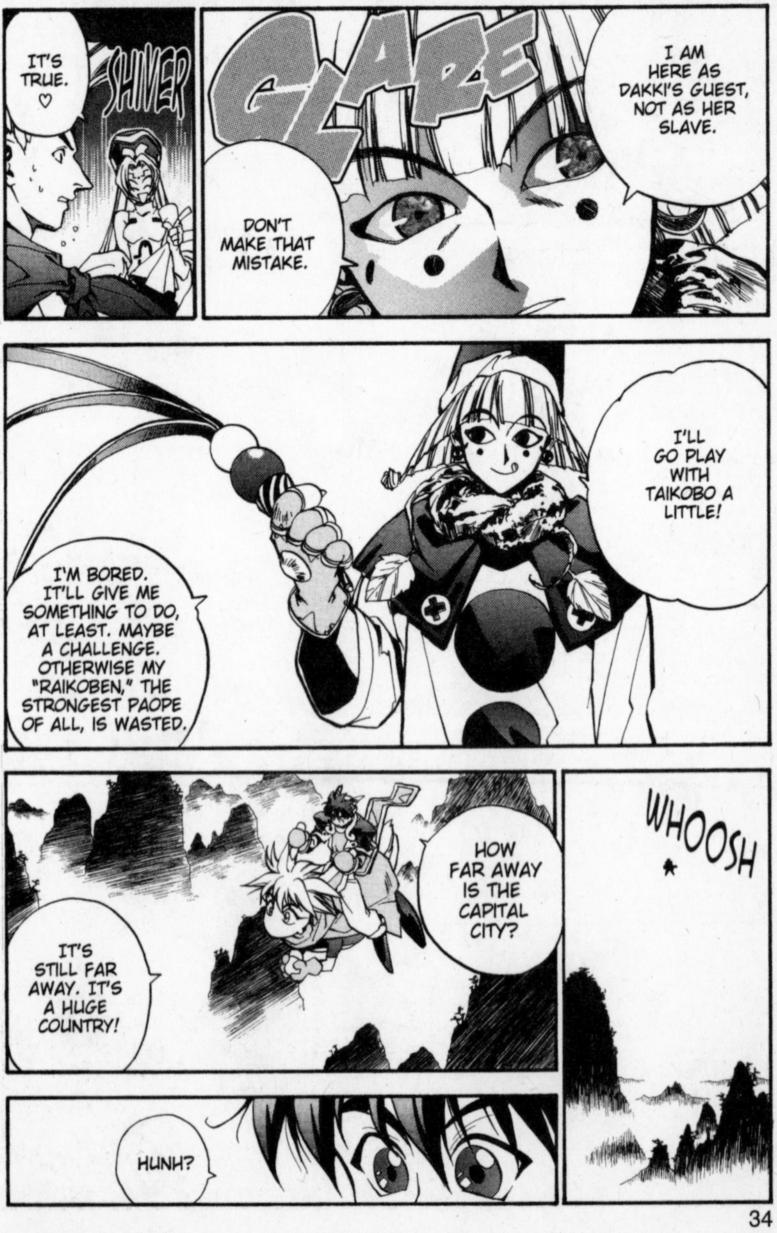
GLARE
I AM HERE AS DAKKI'S GUEST, NOT AS HER SLAVE.
DON'T MAKE THAT MISTAKE.
SHIVER
IT'S TRUE. ♡
I'LL GO PLAY WITH TAIKOBO A LITTLE!
I'M BORED. IT'LL GIVE ME SOMETHING TO DO, AT LEAST. MAYBE A CHALLENGE. OTHERWISE MY "RAIKOBEN," THE STRONGEST PAOPE OF ALL, IS WASTED.
WHOOSH
HOW FAR AWAY IS THE CAPITAL CITY?
IT'S STILL FAR AWAY. IT'S A HUGE COUNTRY!
HUNH?

READ THIS WAY

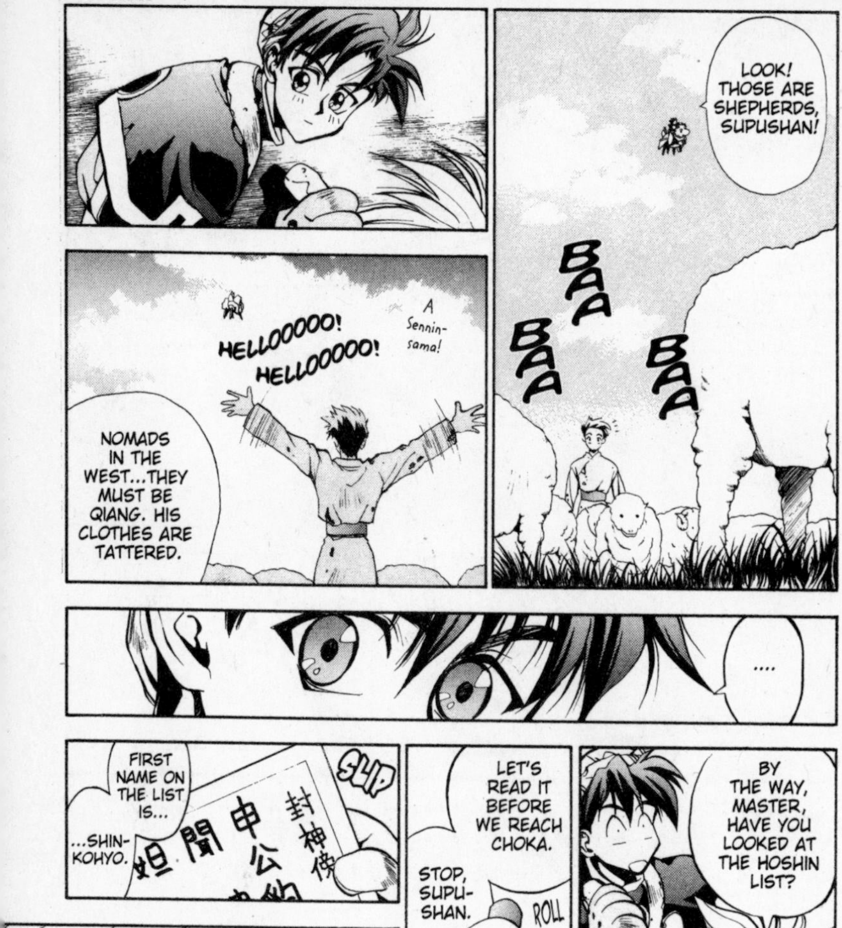
LOOK! THOSE ARE SHEPHERDS, SUPUSHAN!
BAA
BAA
BAA
HELLOOOOO!
HELLOOOOO!
A Sennin-sama!
NOMADS IN THE WEST...THEY MUST BE QIANG. HIS CLOTHES ARE TATTERED.
....
BY THE WAY, MASTER, HAVE YOU LOOKED AT THE HOSHIN LIST?
NOT YET.
LET'S READ IT BEFORE WE REACH CHOKA.
STOP, SUPU-SHAN.
ROLL
RIGHTY!
SLIP
FIRST NAME ON THE LIST IS...
...SHIN-KOHYO.
封神傍
申公
聞
妲
SH-SHINKOHYO-SAMA!?
HIS NAME IS ON THE LIST ?!

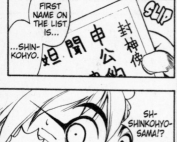

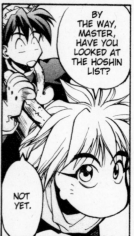

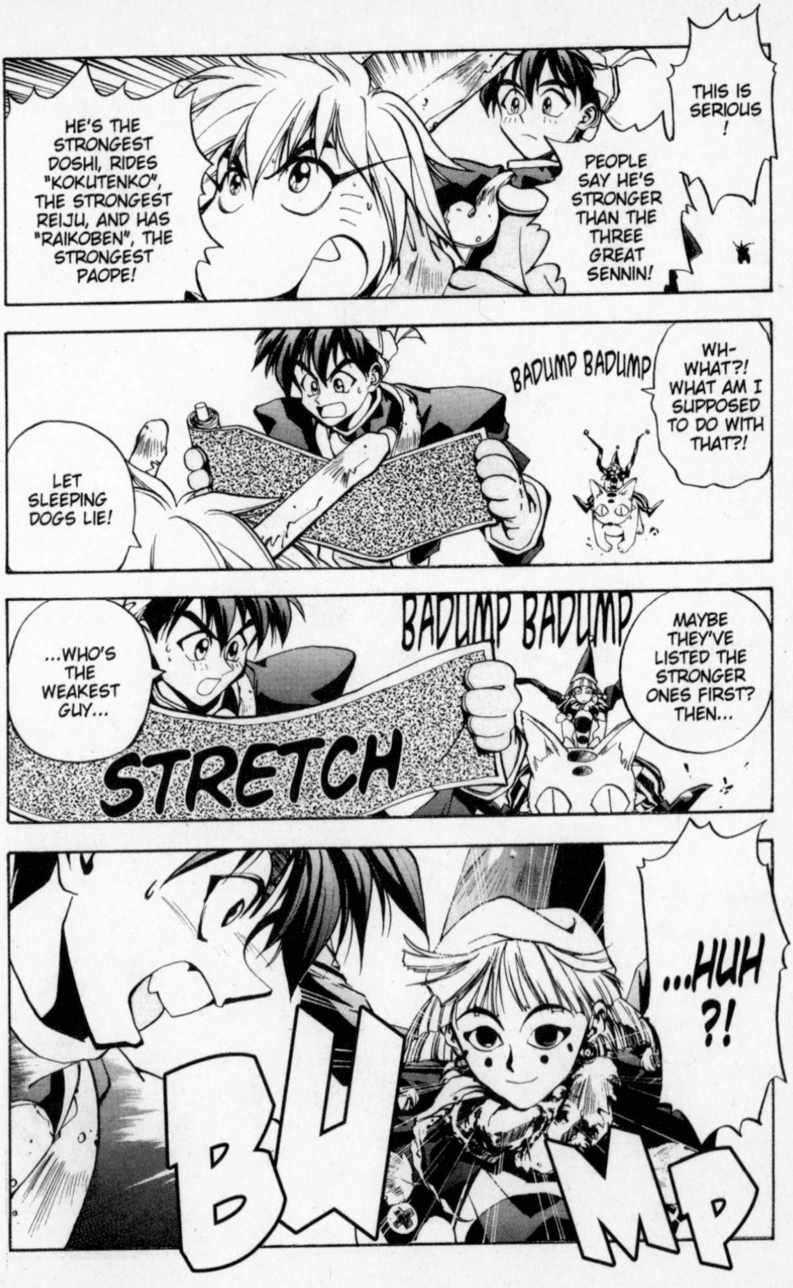
THIS IS SERIOUS!
PEOPLE SAY HE'S STRONGER THAN THE THREE GREAT SENNIN!
HE'S THE STRONGEST DOSHI, RIDES "KOKUTENKO", THE STRONGEST REIJU, AND HAS "RAIKOBEN", THE STRONGEST PAOPE!
WH- WHAT?! WHAT AM I SUPPOSED TO DO WITH THAT?!
BADUMP BADUMP
LET SLEEPING DOGS LIE!
MAYBE THEY'VE LISTED THE STRONGER ONES FIRST? THEN...
BADUMP BADUMP
...WHO'S THE WEAKEST GUY...
STRETCH
...HUH?!
BUMP

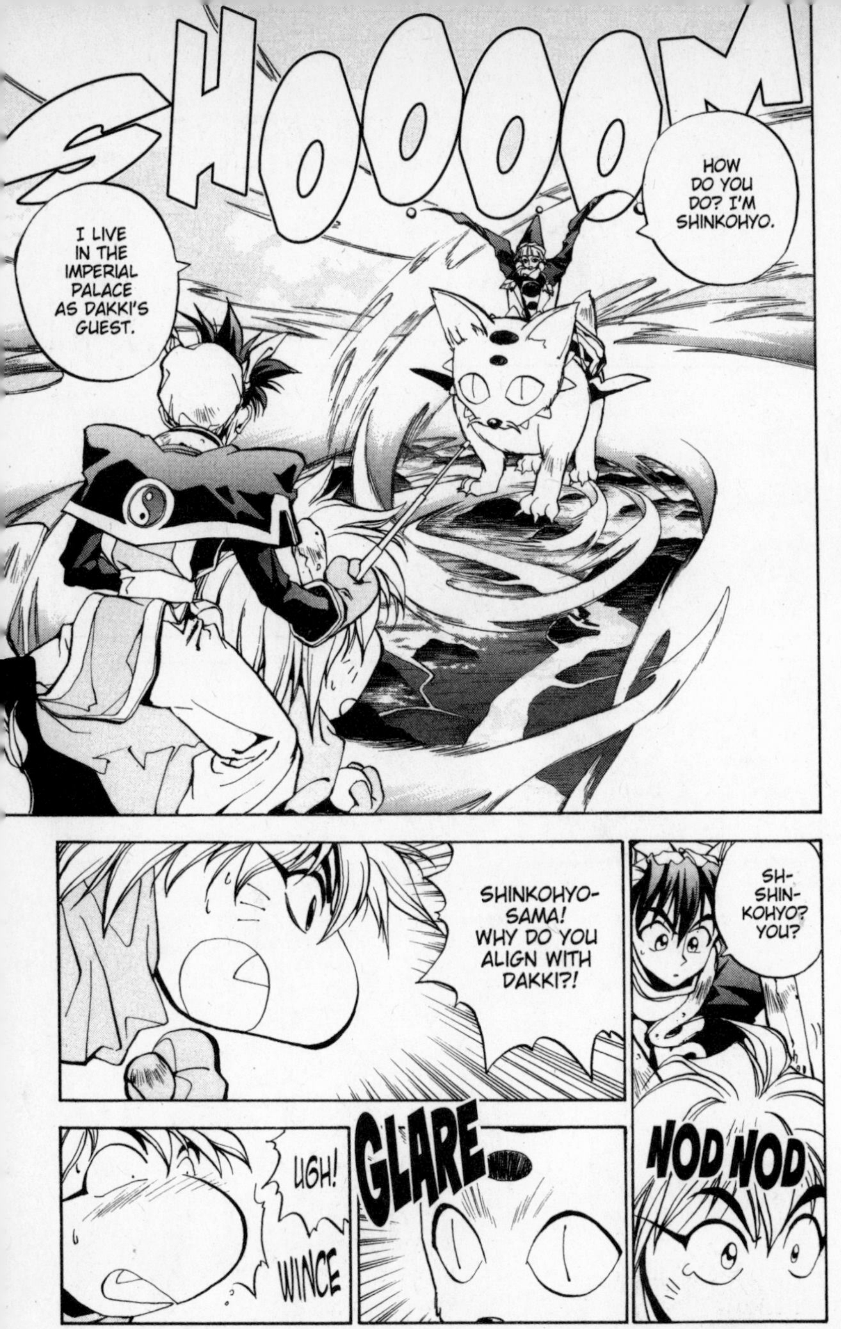
SHOOOOM
HOW DO YOU DO? I'M SHINKOHYO.
I LIVE IN THE IMPERIAL PALACE AS DAKKI'S GUEST.
SH-SHIN-KOHYO? YOU?
SHINKOHYO-SAMA! WHY DO YOU ALIGN WITH DAKKI?!
NOD NOD
GLARE
UGH!
WINCE

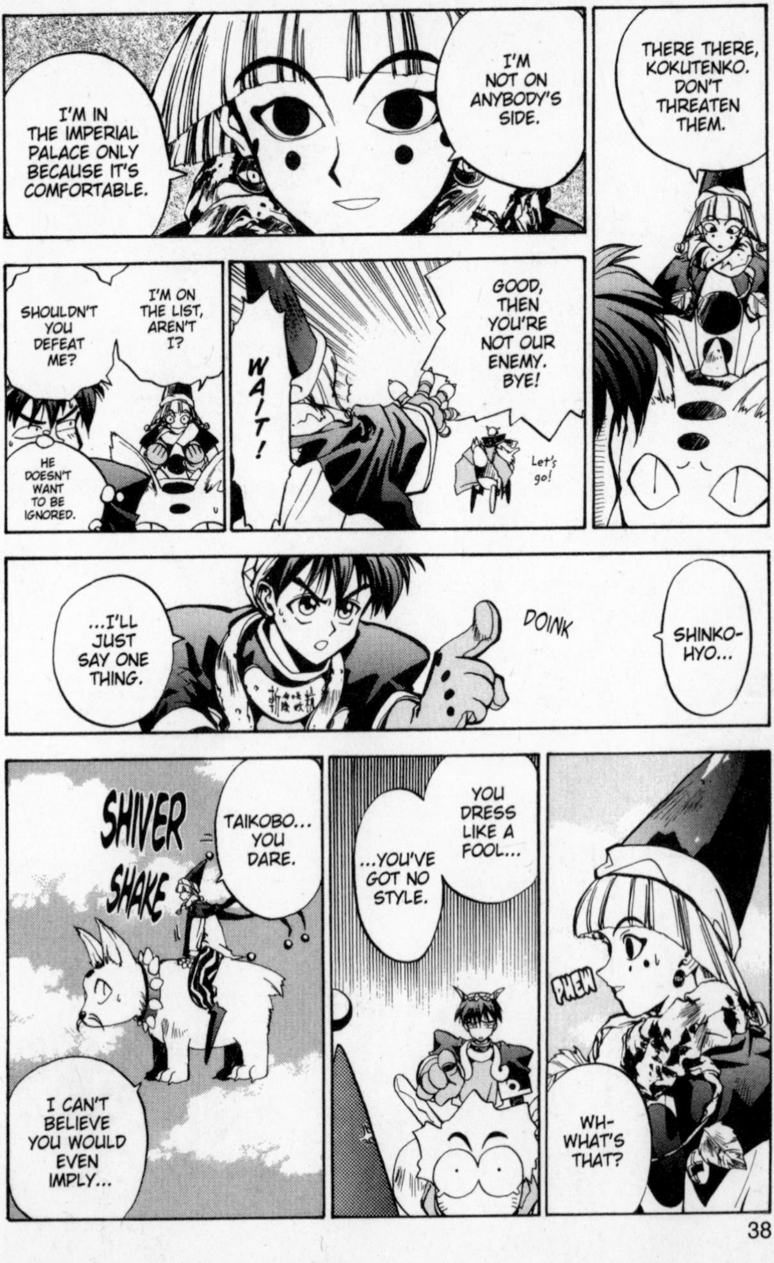
THERE THERE, KOKUTENKO. DON'T THREATEN THEM.
I'M NOT ON ANYBODY'S SIDE.
I'M IN THE IMPERIAL PALACE ONLY BECAUSE IT'S COMFORTABLE.
GOOD, THEN YOU'RE NOT OUR ENEMY. BYE!
Let's go!
WAIT!
I'M ON THE LIST, AREN'T I?
SHOULDN'T YOU DEFEAT ME?
HE DOESN'T WANT TO BE IGNORED.
SHINKO-HYO...
DOINK
...I'LL JUST SAY ONE THING.
PHEW
WH-WHAT'S THAT?
YOU DRESS LIKE A FOOL...
...YOU'VE GOT NO STYLE.
TAIKOBO... YOU DARE.
SHIVER
SHAKE
I CAN'T BELIEVE YOU WOULD EVEN IMPLY...

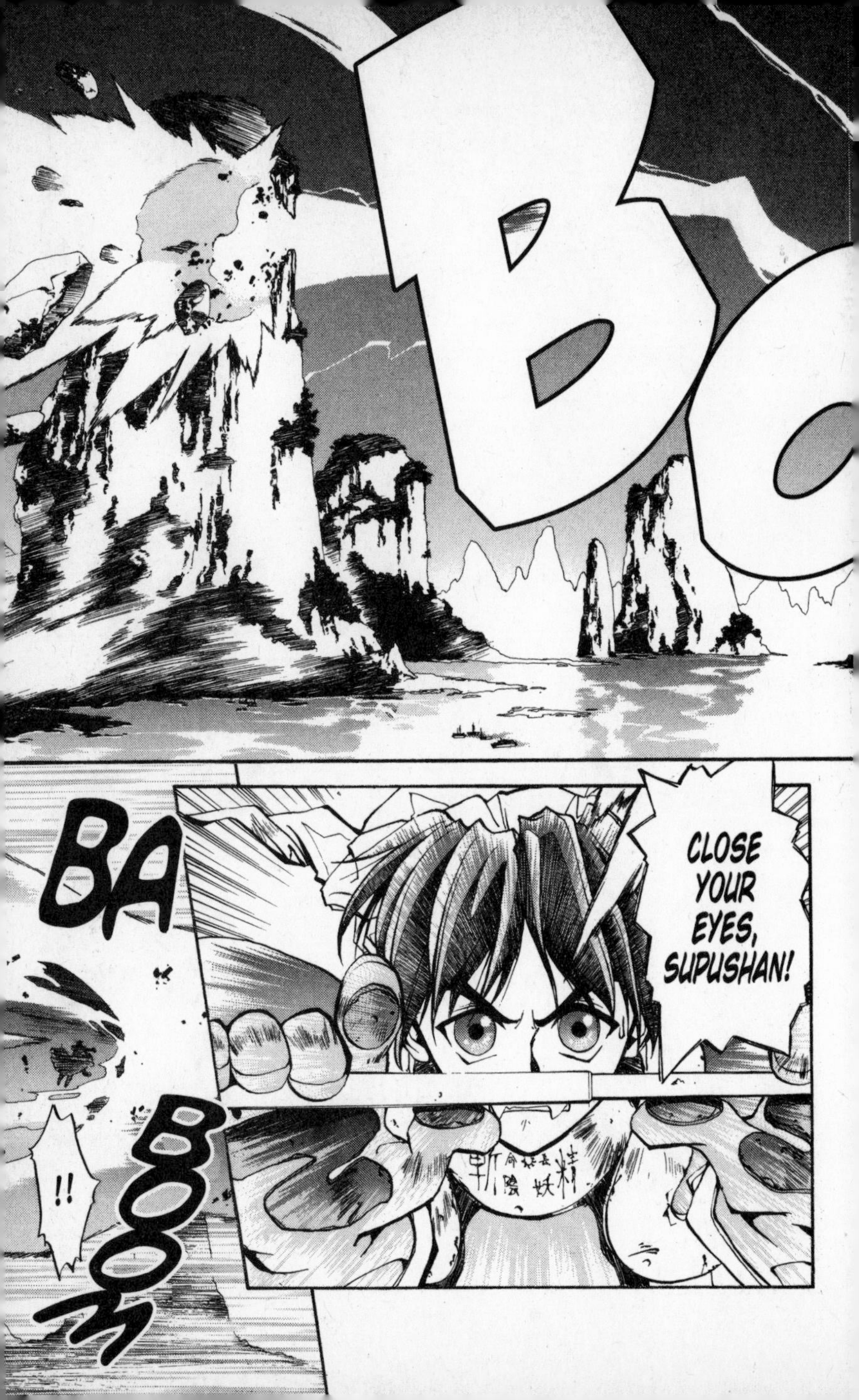
BO
CLOSE YOUR EYES, SUPUSHAN!
BA BOOM
!!

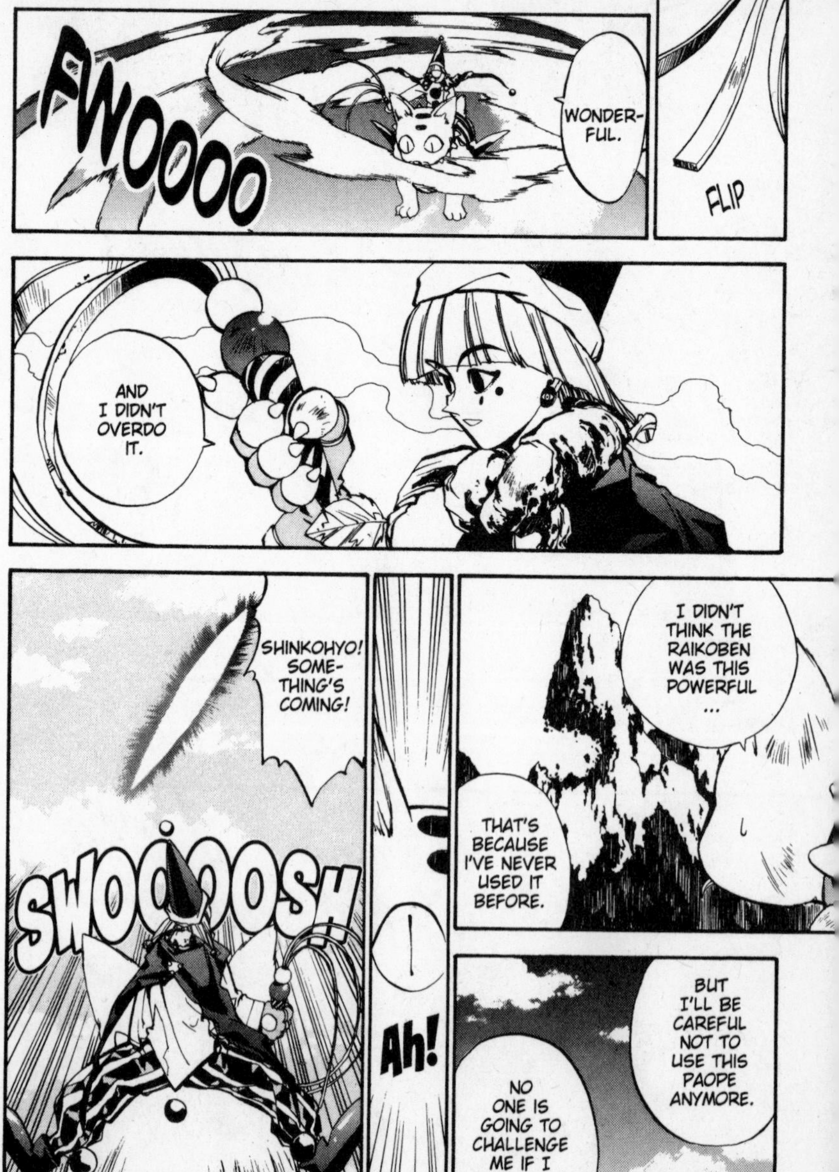
FLIP
WONDER-FUL.
FWOOOO
AND I DIDN'T OVERDO IT.
I DIDN'T THINK THE RAIKOBEN WAS THIS POWERFUL ...
THAT'S BECAUSE I'VE NEVER USED IT BEFORE.
BUT I'LL BE CAREFUL NOT TO USE THIS PAOPE ANYMORE.
NO ONE IS GOING TO CHALLENGE ME IF I HAVE THIS.
!
Ah!
SHINKOHYO! SOME-THING'S COMING!
SWOOOOSH

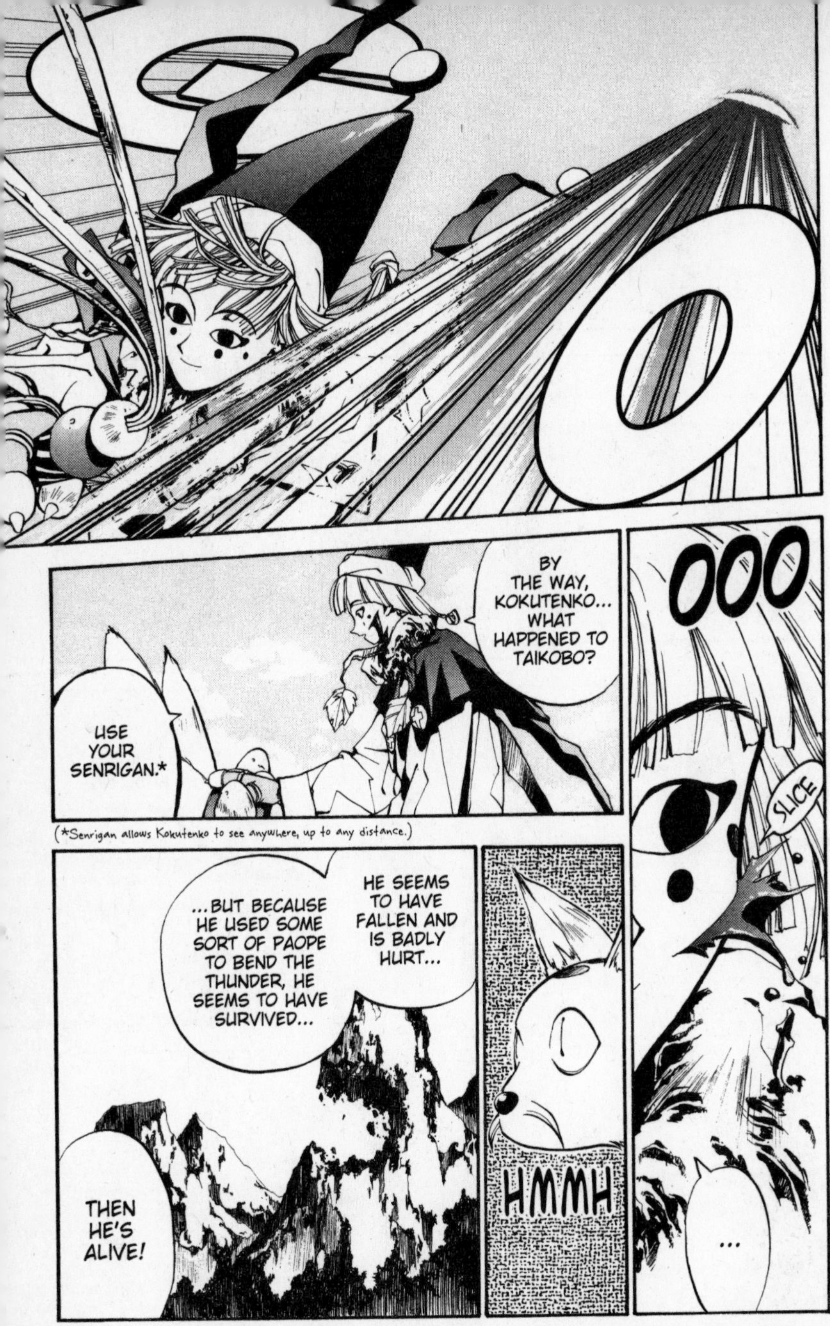
OOO
SLICE
...
BY THE WAY, KOKUTENKO... WHAT HAPPENED TO TAIKOBO?
USE YOUR SENRIGAN.*
HMMH
HE SEEMS TO HAVE FALLEN AND IS BADLY HURT...
...BUT BECAUSE HE USED SOME SORT OF PAOPE TO BEND THE THUNDER, HE SEEMS TO HAVE SURVIVED...
THEN HE'S ALIVE!

(*Senrigan allows Kokutenko to see anywhere, up to any distance.)

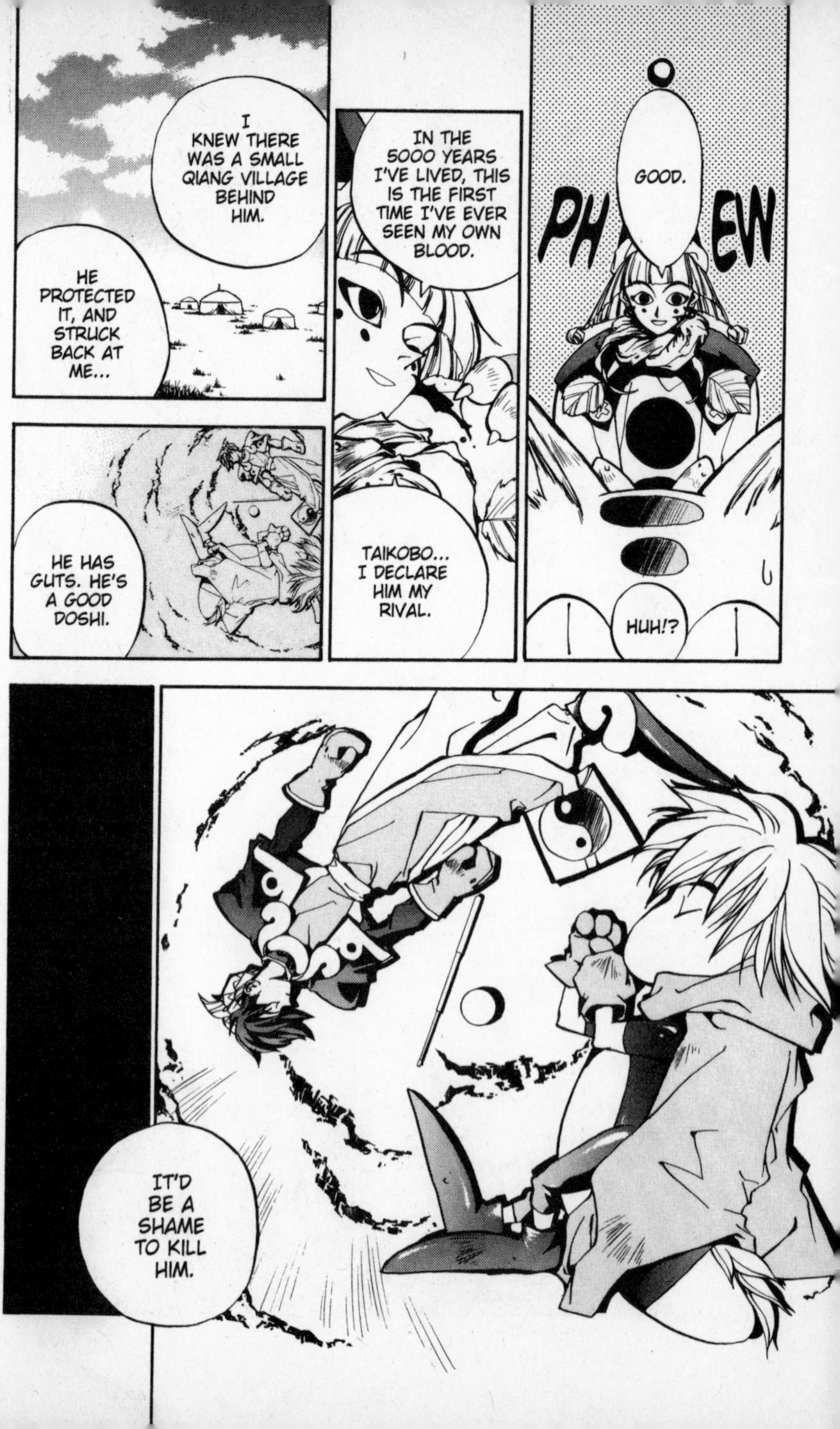
GOOD.
PHEW
HUH!?
IN THE 5000 YEARS I'VE LIVED, THIS IS THE FIRST TIME I'VE EVER SEEN MY OWN BLOOD.
TAIKOBO... I DECLARE HIM MY RIVAL.
I KNEW THERE WAS A SMALL QIANG VILLAGE BEHIND HIM.
HE PROTECTED IT, AND STRUCK BACK AT ME...
HE HAS GUTS. HE'S A GOOD DOSHI.
IT'D BE A SHAME TO KILL HIM.

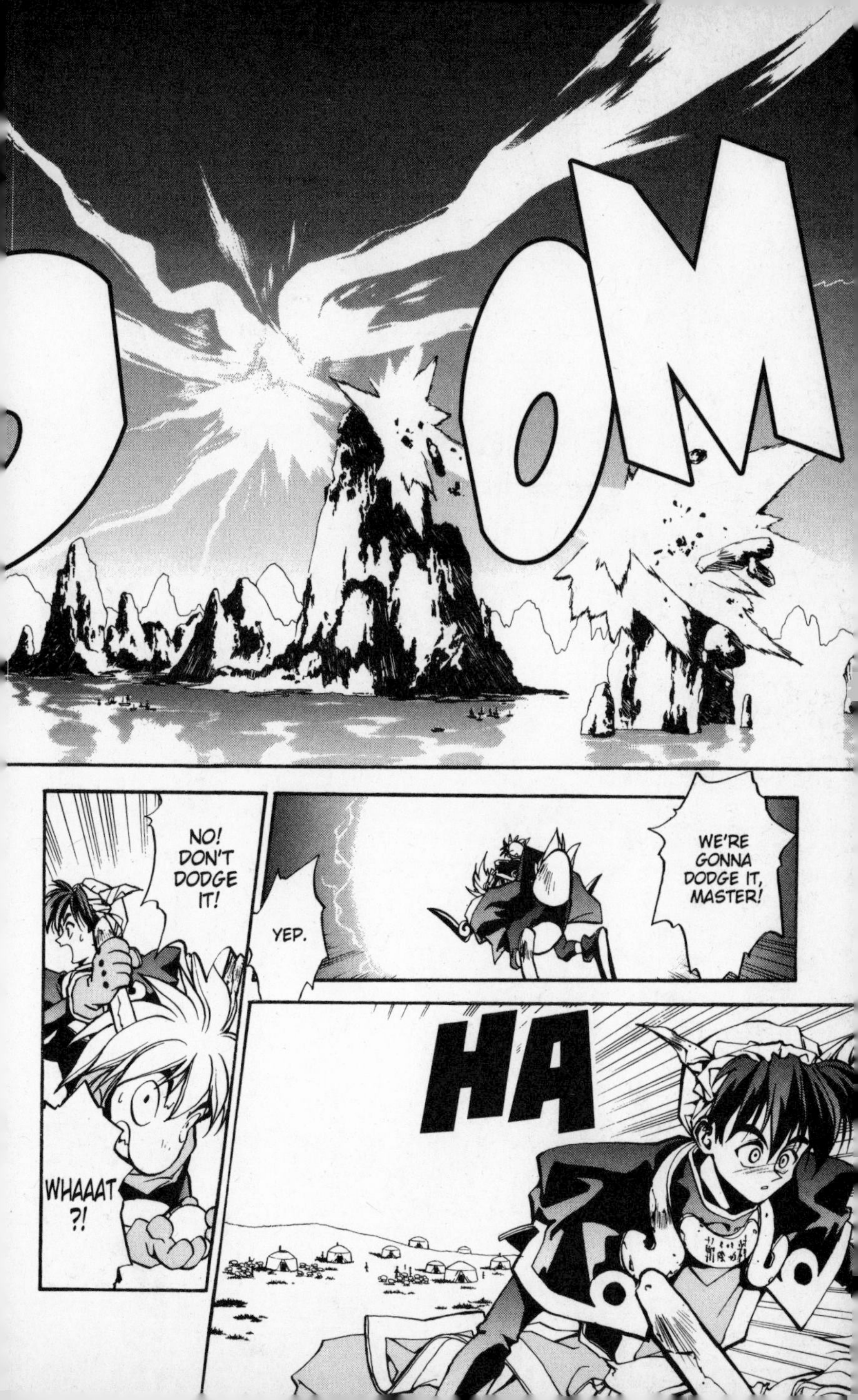
DOM
WE'RE GONNA DODGE IT, MASTER!
YEP.
HA
NO! DON'T DODGE IT!
WHAAAT?!

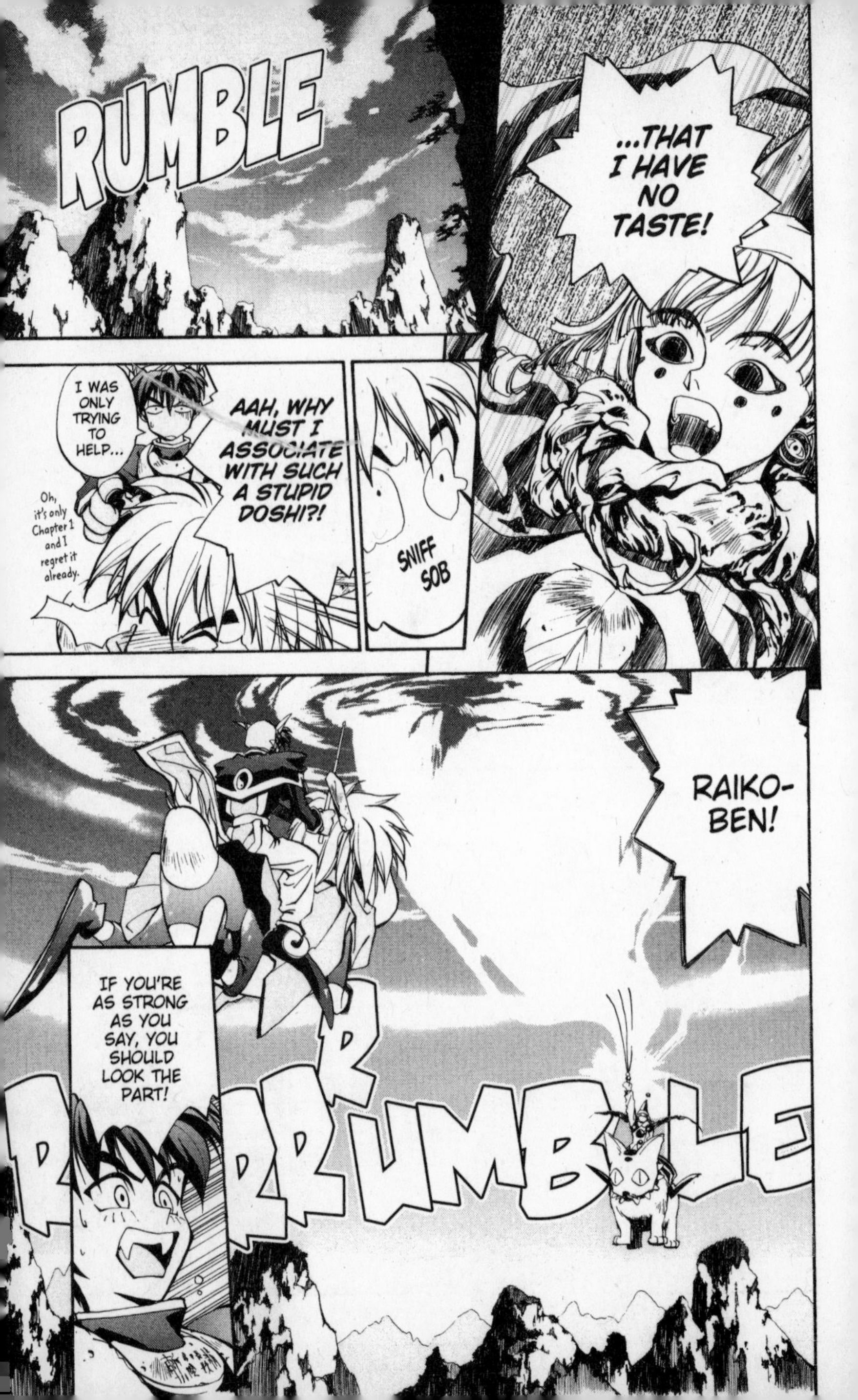
...THAT I HAVE NO TASTE!
RUMBLE
SNIFF SOB
AAH, WHY MUST I ASSOCIATE WITH SUCH A STUPID DOSHI?!
I WAS ONLY TRYING TO HELP...
Oh, it's only Chapter 1 and I regret it already.
RAIKO-BEN!
RRRUMBLE
IF YOU'RE AS STRONG AS YOU SAY, YOU SHOULD LOOK THE PART!

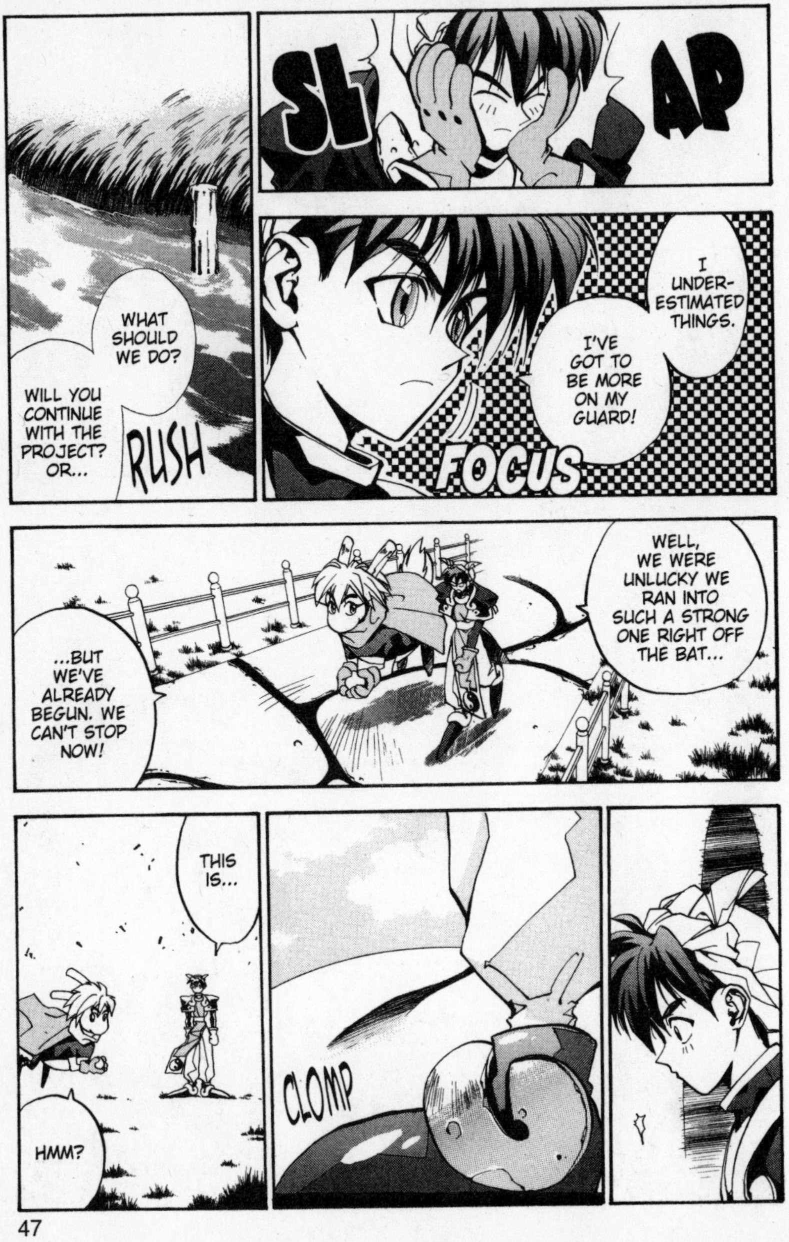
SL AP
I UNDER-ESTIMATED THINGS.
I'VE GOT TO BE MORE ON MY GUARD!
FOCUS
WHAT SHOULD WE DO?
WILL YOU CONTINUE WITH THE PROJECT? OR...
RUSH
WELL, WE WERE UNLUCKY WE RAN INTO SUCH A STRONG ONE RIGHT OFF THE BAT...
...BUT WE'VE ALREADY BEGUN. WE CAN'T STOP NOW!
CLOMP
THIS IS...
HMM?

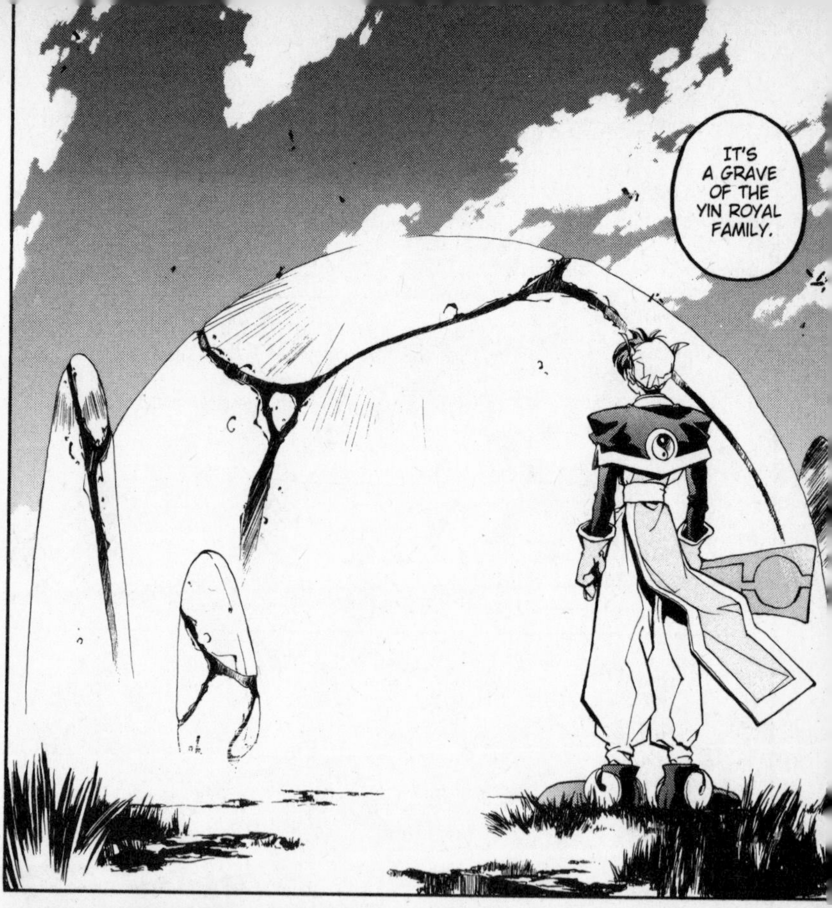
IT'S A GRAVE OF THE YIN ROYAL FAMILY.

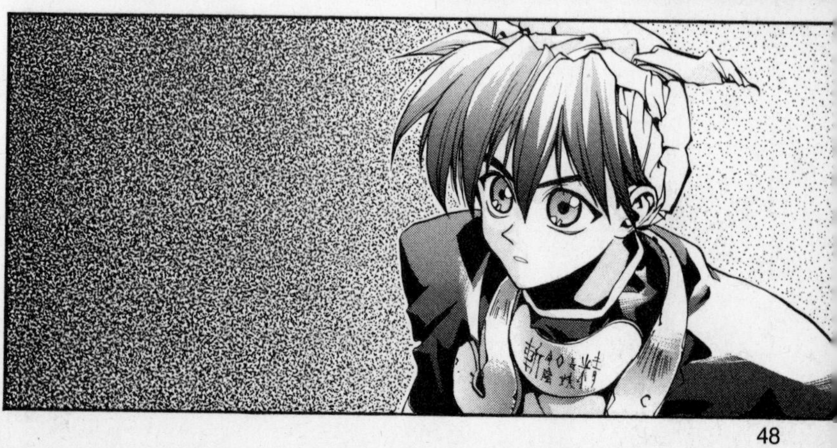

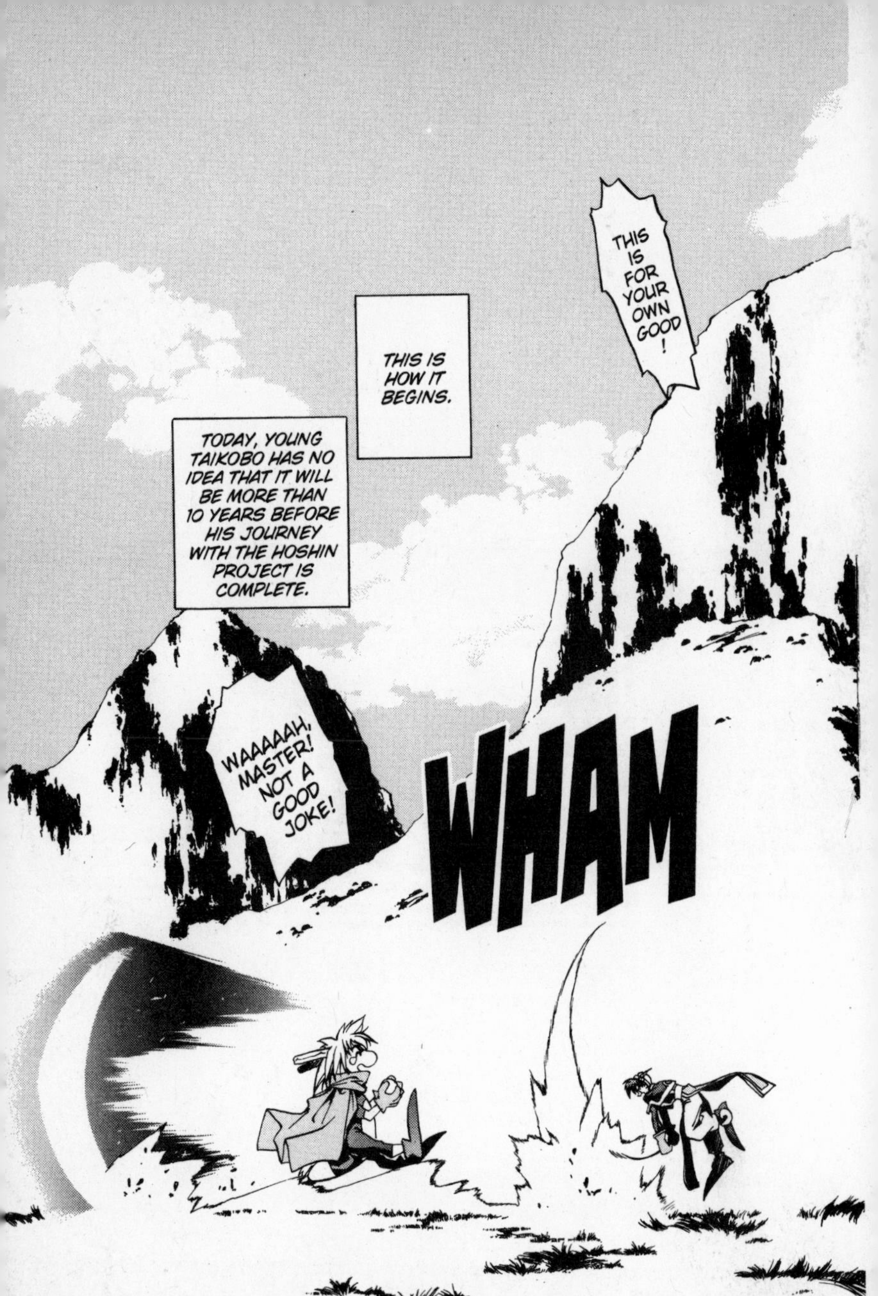
THIS IS FOR YOUR OWN GOOD!
THIS IS HOW IT BEGINS.
TODAY, YOUNG TAIKOBO HAS NO IDEA THAT IT WILL BE MORE THAN 10 YEARS BEFORE HIS JOURNEY WITH THE HOSHIN PROJECT IS COMPLETE.
WHAM
WAAAAAH, MASTER! NOT A GOOD JOKE!

封神演義

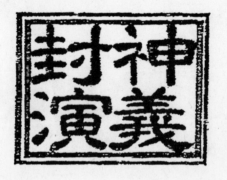

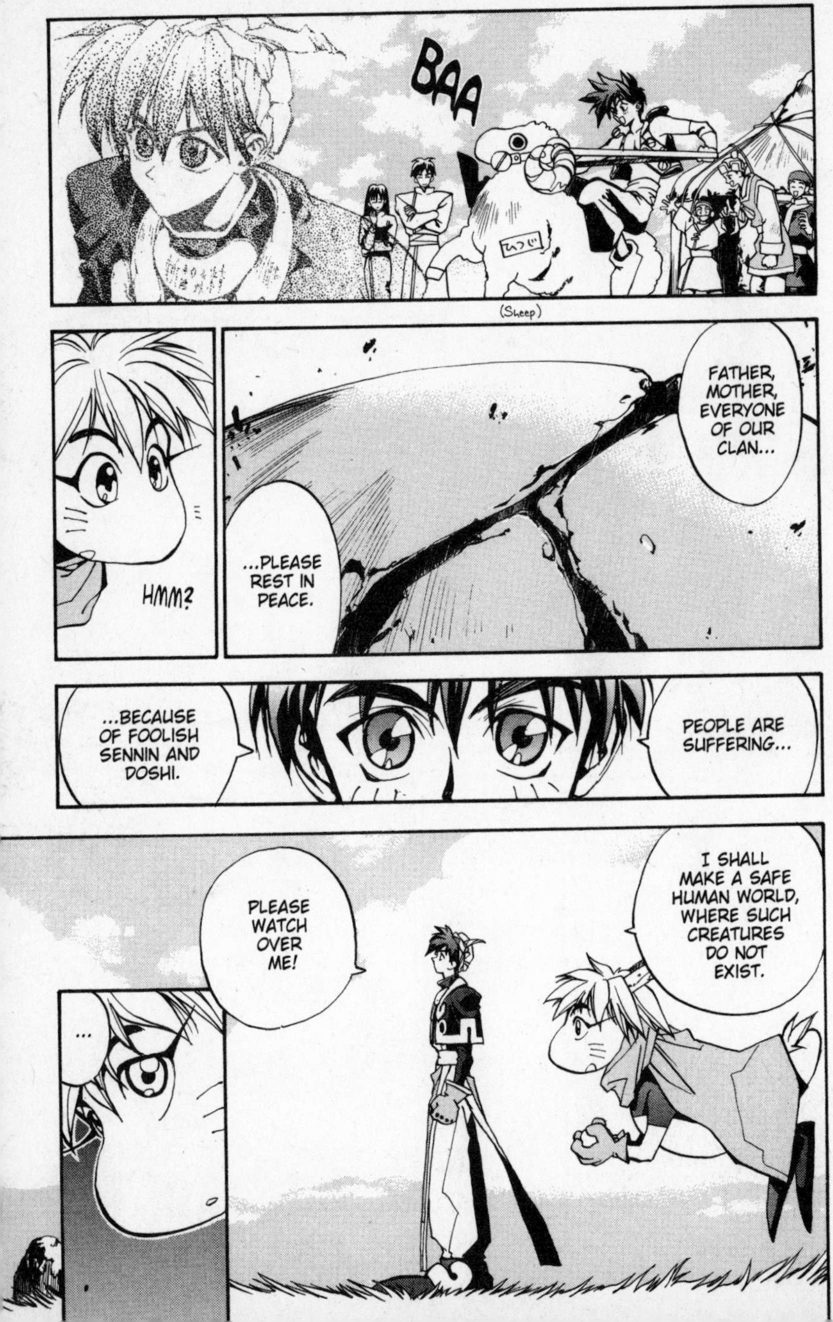
BAA
ひつじ
(Sheep)
FATHER, MOTHER, EVERYONE OF OUR CLAN...
...PLEASE REST IN PEACE.
HMM?
PEOPLE ARE SUFFERING...
...BECAUSE OF FOOLISH SENNIN AND DOSHI.
I SHALL MAKE A SAFE HUMAN WORLD, WHERE SUCH CREATURES DO NOT EXIST.
PLEASE WATCH OVER ME!
...

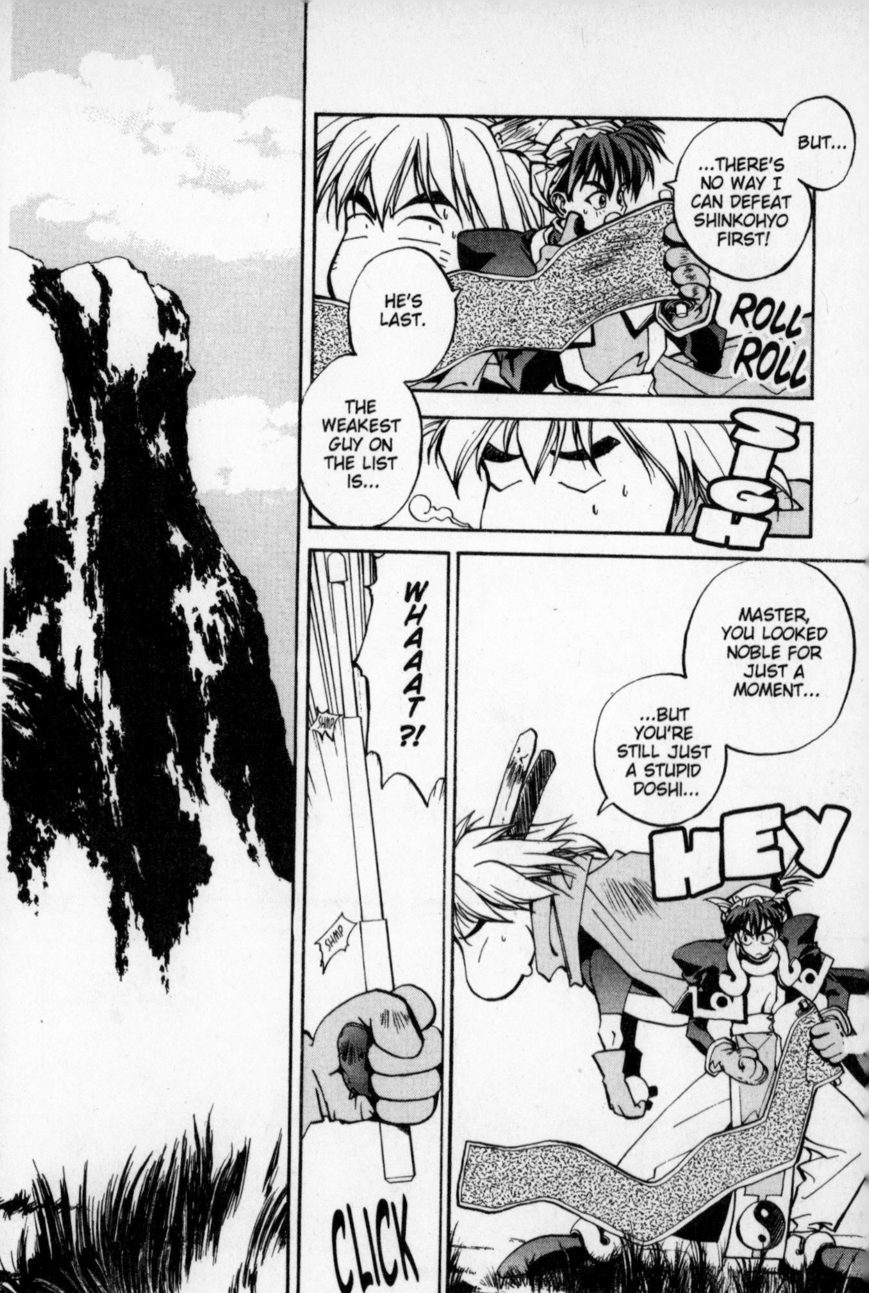
BUT...
...THERE'S NO WAY I CAN DEFEAT SHINKOHYO FIRST!
ROLL-ROLL
HE'S LAST.
THE WEAKEST GUY ON THE LIST IS...
SIGH
MASTER, YOU LOOKED NOBLE FOR JUST A MOMENT...
...BUT YOU'RE STILL JUST A STUPID DOSHI...
HEY
WHAAAAT?!
SHMP
SHMP
CLICK

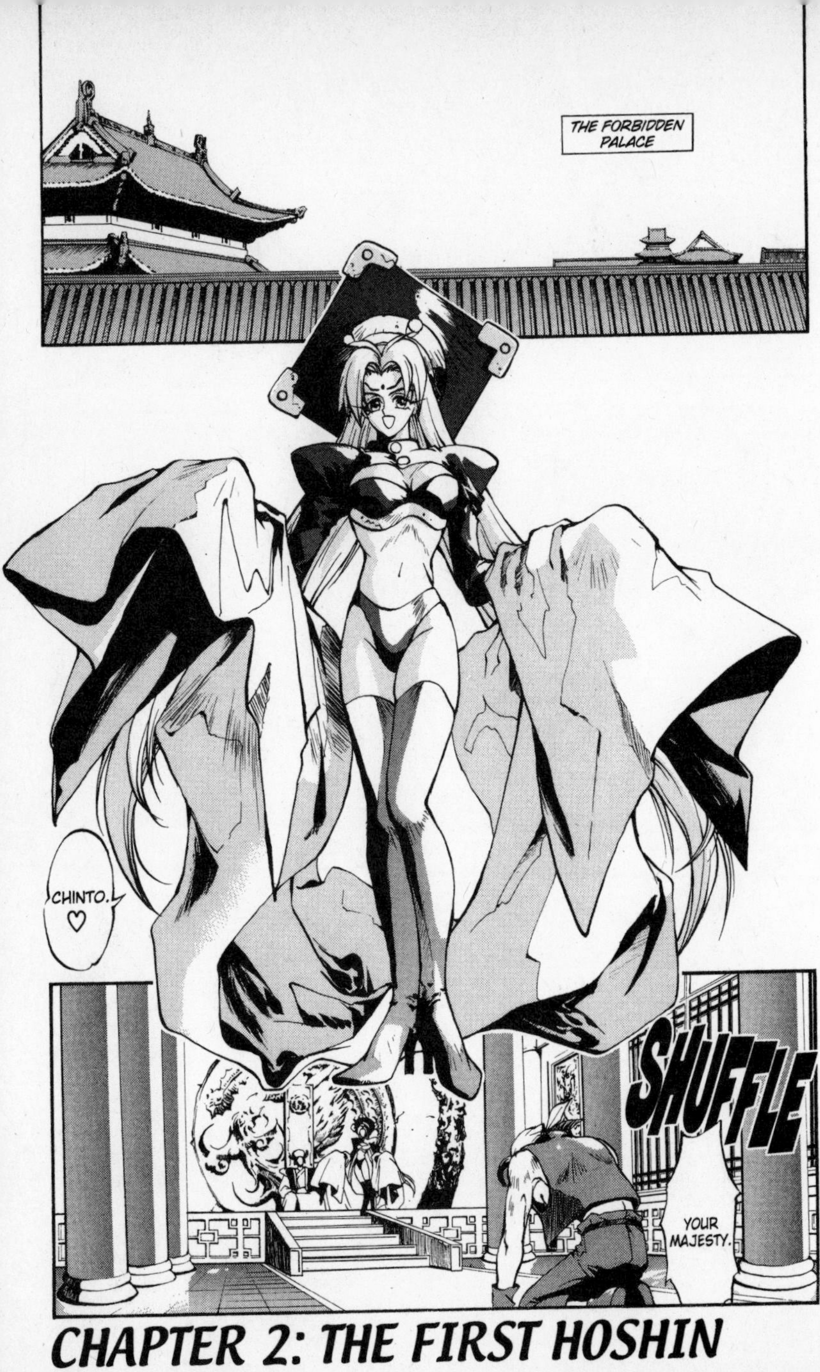
THE FORBIDDEN PALACE
CHINTO. ♡
SHUFFLE
YOUR MAJESTY.

CHAPTER 2: THE FIRST HOSHIN

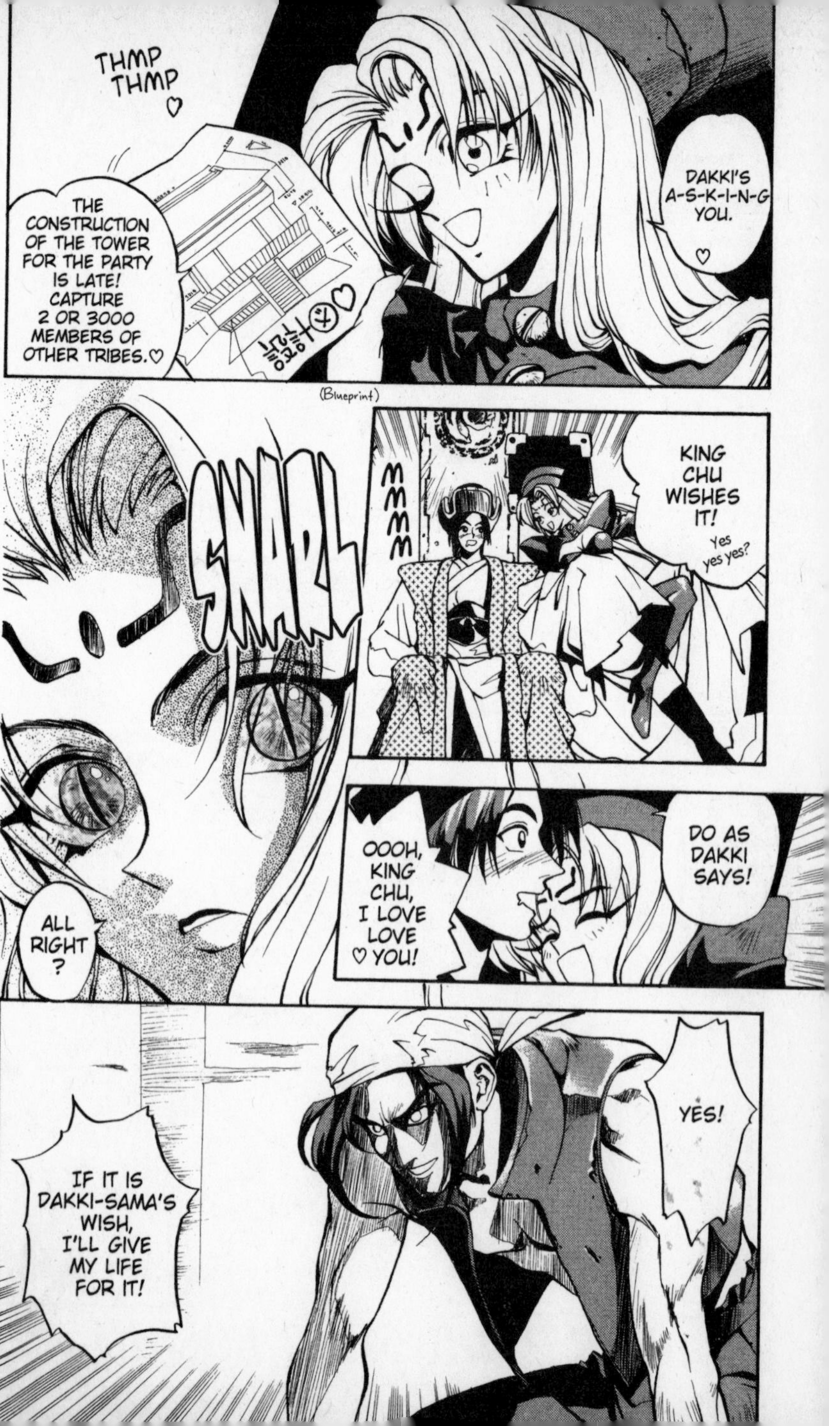
DAKKI'S A-S-K-I-N-G YOU. ♡
THMP THMP ♡
THE CONSTRUCTION OF THE TOWER FOR THE PARTY IS LATE! CAPTURE 2 OR 3000 MEMBERS OF OTHER TRIBES.♡
(Blueprint)
KING CHU WISHES IT!
Yes yes yes?
mmmmm
DO AS DAKKI SAYS!
OOOH, KING CHU, I LOVE LOVE ♡ YOU!
SNARL
ALL RIGHT?
YES!
IF IT IS DAKKI-SAMA'S WISH, I'LL GIVE MY LIFE FOR IT!

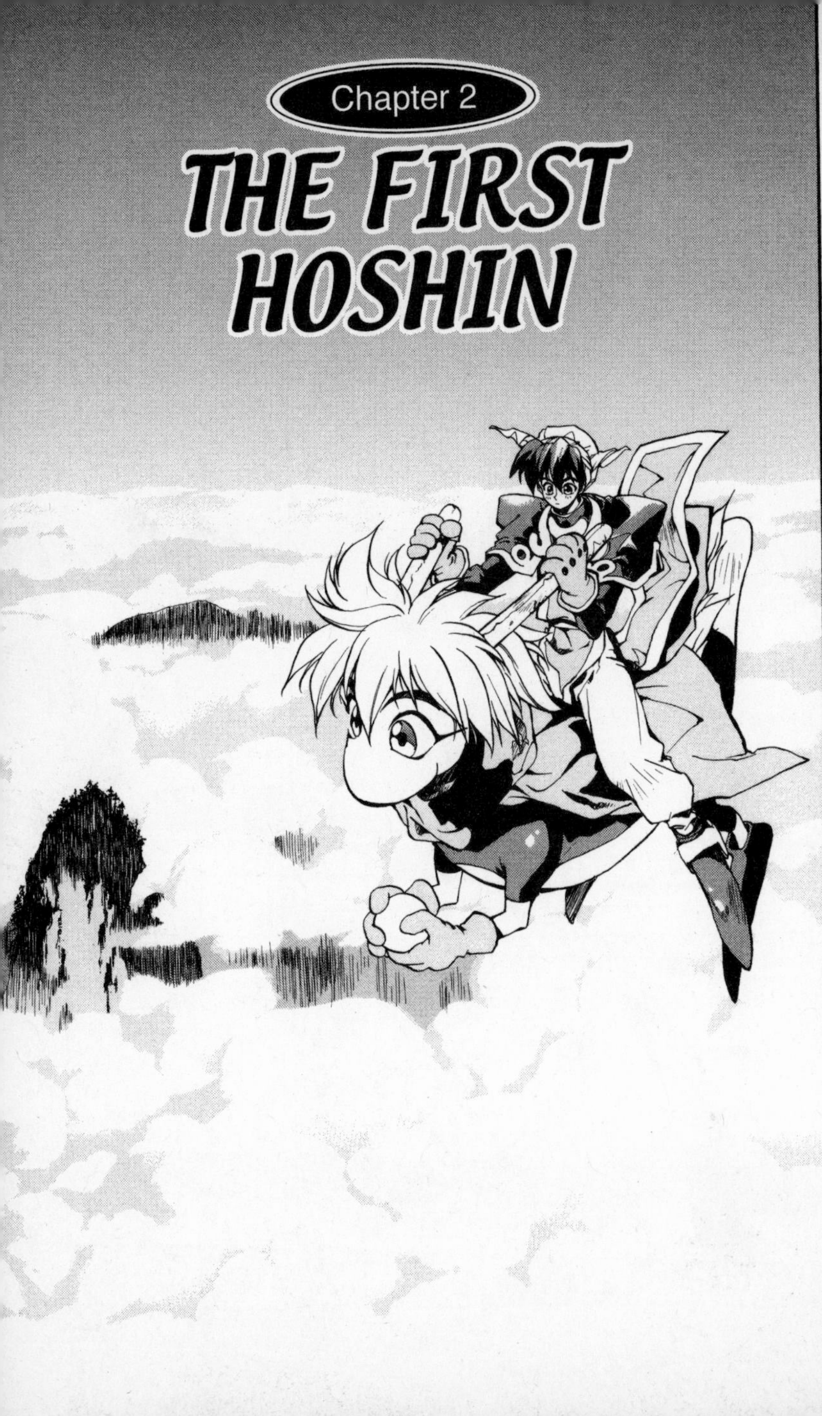
Chapter 2
THE FIRST HOSHIN

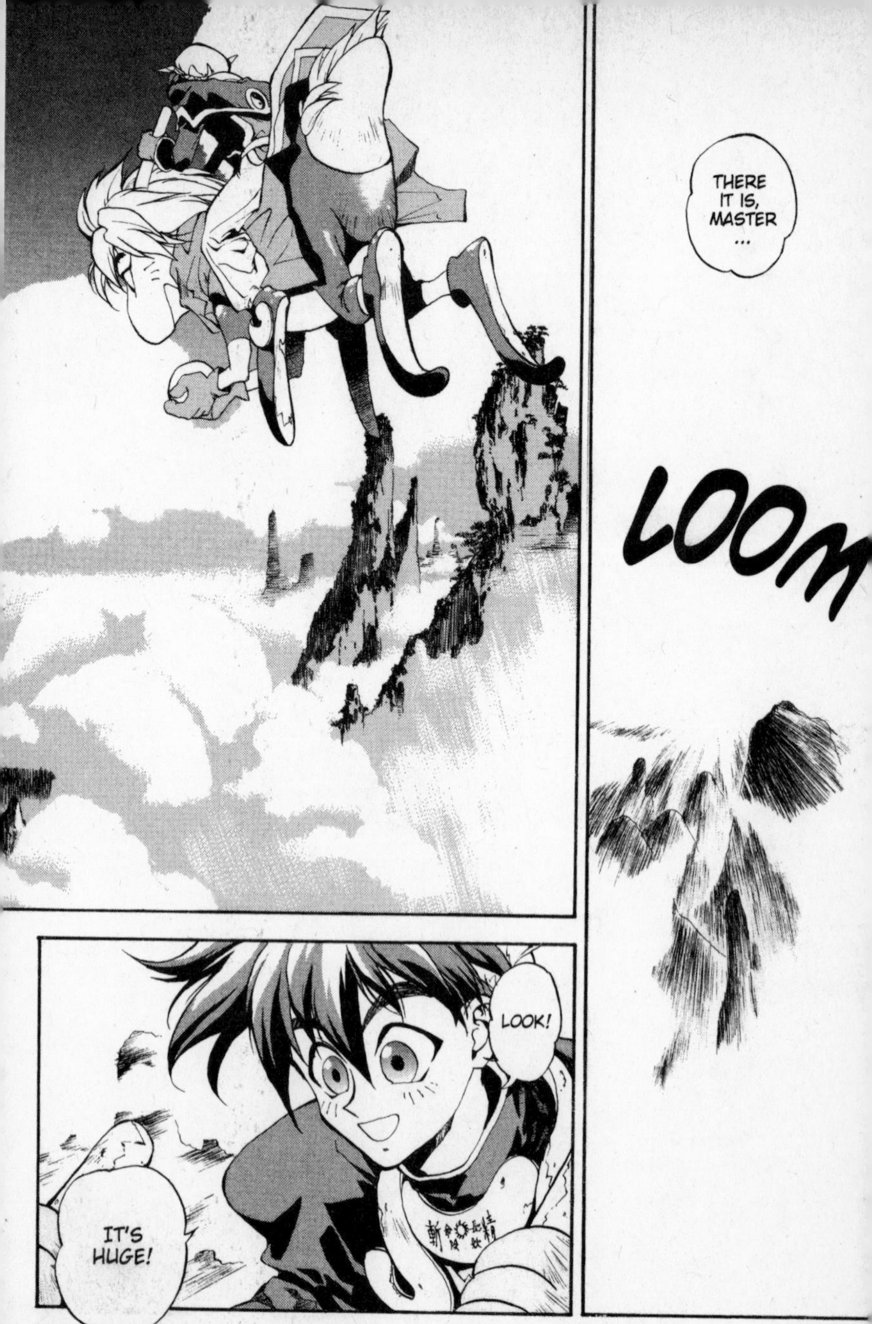
THERE IT IS, MASTER ...
LOOM
LOOK!
IT'S HUGE!

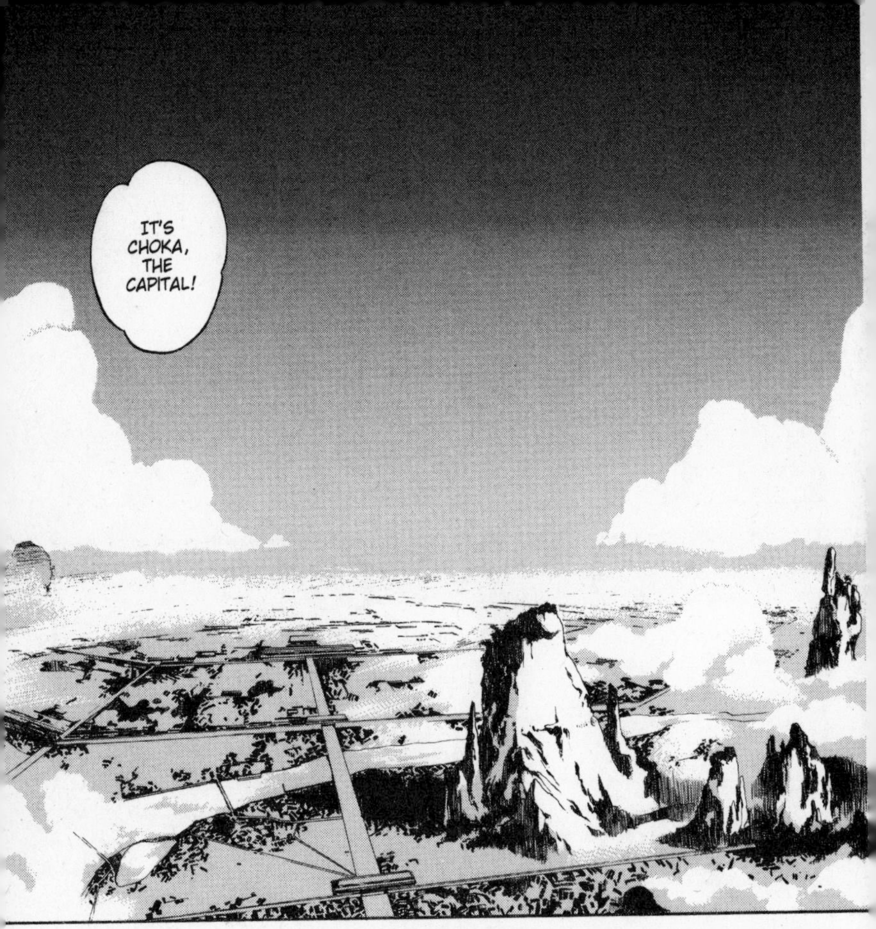
IT'S CHOKA, THE CAPITAL!

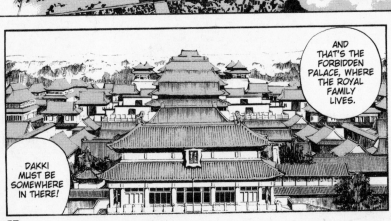

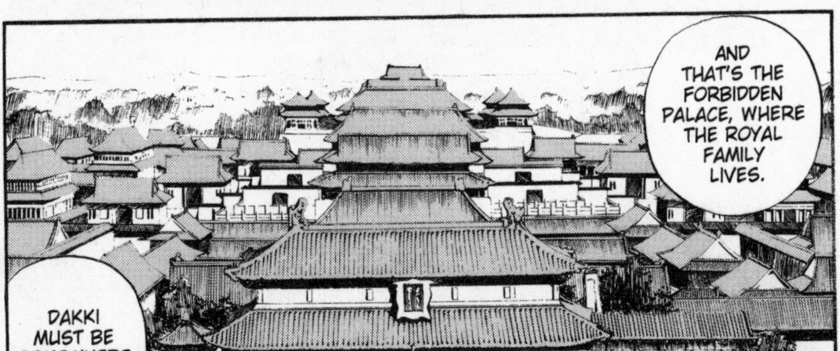
AND THAT'S THE FORBIDDEN PALACE, WHERE THE ROYAL FAMILY LIVES.
DAKKI MUST BE SOMEWHERE IN THERE!

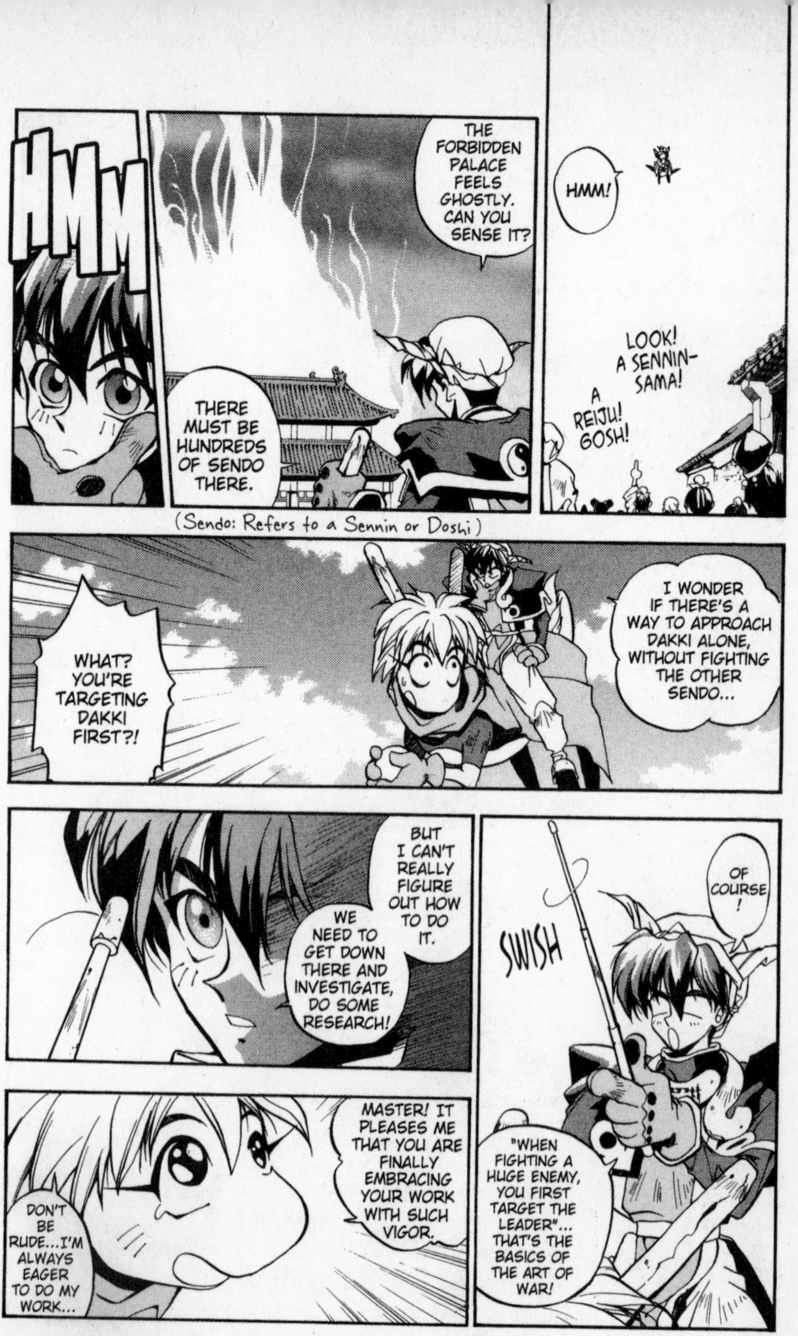
HMM!
LOOK! A SENNIN-SAMA!
A REIJU! GOSH!
THE FORBIDDEN PALACE FEELS GHOSTLY. CAN YOU SENSE IT?
THERE MUST BE HUNDREDS OF SENDO THERE.
HMM
(Sendo: Refers to a Sennin or Doshi)
I WONDER IF THERE'S A WAY TO APPROACH DAKKI ALONE, WITHOUT FIGHTING THE OTHER SENDO...
WHAT? YOU'RE TARGETING DAKKI FIRST?!
OF COURSE!
SWISH
"WHEN FIGHTING A HUGE ENEMY, YOU FIRST TARGET THE LEADER"... THAT'S THE BASICS OF THE ART OF WAR!
BUT I CAN'T REALLY FIGURE OUT HOW TO DO IT.
WE NEED TO GET DOWN THERE AND INVESTIGATE, DO SOME RESEARCH!
MASTER! IT PLEASES ME THAT YOU ARE FINALLY EMBRACING YOUR WORK WITH SUCH VIGOR.
DON'T BE RUDE...I'M ALWAYS EAGER TO DO MY WORK...

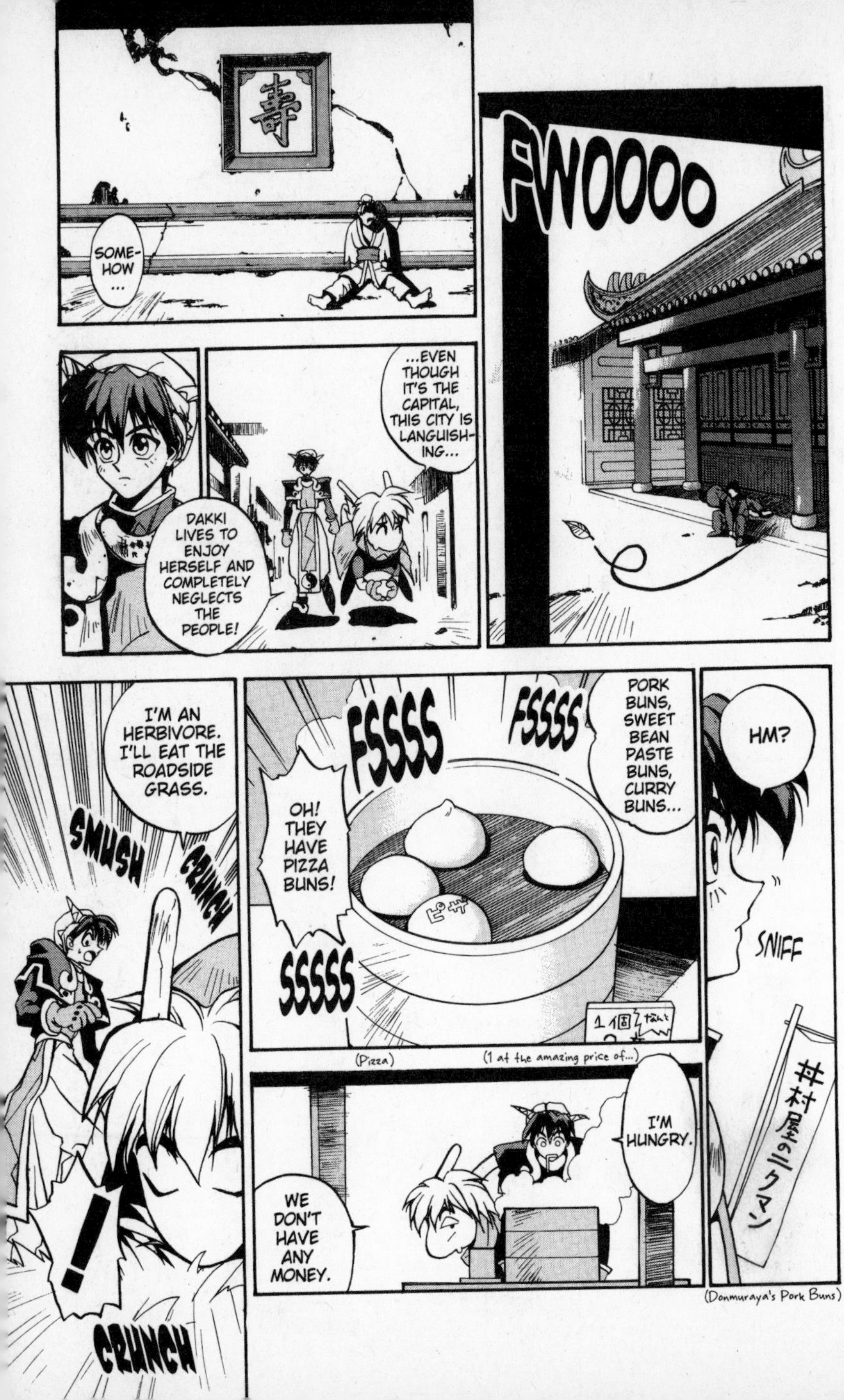
FWOOOO
SOME-HOW...
...EVEN THOUGH IT'S THE CAPITAL, THIS CITY IS LANGUISH-ING...
DAKKI LIVES TO ENJOY HERSELF AND COMPLETELY NEGLECTS THE PEOPLE!
HM?
SNIFF
丼村屋のニクマン
(Donmuraya's Pork Buns)
FSSSS
PORK BUNS, SWEET BEAN PASTE BUNS, CURRY BUNS...
FSSSS
OH! THEY HAVE PIZZA BUNS!
SSSSS
ピザ
(Pizza)
1個 なんと
(1 at the amazing price of...)
I'M HUNGRY.
WE DON'T HAVE ANY MONEY.
I'M AN HERBIVORE. I'LL EAT THE ROADSIDE GRASS.
SMUSH
CRUNCH
!
CRUNCH

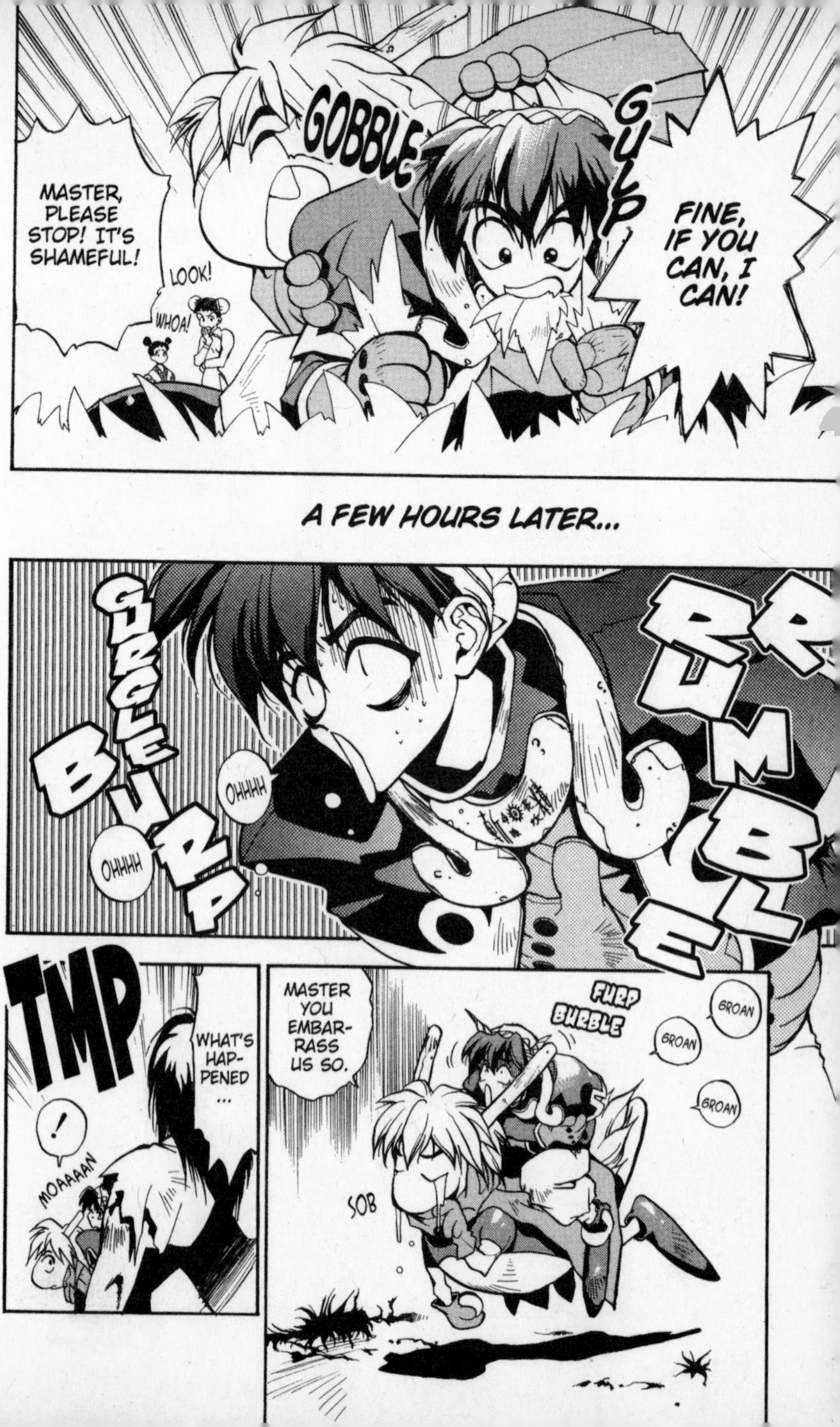
FINE, IF YOU CAN, I CAN!
GULP
GOBBLE
MASTER, PLEASE STOP! IT'S SHAMEFUL!
LOOK!
WHOA!
A FEW HOURS LATER...
RUMBLE
OHHHH
GURGLE
BUMP
OHHHH
GROAN
GROAN
GROAN
FURP BURBLE
MASTER YOU EMBARRASS US SO.
SOB
TMP
WHAT'S HAPPENED...
!
MOAAAAN

READ THIS WAY

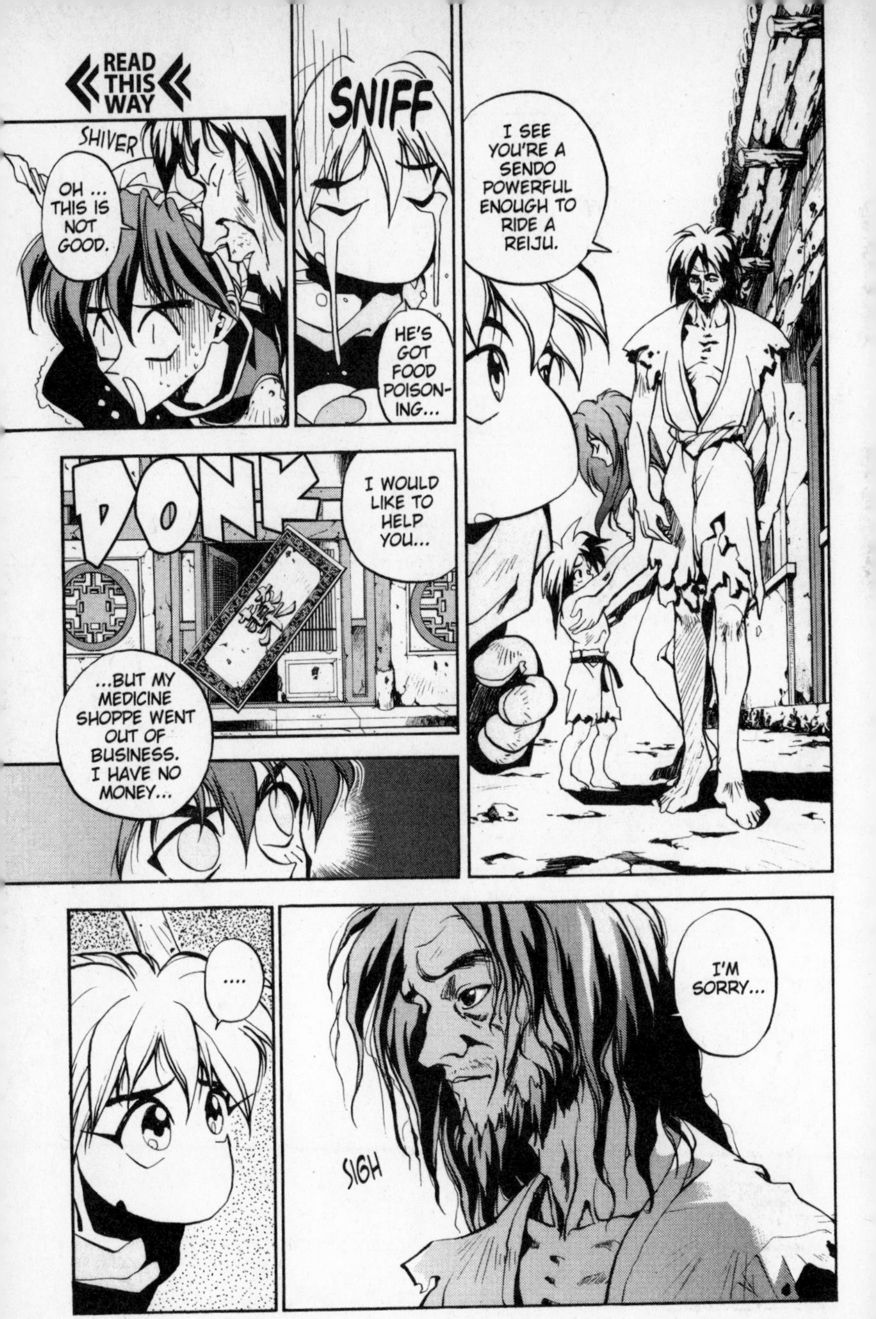
I SEE YOU'RE A SENDO POWERFUL ENOUGH TO RIDE A REIJU.
SNIFF
HE'S GOT FOOD POISONING...
SHIVER
OH ... THIS IS NOT GOOD.
DONK
I WOULD LIKE TO HELP YOU...
...BUT MY MEDICINE SHOPPE WENT OUT OF BUSINESS. I HAVE NO MONEY...
I'M SORRY...
SIGH
....

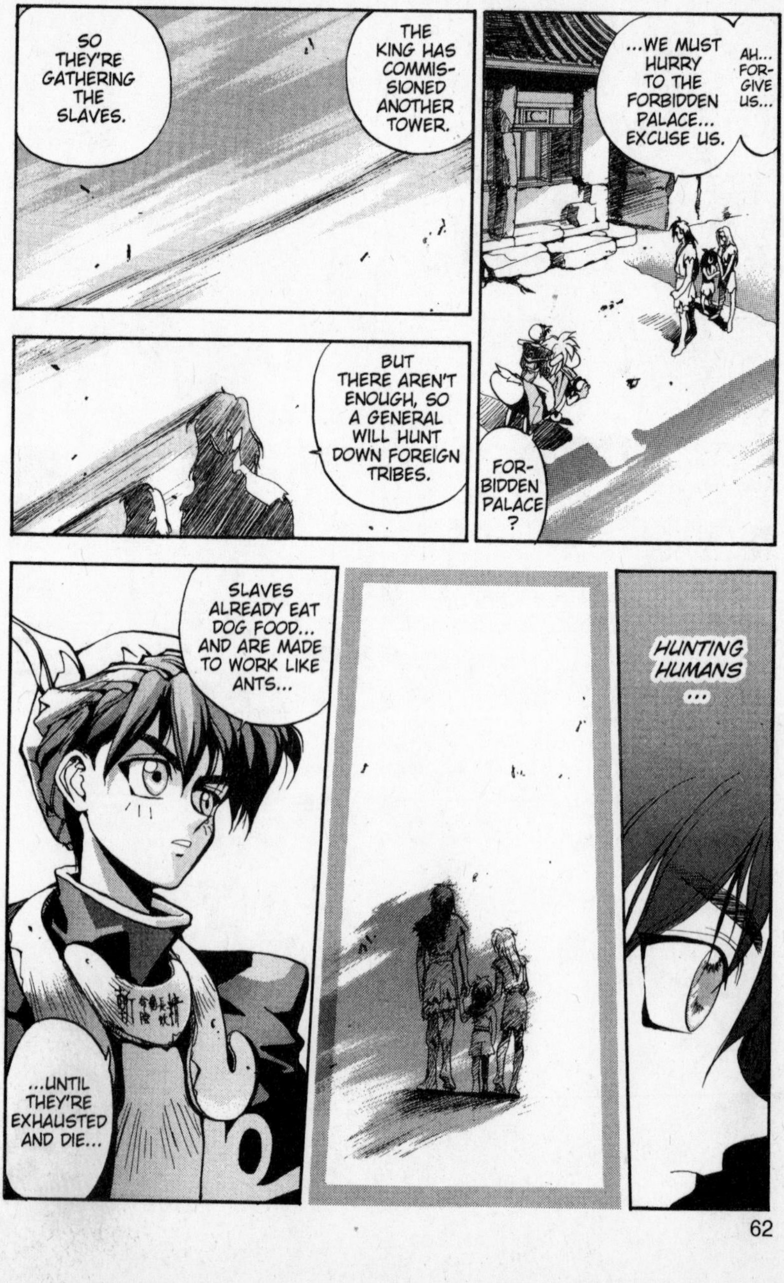
AH... FORGIVE US...
...WE MUST HURRY TO THE FORBIDDEN PALACE... EXCUSE US.
FORBIDDEN PALACE?
THE KING HAS COMMISSIONED ANOTHER TOWER.
SO THEY'RE GATHERING THE SLAVES.
BUT THERE AREN'T ENOUGH, SO A GENERAL WILL HUNT DOWN FOREIGN TRIBES.
HUNTING HUMANS...
SLAVES ALREADY EAT DOG FOOD... AND ARE MADE TO WORK LIKE ANTS...
...UNTIL THEY'RE EXHAUSTED AND DIE...

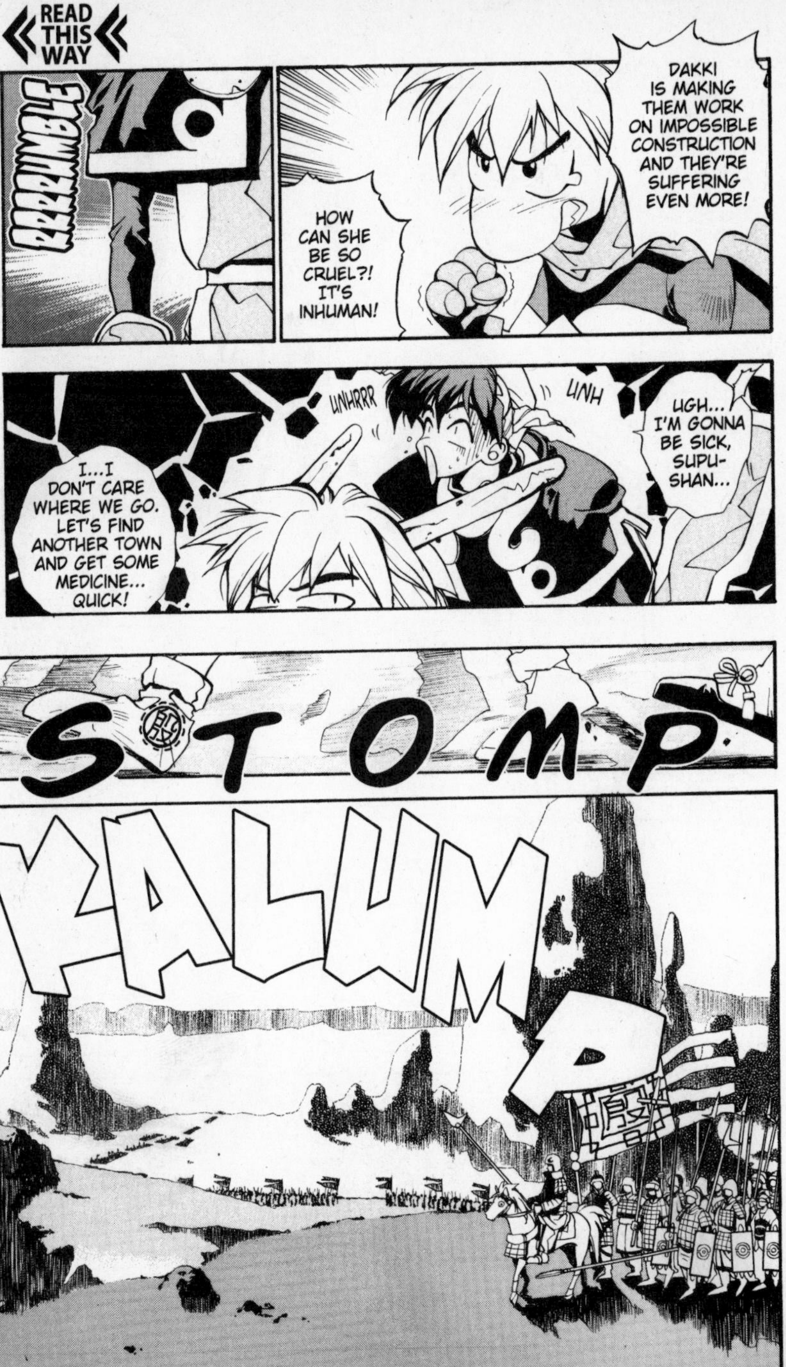
READ THIS WAY
DAKKI IS MAKING THEM WORK ON IMPOSSIBLE CONSTRUCTION AND THEY'RE SUFFERING EVEN MORE!
HOW CAN SHE BE SO CRUEL?! IT'S INHUMAN!
RRRRUMBLE
UNH
UGH... I'M GONNA BE SICK, SUPU-SHAN...
UNHRRR
I...I DON'T CARE WHERE WE GO. LET'S FIND ANOTHER TOWN AND GET SOME MEDICINE... QUICK!
STOMP
KALUMP

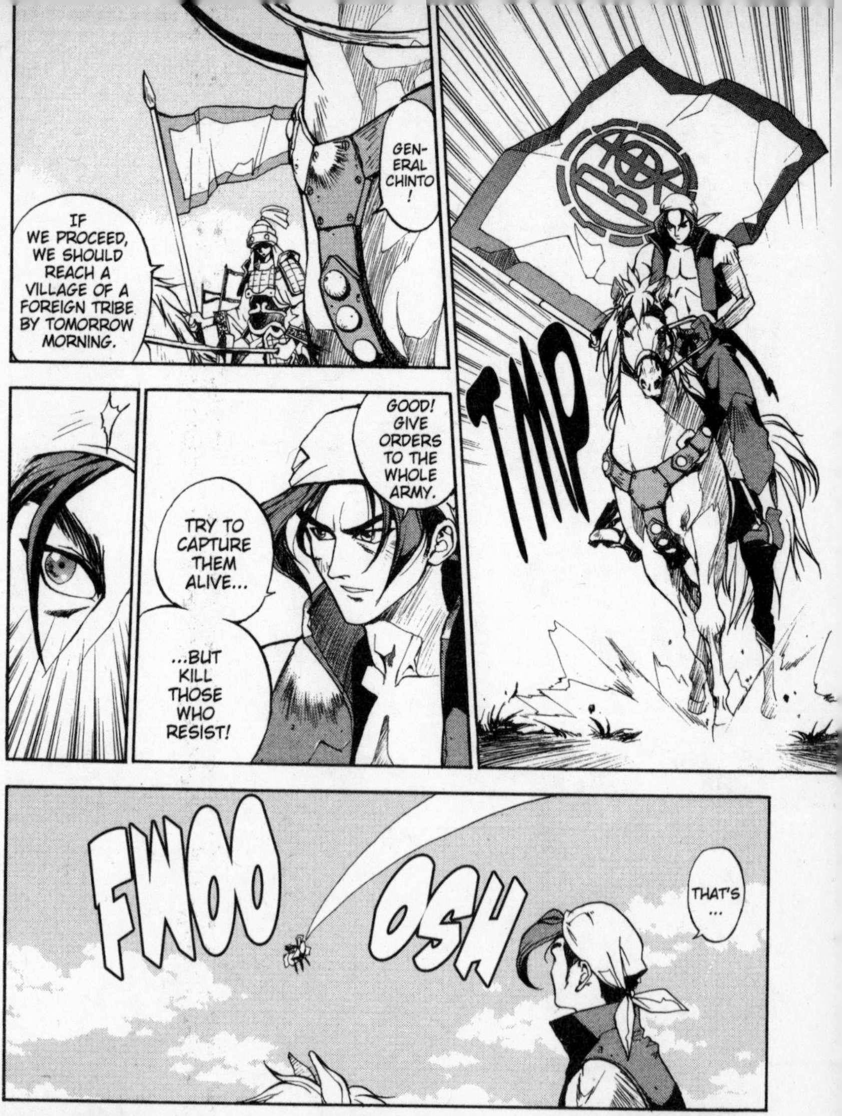
TMP
GEN-
ERAL
CHINTO
!
IF
WE PROCEED,
WE SHOULD
REACH A
VILLAGE OF A
FOREIGN TRIBE
BY TOMORROW
MORNING.
GOOD!
GIVE
ORDERS
TO THE
WHOLE
ARMY.
TRY TO
CAPTURE
THEM
ALIVE...
...BUT
KILL
THOSE
WHO
RESIST!
THAT'S
...
FWOO OSH
...A
SENNIN?
I'VE
NEVER
SEEN HIM
BEFORE...

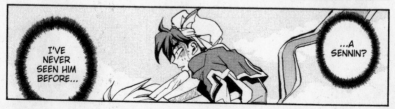

READ THIS WAY

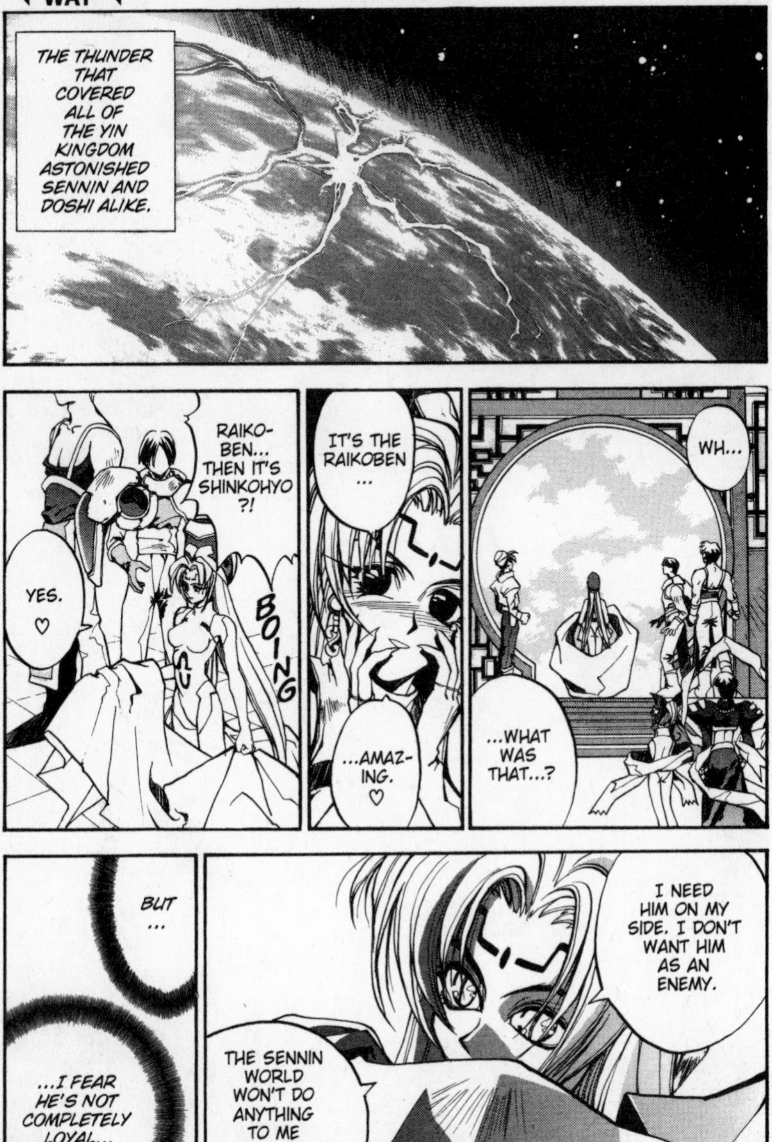
THE THUNDER THAT COVERED ALL OF THE YIN KINGDOM ASTONISHED SENNIN AND DOSHI ALIKE.
WH...
...WHAT WAS THAT...?
IT'S THE RAIKOBEN ...
...AMAZ-ING. ♡
RAIKO-BEN... THEN IT'S SHINKOHYO ?!
YES. ♡
BOING
I NEED HIM ON MY SIDE. I DON'T WANT HIM AS AN ENEMY.
THE SENNIN WORLD WON'T DO ANYTHING TO ME WHILE THEY ARE AFRAID OF HIM.
BUT ...
...I FEAR HE'S NOT COMPLETELY LOYAL...

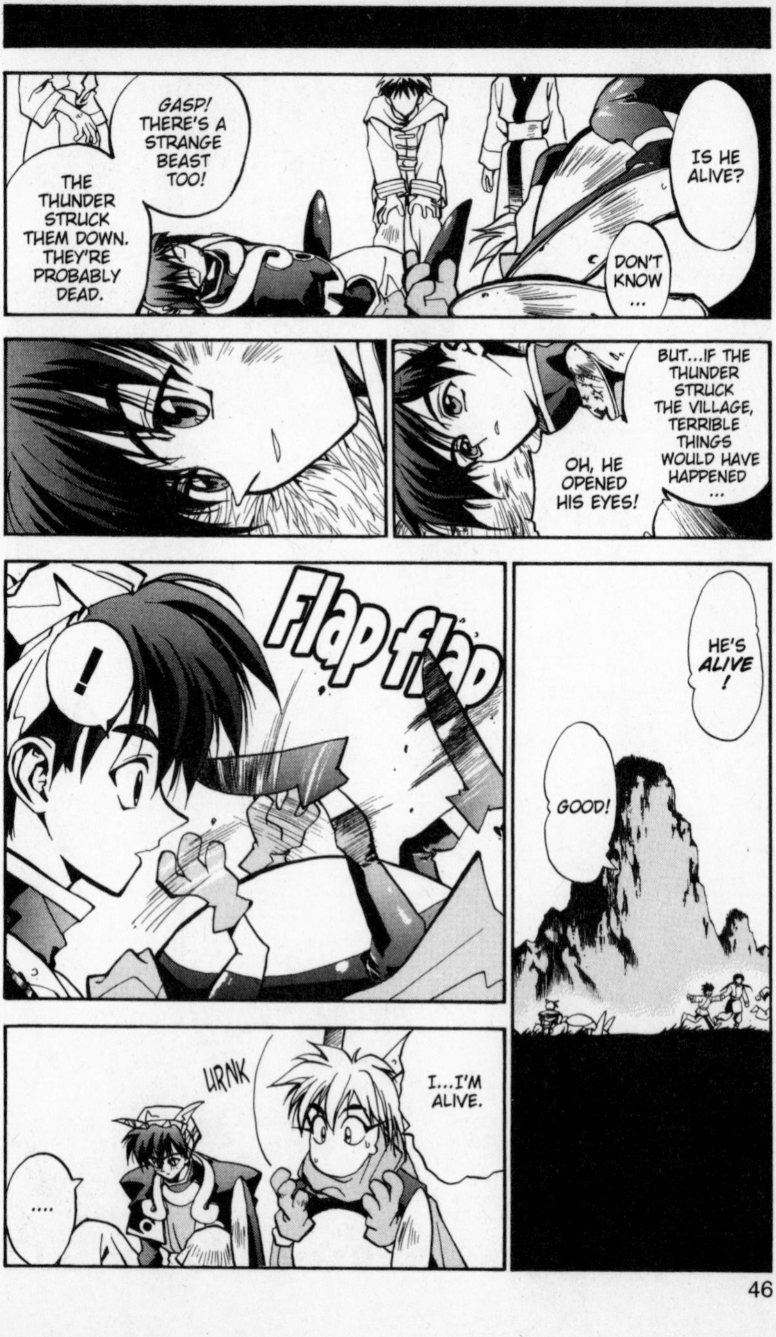
IS HE ALIVE?
DON'T KNOW ...
GASP! THERE'S A STRANGE BEAST TOO!
THE THUNDER STRUCK THEM DOWN. THEY'RE PROBABLY DEAD.
BUT...IF THE THUNDER STRUCK THE VILLAGE, TERRIBLE THINGS WOULD HAVE HAPPENED ...
OH, HE OPENED HIS EYES!
HE'S ALIVE!
GOOD!
Flap flap
!
I...I'M ALIVE.
URNK
....

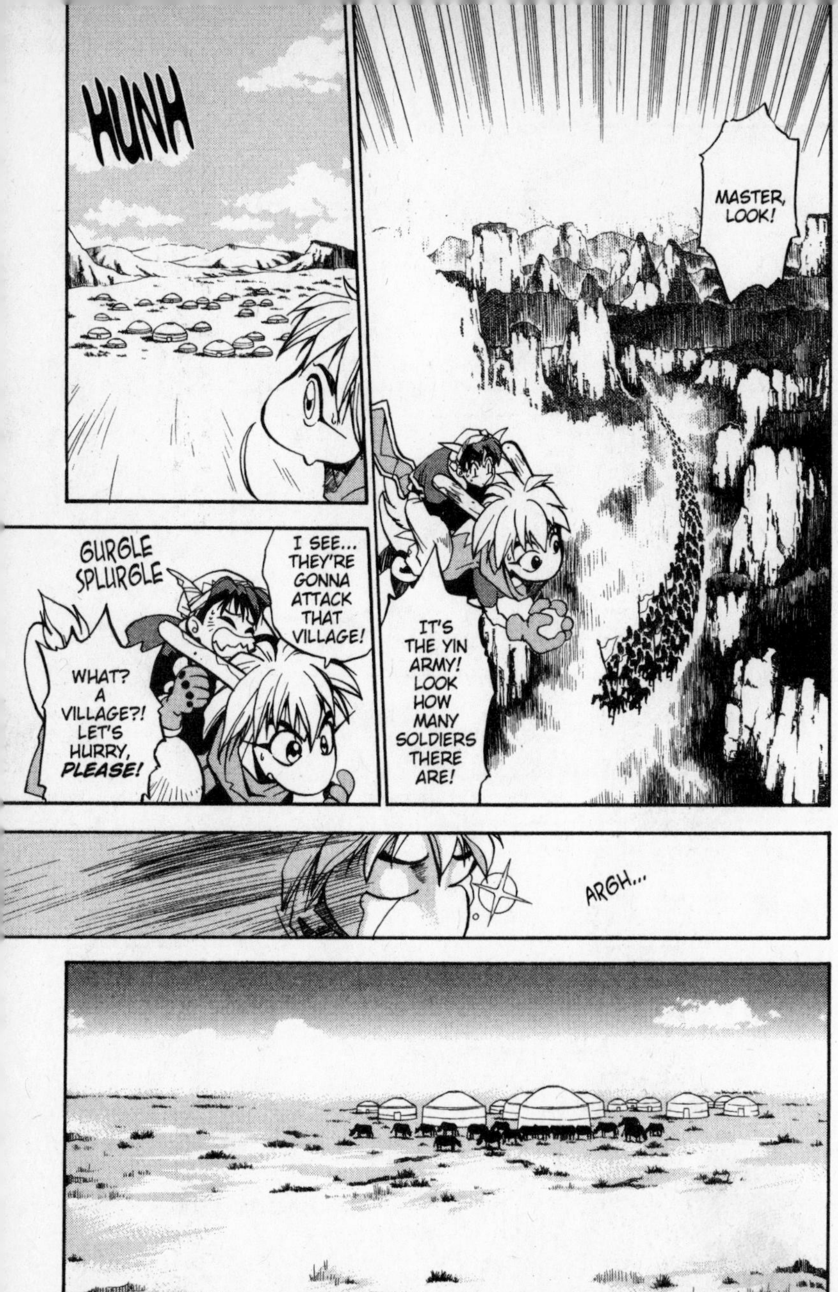
MASTER, LOOK!
IT'S THE YIN ARMY! LOOK HOW MANY SOLDIERS THERE ARE!
HUNH
I SEE... THEY'RE GONNA ATTACK THAT VILLAGE!
GURGLE SPLURGLE
WHAT? A VILLAGE?! LET'S HURRY, *PLEASE!*
ARGH...

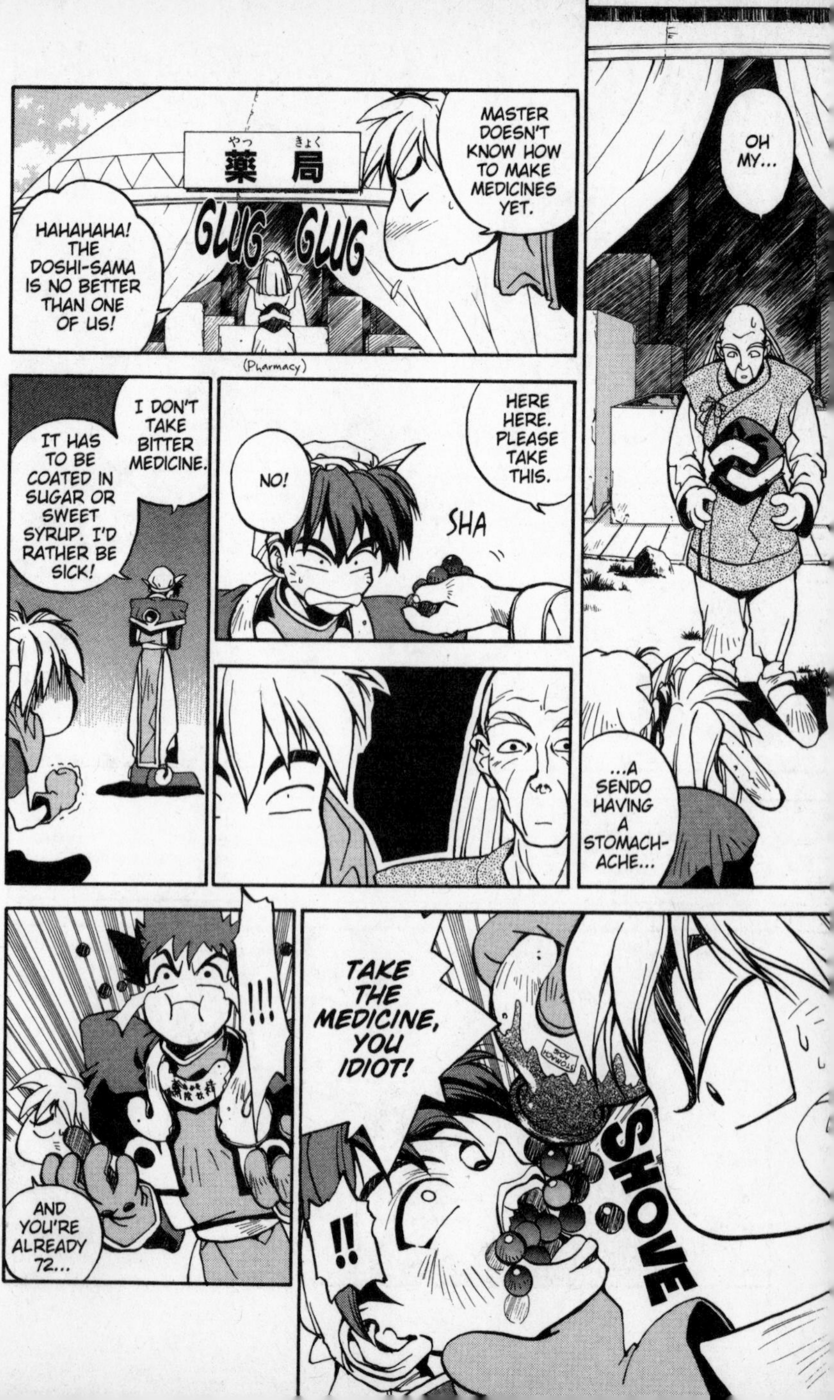
OH MY...
...A SENDO HAVING A STOMACH-ACHE...
MASTER DOESN'T KNOW HOW TO MAKE MEDICINES YET.
やっきょく
薬局
GLUG GLUG
HAHAHAHA! THE DOSHI-SAMA IS NO BETTER THAN ONE OF US!
(Pharmacy)
HERE HERE. PLEASE TAKE THIS.
SHA
NO!
I DON'T TAKE BITTER MEDICINE.
IT HAS TO BE COATED IN SUGAR OR SWEET SYRUP. I'D RATHER BE SICK!
TAKE THE MEDICINE, YOU IDIOT!
STOMACH ACHE
SHOVE
!!
!!!
AND YOU'RE ALREADY 72...

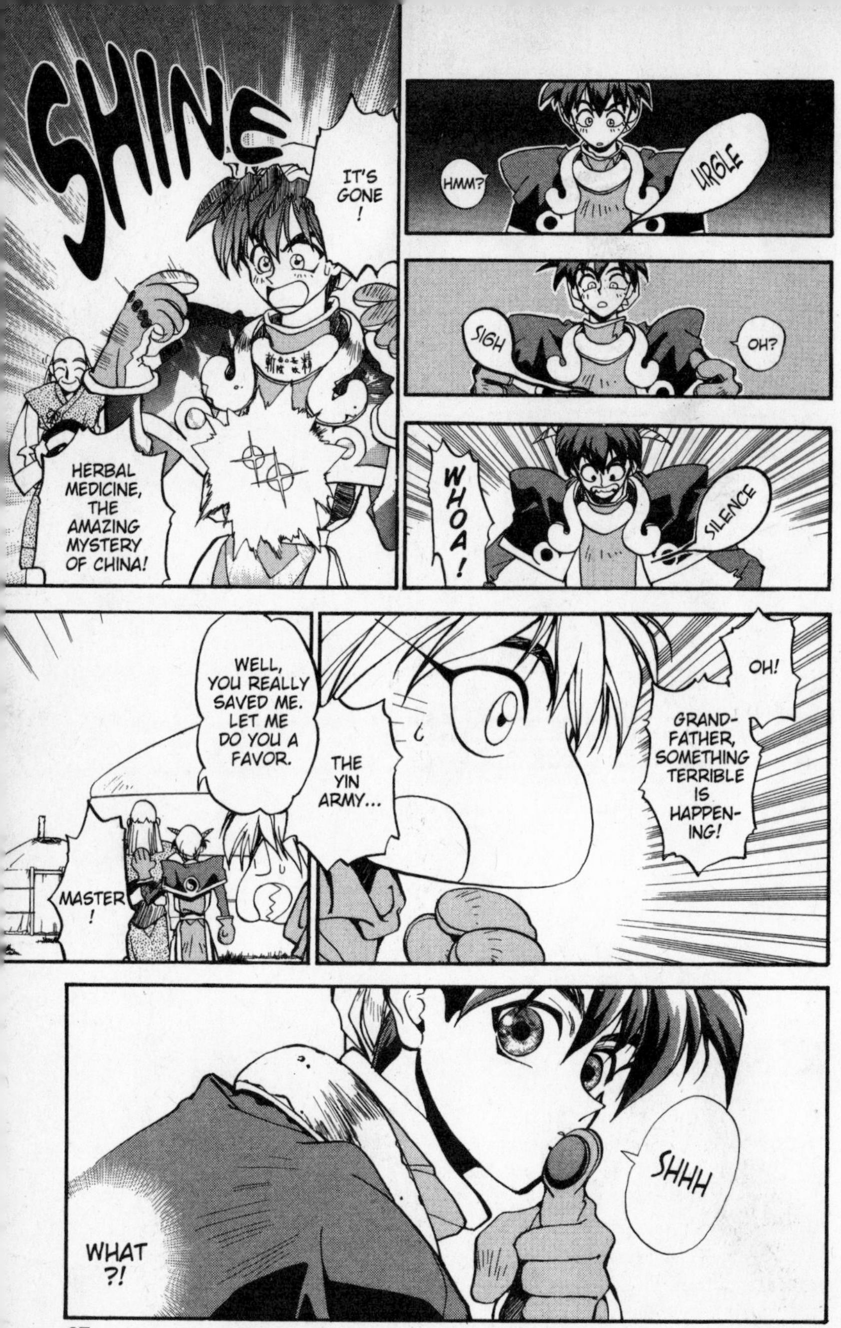
URGLE
HMM?
OH?
SIGH
SILENCE
WHOA!
IT'S GONE!
SHINE
HERBAL MEDICINE, THE AMAZING MYSTERY OF CHINA!
OH!
GRANDFATHER, SOMETHING TERRIBLE IS HAPPENING!
THE YIN ARMY...
WELL, YOU REALLY SAVED ME. LET ME DO YOU A FAVOR.
MASTER!
SHHH
WHAT?!

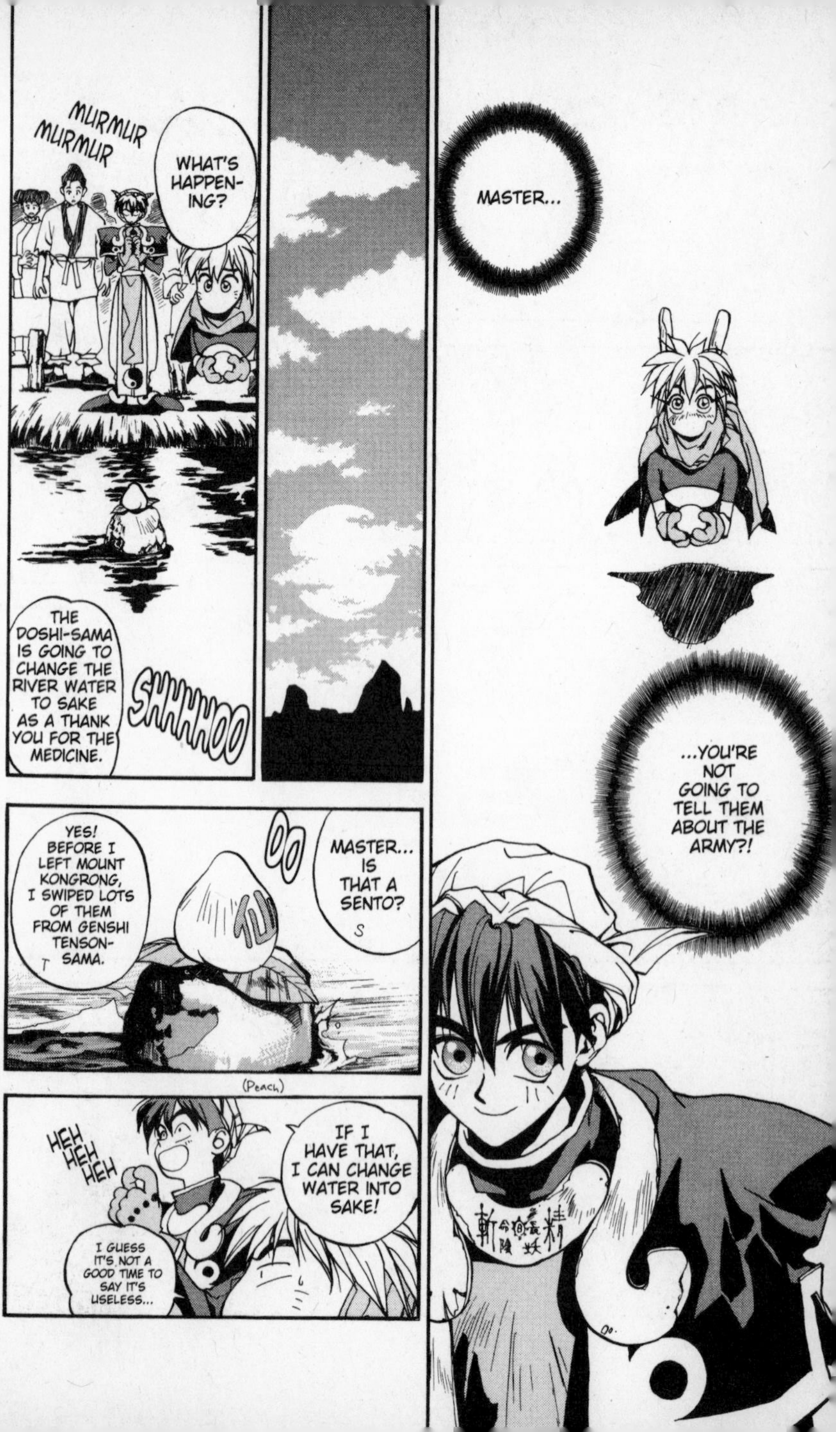
MASTER...
...YOU'RE NOT GOING TO TELL THEM ABOUT THE ARMY?!
WHAT'S HAPPEN-ING?
MURMUR MURMUR
SHHHHOO
THE DOSHI-SAMA IS GOING TO CHANGE THE RIVER WATER TO SAKE AS A THANK YOU FOR THE MEDICINE.
OO
MASTER... IS THAT A SENTO?
YES! BEFORE I LEFT MOUNT KONGRONG, I SWIPED LOTS OF THEM FROM GENSHI TENSON-SAMA.
(Peach)
IF I HAVE THAT, I CAN CHANGE WATER INTO SAKE!
HEH HEH HEH
I GUESS IT'S NOT A GOOD TIME TO SAY IT'S USELESS...

READ THIS WAY

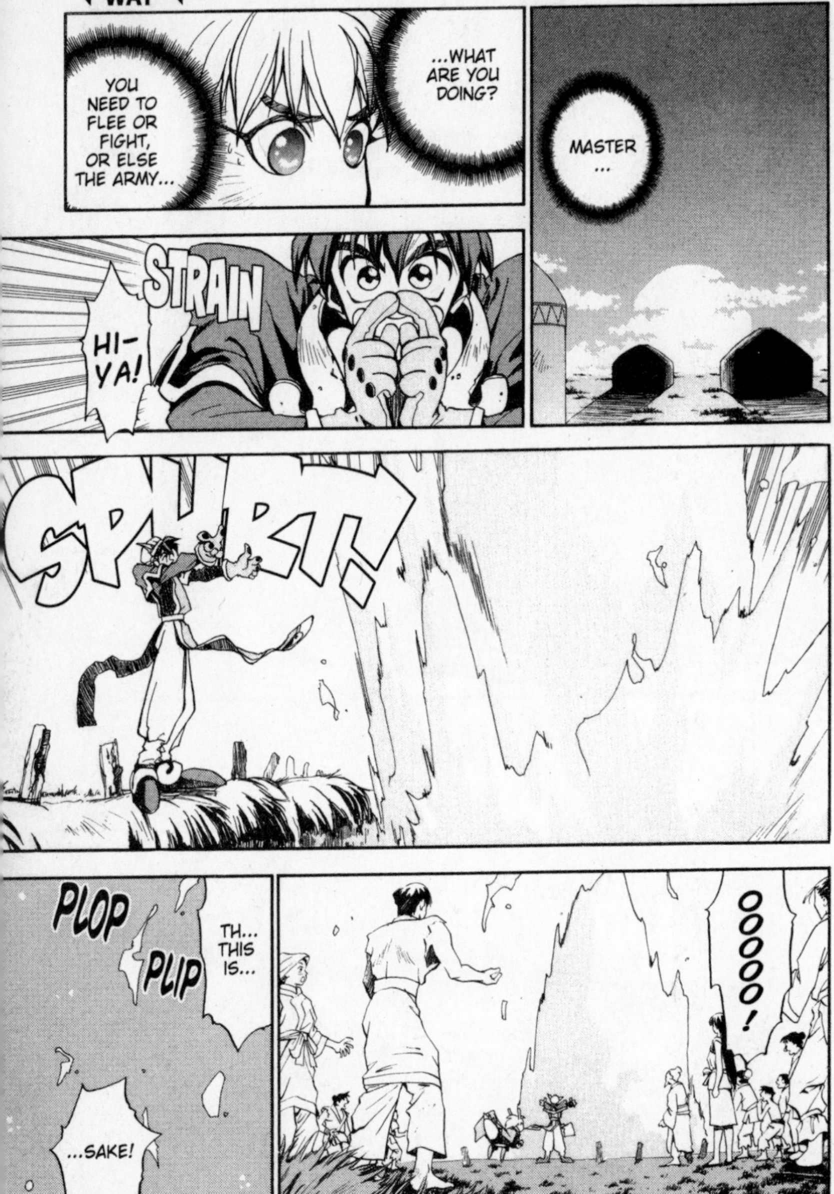
MASTER ...
...WHAT ARE YOU DOING?
YOU NEED TO FLEE OR FIGHT, OR ELSE THE ARMY...
STRAIN
HI-YA!
SPURT!
OOOOOO!
TH... THIS IS...
PLOP
PLIP
...SAKE!

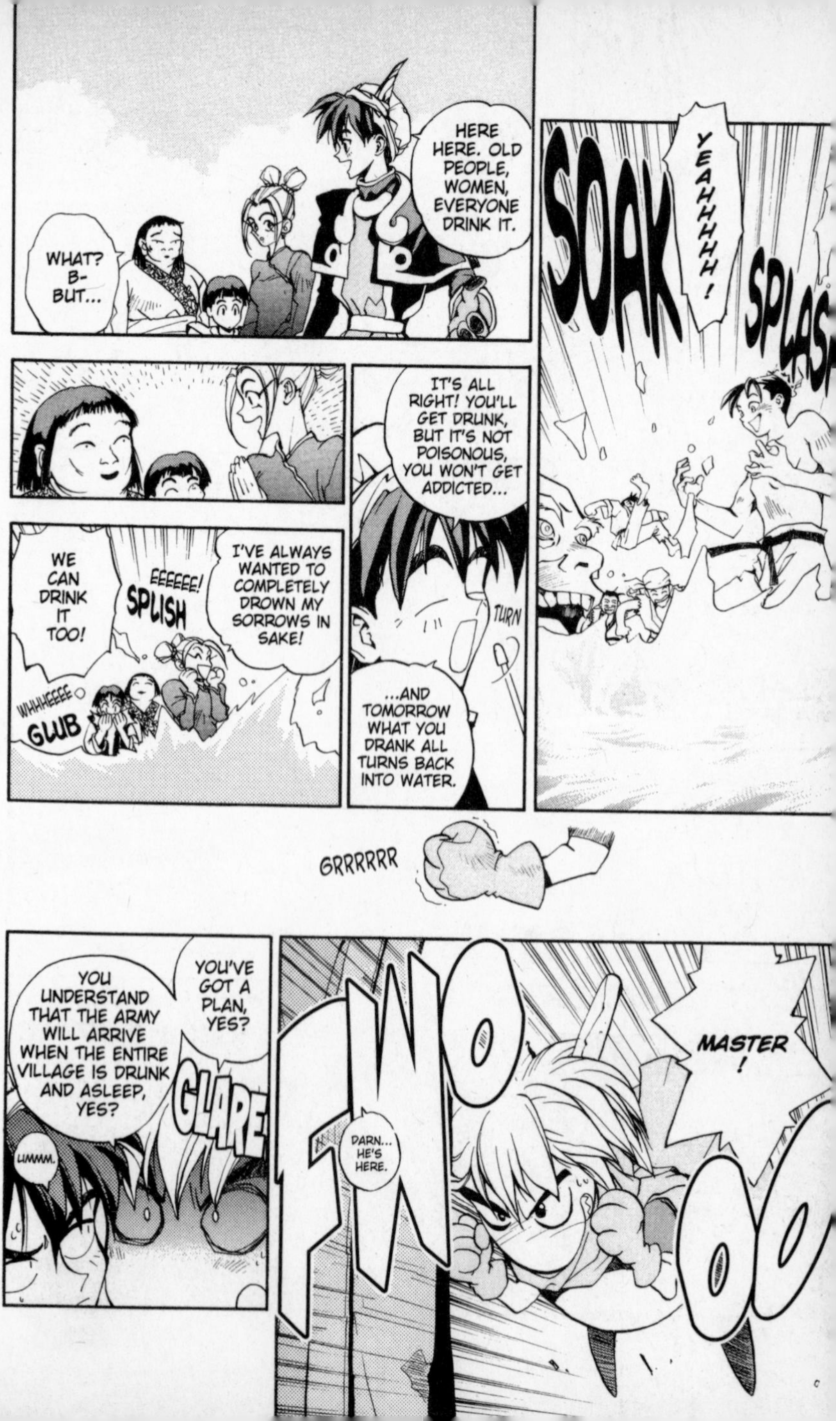
SOAK
YEAHHHHH!
SPLASH
HERE HERE. OLD PEOPLE, WOMEN, EVERYONE DRINK IT.
WHAT? B-BUT...
IT'S ALL RIGHT! YOU'LL GET DRUNK, BUT IT'S NOT POISONOUS, YOU WON'T GET ADDICTED...
TURN
...AND TOMORROW WHAT YOU DRANK ALL TURNS BACK INTO WATER.
I'VE ALWAYS WANTED TO COMPLETELY DROWN MY SORROWS IN SAKE!
EEEEEE!
SPLISH
WE CAN DRINK IT TOO!
WHHHEEEE
GLUB
GRRRRRR
MASTER!
WOOF
DARN... HE'S HERE.
YOU'VE GOT A PLAN, YES?
YOU UNDERSTAND THAT THE ARMY WILL ARRIVE WHEN THE ENTIRE VILLAGE IS DRUNK AND ASLEEP, YES?
GLARE
UMMM.

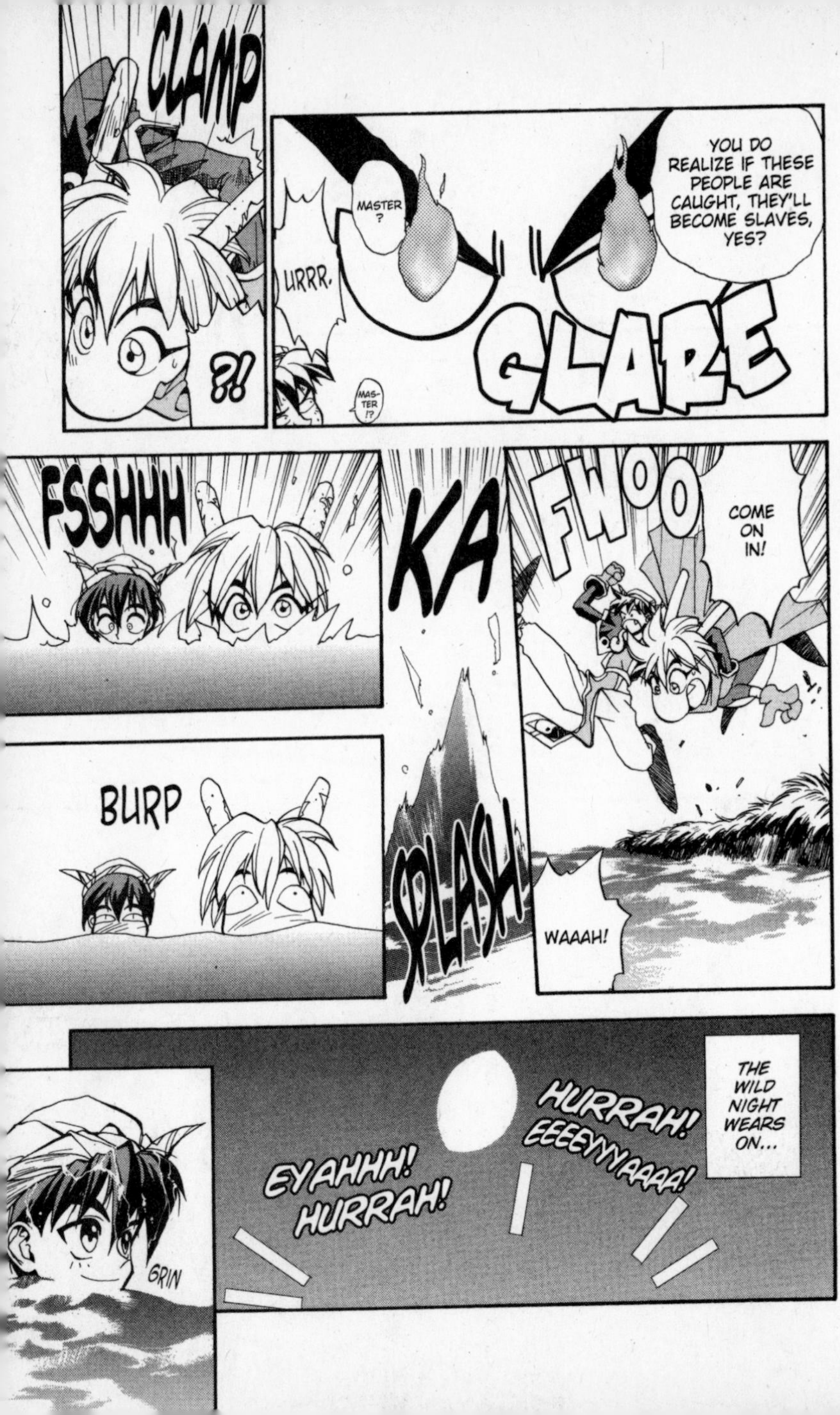
YOU DO REALIZE IF THESE PEOPLE ARE CAUGHT, THEY'LL BECOME SLAVES, YES?
MASTER ?
URRR.
GLARE
MAS-TER !?
CLAMP
?!
FWOO
COME ON IN!
WAAAH!
KA
SPLASH
FSSHHH
BURP
THE WILD NIGHT WEARS ON...
HURRAH! EEEEYYYAAAA!
EYAHHH! HURRAH!
GRIN

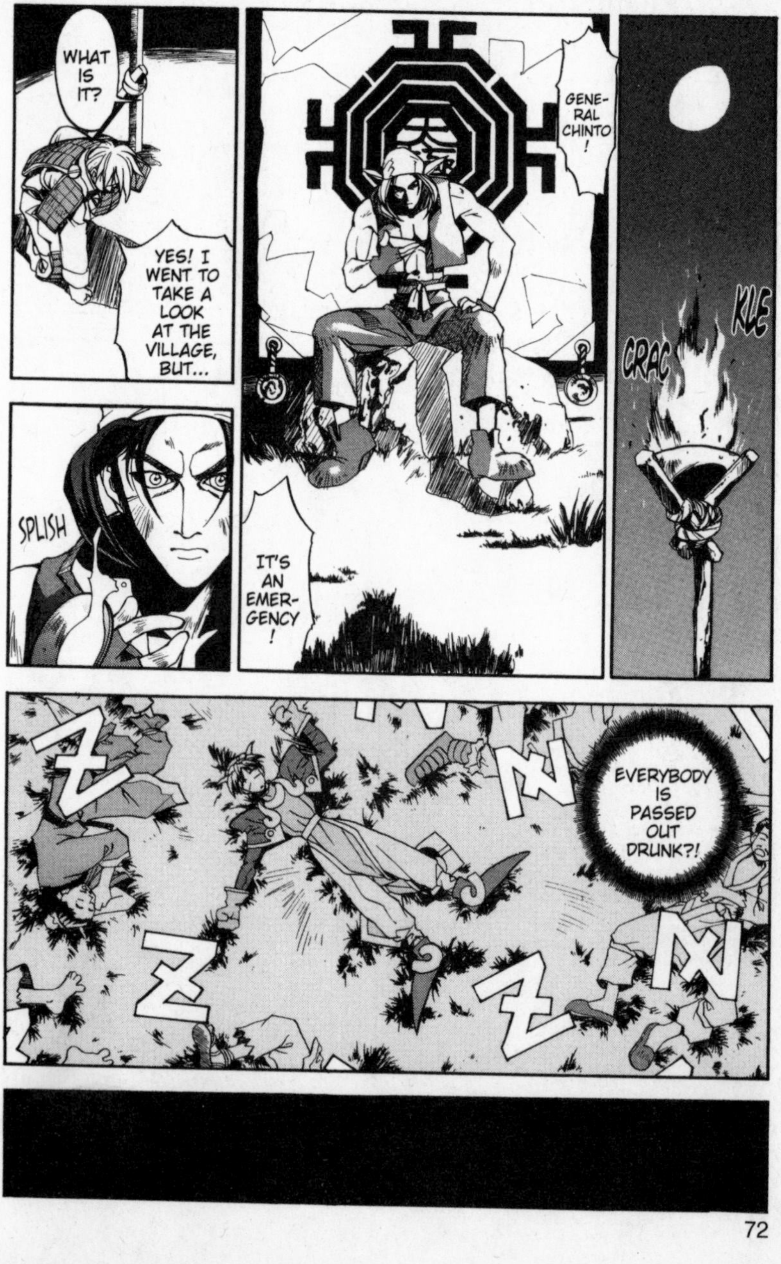
CRAC
KLE
GENERAL CHINTO!
IT'S AN EMERGENCY!
WHAT IS IT?
YES! I WENT TO TAKE A LOOK AT THE VILLAGE, BUT...
SPLISH
EVERYBODY IS PASSED OUT DRUNK?!
Z
Z
Z
Z
Z

READ THIS WAY

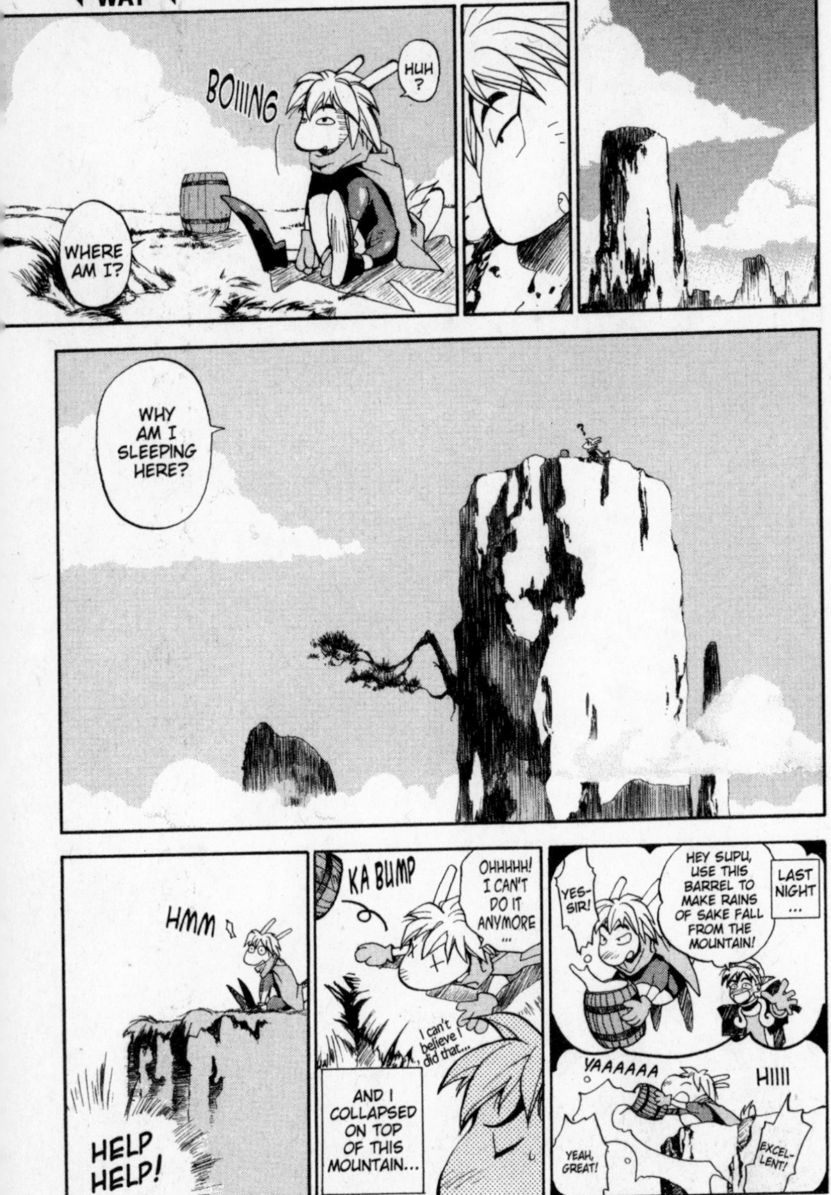

HUH?
BOIIING
WHERE AM I?
WHY AM I SLEEPING HERE?
LAST NIGHT...
HEY SUPU, USE THIS BARREL TO MAKE RAINS OF SAKE FALL FROM THE MOUNTAIN!
YES-SIR!
YAAAAAA
HIIII
EXCEL-LENT!
YEAH, GREAT!
OHHHHH! I CAN'T DO IT ANYMORE...
KA BUMP
I can't believe I did that...
AND I COLLAPSED ON TOP OF THIS MOUNTAIN...
HMM
HELP HELP!

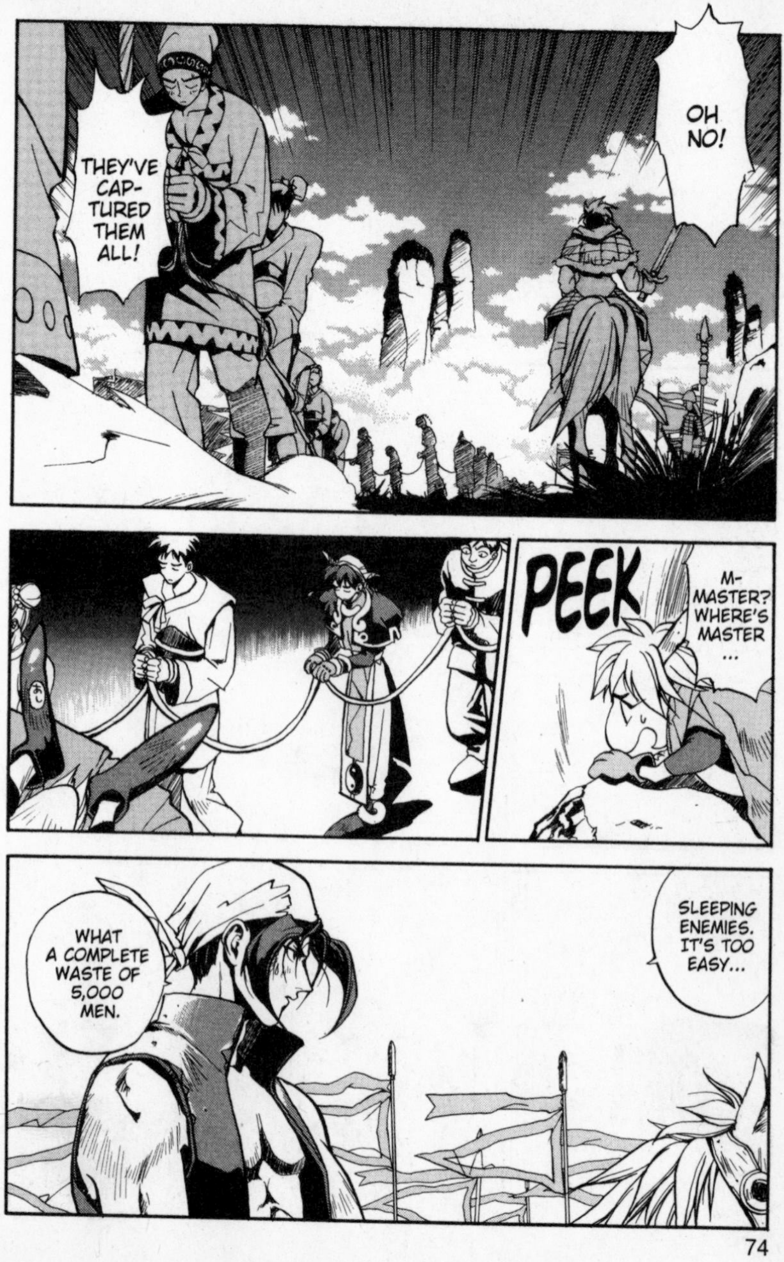
OH NO!
THEY'VE CAPTURED THEM ALL!
PEEK
M-MASTER? WHERE'S MASTER ...
SLEEPING ENEMIES. IT'S TOO EASY...
WHAT A COMPLETE WASTE OF 5,000 MEN.

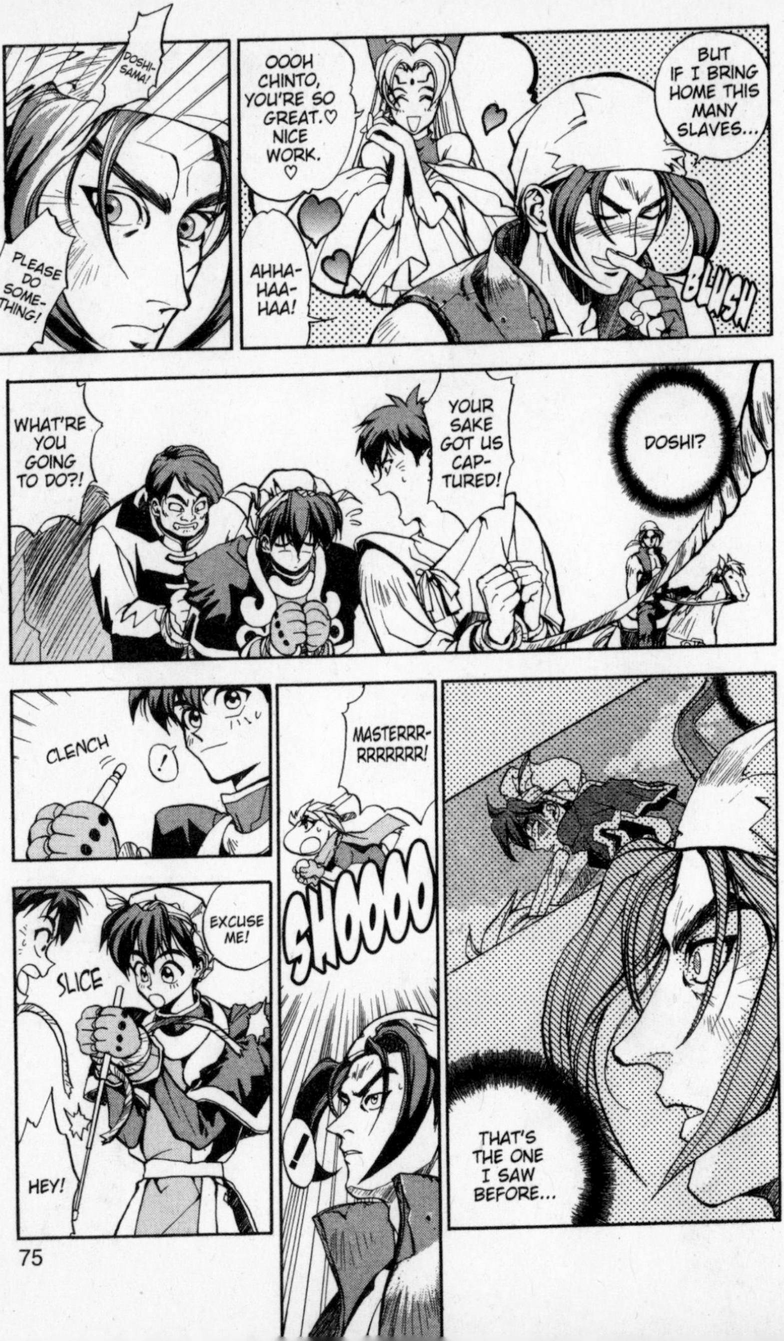
BUT IF I BRING HOME THIS MANY SLAVES...
BLUSH
OOOH CHINTO, YOU'RE SO GREAT.♡ NICE WORK. ♡
AHHA-HAA-HAA!
DOSHI-SAMA!
PLEASE DO SOME-THING!
DOSHI?
YOUR SAKE GOT US CAP-TURED!
WHAT'RE YOU GOING TO DO?!
THAT'S THE ONE I SAW BEFORE...
MASTERRR-RRRRRRR!
SHOOOO
!
CLENCH
!
EXCUSE ME!
SLICE
HEY!

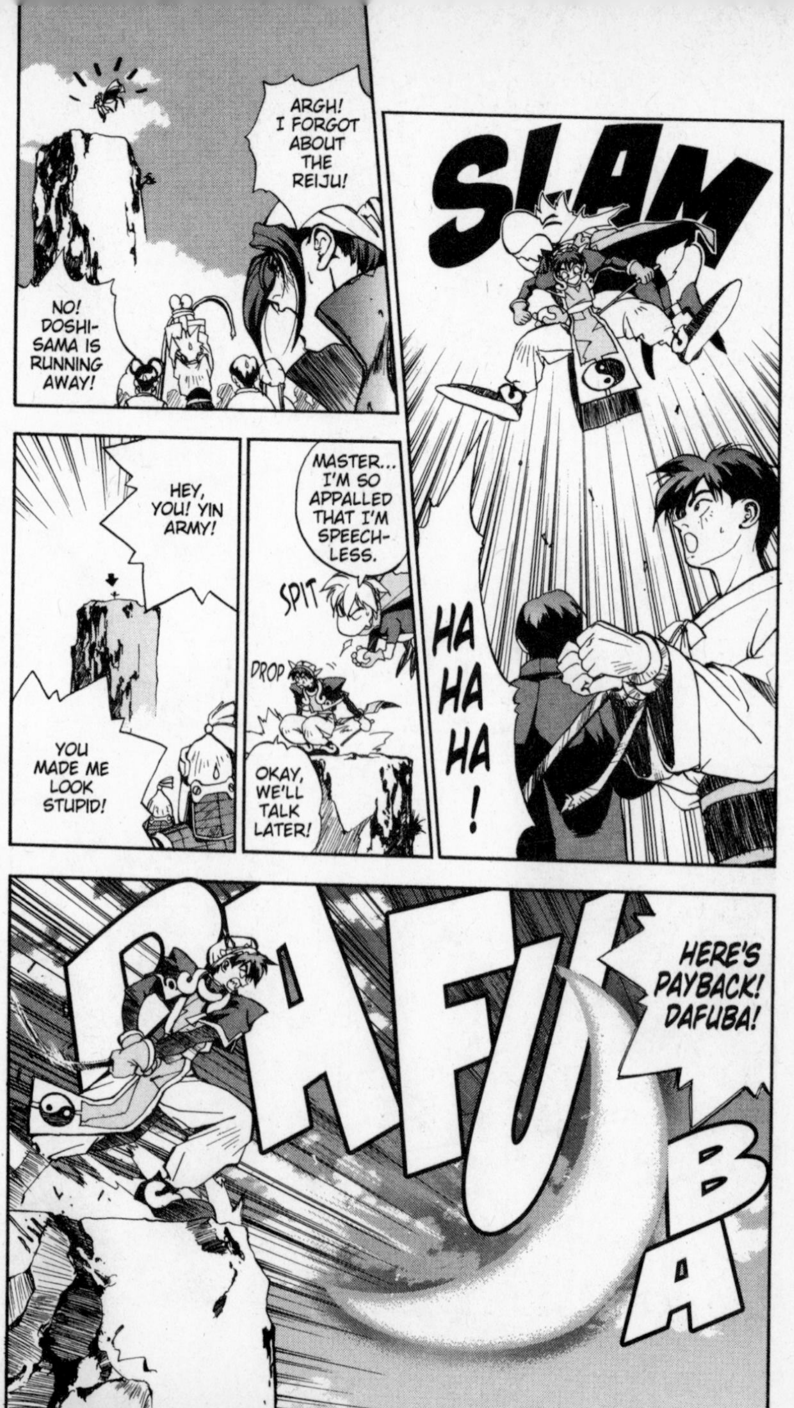
SLAM
HA HA HA!
ARGH! I FORGOT ABOUT THE REIJU!
NO! DOSHI-SAMA IS RUNNING AWAY!
MASTER... I'M SO APPALLED THAT I'M SPEECHLESS.
SPIT
DROP
OKAY, WE'LL TALK LATER!
HEY, YOU! YIN ARMY!
YOU MADE ME LOOK STUPID!
HERE'S PAYBACK! DAFUBA!
DAFUBA

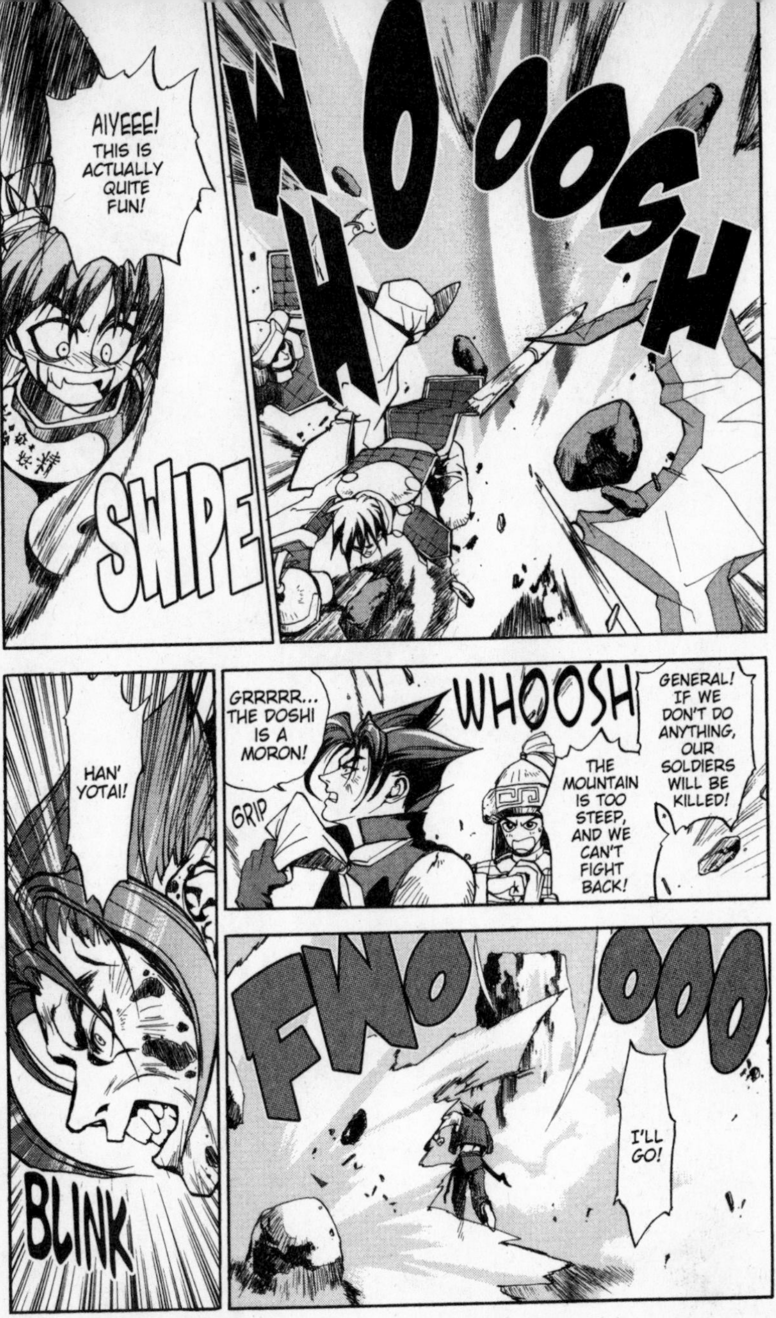
WHOOOOSH
AIYEEE! THIS IS ACTUALLY QUITE FUN!
SWIPE
GENERAL! IF WE DON'T DO ANYTHING, OUR SOLDIERS WILL BE KILLED!
THE MOUNTAIN IS TOO STEEP, AND WE CAN'T FIGHT BACK!
WHOOSH
GRRRRR... THE DOSHI IS A MORON!
GRIP
FWOOOO
I'LL GO!
HAN' YOTAI!
BLINK

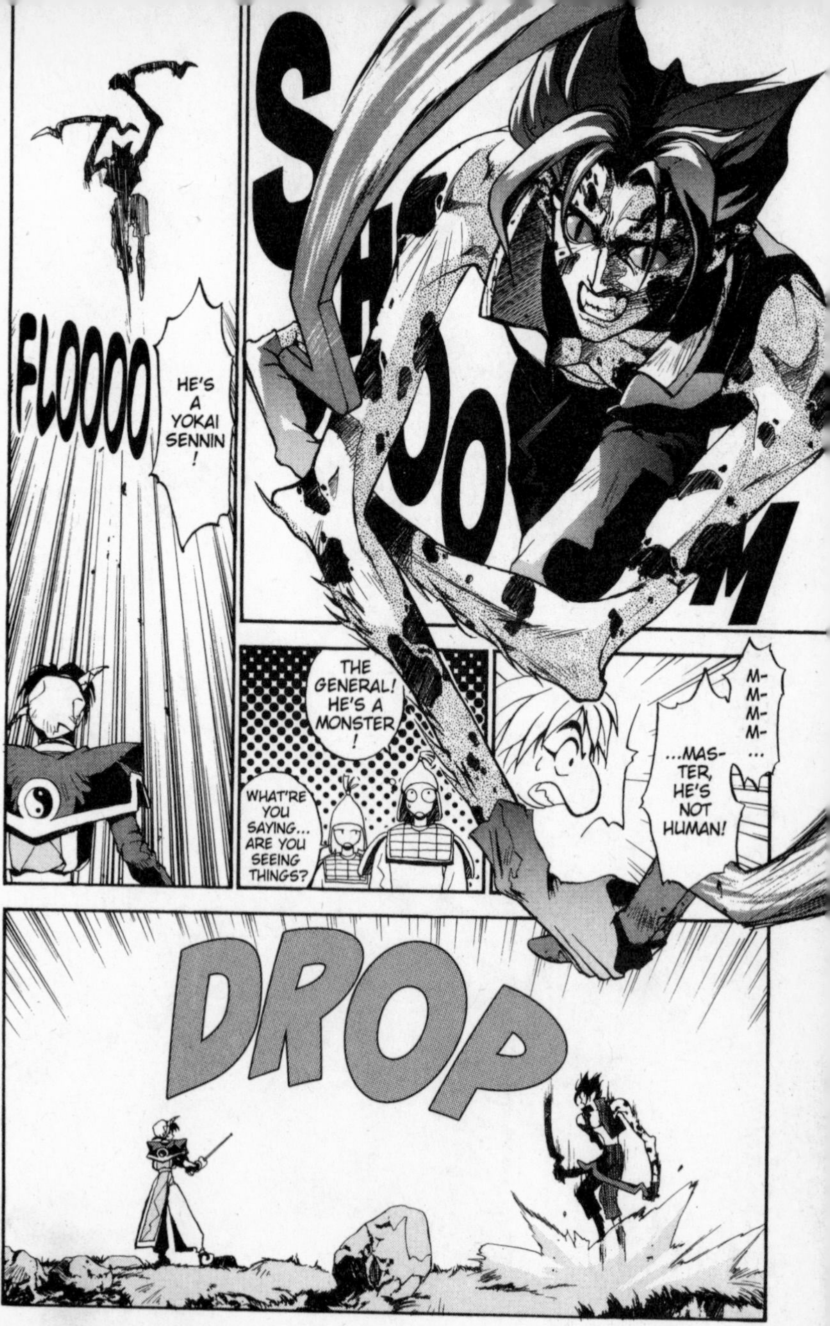
SHOOOM
M-M-M-M-...
...MASTER, HE'S NOT HUMAN!
THE GENERAL! HE'S A MONSTER!
WHAT'RE YOU SAYING... ARE YOU SEEING THINGS?
FLOOOO
HE'S A YOKAI SENNIN!
DROP

READ THIS WAY

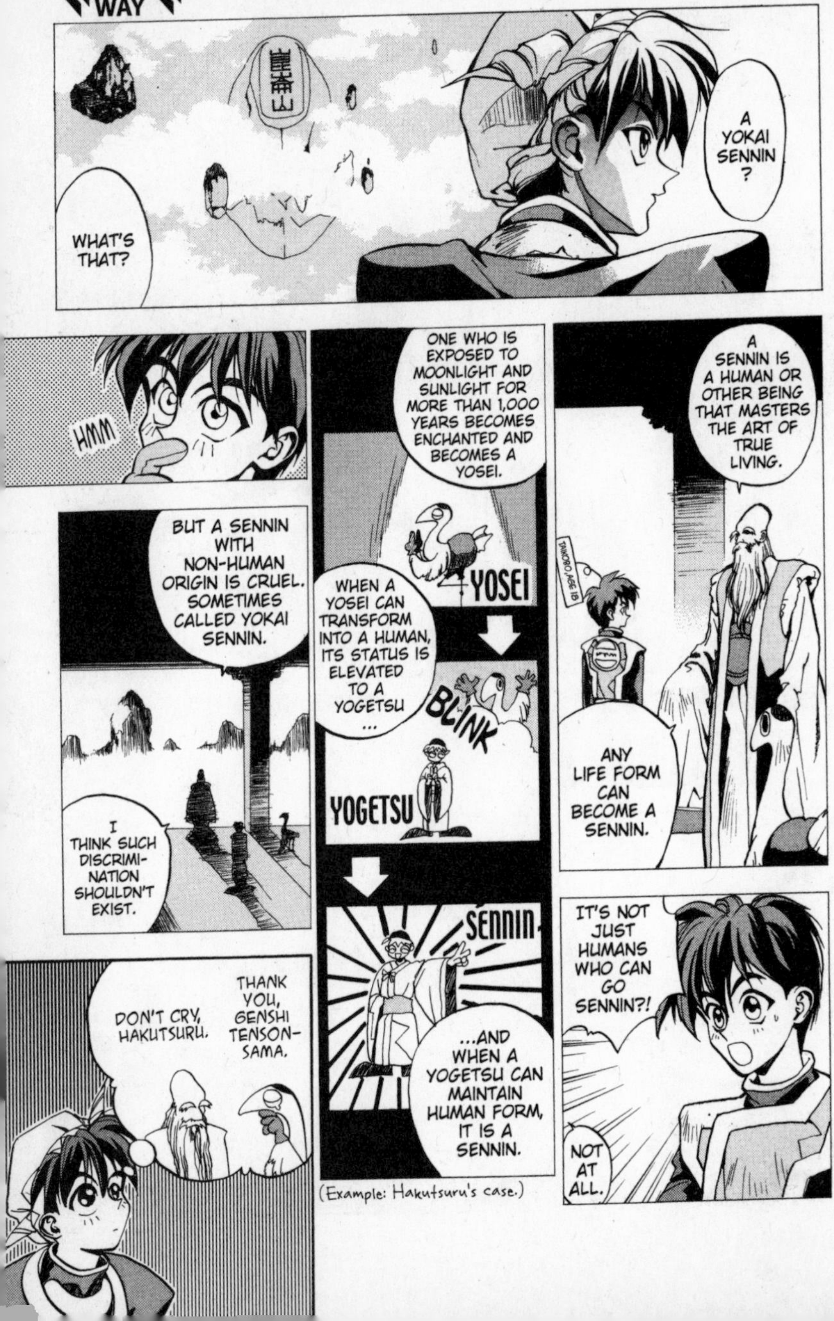

A YOKAI SENNIN?
WHAT'S THAT?
A SENNIN IS A HUMAN OR OTHER BEING THAT MASTERS THE ART OF TRUE LIVING.
TAIKOBO, AGE 18
ANY LIFE FORM CAN BECOME A SENNIN.
IT'S NOT JUST HUMANS WHO CAN GO SENNIN?!
NOT AT ALL.
ONE WHO IS EXPOSED TO MOONLIGHT AND SUNLIGHT FOR MORE THAN 1,000 YEARS BECOMES ENCHANTED AND BECOMES A YOSEI.
YOSEI
WHEN A YOSEI CAN TRANSFORM INTO A HUMAN, ITS STATUS IS ELEVATED TO A YOGETSU ...
BLINK
YOGETSU
SENNIN
...AND WHEN A YOGETSU CAN MAINTAIN HUMAN FORM, IT IS A SENNIN.
(Example: Hakutsuru's case.)
HMM
BUT A SENNIN WITH NON-HUMAN ORIGIN IS CRUEL. SOMETIMES CALLED YOKAI SENNIN.
I THINK SUCH DISCRIMINATION SHOULDN'T EXIST.
THANK YOU, GENSHI TENSON-SAMA.
DON'T CRY, HAKUTSURU.

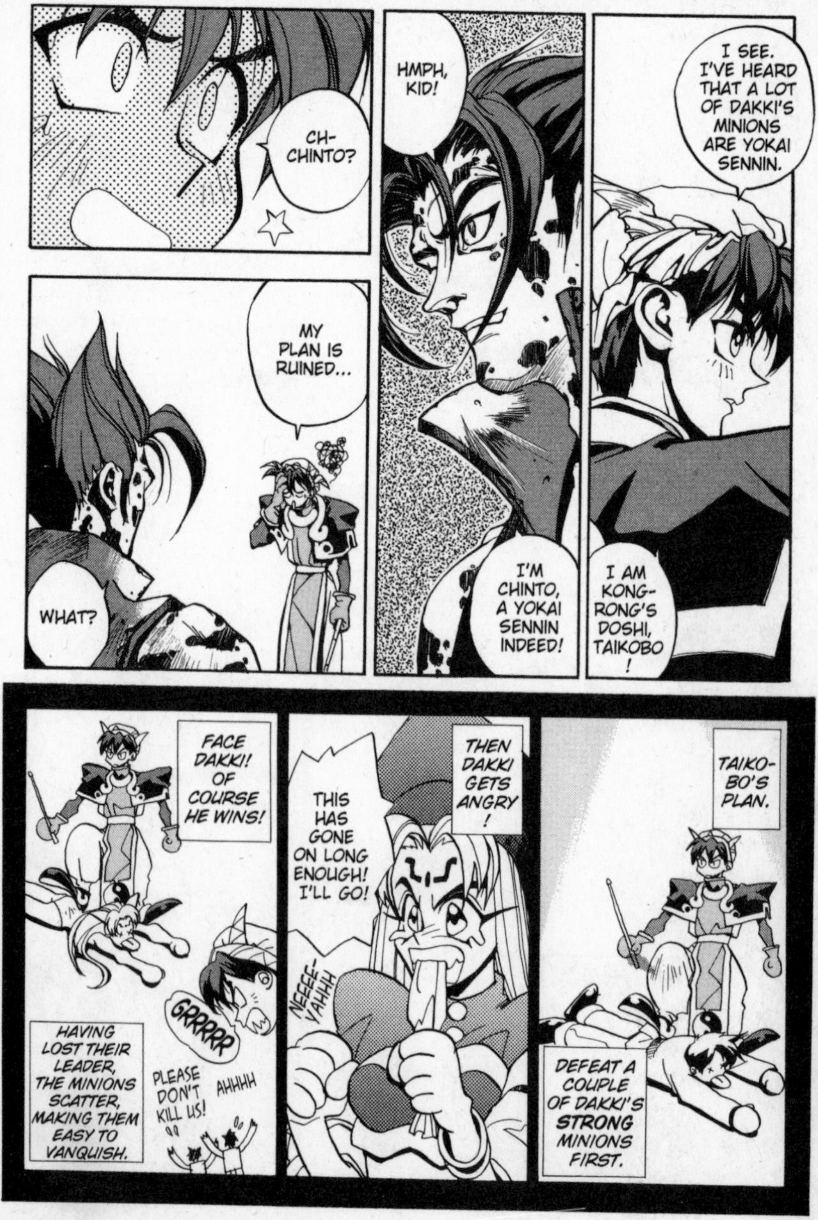
I SEE. I'VE HEARD THAT A LOT OF DAKKI'S MINIONS ARE YOKAI SENNIN.
I AM KONG-RONG'S DOSHI, TAIKOBO!
HMPH, KID!
I'M CHINTO, A YOKAI SENNIN INDEED!
CH-CHINTO?
MY PLAN IS RUINED...
WHAT?
TAIKO-BO'S PLAN.
DEFEAT A COUPLE OF DAKKI'S STRONG MINIONS FIRST.
THEN DAKKI GETS ANGRY!
THIS HAS GONE ON LONG ENOUGH! I'LL GO!
NEEEE-YAHHH
FACE DAKKI! OF COURSE HE WINS!
GRRRRRR
HAVING LOST THEIR LEADER, THE MINIONS SCATTER, MAKING THEM EASY TO VANQUISH.
PLEASE DON'T KILL US!
AHHHH

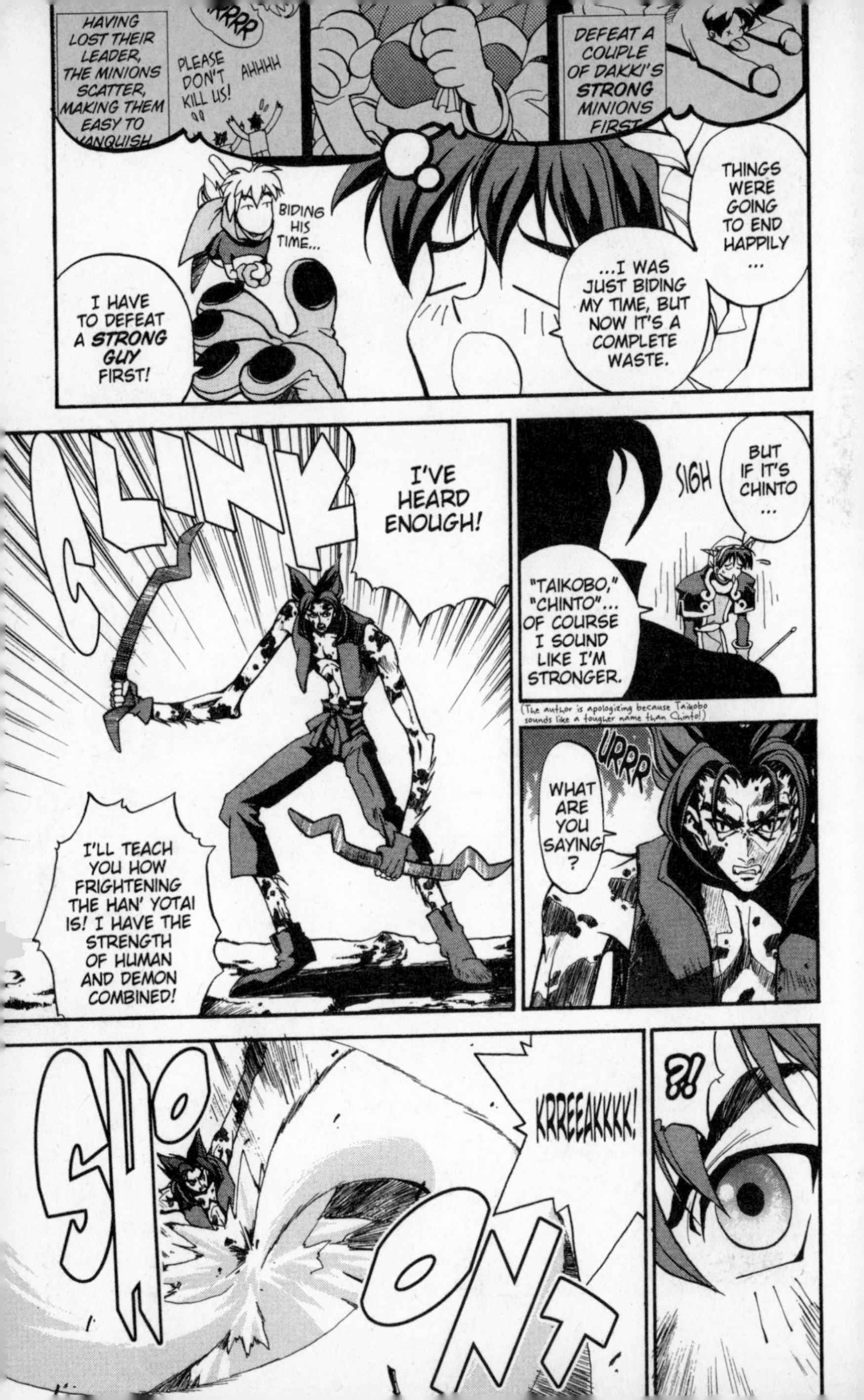
DEFEAT A COUPLE OF DAKKI'S **STRONG** MINIONS FIRST
HAVING LOST THEIR LEADER, THE MINIONS SCATTER, MAKING THEM EASY TO VANQUISH
RRRR
PLEASE DON'T KILL US!
AHHHH
THINGS WERE GOING TO END HAPPILY ...
...I WAS JUST BIDING MY TIME, BUT NOW IT'S A COMPLETE WASTE.
BIDING HIS TIME...
I HAVE TO DEFEAT A **STRONG GUY** FIRST!
BUT IF IT'S CHINTO ...
SIGH
"TAIKOBO," "CHINTO"... OF COURSE I SOUND LIKE I'M STRONGER.
(The author is apologizing because Taikobo sounds like a tougher name than Chinto!)
URRR
WHAT ARE YOU SAYING?
CLINK
I'VE HEARD ENOUGH!
I'LL TEACH YOU HOW FRIGHTENING THE HAN' YOTAI IS! I HAVE THE STRENGTH OF HUMAN AND DEMON COMBINED!
?!
KRREEAKKK!
SHOONT

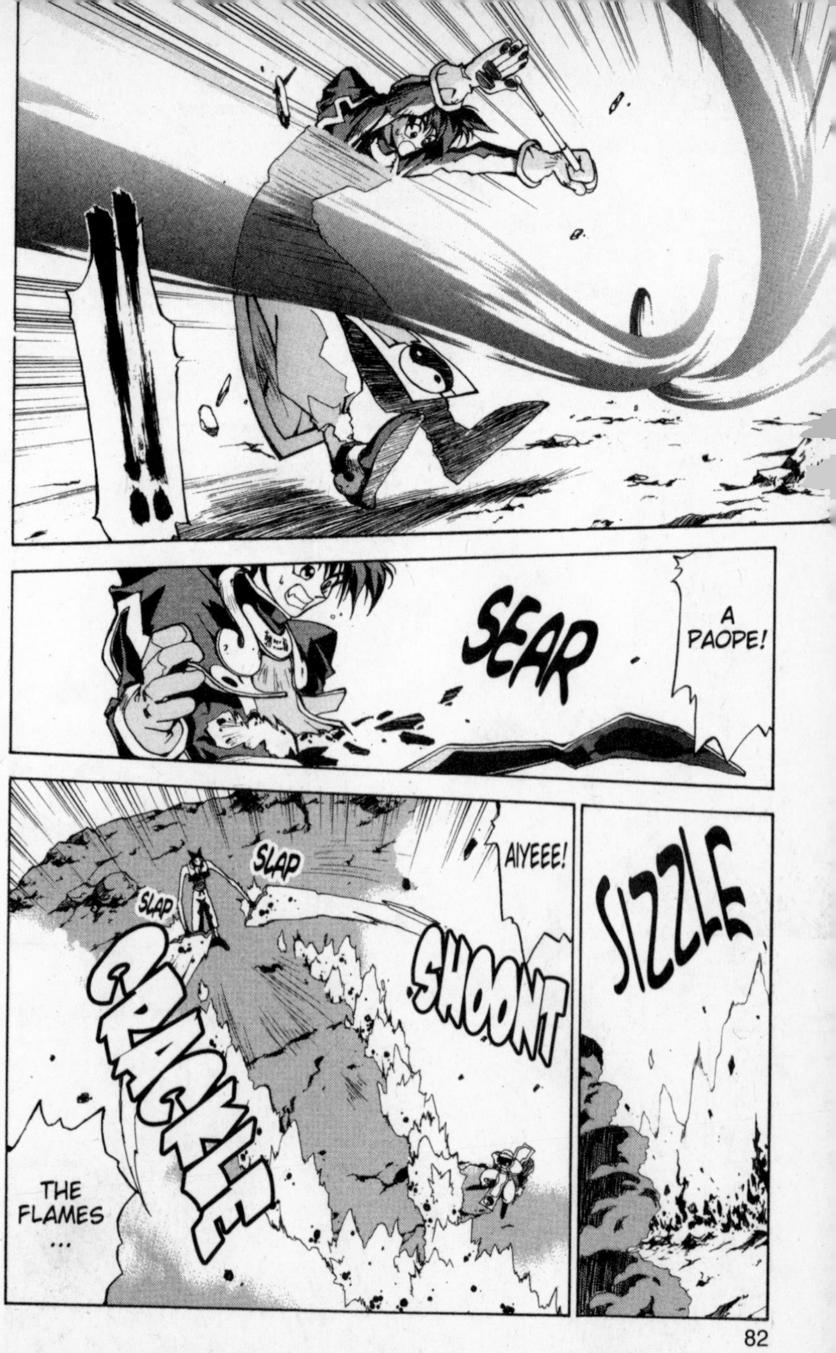
!!
A PAOPE!
SEAR
SIZZLE
AIYEEE!
SLAP
SHOONT
SLAP
CRACKLE
THE FLAMES ...

READ THIS WAY

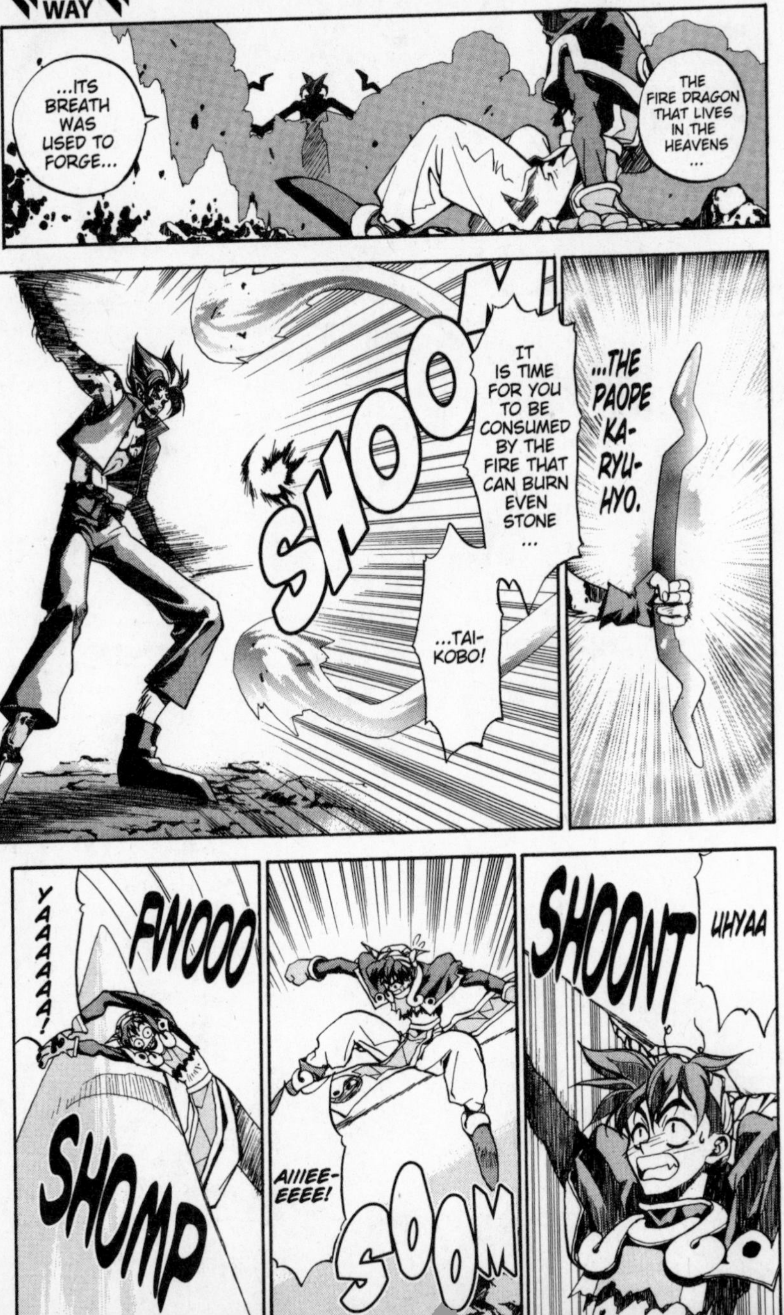
THE FIRE DRAGON THAT LIVES IN THE HEAVENS ...
...ITS BREATH WAS USED TO FORGE...
...THE PAOPE KA-RYU-HYO.
IT IS TIME FOR YOU TO BE CONSUMED BY THE FIRE THAT CAN BURN EVEN STONE ...
...TAI-KOBO!
SHOOOM!
SHOONT
UHYAA
AIIIEE-EEEE!
SOOM
YAAAAAAA!
FWOOO
SHOMP

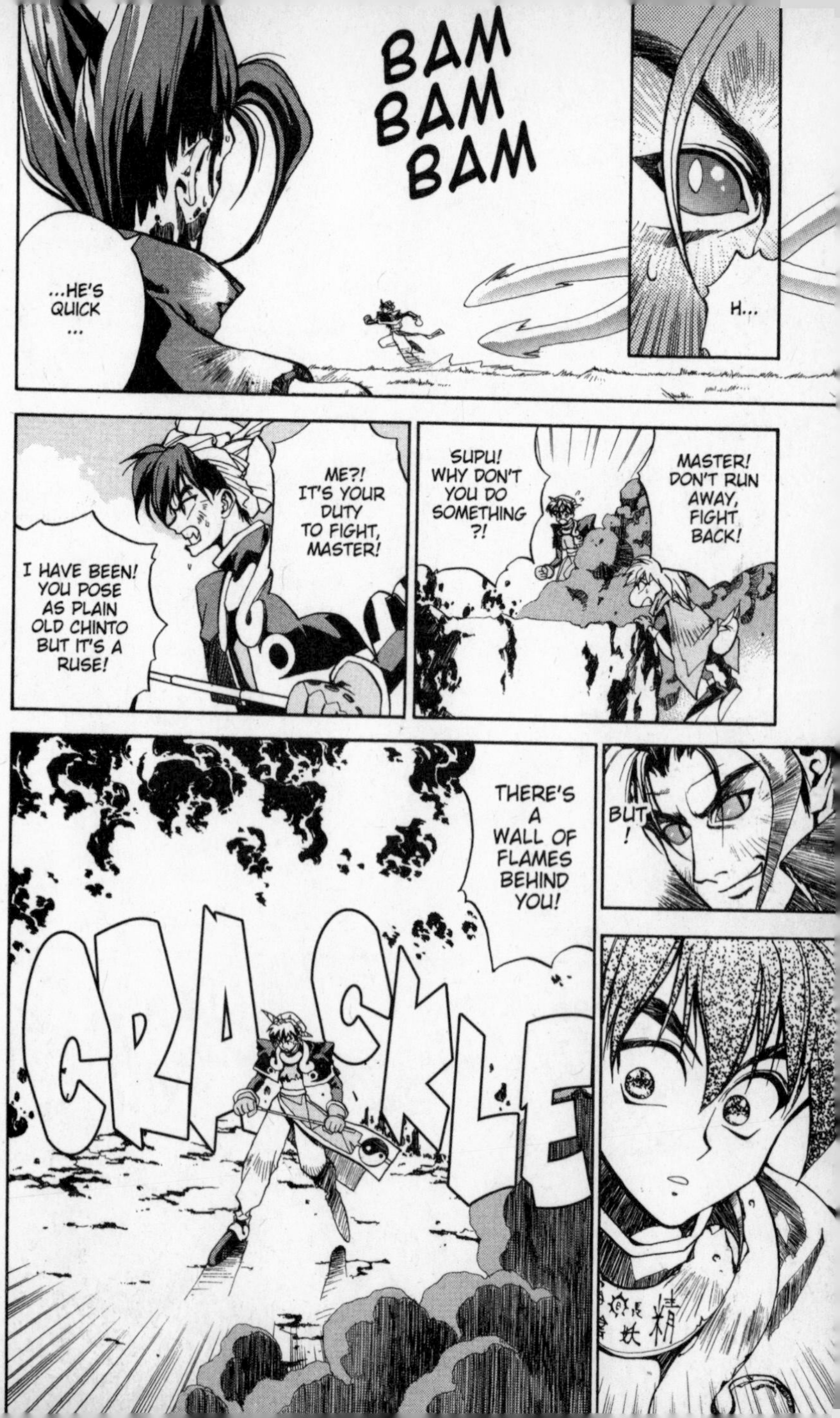
H...
BAM BAM BAM
...HE'S QUICK ...
MASTER! DON'T RUN AWAY, FIGHT BACK!
SUPU! WHY DON'T YOU DO SOMETHING ?!
ME?! IT'S YOUR DUTY TO FIGHT, MASTER!
I HAVE BEEN! YOU POSE AS PLAIN OLD CHINTO BUT IT'S A RUSE!
BUT !
THERE'S A WALL OF FLAMES BEHIND YOU!
CRACKLE

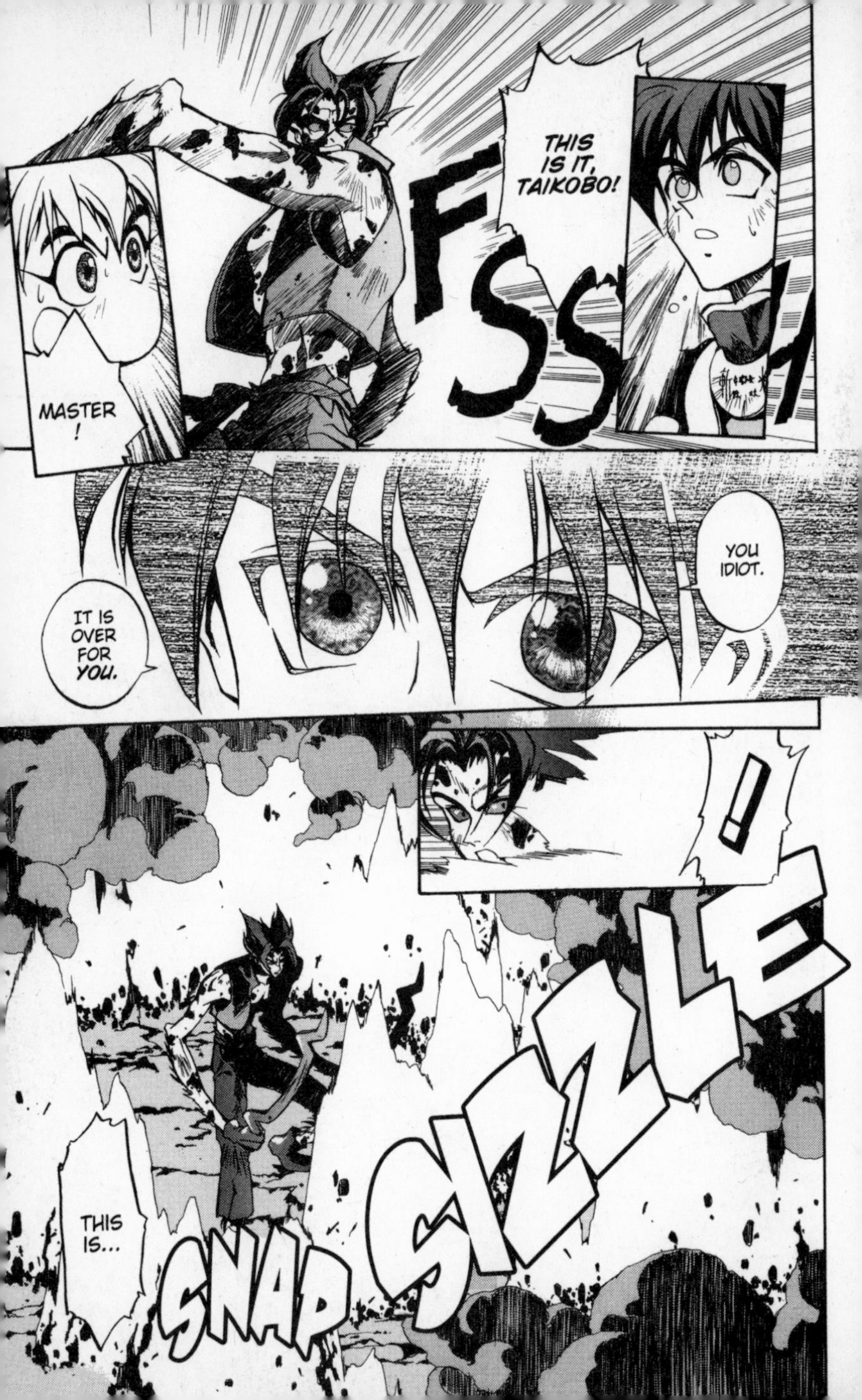
THIS IS IT, TAIKOBO!
FSSH
MASTER!
YOU IDIOT.
IT IS OVER FOR YOU.
!
SIZZLE
SNAP
THIS IS...

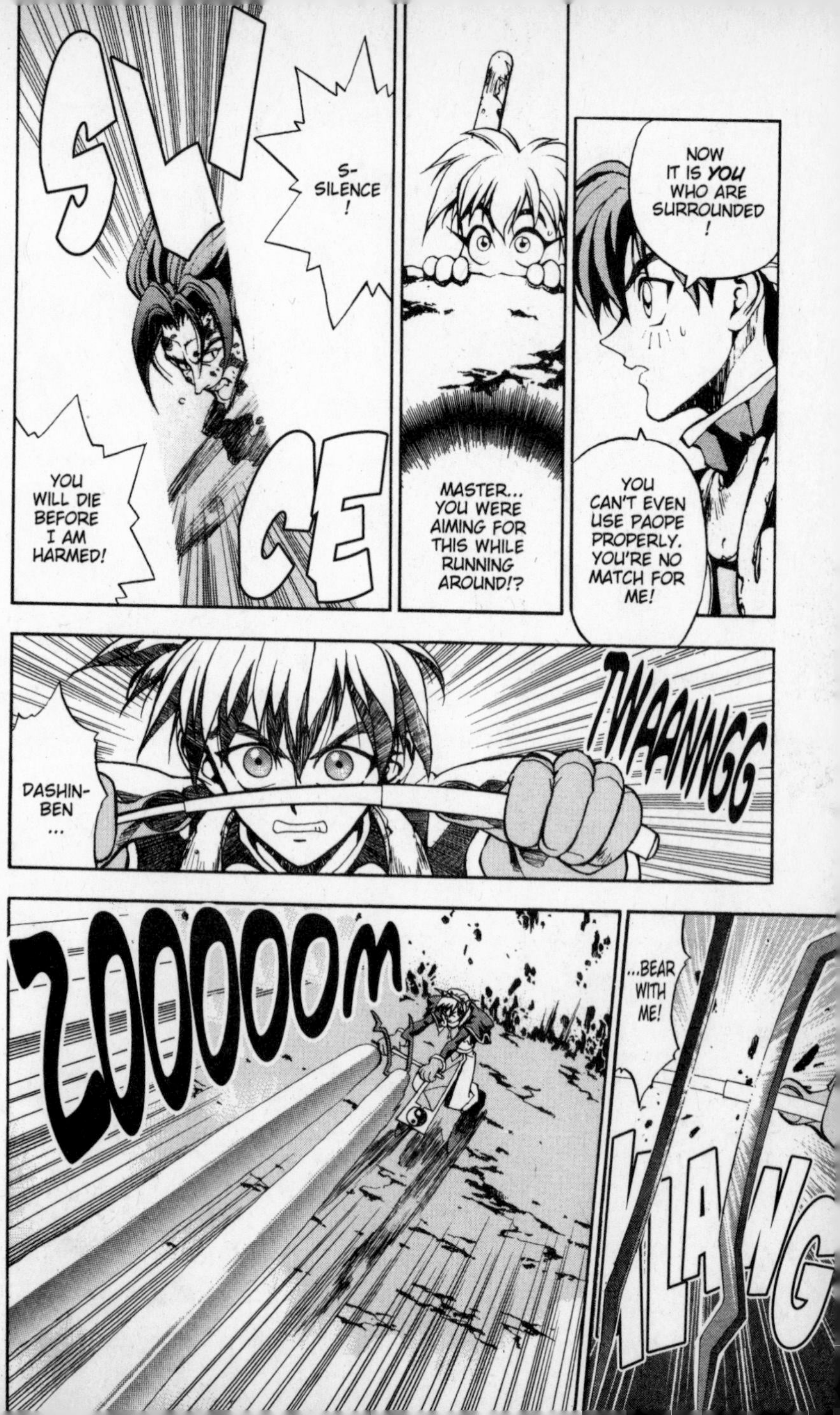
NOW IT IS *YOU* WHO ARE SURROUNDED!
YOU CAN'T EVEN USE PAOPE PROPERLY. YOU'RE NO MATCH FOR ME!
MASTER... YOU WERE AIMING FOR THIS WHILE RUNNING AROUND!?
S-SILENCE!
SLICE
YOU WILL DIE BEFORE I AM HARMED!
TWAANNGG
DASHIN-BEN...
...BEAR WITH ME!
KLANG
ZOOOOOM

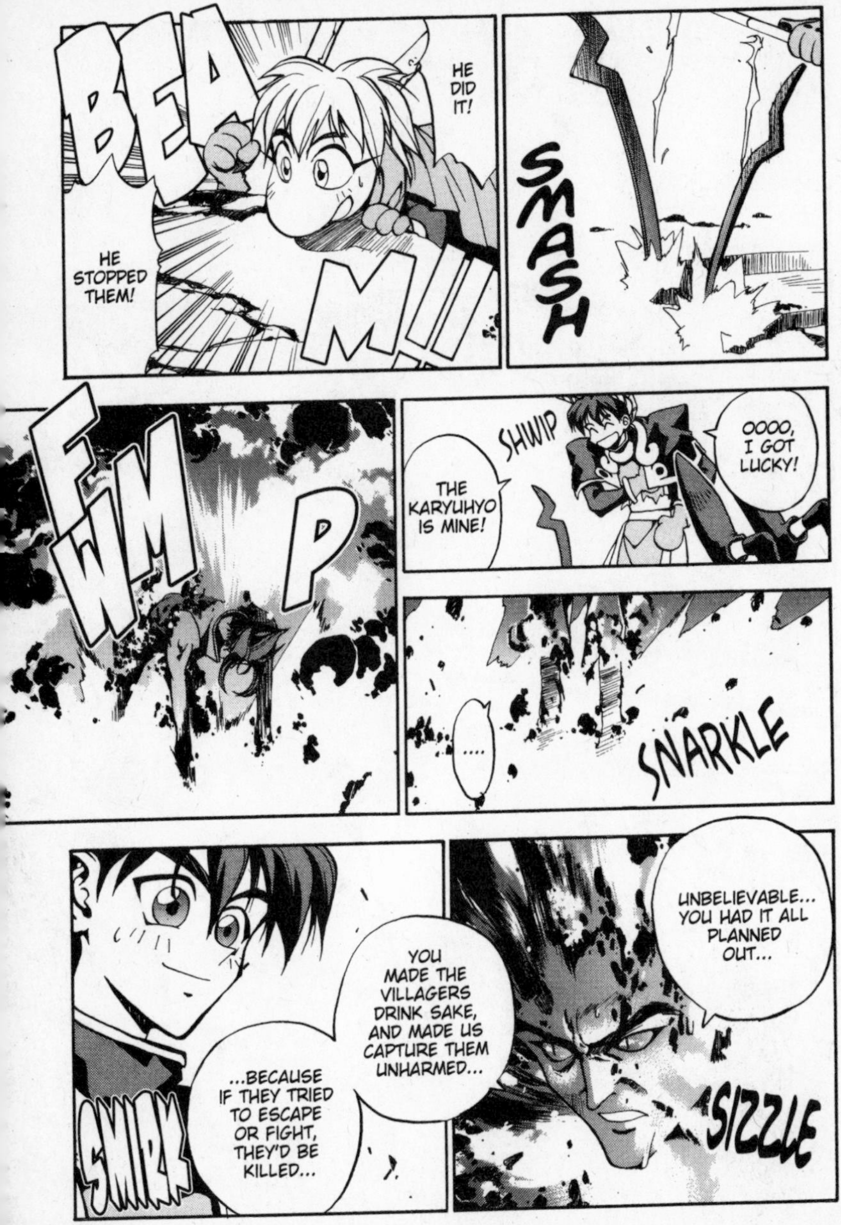
SMASH
HE DID IT!
HE STOPPED THEM!
BEAM
OOOO, I GOT LUCKY!
THE KARYUHYO IS MINE!
SHWIP
....
SNARKLE
FWMP
UNBELIEVABLE... YOU HAD IT ALL PLANNED OUT...
YOU MADE THE VILLAGERS DRINK SAKE, AND MADE US CAPTURE THEM UNHARMED...
SIZZLE
...BECAUSE IF THEY TRIED TO ESCAPE OR FIGHT, THEY'D BE KILLED...
SMIRK

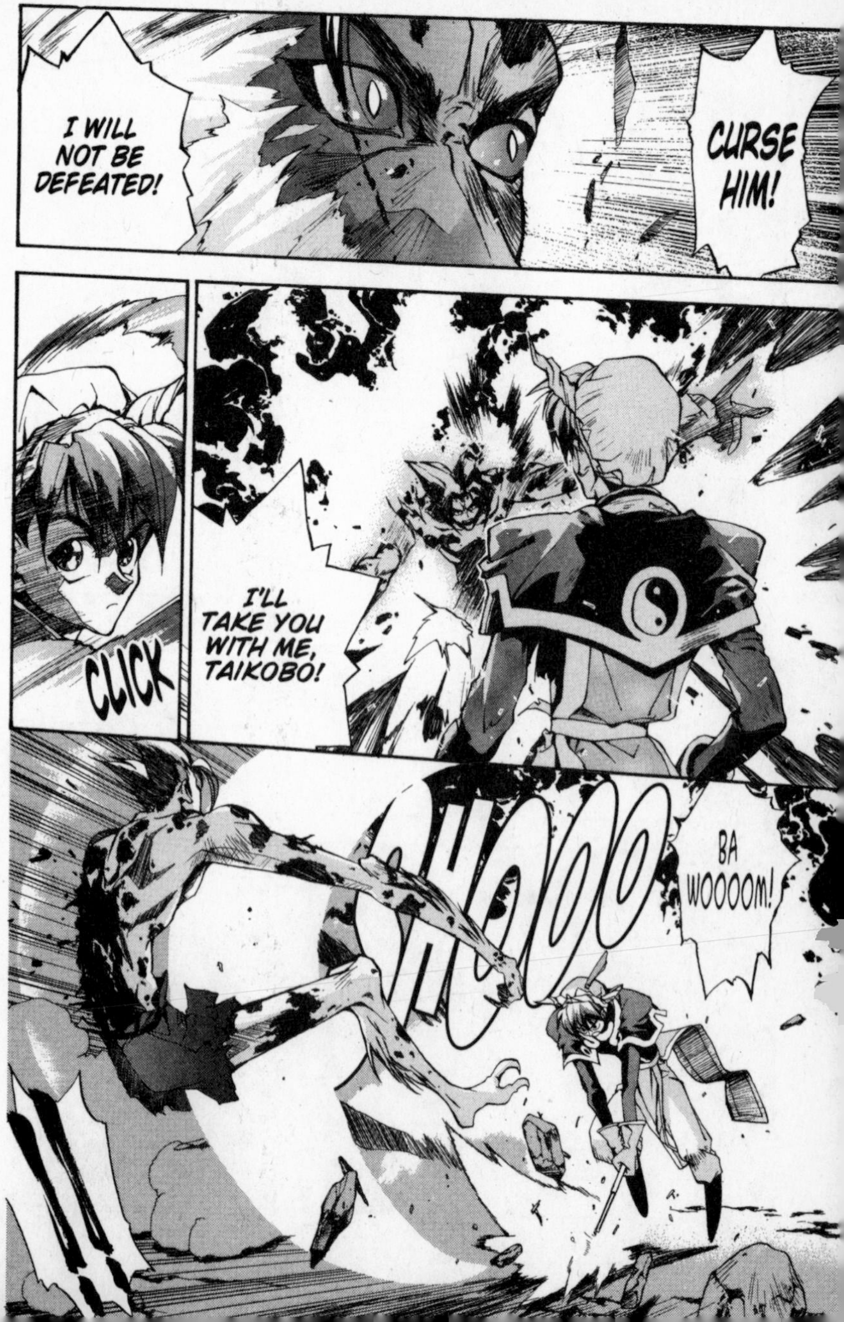
CURSE HIM!
I WILL NOT BE DEFEATED!
I'LL TAKE YOU WITH ME, TAIKOBO!
CLICK
BA WOOOOM!

READ THIS WAY

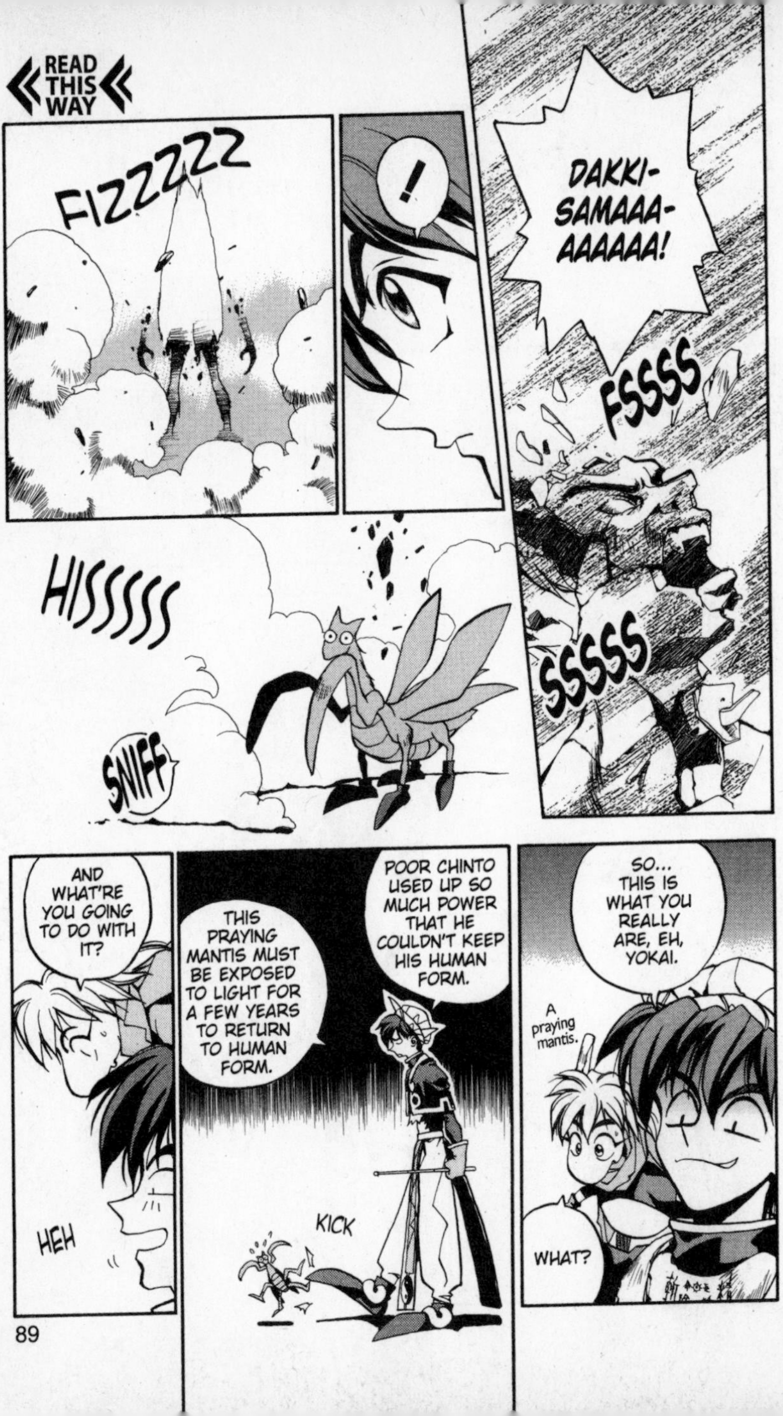
DAKKI-SAMAAA-AAAAAA!
FSSSS
SSSSS
!
FIZZZZZ
HISSSSS
SNIFF
SO... THIS IS WHAT YOU REALLY ARE, EH, YOKAI.
A praying mantis.
WHAT?
POOR CHINTO USED UP SO MUCH POWER THAT HE COULDN'T KEEP HIS HUMAN FORM.
THIS PRAYING MANTIS MUST BE EXPOSED TO LIGHT FOR A FEW YEARS TO RETURN TO HUMAN FORM.
KICK
AND WHAT'RE YOU GOING TO DO WITH IT?
HEH

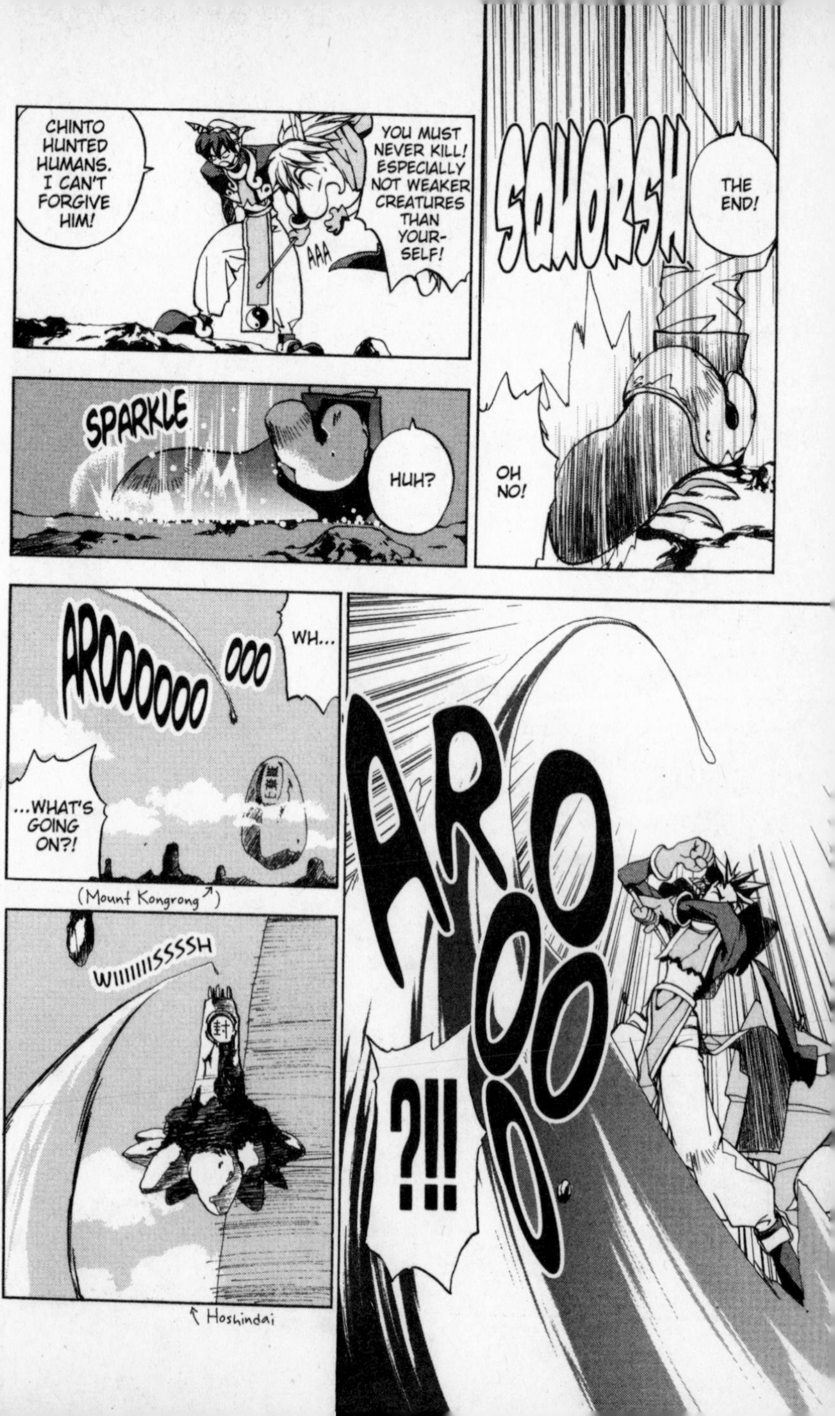
THE END!
SQUORSH
OH NO!
YOU MUST NEVER KILL! ESPECIALLY NOT WEAKER CREATURES THAN YOURSELF!
AAA
CHINTO HUNTED HUMANS. I CAN'T FORGIVE HIM!
HUH?
SPARKLE
AROOOOOO
?!!!
WH...
AROOOOOO OOO
...WHAT'S GOING ON?!
(Mount Kongrong)
WIIIIIISSSSH
Hoshindai

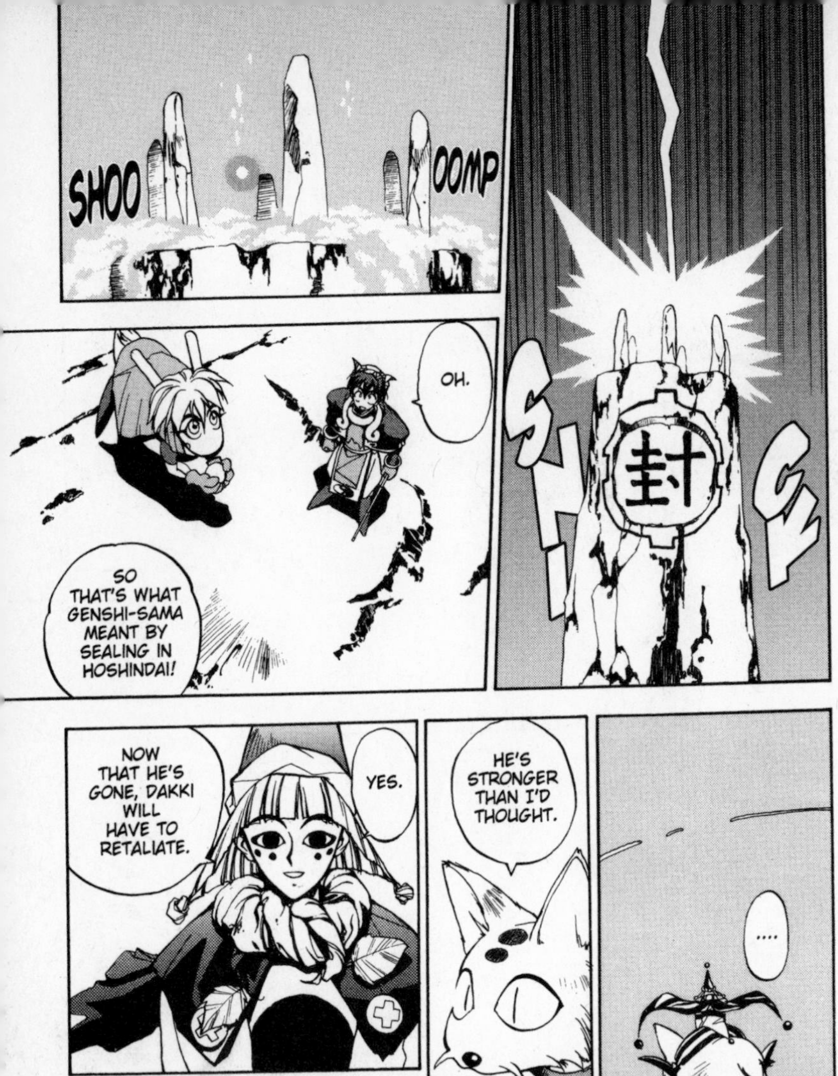
封
SHOO
OOMP
OH.
SO THAT'S WHAT GENSHI-SAMA MEANT BY SEALING IN HOSHINDAI!
....
TAIKOBO DEFEATED CHINTO...
HE'S STRONGER THAN I'D THOUGHT.
CHINTO WAS NOT THE MOST POWERFUL OF DAKKI'S MINIONS, CORRECT?
YES.
NOW THAT HE'S GONE, DAKKI WILL HAVE TO RETALIATE.
WELL... BEFORE THAT...

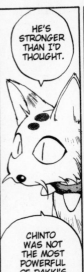

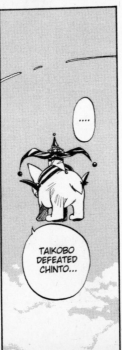

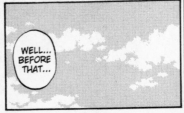

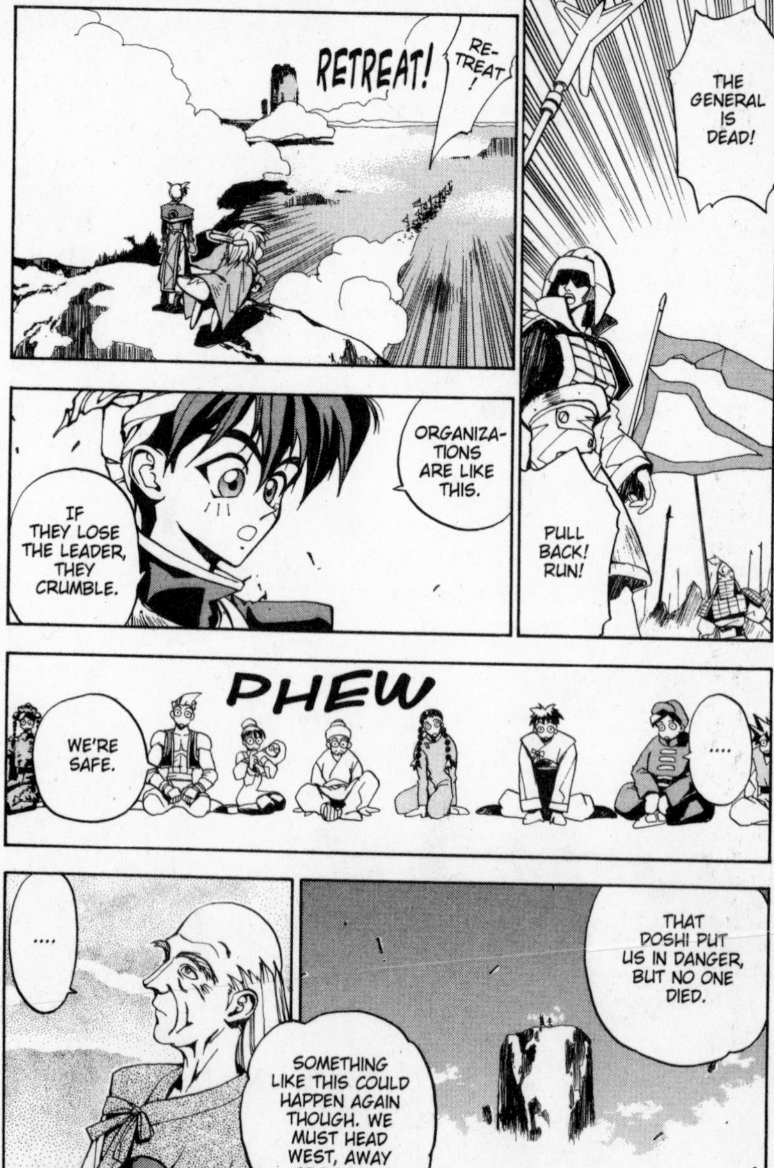
THE GENERAL IS DEAD!
PULL BACK! RUN!
RE-TREAT!
RETREAT!
ORGANIZA-TIONS ARE LIKE THIS.
IF THEY LOSE THE LEADER, THEY CRUMBLE.
PHEW
....
WE'RE SAFE.
THAT DOSHI PUT US IN DANGER, BUT NO ONE DIED.
....
SOMETHING LIKE THIS COULD HAPPEN AGAIN THOUGH. WE MUST HEAD WEST, AWAY FROM THIS!

READ THIS WAY

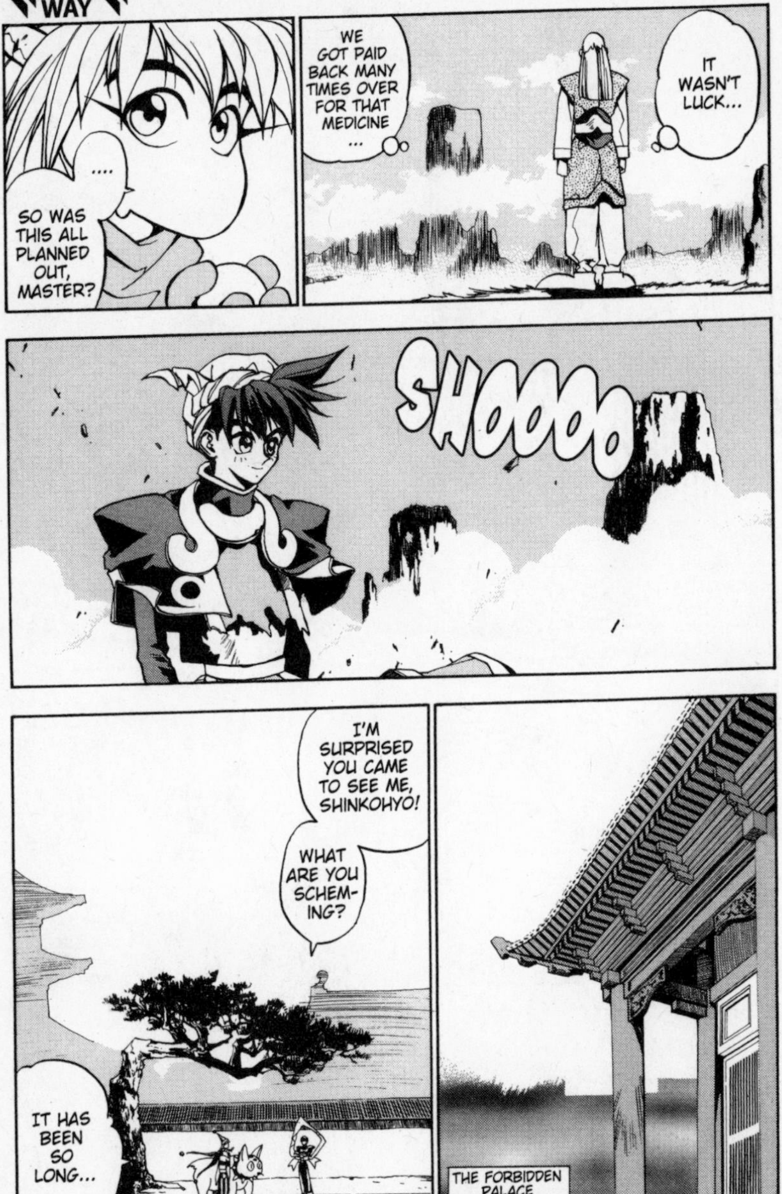
IT WASN'T LUCK...
WE GOT PAID BACK MANY TIMES OVER FOR THAT MEDICINE ...
....
SO WAS THIS ALL PLANNED OUT, MASTER?
SHOOOO
THE FORBIDDEN PALACE
I'M SURPRISED YOU CAME TO SEE ME, SHINKOHYO!
WHAT ARE YOU SCHEMING?
IT HAS BEEN SO LONG...

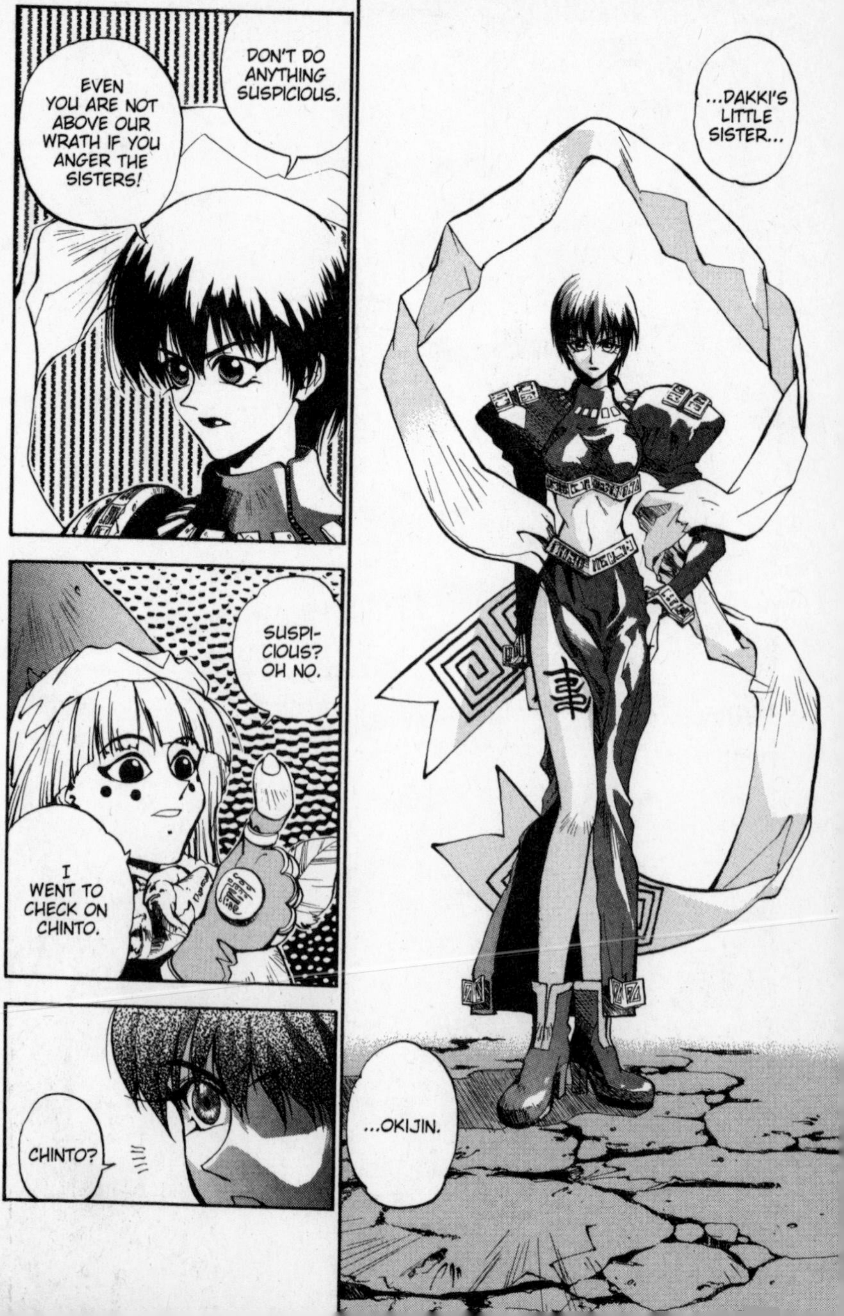
...DAKKI'S LITTLE SISTER...
...OKIJIN.
DON'T DO ANYTHING SUSPICIOUS.
EVEN YOU ARE NOT ABOVE OUR WRATH IF YOU ANGER THE SISTERS!
SUSPI-CIOUS? OH NO.
I WENT TO CHECK ON CHINTO.
CHINTO?

READ THIS WAY

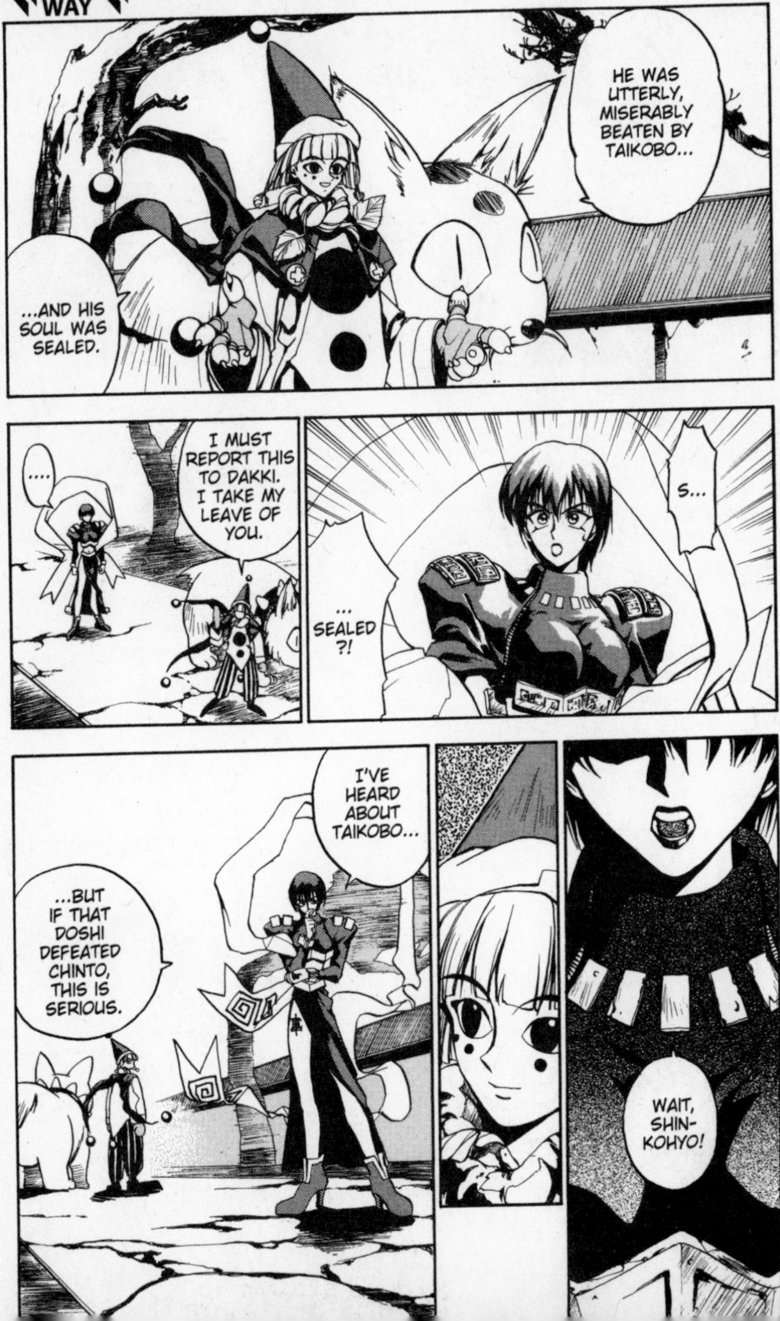
HE WAS UTTERLY, MISERABLY BEATEN BY TAIKOBO...
...AND HIS SOUL WAS SEALED.
S...
...SEALED?!
I MUST REPORT THIS TO DAKKI. I TAKE MY LEAVE OF YOU.
....
WAIT, SHIN-KOHYO!
I'VE HEARD ABOUT TAIKOBO...
...BUT IF THAT DOSHI DEFEATED CHINTO, THIS IS SERIOUS.

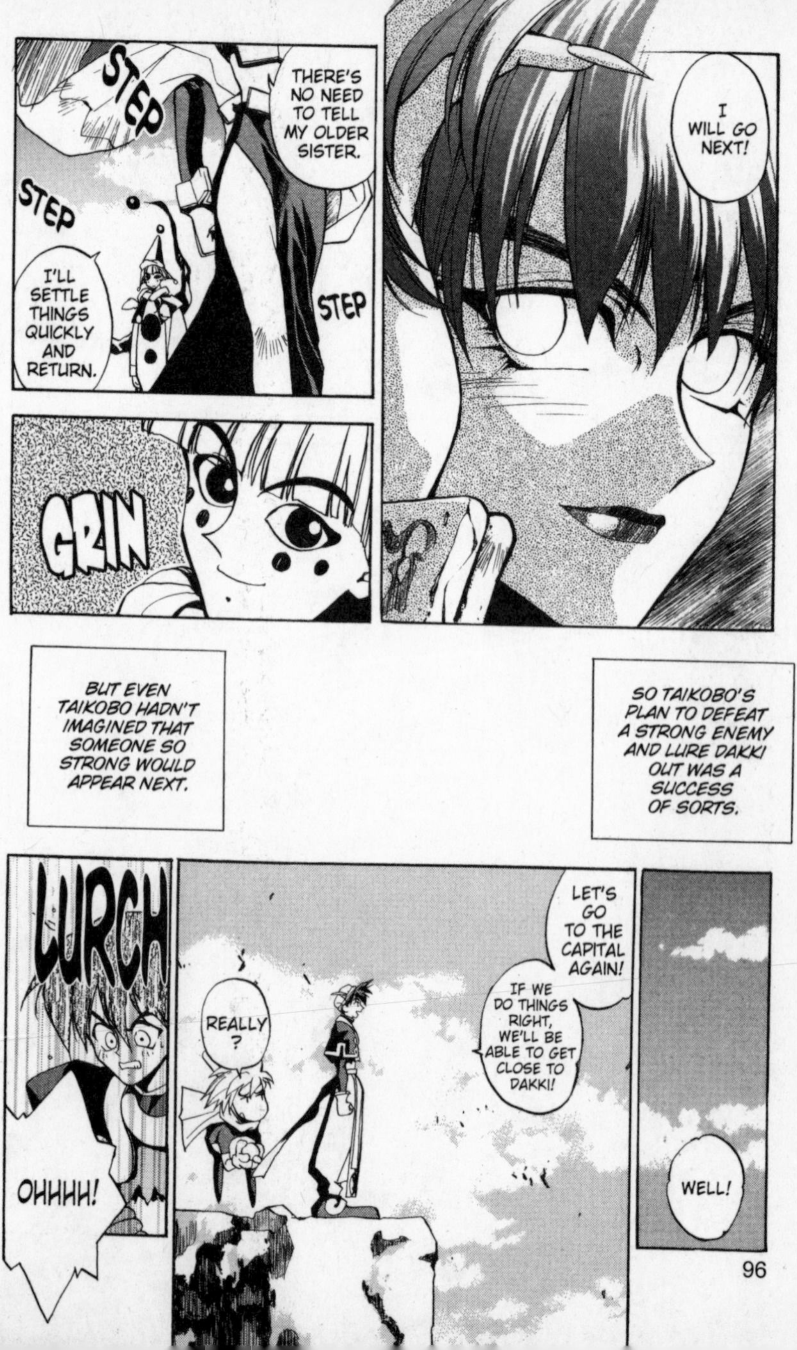
I WILL GO NEXT!
STEP
THERE'S NO NEED TO TELL MY OLDER SISTER.
STEP
STEP
I'LL SETTLE THINGS QUICKLY AND RETURN.
GRIN
SO TAIKOBO'S PLAN TO DEFEAT A STRONG ENEMY AND LURE DAKKI OUT WAS A SUCCESS OF SORTS.
BUT EVEN TAIKOBO HADN'T IMAGINED THAT SOMEONE SO STRONG WOULD APPEAR NEXT.
WELL!
LET'S GO TO THE CAPITAL AGAIN!
IF WE DO THINGS RIGHT, WE'LL BE ABLE TO GET CLOSE TO DAKKI!
REALLY?
LURCH
OHHHH!

READ THIS WAY

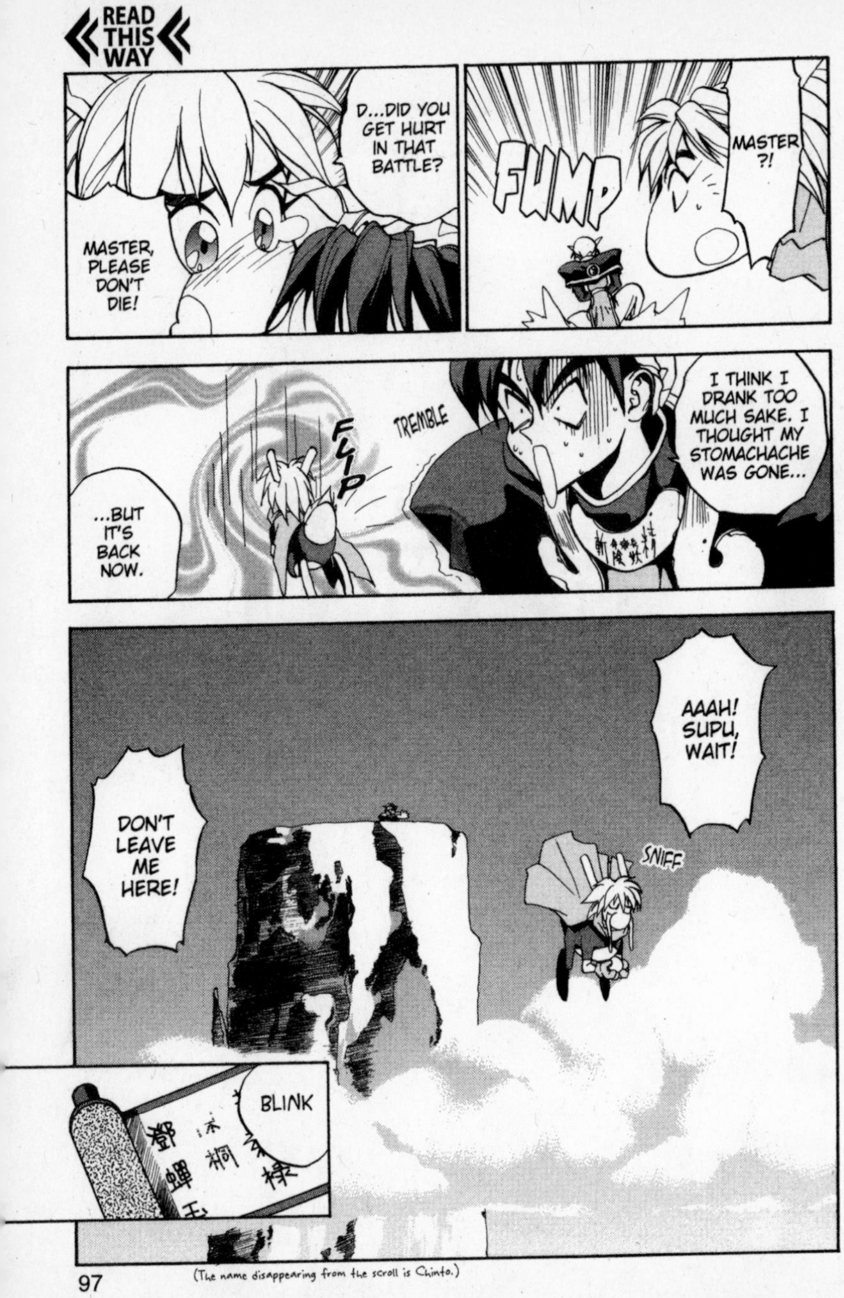
MASTER ?!
FUMP
D...DID YOU GET HURT IN THAT BATTLE?
MASTER, PLEASE DON'T DIE!
I THINK I DRANK TOO MUCH SAKE. I THOUGHT MY STOMACHACHE WAS GONE...
TREMBLE
FLIP
...BUT IT'S BACK NOW.
AAAH! SUPU, WAIT!
SNIFF
DON'T LEAVE ME HERE!
BLINK

(The name disappearing from the scroll is Chinto.)

封神演義

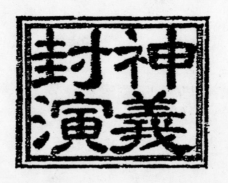

CHAPTER 3: THE HORAKU

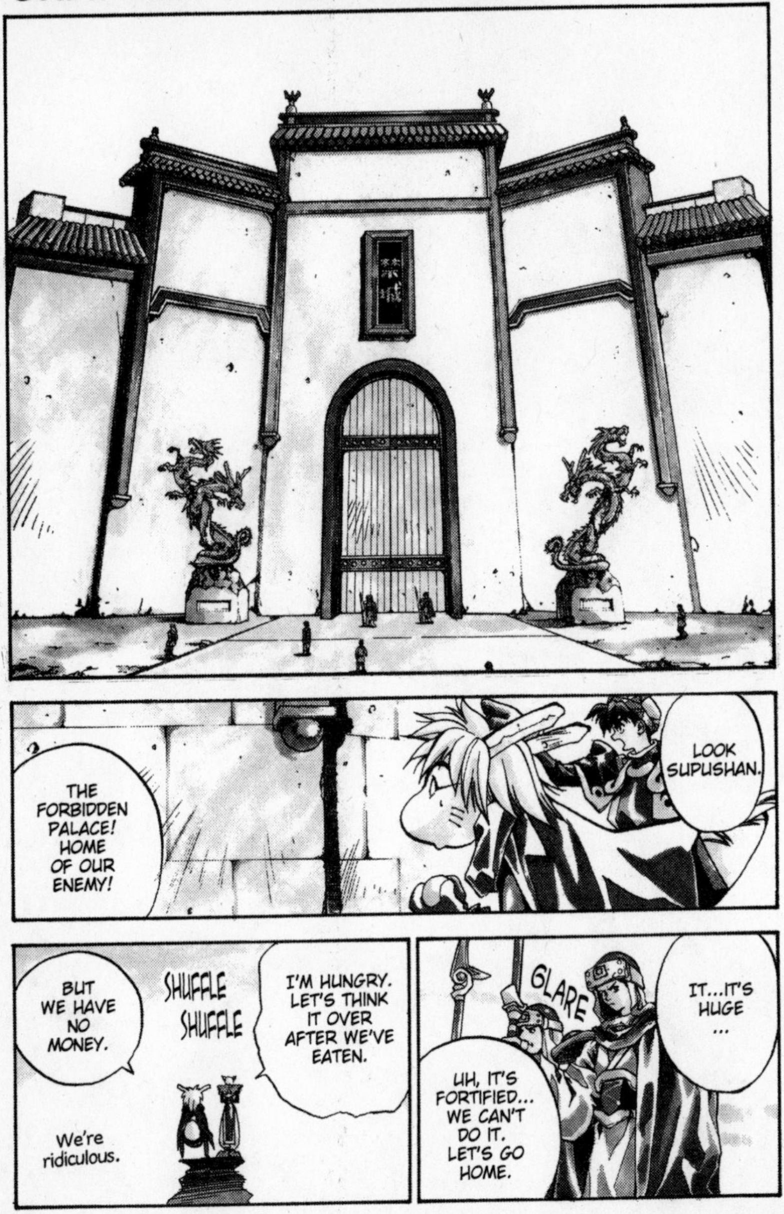
LOOK SUPUSHAN.
THE FORBIDDEN PALACE! HOME OF OUR ENEMY!
IT...IT'S HUGE ...
GLARE
UH, IT'S FORTIFIED... WE CAN'T DO IT. LET'S GO HOME.
I'M HUNGRY. LET'S THINK IT OVER AFTER WE'VE EATEN.
SHUFFLE SHUFFLE
BUT WE HAVE NO MONEY.
We're ridiculous.

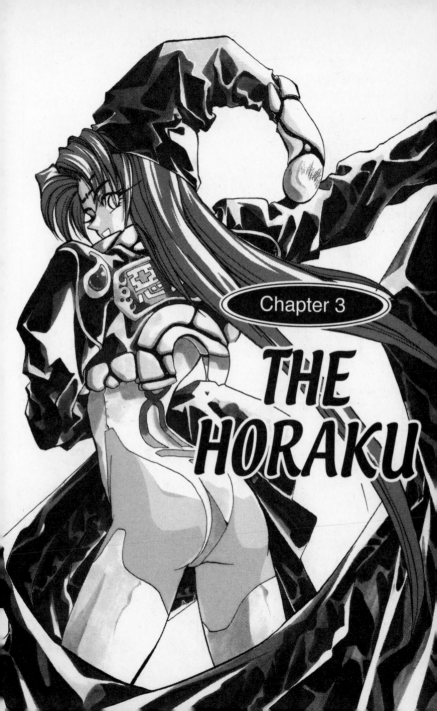

Chapter 3

THE
HORAKU

READ THIS WAY

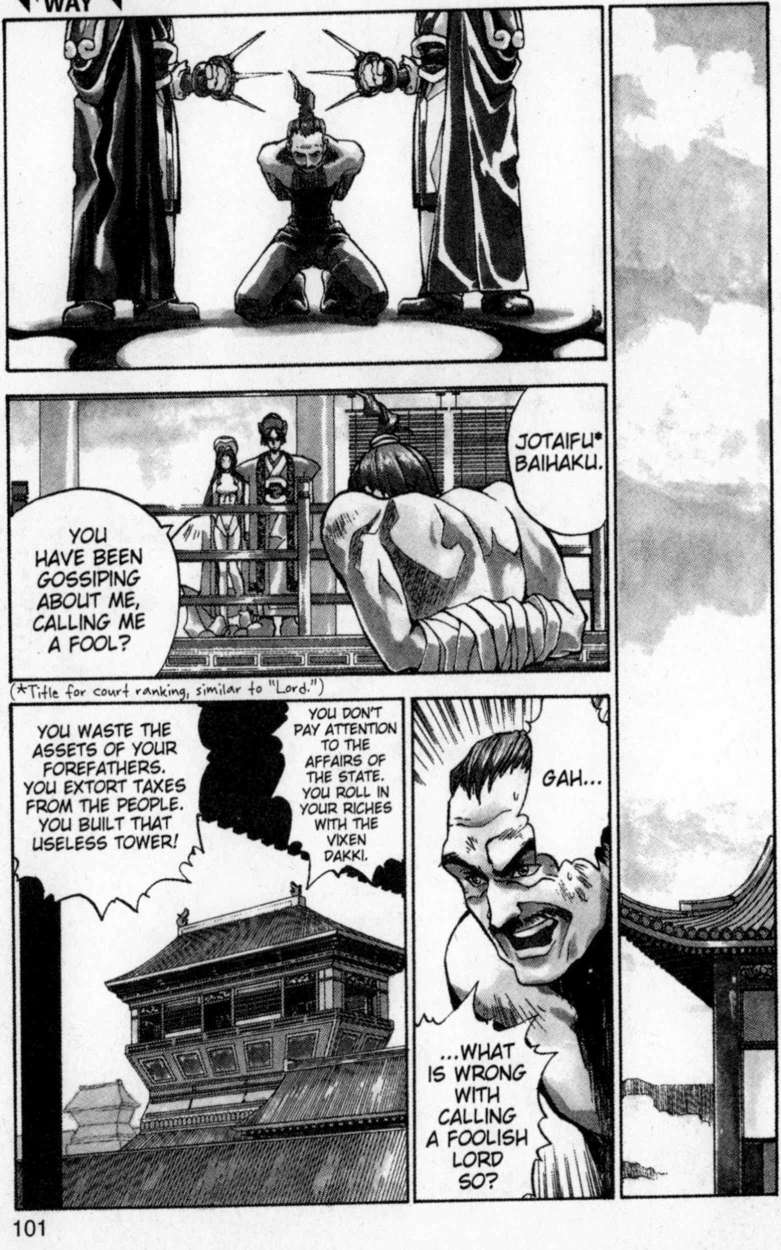
JOTAIFU* BAIHAKU.
YOU HAVE BEEN GOSSIPING ABOUT ME, CALLING ME A FOOL?
(*Title for court ranking, similar to "Lord.")
GAH...
...WHAT IS WRONG WITH CALLING A FOOLISH LORD SO?
YOU DON'T PAY ATTENTION TO THE AFFAIRS OF THE STATE. YOU ROLL IN YOUR RICHES WITH THE VIXEN DAKKI.
YOU WASTE THE ASSETS OF YOUR FOREFATHERS. YOU EXTORT TAXES FROM THE PEOPLE. YOU BUILT THAT USELESS TOWER!

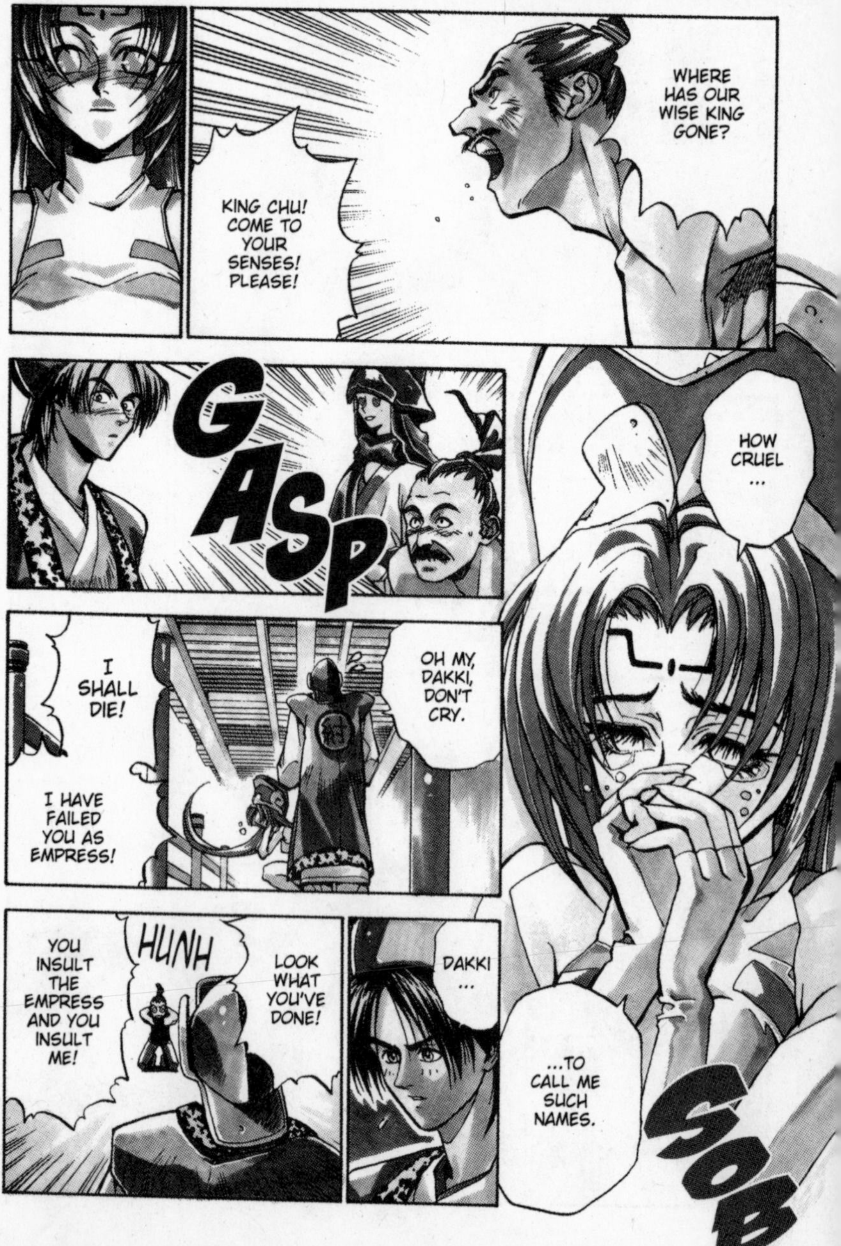
WHERE HAS OUR WISE KING GONE?
KING CHU! COME TO YOUR SENSES! PLEASE!
HOW CRUEL ...
...TO CALL ME SUCH NAMES.
SOB
GASP
OH MY, DAKKI, DON'T CRY.
I SHALL DIE!
I HAVE FAILED YOU AS EMPRESS!
DAKKI ...
LOOK WHAT YOU'VE DONE!
HUNH
YOU INSULT THE EMPRESS AND YOU INSULT ME!

READ THIS WAY

TSSSS
OFF WITH HIS HEAD!
WAIT!
FORGET ABOUT MY OWN INSULT, HE CALLED OUR KING A *FOOL*.
HE MUST BE EXECUTED MUCH MORE BRUTALLY, AS A LESSON TO SUCH INSOLENCE.
AND I KNOW JUST THE RIGHT METHOD. ♡
FLIP
THE FOLLOWING DAY
CLANK
CLANG
ALL RIGHT.
ALL RIGHT.
STOP. ♡
WAVE
LOWER IT STRAIGHT DOWN. ♡

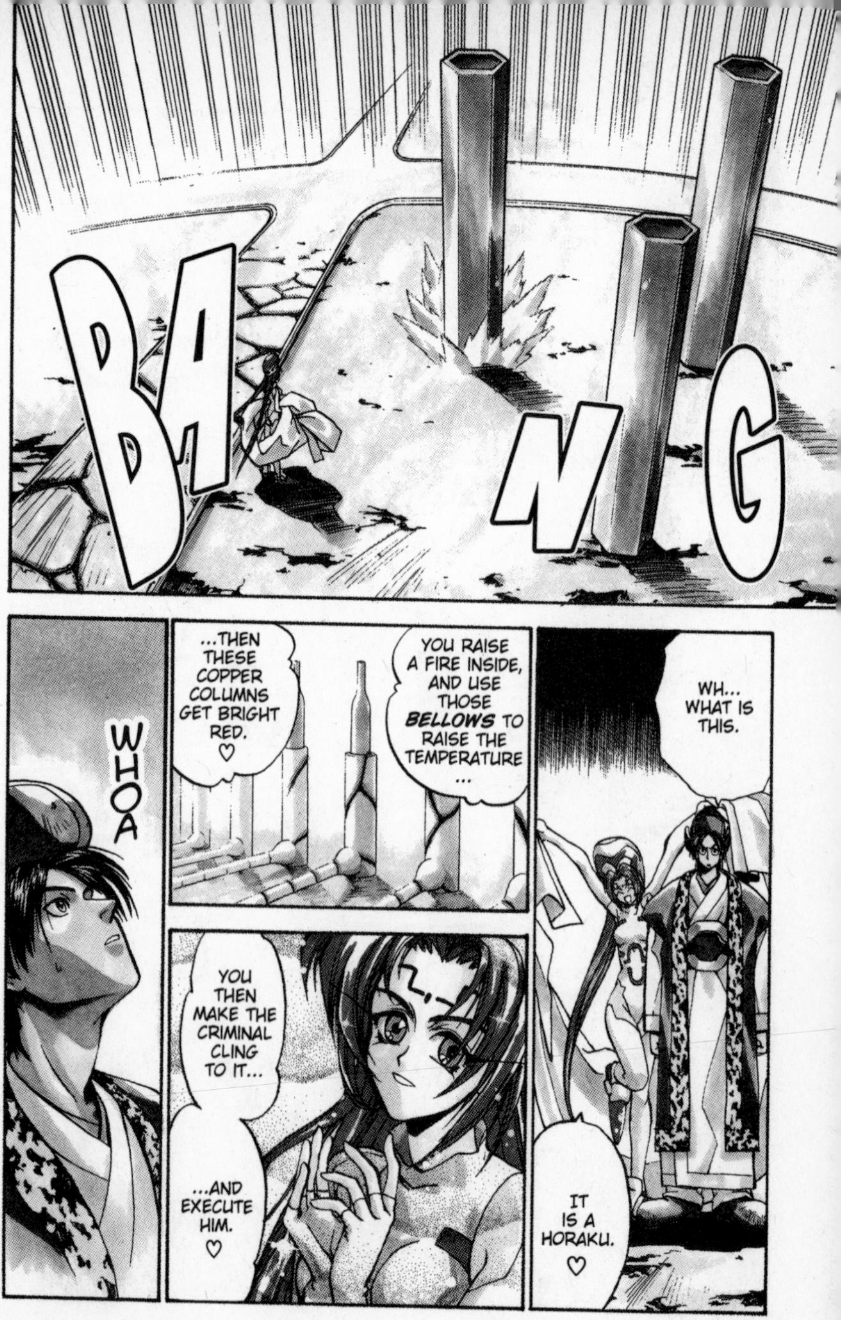
BANG
WH... WHAT IS THIS.
IT IS A HORAKU. ♡
YOU RAISE A FIRE INSIDE, AND USE THOSE **BELLOWS** TO RAISE THE TEMPERATURE ...
...THEN THESE COPPER COLUMNS GET BRIGHT RED. ♡
YOU THEN MAKE THE CRIMINAL CLING TO IT...
...AND EXECUTE HIM. ♡
WHOA

READ THIS WAY

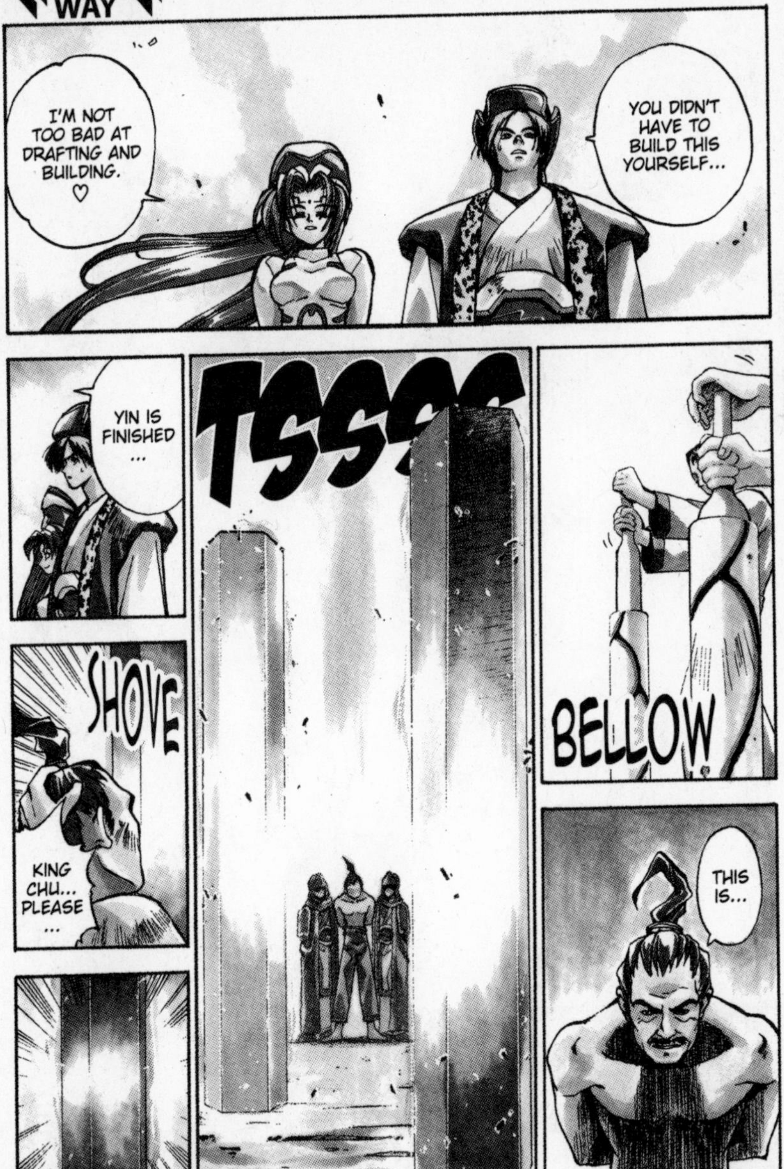

YOU DIDN'T HAVE TO BUILD THIS YOURSELF...
I'M NOT TOO BAD AT DRAFTING AND BUILDING. ♡
BELLOW
THIS IS...
TSSSS
YIN IS FINISHED...
SHOVE
KING CHU... PLEASE...

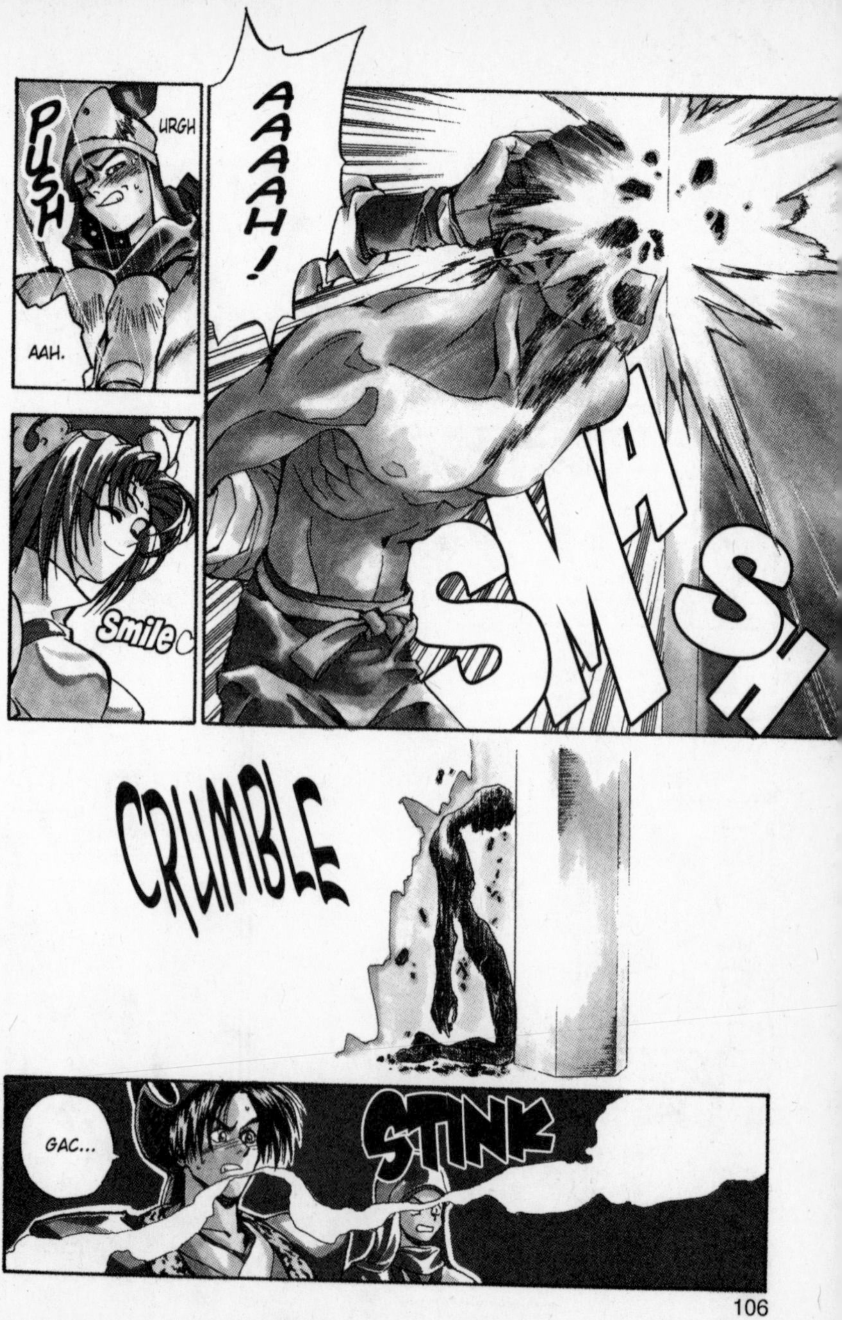
AAAAAH!
SMASH
URGH
PUSH
AAH.
Smile
CRUMBLE
STINK
GAC...

READ THIS WAY

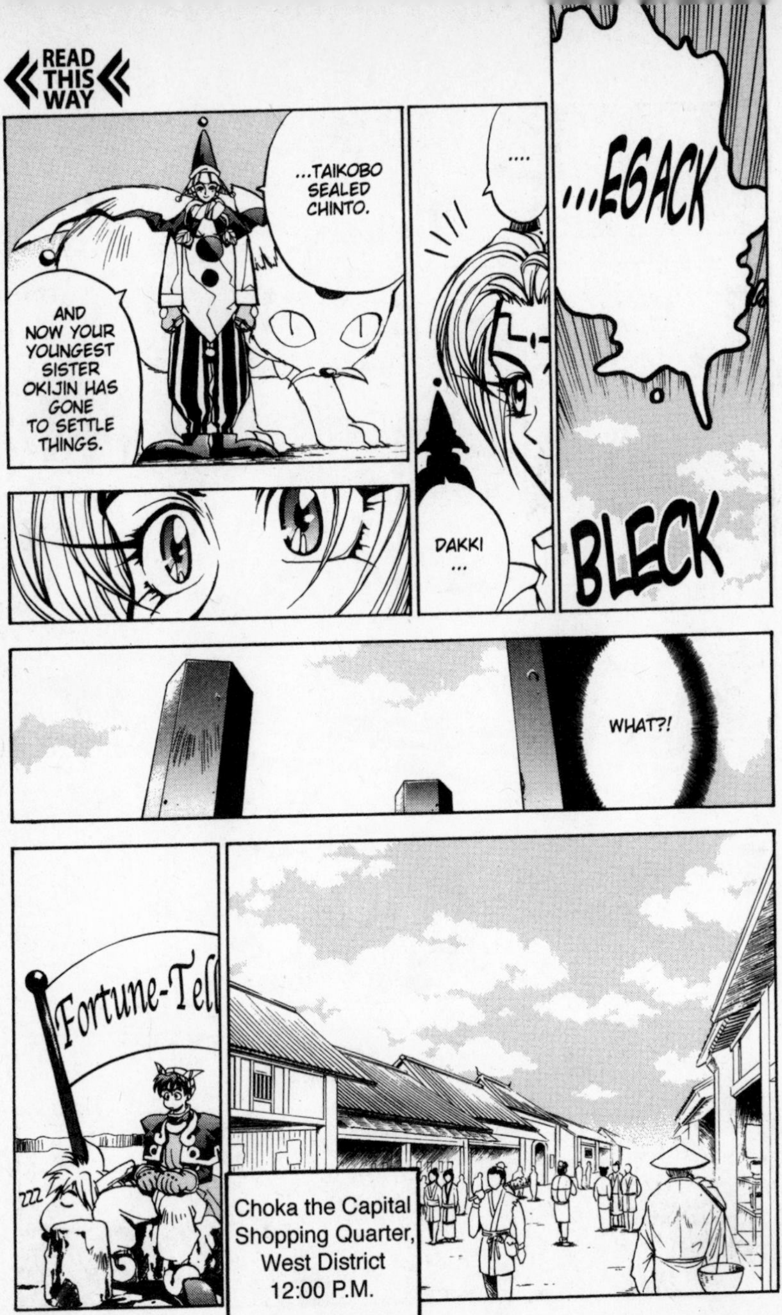
...EGACK
BLECK
....
DAKKI ...
...TAIKOBO SEALED CHINTO.
AND NOW YOUR YOUNGEST SISTER OKIJIN HAS GONE TO SETTLE THINGS.
WHAT?!
Choka the Capital Shopping Quarter, West District 12:00 P.M.
Fortune-Tell
zzz

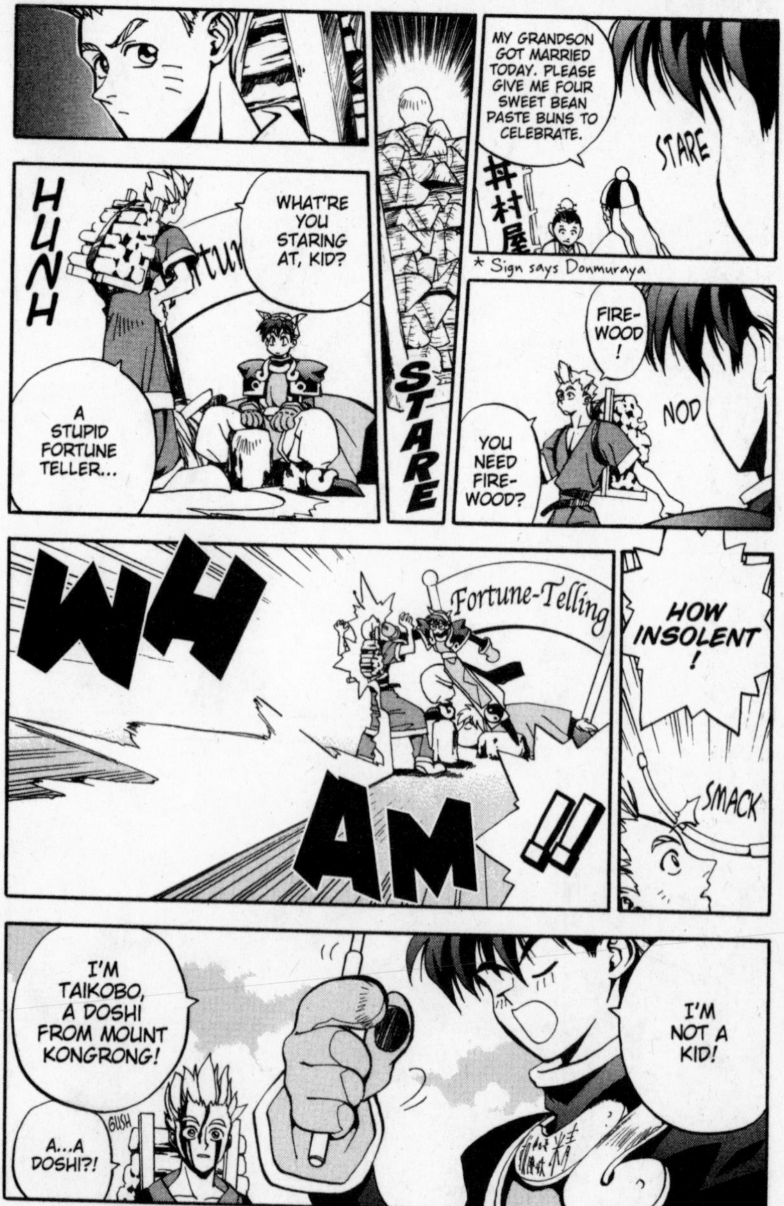
MY GRANDSON GOT MARRIED TODAY. PLEASE GIVE ME FOUR SWEET BEAN PASTE BUNS TO CELEBRATE.
STARE
丼村屋
* Sign says Donmuraya
FIRE-WOOD!
NOD
YOU NEED FIRE-WOOD?
STARE
WHAT'RE YOU STARING AT, KID?
HUNH
Fortun
A STUPID FORTUNE TELLER...
HOW INSOLENT!
SMACK
WHAM!!
Fortune-Telling
I'M NOT A KID!
I'M TAIKOBO, A DOSHI FROM MOUNT KONGRONG!
GUSH
A...A DOSHI?!

READ THIS WAY

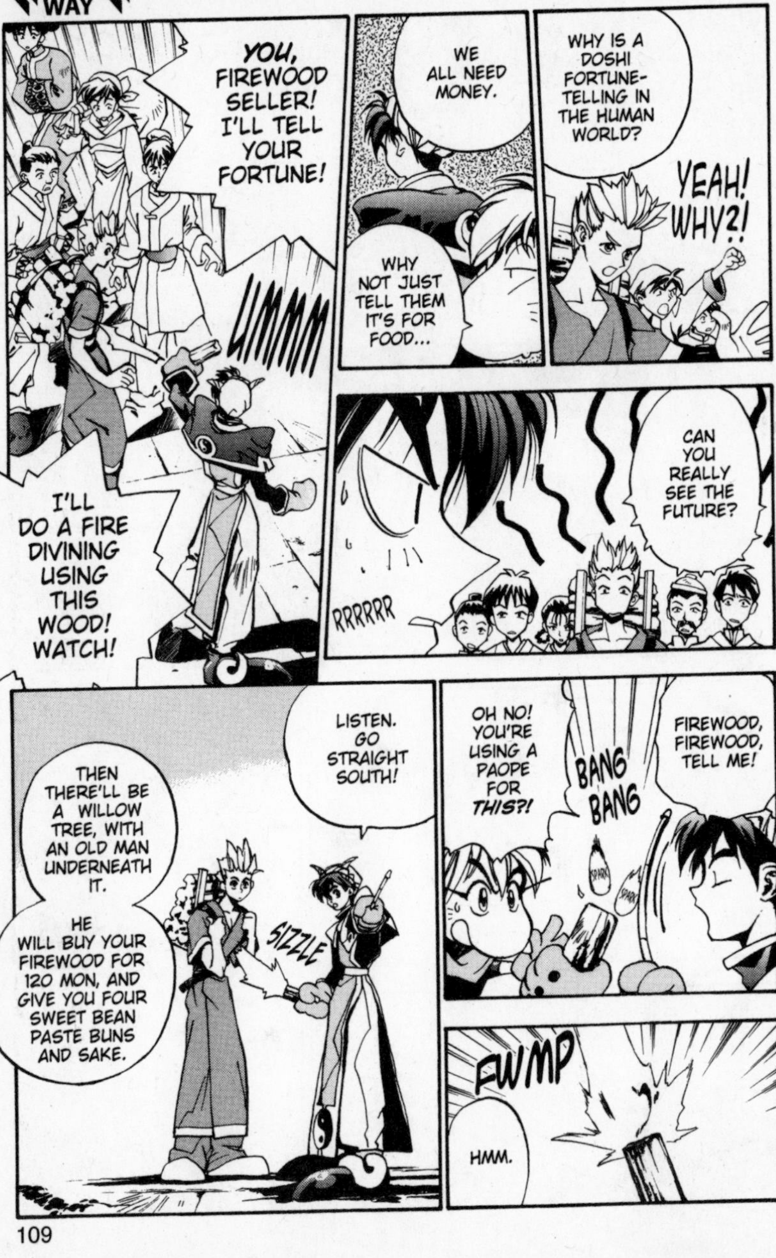
WHY IS A DOSHI FORTUNE-TELLING IN THE HUMAN WORLD?
YEAH! WHY?!
WE ALL NEED MONEY.
WHY NOT JUST TELL THEM IT'S FOR FOOD...
CAN YOU REALLY SEE THE FUTURE?
RRRRRR
YOU, FIREWOOD SELLER! I'LL TELL YOUR FORTUNE!
UMMM
I'LL DO A FIRE DIVINING USING THIS WOOD! WATCH!
FIREWOOD, FIREWOOD, TELL ME!
BANG BANG
SPARK
SPARK
OH NO! YOU'RE USING A PAOPE FOR *THIS*?!
FWUMP
HMM.
LISTEN. GO STRAIGHT SOUTH!
THEN THERE'LL BE A WILLOW TREE, WITH AN OLD MAN UNDERNEATH IT.
HE WILL BUY YOUR FIREWOOD FOR 120 MON, AND GIVE YOU FOUR SWEET BEAN PASTE BUNS AND SAKE.
SIZZLE

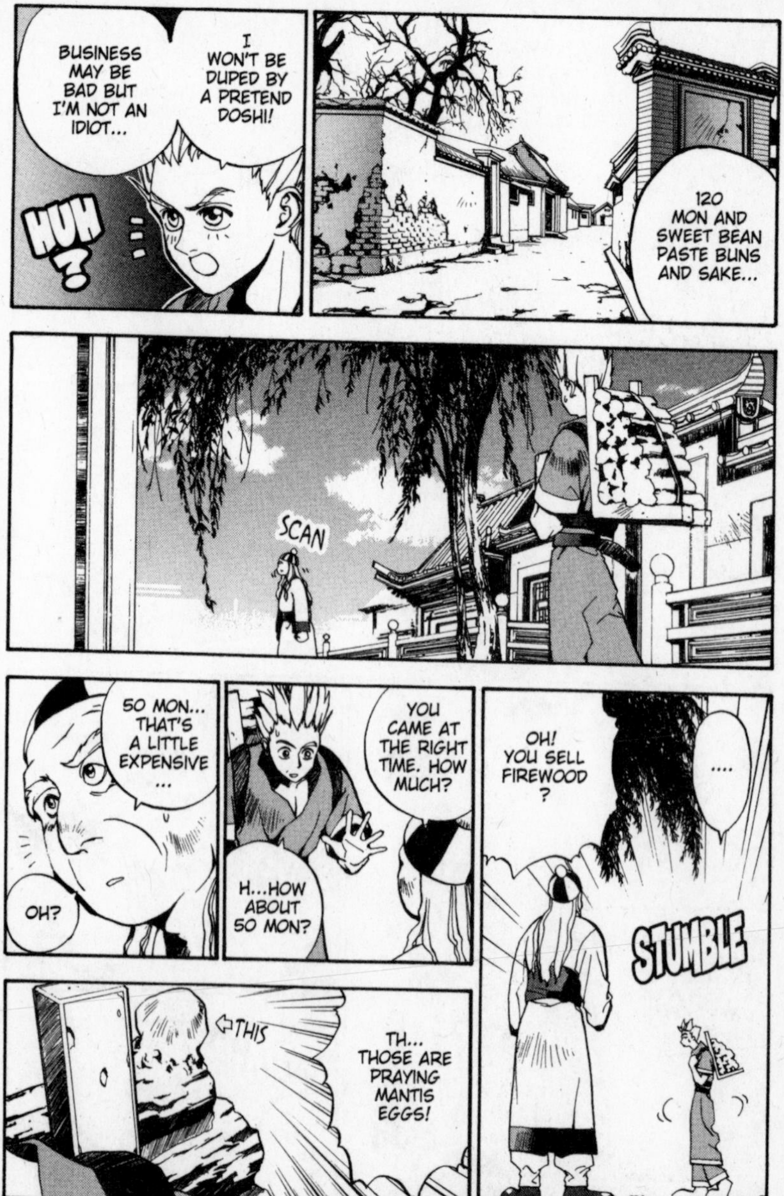

120 MON AND SWEET BEAN PASTE BUNS AND SAKE...
I WON'T BE DUPED BY A PRETEND DOSHI!
BUSINESS MAY BE BAD BUT I'M NOT AN IDIOT...
HUH?
SCAN
....
OH! YOU SELL FIREWOOD?
STUMBLE
YOU CAME AT THE RIGHT TIME. HOW MUCH?
H...HOW ABOUT 50 MON?
50 MON... THAT'S A LITTLE EXPENSIVE ...
OH?
TH... THOSE ARE PRAYING MANTIS EGGS!
THIS

READ THIS WAY

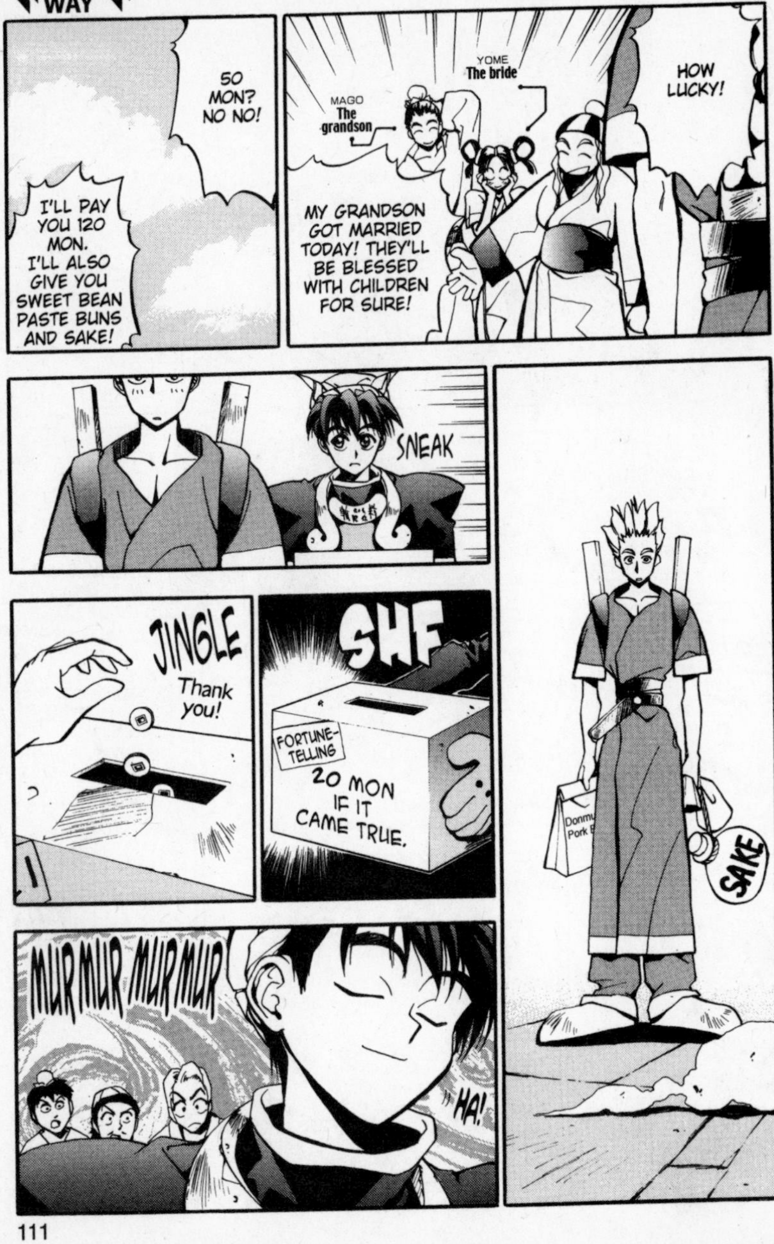
YOME
The bride
MAGO
The grandson
HOW LUCKY!
MY GRANDSON GOT MARRIED TODAY! THEY'LL BE BLESSED WITH CHILDREN FOR SURE!
50 MON? NO NO!
I'LL PAY YOU 120 MON. I'LL ALSO GIVE YOU SWEET BEAN PASTE BUNS AND SAKE!
SAKE
SNEAK
SHF
FORTUNE-TELLING
20 MON IF IT CAME TRUE.
JINGLE
Thank you!
MURMUR MURMUR
HA!

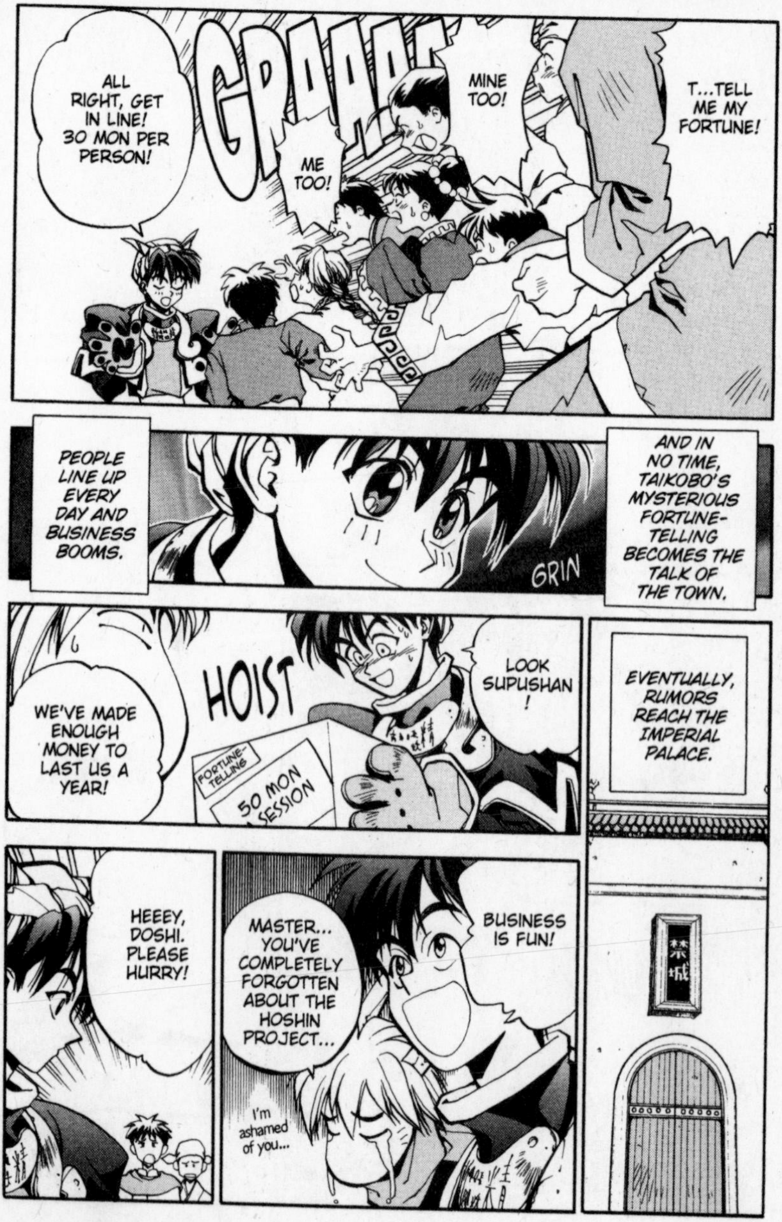
T...TELL ME MY FORTUNE!
MINE TOO!
ME TOO!
ALL RIGHT, GET IN LINE! 30 MON PER PERSON!
AND IN NO TIME, TAIKOBO'S MYSTERIOUS FORTUNE-TELLING BECOMES THE TALK OF THE TOWN.
GRIN
PEOPLE LINE UP EVERY DAY AND BUSINESS BOOMS.
EVENTUALLY, RUMORS REACH THE IMPERIAL PALACE.
LOOK SUPUSHAN!
HOIST
FORTUNE-TELLING
50 MON SESSION
WE'VE MADE ENOUGH MONEY TO LAST US A YEAR!
BUSINESS IS FUN!
MASTER... YOU'VE COMPLETELY FORGOTTEN ABOUT THE HOSHIN PROJECT...
I'm ashamed of you...
HEEEY, DOSHI. PLEASE HURRY!

READ THIS WAY

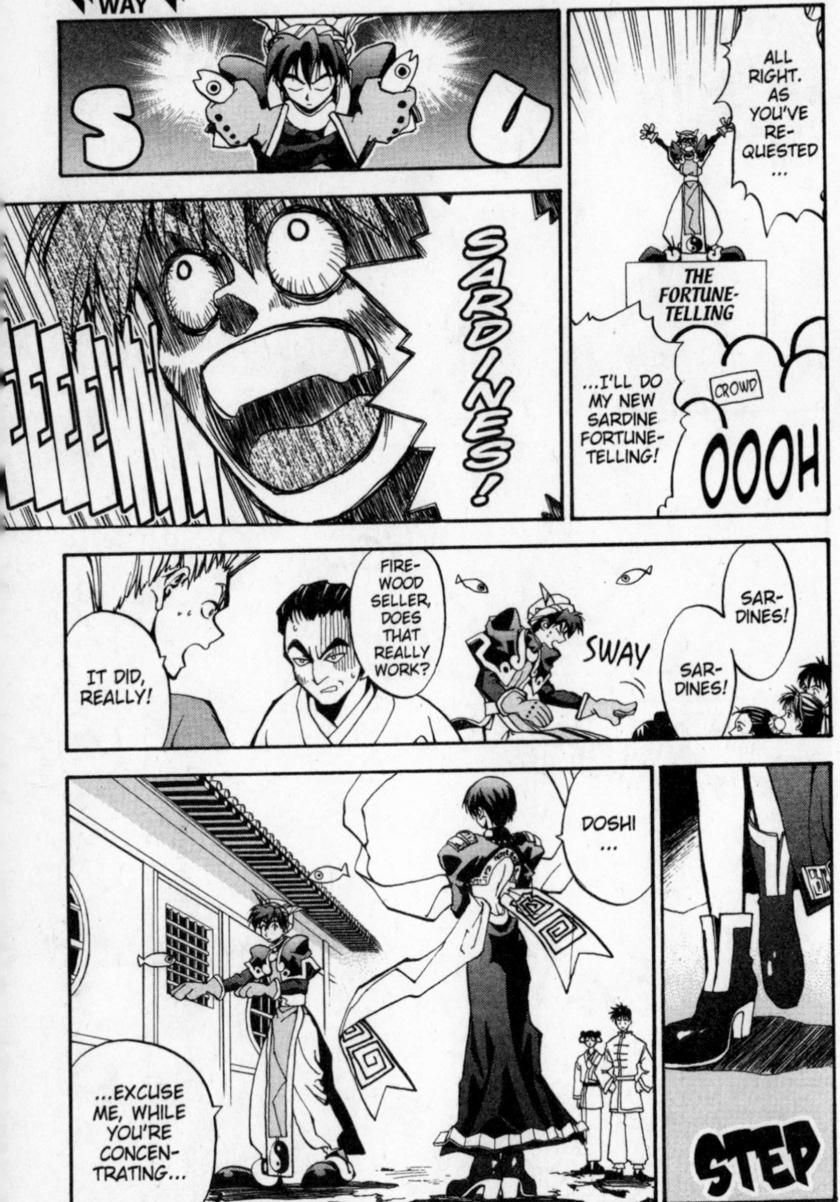
ALL RIGHT. AS YOU'VE RE-QUESTED ...
THE FORTUNE-TELLING
...I'LL DO MY NEW SARDINE FORTUNE-TELLING!
CROWD
OOOH
S
U
SARDINES!
SAR-DINES!
SAR-DINES!
SWAY
FIRE-WOOD SELLER, DOES THAT REALLY WORK?
IT DID, REALLY!
STEP
DOSHI ...
...EXCUSE ME, WHILE YOU'RE CONCEN-TRATING...

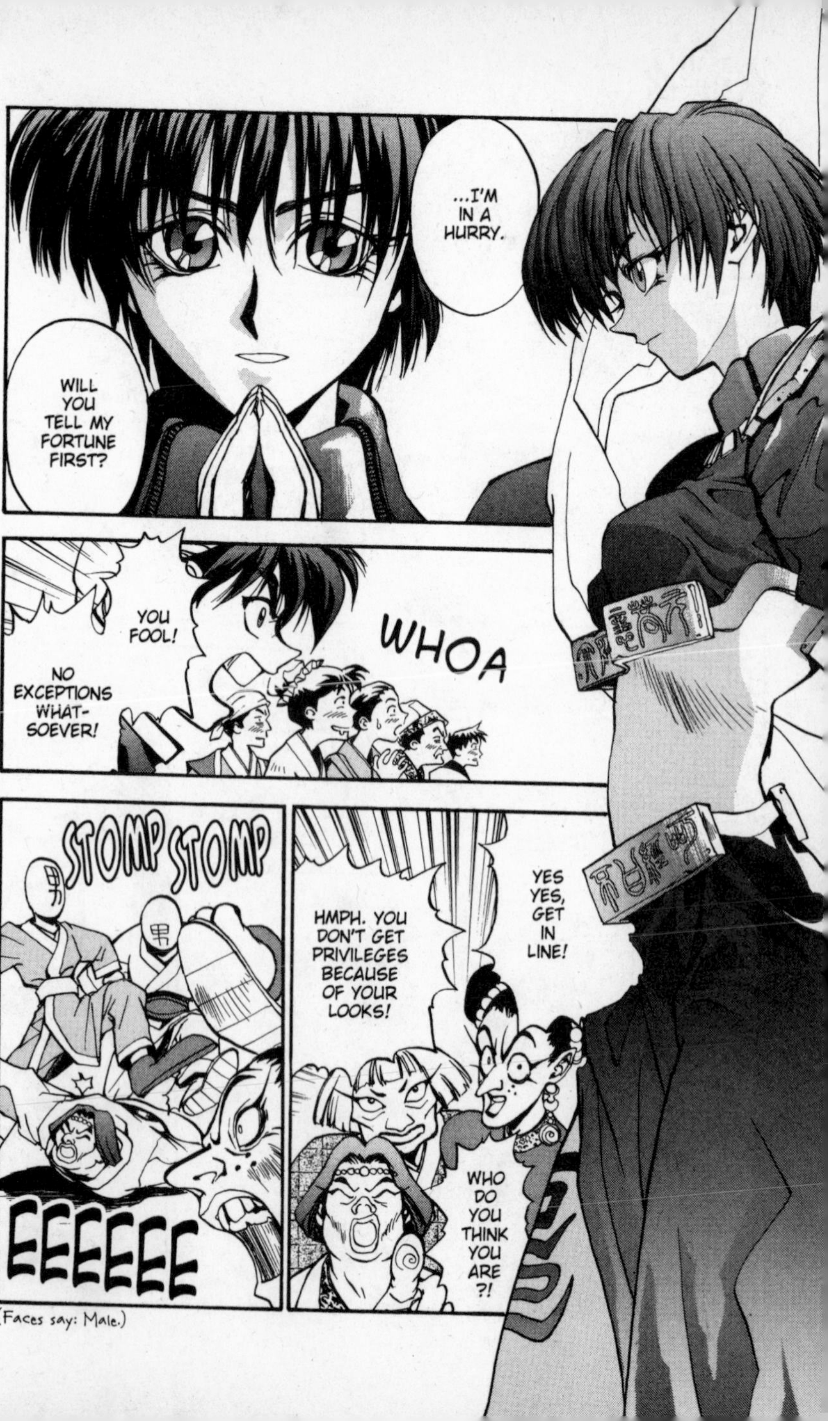
...I'M IN A HURRY.
WILL YOU TELL MY FORTUNE FIRST?
WHOA
YOU FOOL!
NO EXCEPTIONS WHAT-SOEVER!
YES YES, GET IN LINE!
HMPH. YOU DON'T GET PRIVILEGES BECAUSE OF YOUR LOOKS!
WHO DO YOU THINK YOU ARE?!
STOMP STOMP
EEEEEE
(Faces say: Male.)

READ THIS WAY

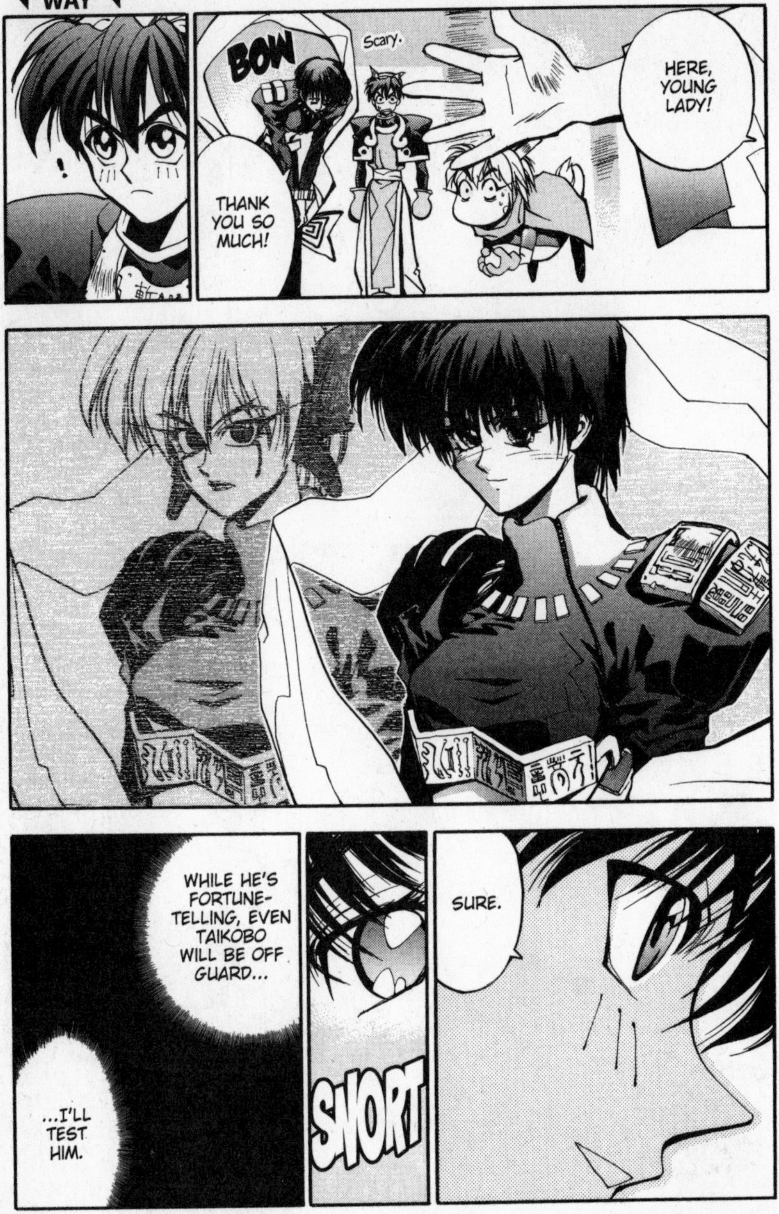

HERE, YOUNG LADY!
Scary.
BOW
THANK YOU SO MUCH!
!
SURE.
SNORT
WHILE HE'S FORTUNE-TELLING, EVEN TAIKOBO WILL BE OFF GUARD...
...I'LL TEST HIM.

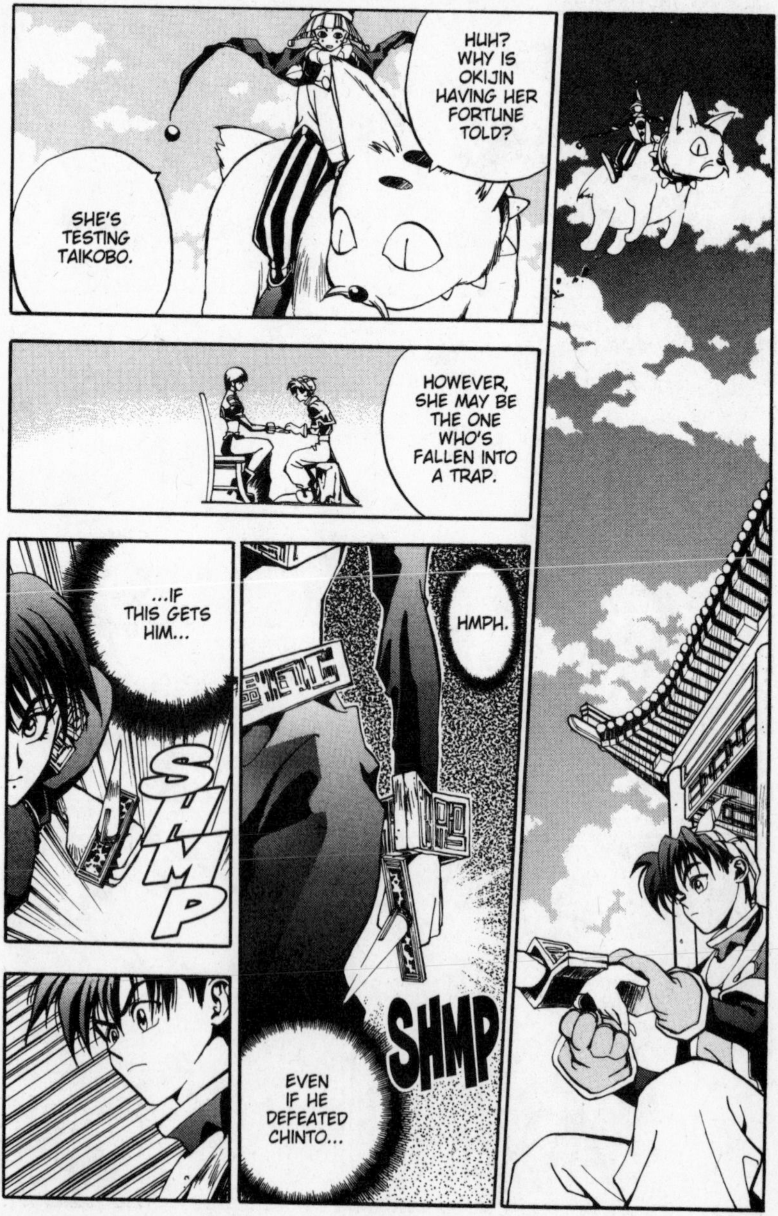
HUH? WHY IS OKIJIN HAVING HER FORTUNE TOLD?
SHE'S TESTING TAIKOBO.
HOWEVER, SHE MAY BE THE ONE WHO'S FALLEN INTO A TRAP.
HMPH.
SHMP
EVEN IF HE DEFEATED CHINTO...
...IF THIS GETS HIM...
SHMP

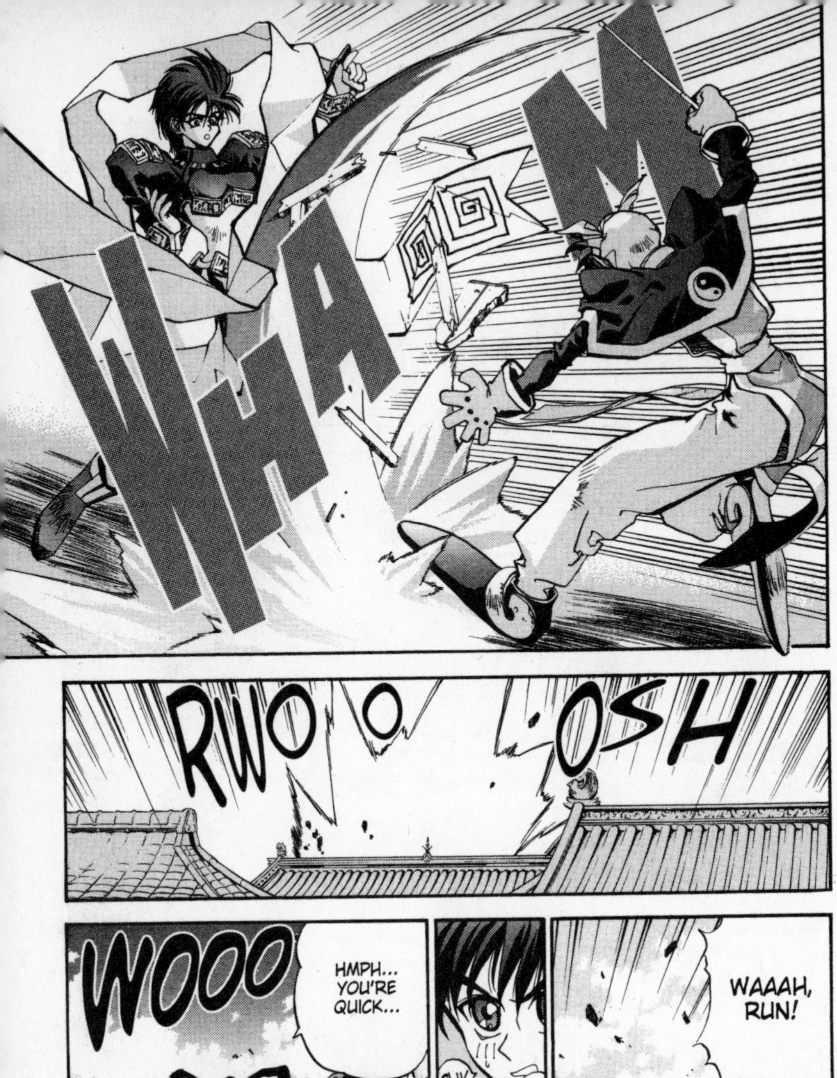
WHAM
RWOOOSH
WAAAH, RUN!
DOSHI HAS GONE BERSERK!
CLIK
WOOO
HMPH... YOU'RE QUICK...
...YOU ALREADY KNEW WHO I WAS... WELL, FINE THEN...

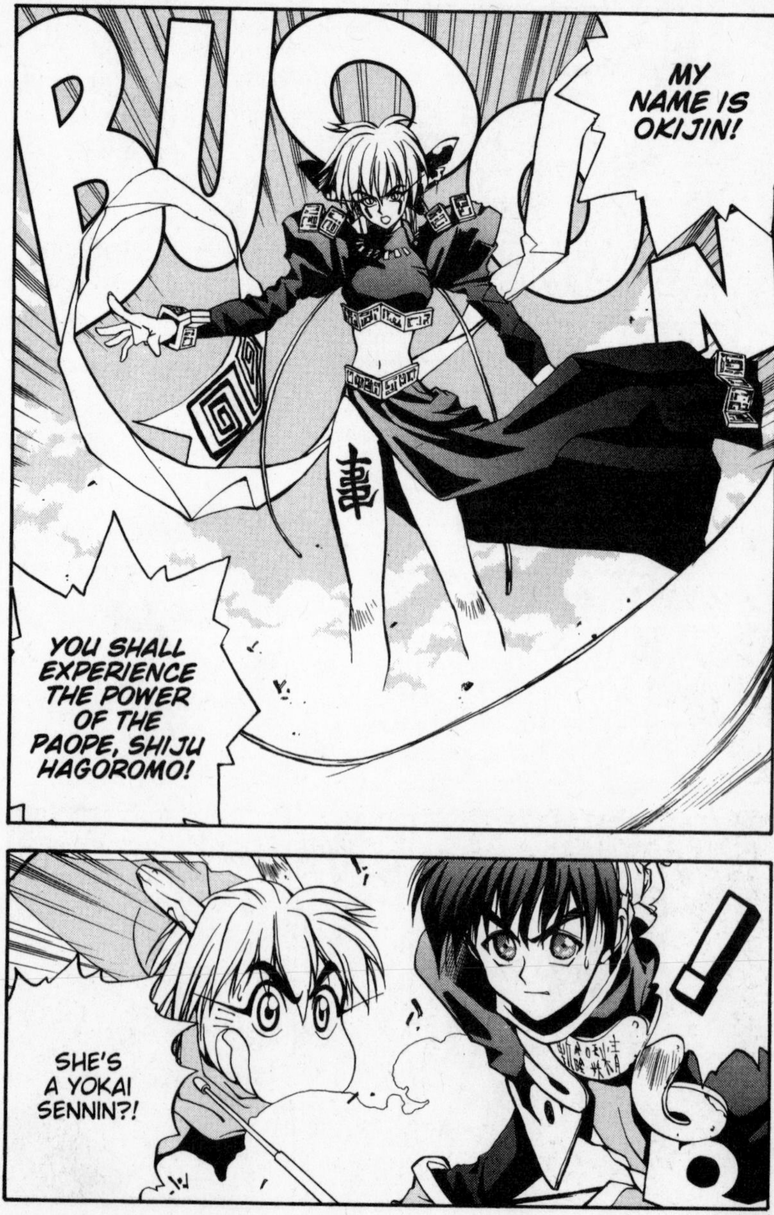
MY NAME IS OKIJIN!
YOU SHALL EXPERIENCE THE POWER OF THE PAOPE, SHIJU HAGOROMO!
!
SHE'S A YOKAI SENNIN?!

READ THIS WAY

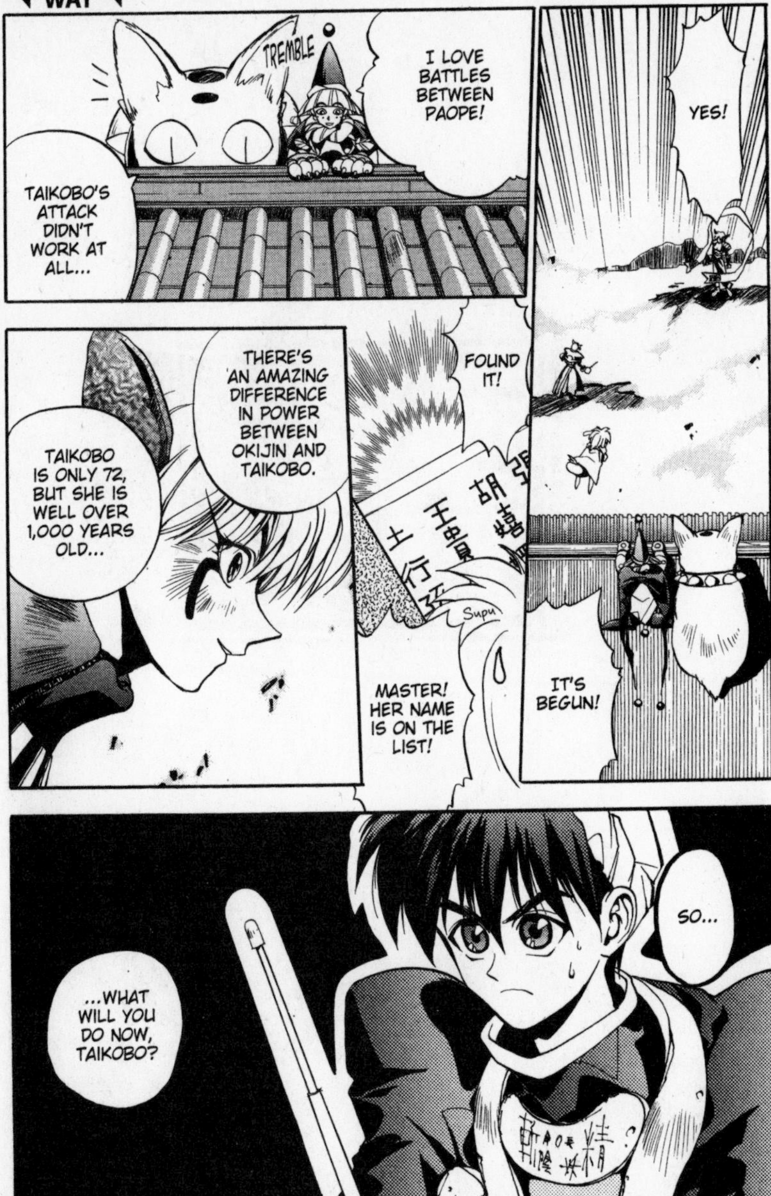
YES!
IT'S BEGUN!
I LOVE BATTLES BETWEEN PAOPE!
TREMBLE
TAIKOBO'S ATTACK DIDN'T WORK AT ALL...
FOUND IT!
MASTER! HER NAME IS ON THE LIST!
Supu
THERE'S AN AMAZING DIFFERENCE IN POWER BETWEEN OKIJIN AND TAIKOBO.
TAIKOBO IS ONLY 72, BUT SHE IS WELL OVER 1,000 YEARS OLD...
SO...
...WHAT WILL YOU DO NOW, TAIKOBO?

封神演義

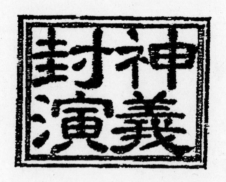

Chapter 4

OKIJIN

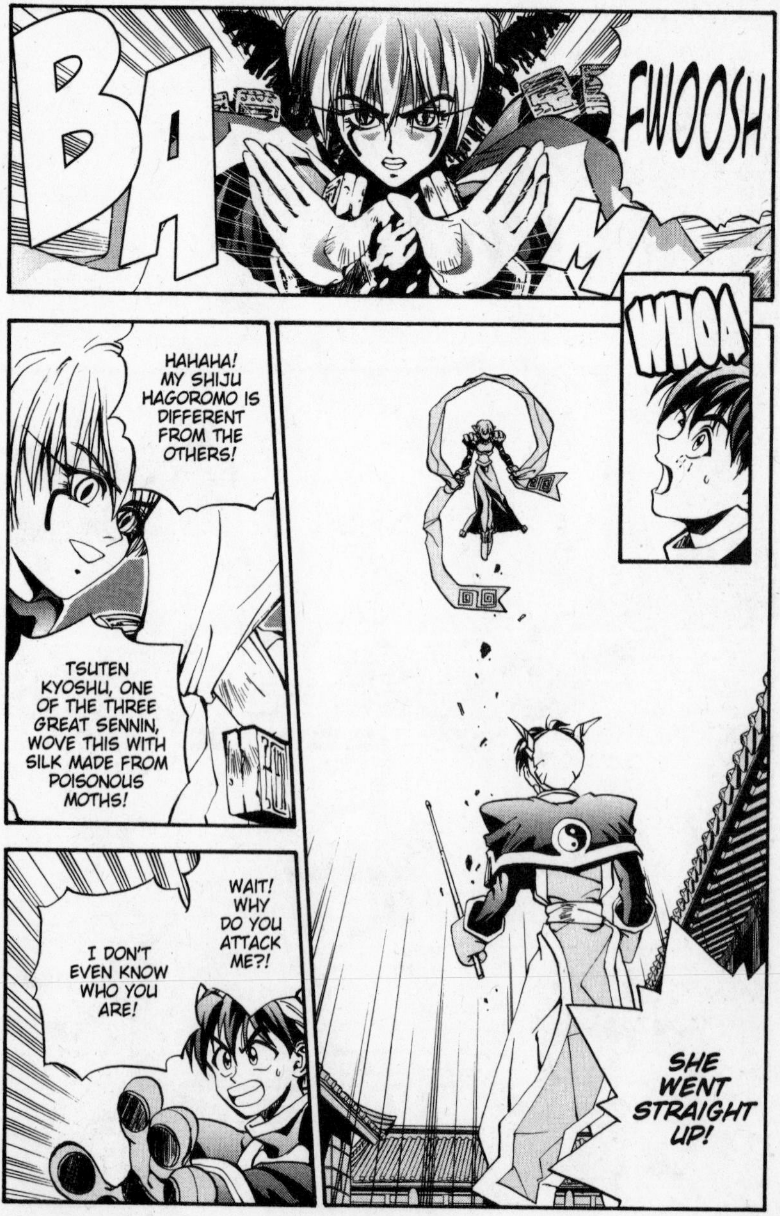
FWOOSH
BAM
WHOA
SHE WENT STRAIGHT UP!
HAHAHA! MY SHIJU HAGOROMO IS DIFFERENT FROM THE OTHERS!
TSUTEN KYOSHU, ONE OF THE THREE GREAT SENNIN, WOVE THIS WITH SILK MADE FROM POISONOUS MOTHS!
WAIT! WHY DO YOU ATTACK ME?!
I DON'T EVEN KNOW WHO YOU ARE!

READ THIS WAY

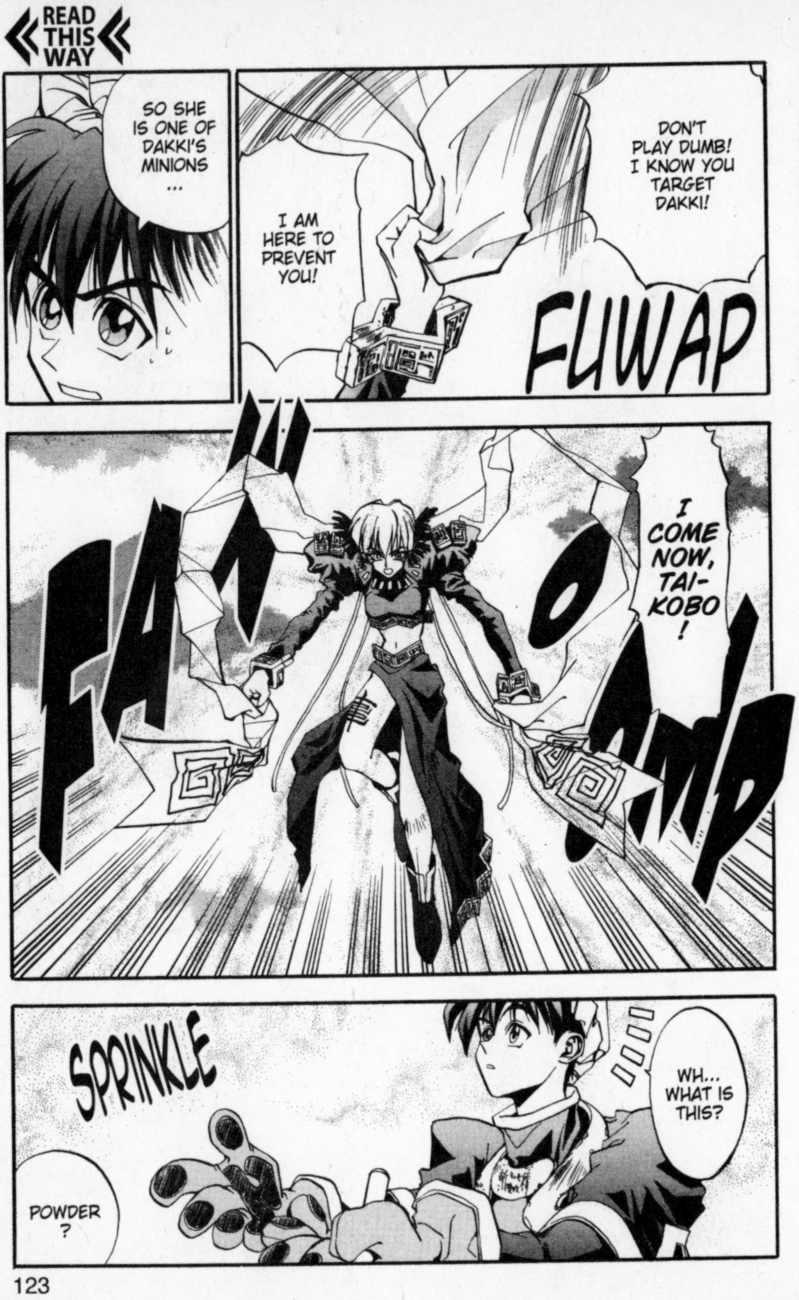
DON'T PLAY DUMB! I KNOW YOU TARGET DAKKI!
I AM HERE TO PREVENT YOU!
FUWAP
SO SHE IS ONE OF DAKKI'S MINIONS ...
I COME NOW, TAI-KOBO!
WH... WHAT IS THIS?
SPRINKLE
POWDER ?

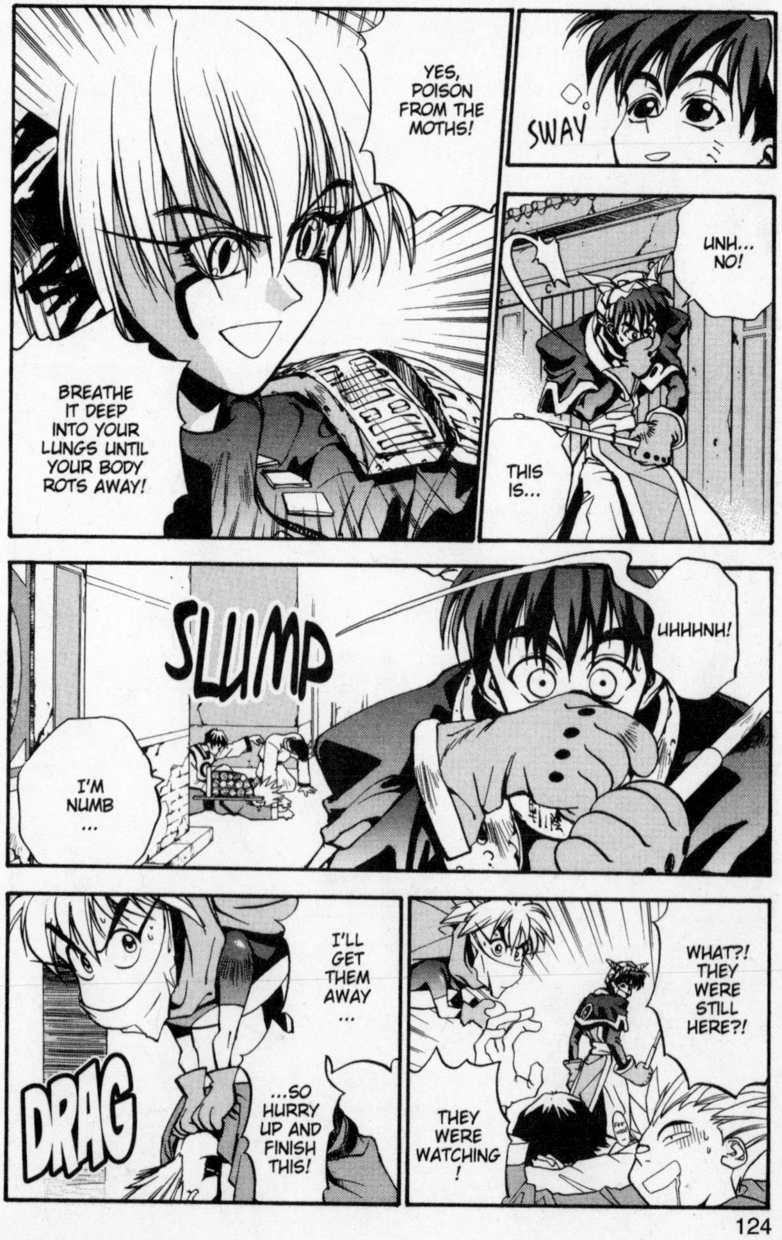
SWAY
UNH... NO!
THIS IS...
YES, POISON FROM THE MOTHS!
BREATHE IT DEEP INTO YOUR LUNGS UNTIL YOUR BODY ROTS AWAY!
UHHHNH!
SLUMP
I'M NUMB ...
WHAT?! THEY WERE STILL HERE?!
THEY WERE WATCHING!
I'LL GET THEM AWAY ...
DRAG
...SO HURRY UP AND FINISH THIS!

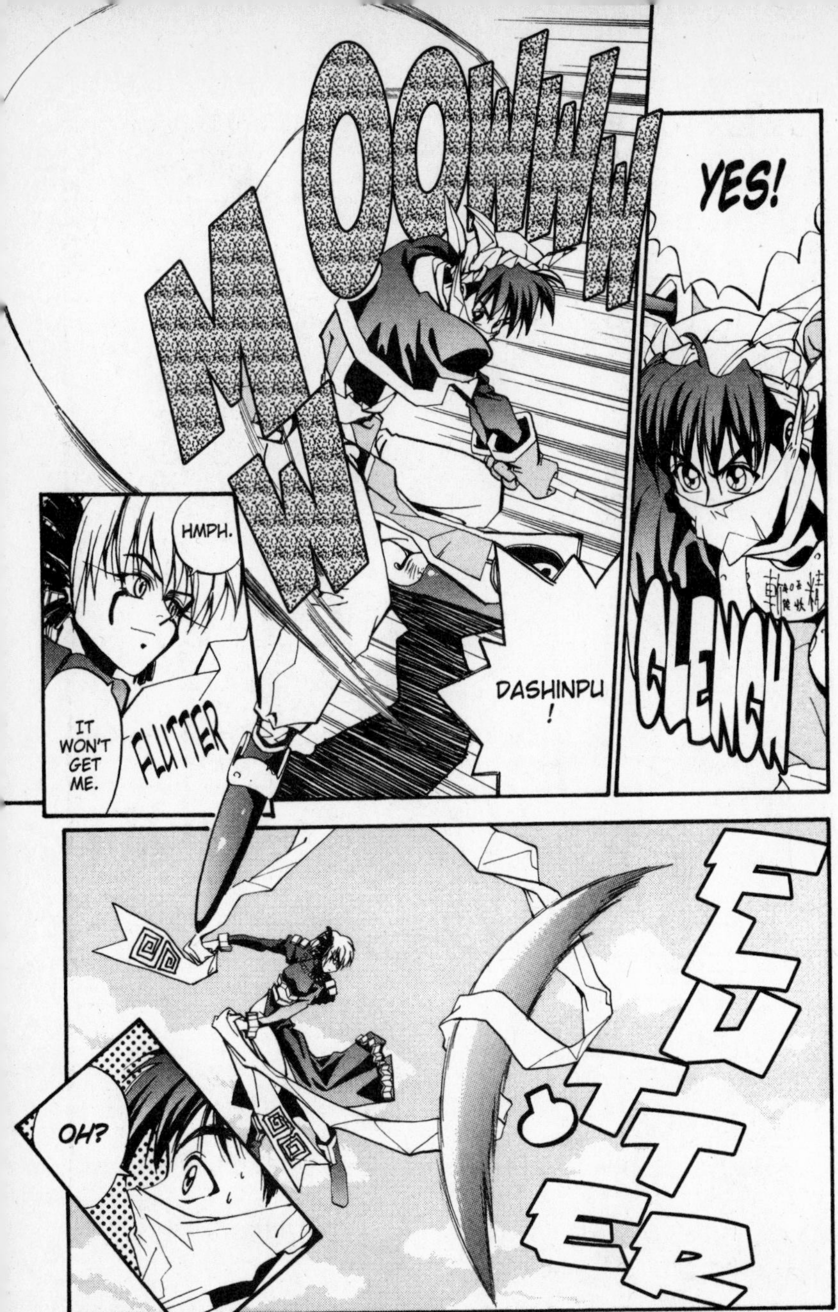
YES!
CLENCH
MOOWWWW
DASHINPU!
HMPH.
IT WON'T GET ME.
FLUTTER
FLUTTER
OH?

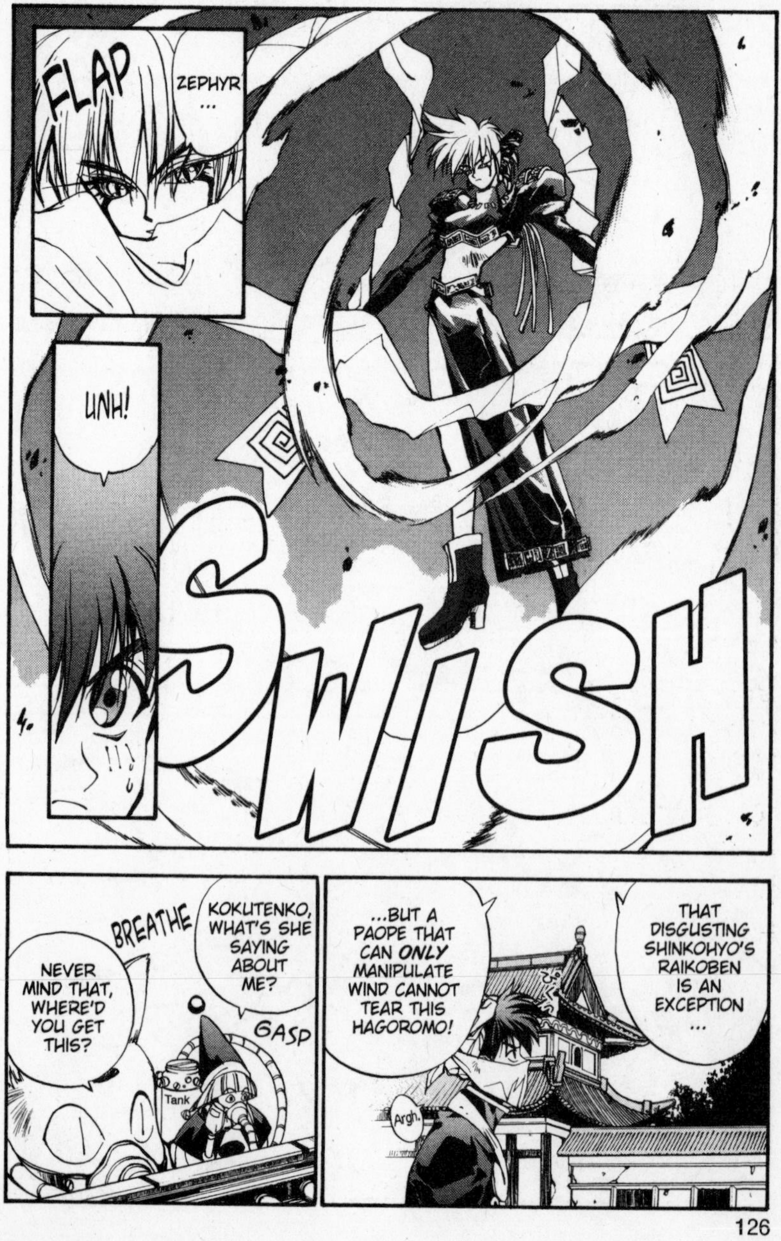
SWISH
ZEPHYR ...
FLAP
UNH!
THAT DISGUSTING SHINKOHYO'S RAIKOBEN IS AN EXCEPTION ...
...BUT A PAOPE THAT CAN ***ONLY*** MANIPULATE WIND CANNOT TEAR THIS HAGOROMO!
Argh.
KOKUTENKO, WHAT'S SHE SAYING ABOUT ME?
BREATHE
GASP
NEVER MIND THAT, WHERE'D YOU GET THIS?
Tank

READ THIS WAY

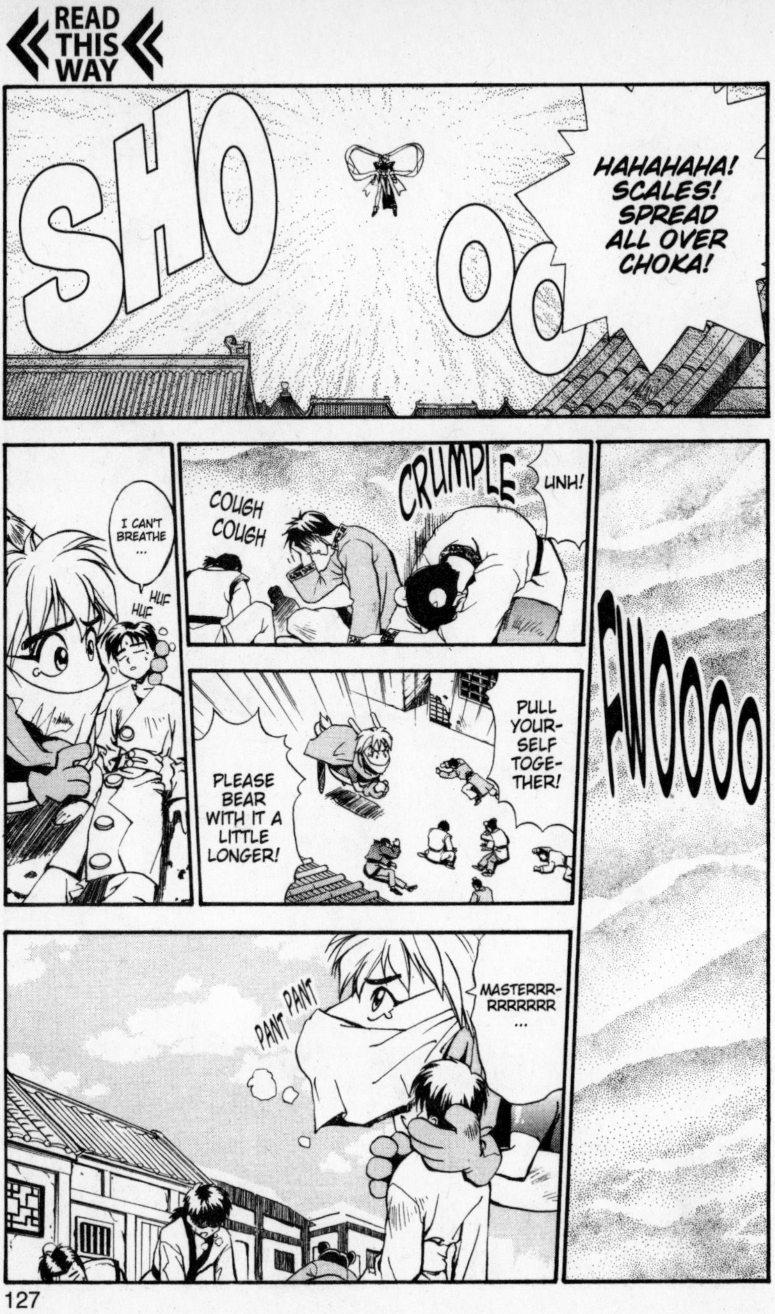
SHOOOO
HAHAHAHA! SCALES! SPREAD ALL OVER CHOKA!
FWOOOO
UNH!
CRUMPLE
COUGH COUGH
PULL YOUR-SELF TOGE-THER!
PLEASE BEAR WITH IT A LITTLE LONGER!
I CAN'T BREATHE ...
HUF HUF
MASTERRR-RRRRRRR ...
PANT PANT

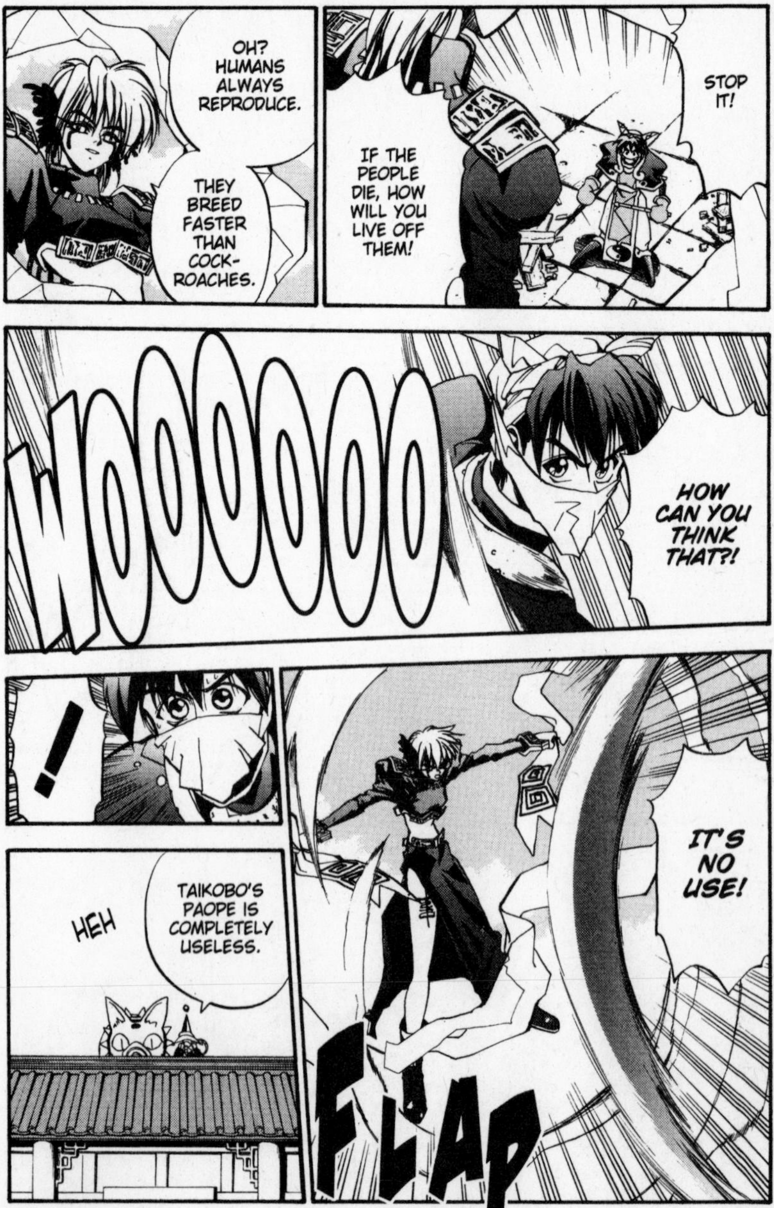
STOP IT!
IF THE PEOPLE DIE, HOW WILL YOU LIVE OFF THEM!
OH? HUMANS ALWAYS REPRODUCE.
THEY BREED FASTER THAN COCK-ROACHES.
HOW CAN YOU THINK THAT?!
WOOOOOOO
IT'S NO USE!
FLAP
!
HEH
TAIKOBO'S PAOPE IS COMPLETELY USELESS.

READ THIS WAY

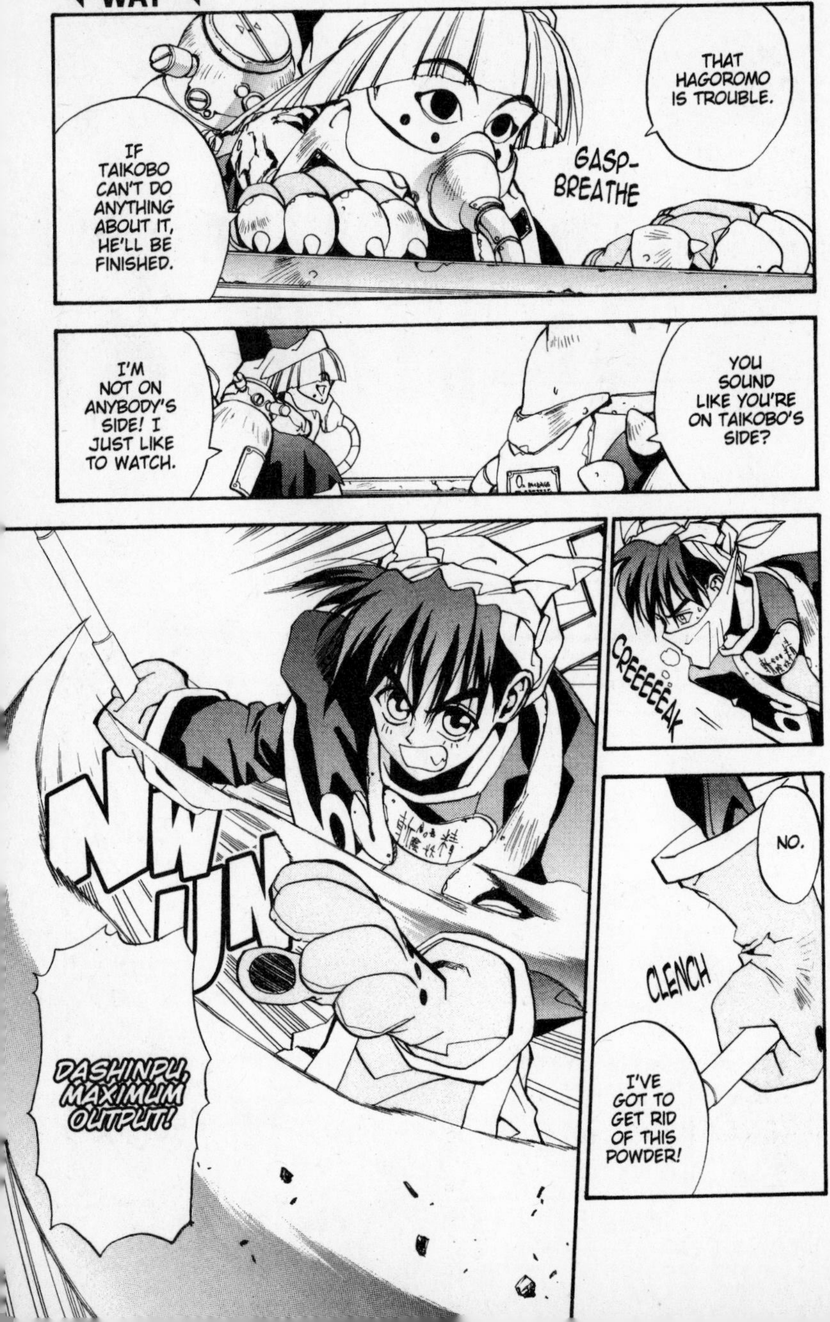
THAT HAGOROMO IS TROUBLE.
GASP-BREATHE
IF TAIKOBO CAN'T DO ANYTHING ABOUT IT, HE'LL BE FINISHED.
YOU SOUND LIKE YOU'RE ON TAIKOBO'S SIDE?
I'M NOT ON ANYBODY'S SIDE! I JUST LIKE TO WATCH.
CREEEEEEAK
NO.
CLENCH
I'VE GOT TO GET RID OF THIS POWDER!
DASHINPU, MAXIMUM OUTPUT!

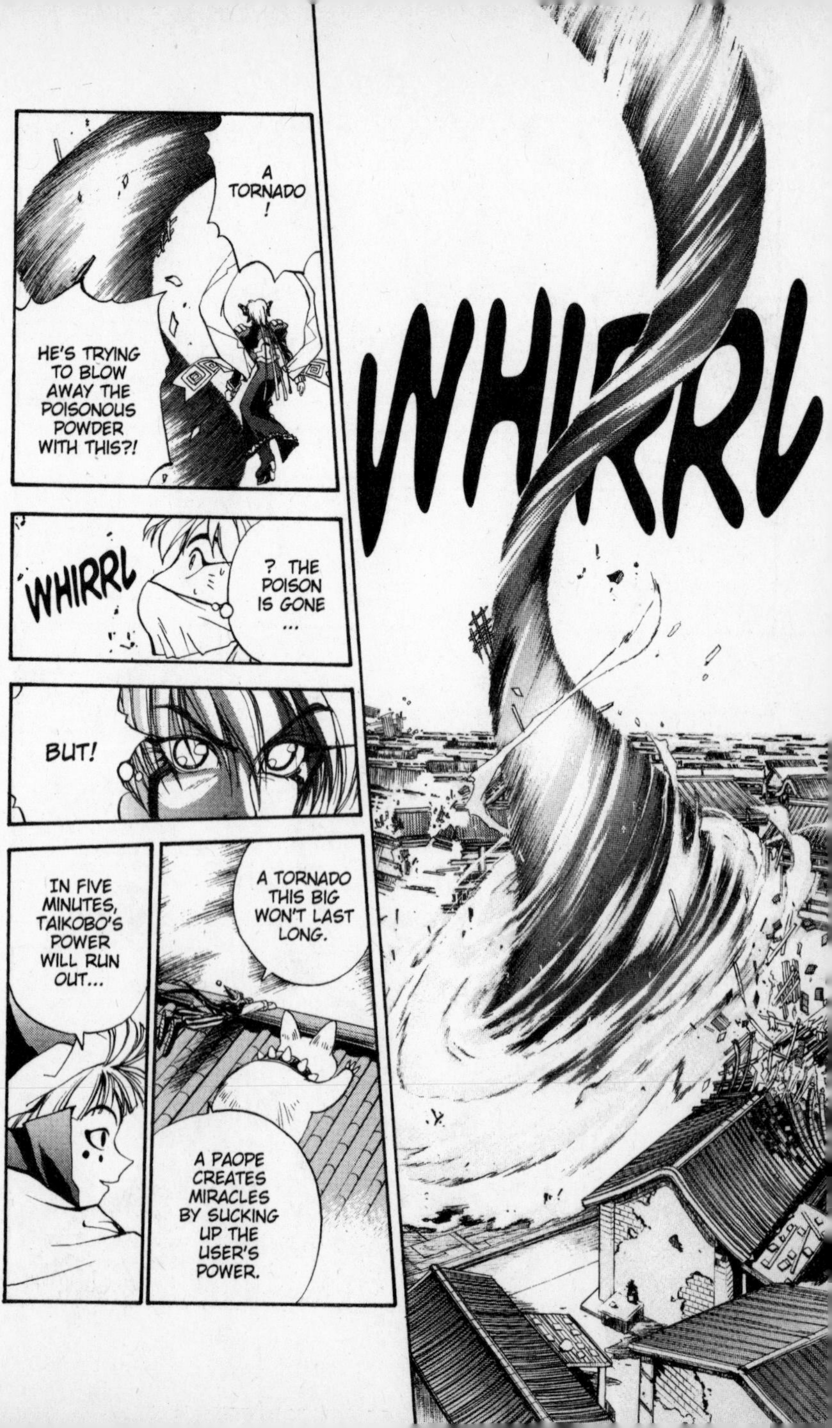
WHIRRL
A TORNADO!
HE'S TRYING TO BLOW AWAY THE POISONOUS POWDER WITH THIS?!
? THE POISON IS GONE ...
WHIRRL
BUT!
A TORNADO THIS BIG WON'T LAST LONG.
A PAOPE CREATES MIRACLES BY SUCKING UP THE USER'S POWER.
IN FIVE MINUTES, TAIKOBO'S POWER WILL RUN OUT...

READ THIS WAY

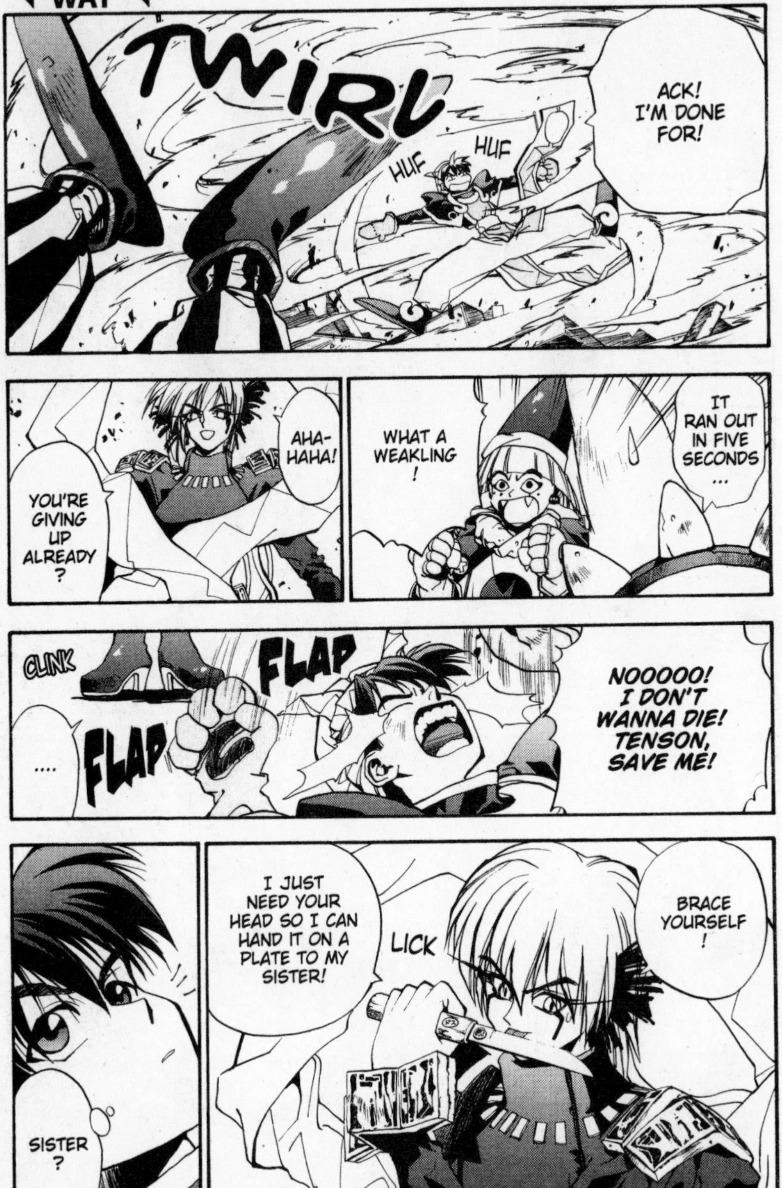

ACK! I'M DONE FOR!
HUF HUF
TWIRL
IT RAN OUT IN FIVE SECONDS ...
WHAT A WEAKLING!
AHA-HAHA!
YOU'RE GIVING UP ALREADY?
NOOOOO! I DON'T WANNA DIE! TENSON, SAVE ME!
FLAP
FLAP
CLINK
....
BRACE YOURSELF!
LICK
I JUST NEED YOUR HEAD SO I CAN HAND IT ON A PLATE TO MY SISTER!
SISTER?

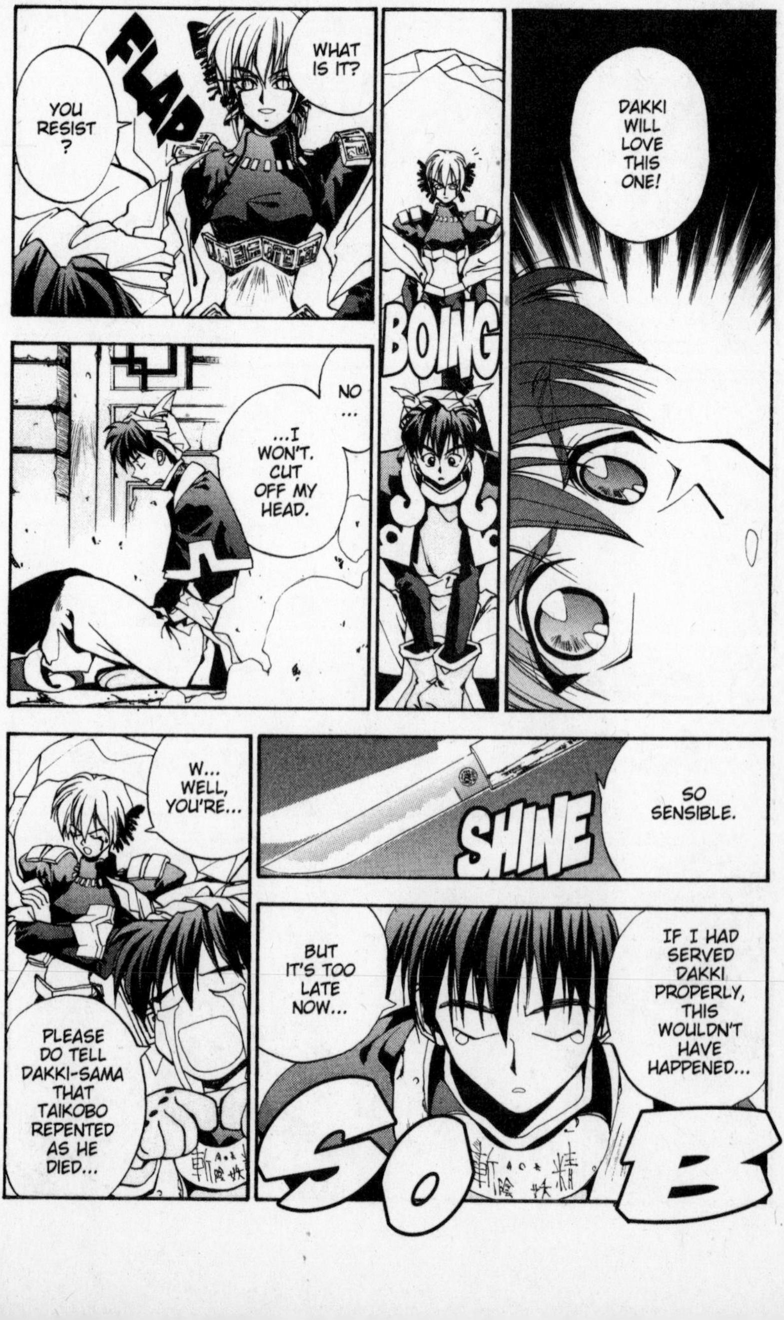

DAKKI WILL LOVE THIS ONE!
BOING
FLAP
WHAT IS IT?
YOU RESIST ?
NO ...
...I WON'T. CUT OFF MY HEAD.
SO SENSIBLE.
SHINE
IF I HAD SERVED DAKKI PROPERLY, THIS WOULDN'T HAVE HAPPENED...
BUT IT'S TOO LATE NOW...
SOB
W... WELL, YOU'RE...
PLEASE DO TELL DAKKI-SAMA THAT TAIKOBO REPENTED AS HE DIED...

READ THIS WAY

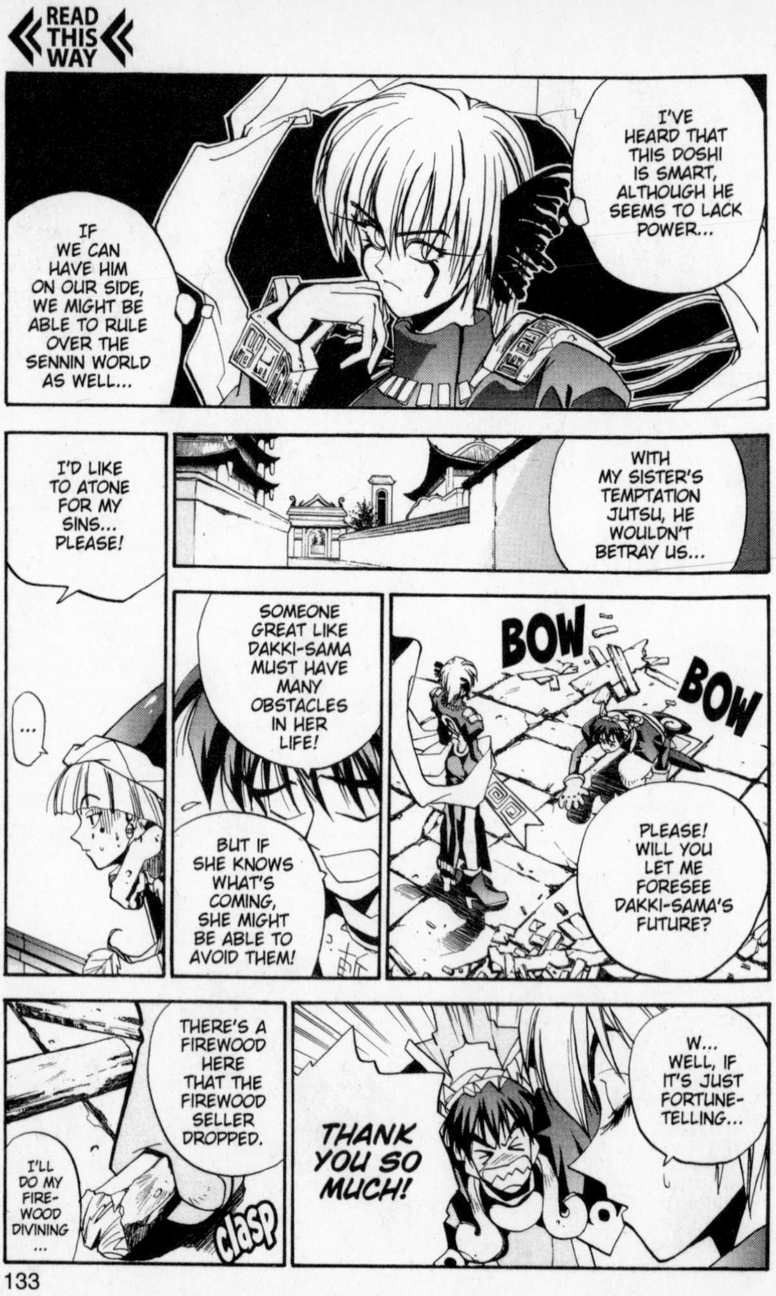

I'VE HEARD THAT THIS DOSHI IS SMART, ALTHOUGH HE SEEMS TO LACK POWER...
IF WE CAN HAVE HIM ON OUR SIDE, WE MIGHT BE ABLE TO RULE OVER THE SENNIN WORLD AS WELL...
WITH MY SISTER'S TEMPTATION JUTSU, HE WOULDN'T BETRAY US...
BOW
BOW
PLEASE! WILL YOU LET ME FORESEE DAKKI-SAMA'S FUTURE?
SOMEONE GREAT LIKE DAKKI-SAMA MUST HAVE MANY OBSTACLES IN HER LIFE!
BUT IF SHE KNOWS WHAT'S COMING, SHE MIGHT BE ABLE TO AVOID THEM!
I'D LIKE TO ATONE FOR MY SINS... PLEASE!
...
W... WELL, IF IT'S JUST FORTUNE-TELLING...
THANK YOU SO MUCH!
THERE'S A FIREWOOD HERE THAT THE FIREWOOD SELLER DROPPED.
I'LL DO MY FIRE-WOOD DIVINING ...
clasp

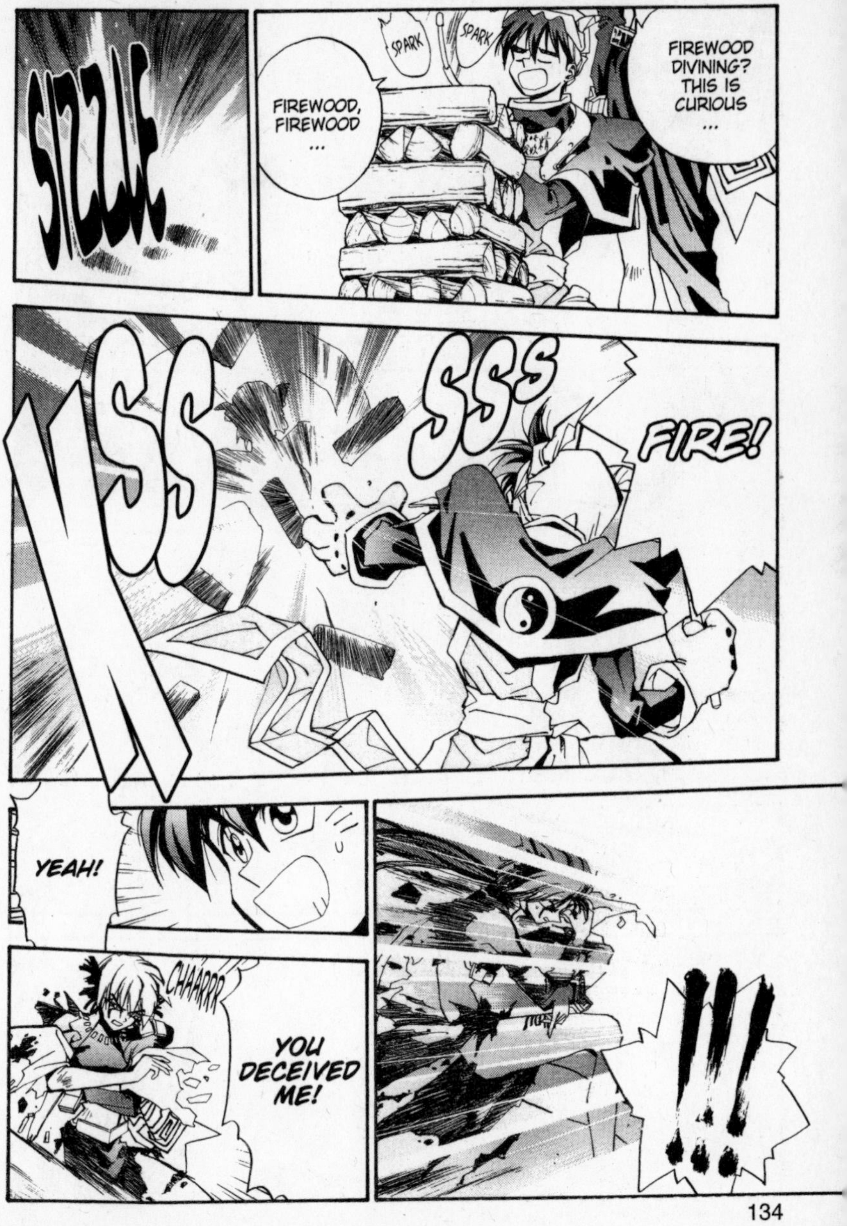
FIREWOOD DIVINING? THIS IS CURIOUS ...
SPARK
SPARK
FIREWOOD, FIREWOOD ...
SIZZLE
FIRE!
VSSSSS
!!!
YEAH!
CHAARRR
YOU DECEIVED ME!

READ THIS WAY

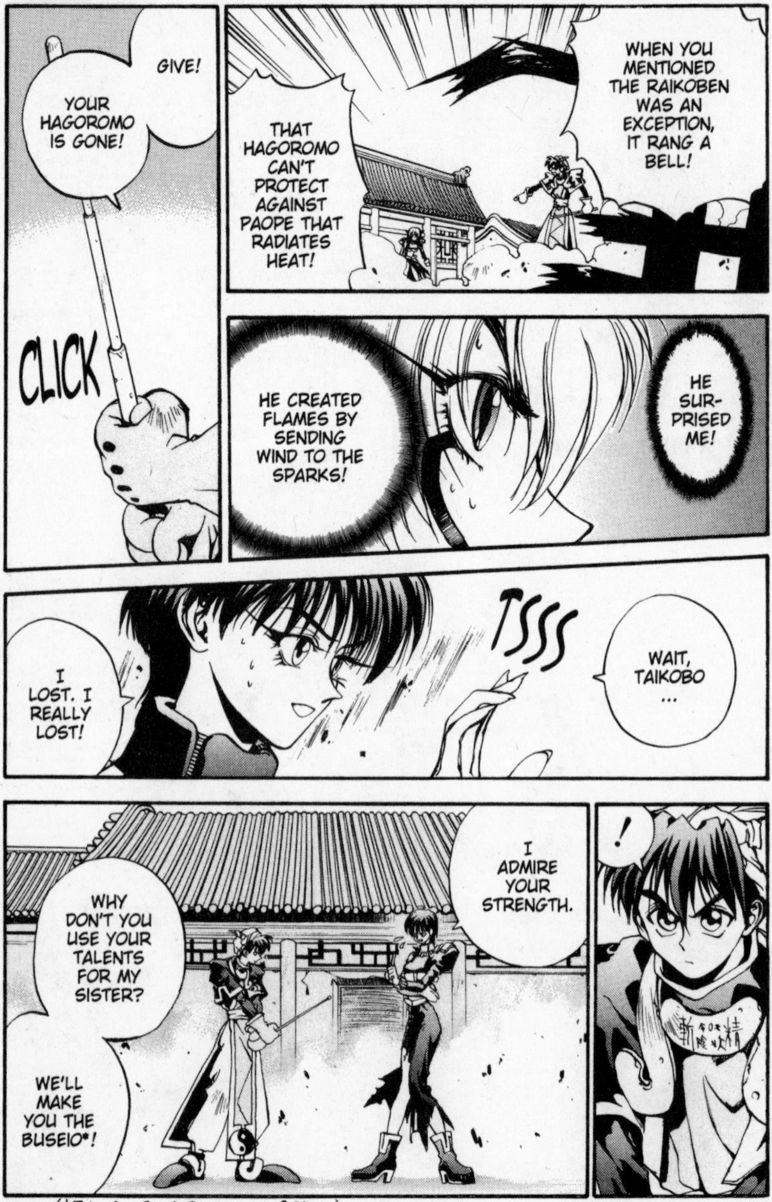
WHEN YOU MENTIONED THE RAIKOBEN WAS AN EXCEPTION, IT RANG A BELL!
THAT HAGOROMO CAN'T PROTECT AGAINST PAOPE THAT RADIATES HEAT!
HE SURPRISED ME!
HE CREATED FLAMES BY SENDING WIND TO THE SPARKS!
GIVE!
YOUR HAGOROMO IS GONE!
CLICK
WAIT, TAIKOBO ...
TSSS
I LOST. I REALLY LOST!
!
I ADMIRE YOUR STRENGTH.
WHY DON'T YOU USE YOUR TALENTS FOR MY SISTER?
WE'LL MAKE YOU THE BUSEIO*!

(*Title for Chief Commanding Officer)

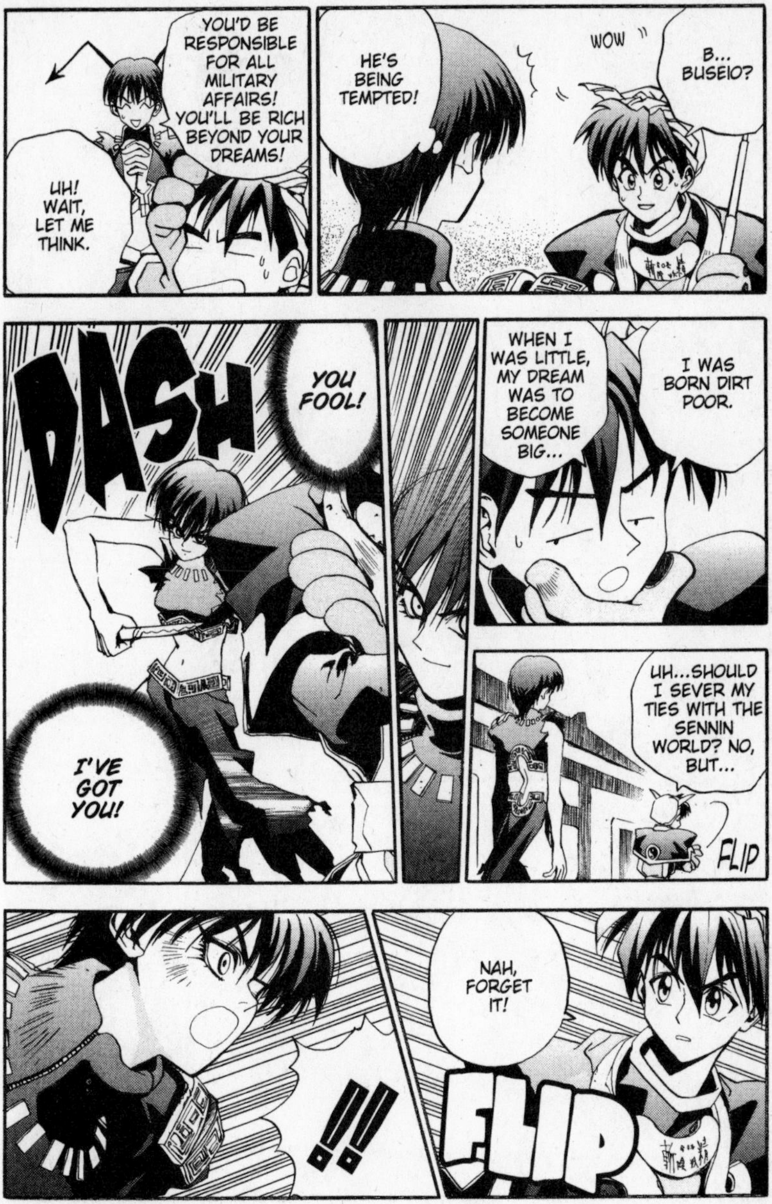
B...
BUSEIO?
WOW
HE'S BEING TEMPTED!
YOU'D BE RESPONSIBLE FOR ALL MILITARY AFFAIRS! YOU'LL BE RICH BEYOND YOUR DREAMS!
UH! WAIT, LET ME THINK.
I WAS BORN DIRT POOR.
WHEN I WAS LITTLE, MY DREAM WAS TO BECOME SOMEONE BIG...
UH...SHOULD I SEVER MY TIES WITH THE SENNIN WORLD? NO, BUT...
FLIP
YOU FOOL!
DASH
I'VE GOT YOU!
NAH, FORGET IT!
FLIP
!!

READ THIS WAY

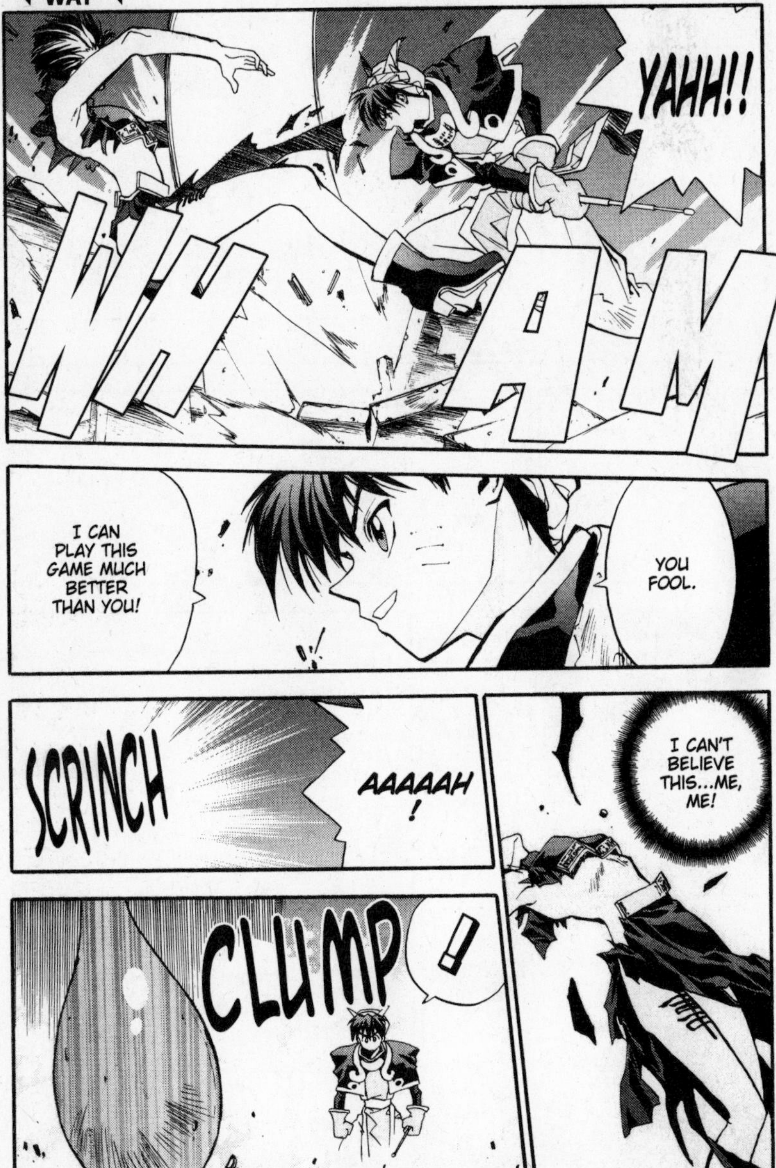

YAHH!!
WHAM
YOU FOOL.
I CAN PLAY THIS GAME MUCH BETTER THAN YOU!
I CAN'T BELIEVE THIS...ME, ME!
SCRINCH
AAAAAH!
CLUMP
!

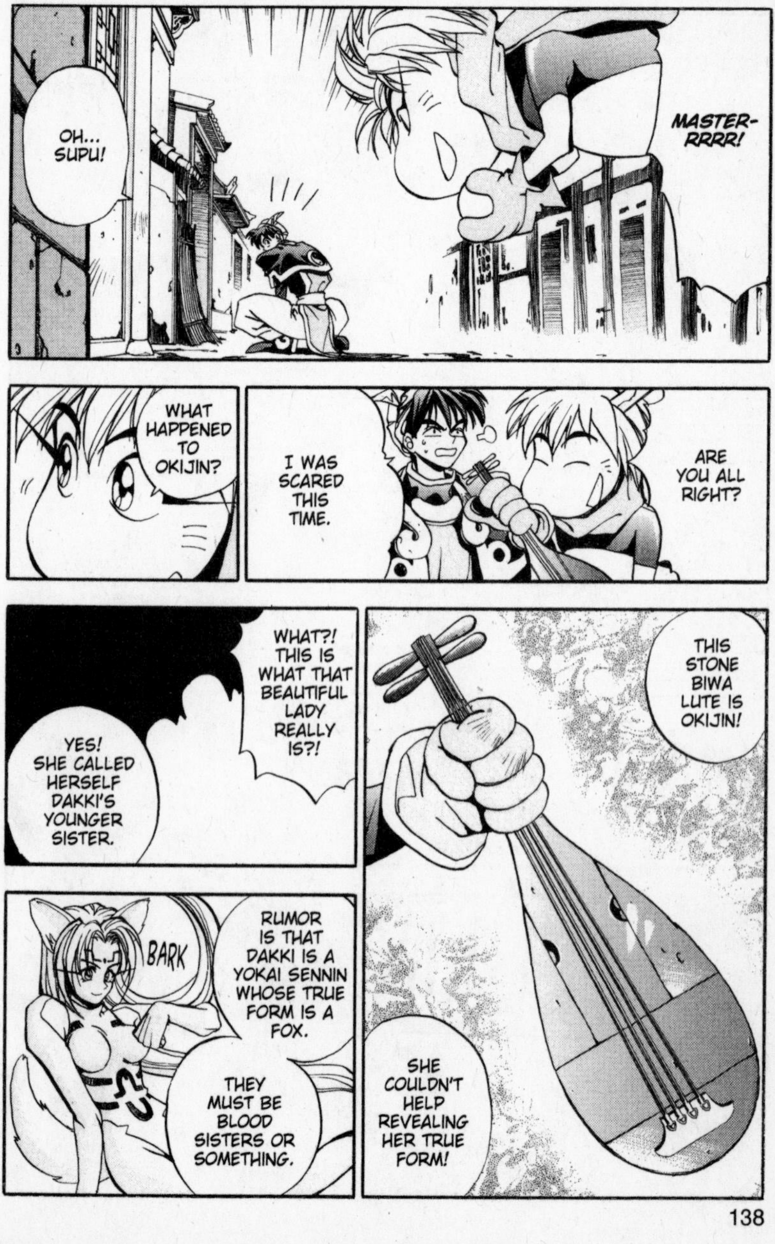
MASTER-RRRR!
OH... SUPU!
ARE YOU ALL RIGHT?
I WAS SCARED THIS TIME.
WHAT HAPPENED TO OKIJIN?
THIS STONE BIWA LUTE IS OKIJIN!
SHE COULDN'T HELP REVEALING HER TRUE FORM!
WHAT?! THIS IS WHAT THAT BEAUTIFUL LADY REALLY IS?!
YES! SHE CALLED HERSELF DAKKI'S YOUNGER SISTER.
RUMOR IS THAT DAKKI IS A YOKAI SENNIN WHOSE TRUE FORM IS A FOX.
BARK
THEY MUST BE BLOOD SISTERS OR SOMETHING.

READ THIS WAY

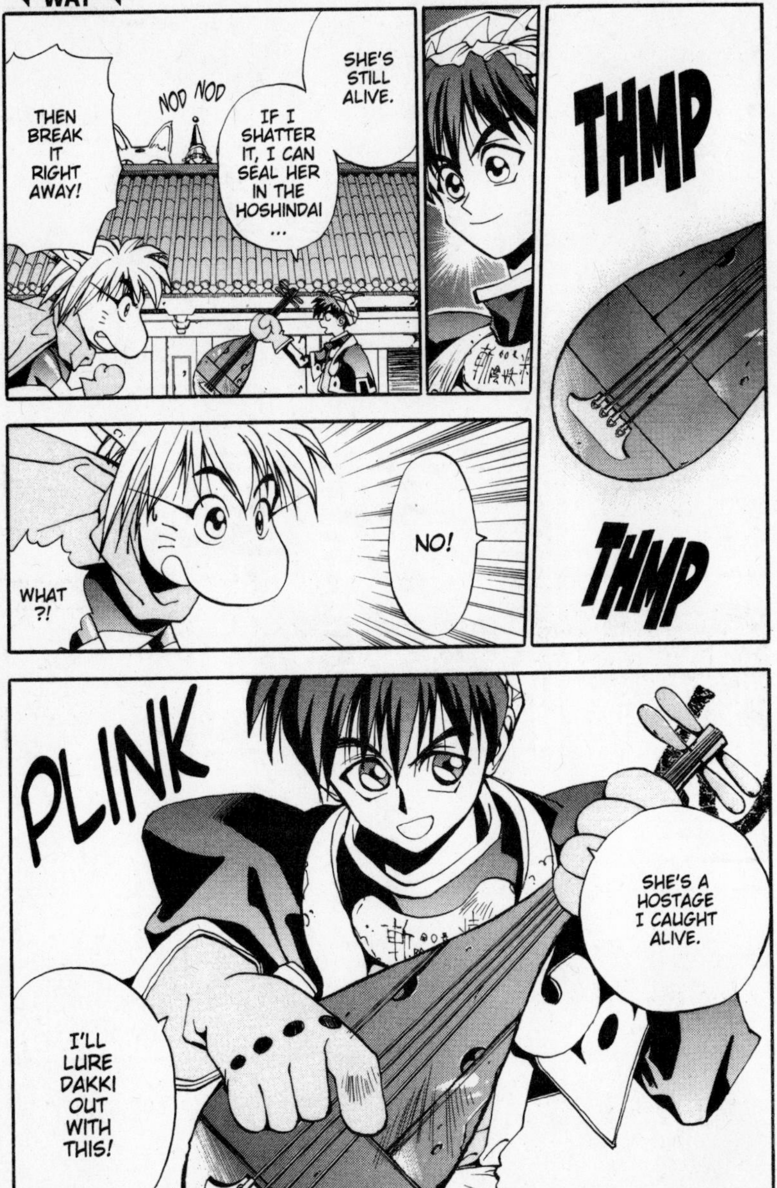
THMP
THMP
SHE'S STILL ALIVE.
IF I SHATTER IT, I CAN SEAL HER IN THE HOSHINDAI ...
NOD NOD
THEN BREAK IT RIGHT AWAY!
NO!
WHAT ?!
PLINK
SHE'S A HOSTAGE I CAUGHT ALIVE.
I'LL LURE DAKKI OUT WITH THIS!

封神演義

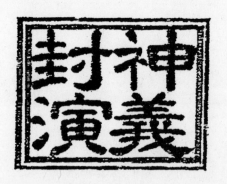

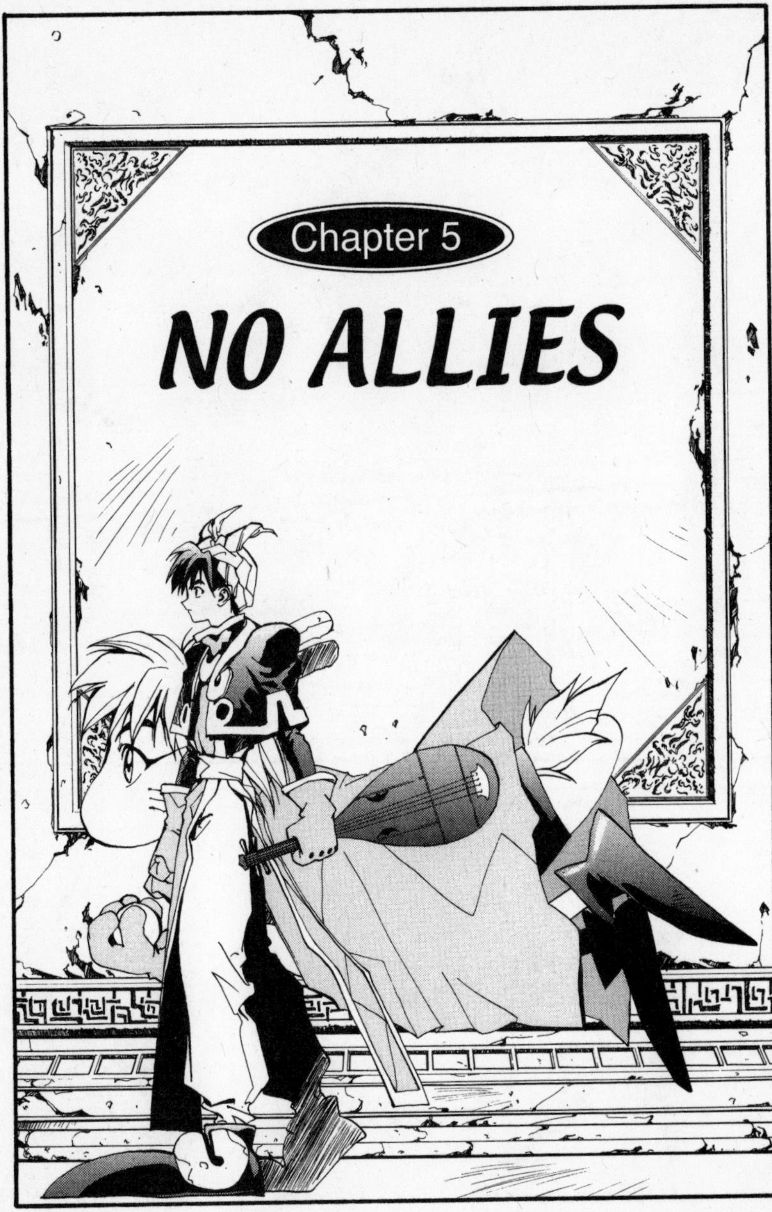
Chapter 5
NO ALLIES

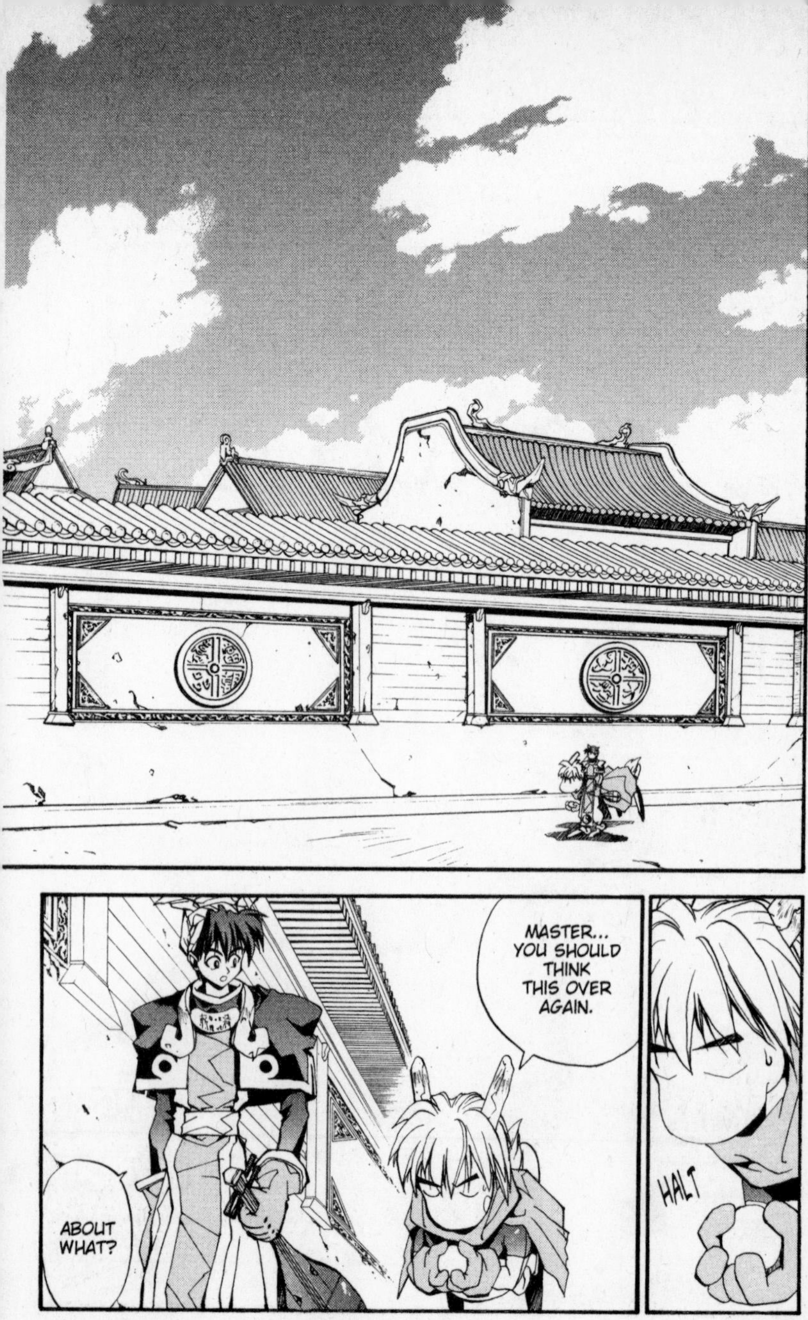
HALT
MASTER... YOU SHOULD THINK THIS OVER AGAIN.
ABOUT WHAT?

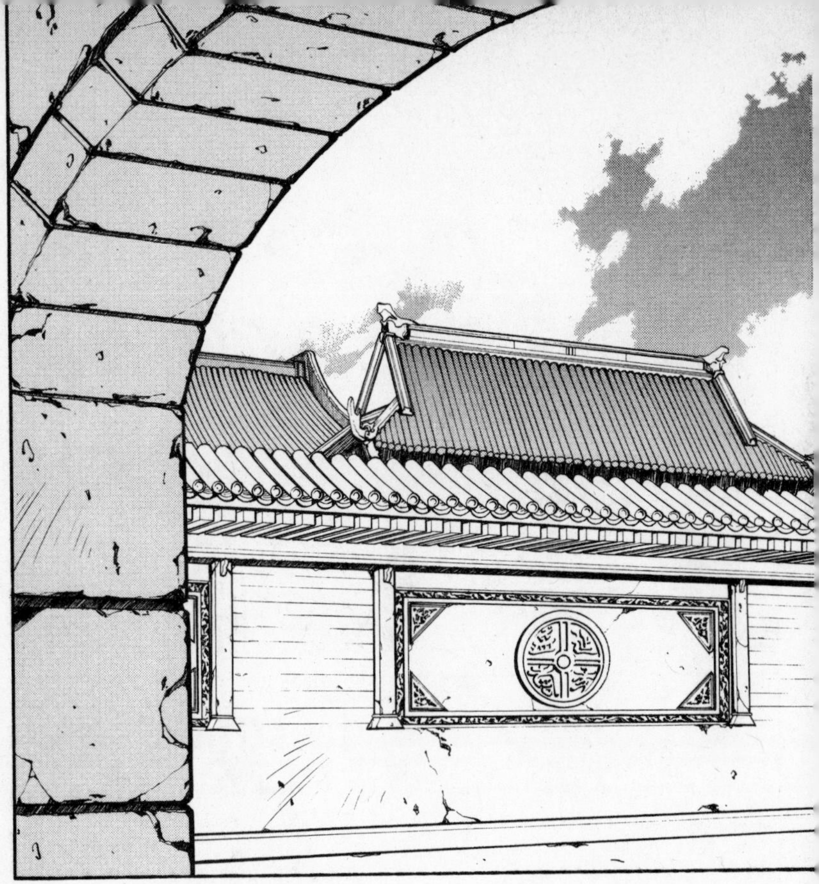

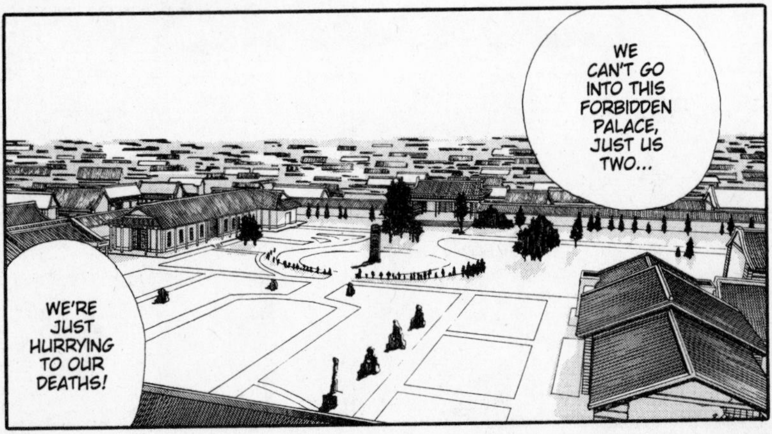
WE CAN'T GO INTO THIS FORBIDDEN PALACE, JUST US TWO...
WE'RE JUST HURRYING TO OUR DEATHS!

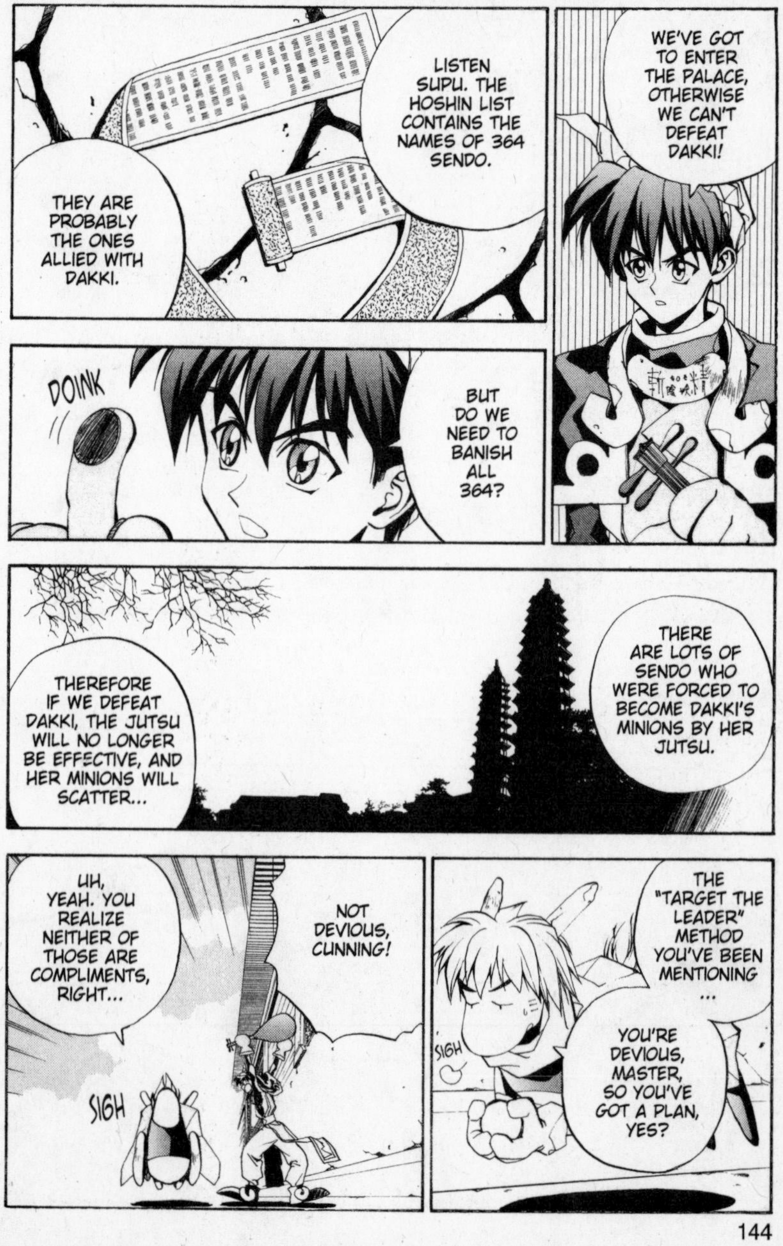
WE'VE GOT TO ENTER THE PALACE, OTHERWISE WE CAN'T DEFEAT DAKKI!
LISTEN SUPU. THE HOSHIN LIST CONTAINS THE NAMES OF 364 SENDO.
THEY ARE PROBABLY THE ONES ALLIED WITH DAKKI.
BUT DO WE NEED TO BANISH ALL 364?
DOINK
THERE ARE LOTS OF SENDO WHO WERE FORCED TO BECOME DAKKI'S MINIONS BY HER JUTSU.
THEREFORE IF WE DEFEAT DAKKI, THE JUTSU WILL NO LONGER BE EFFECTIVE, AND HER MINIONS WILL SCATTER...
THE "TARGET THE LEADER" METHOD YOU'VE BEEN MENTIONING ...
YOU'RE DEVIOUS, MASTER, SO YOU'VE GOT A PLAN, YES?
SIGH
NOT DEVIOUS, CUNNING!
UH, YEAH. YOU REALIZE NEITHER OF THOSE ARE COMPLIMENTS, RIGHT...
SIGH

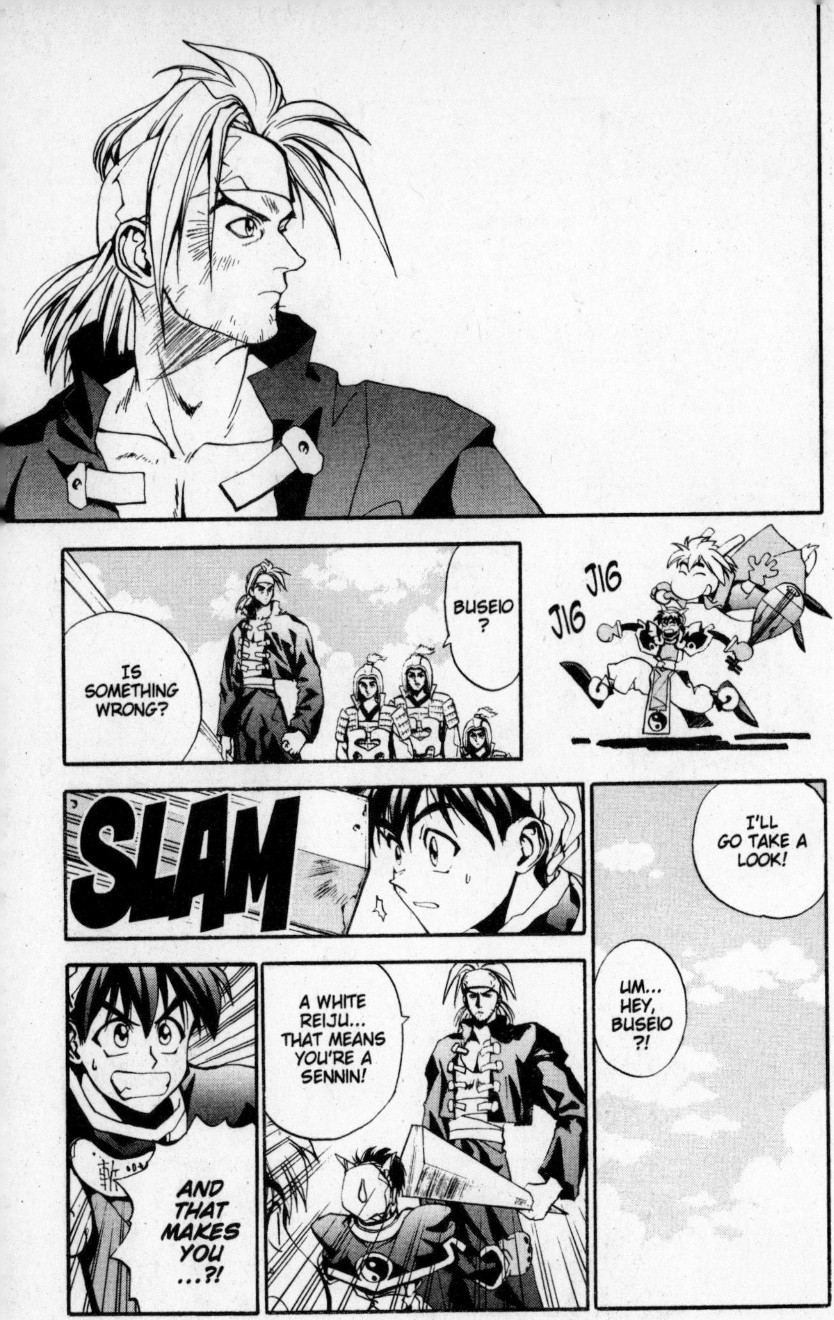
JIG JIG
BUSEIO?
IS SOMETHING WRONG?
I'LL GO TAKE A LOOK!
UM... HEY, BUSEIO?!
SLAM
A WHITE REIJU... THAT MEANS YOU'RE A SENNIN!
AND THAT MAKES YOU...?!

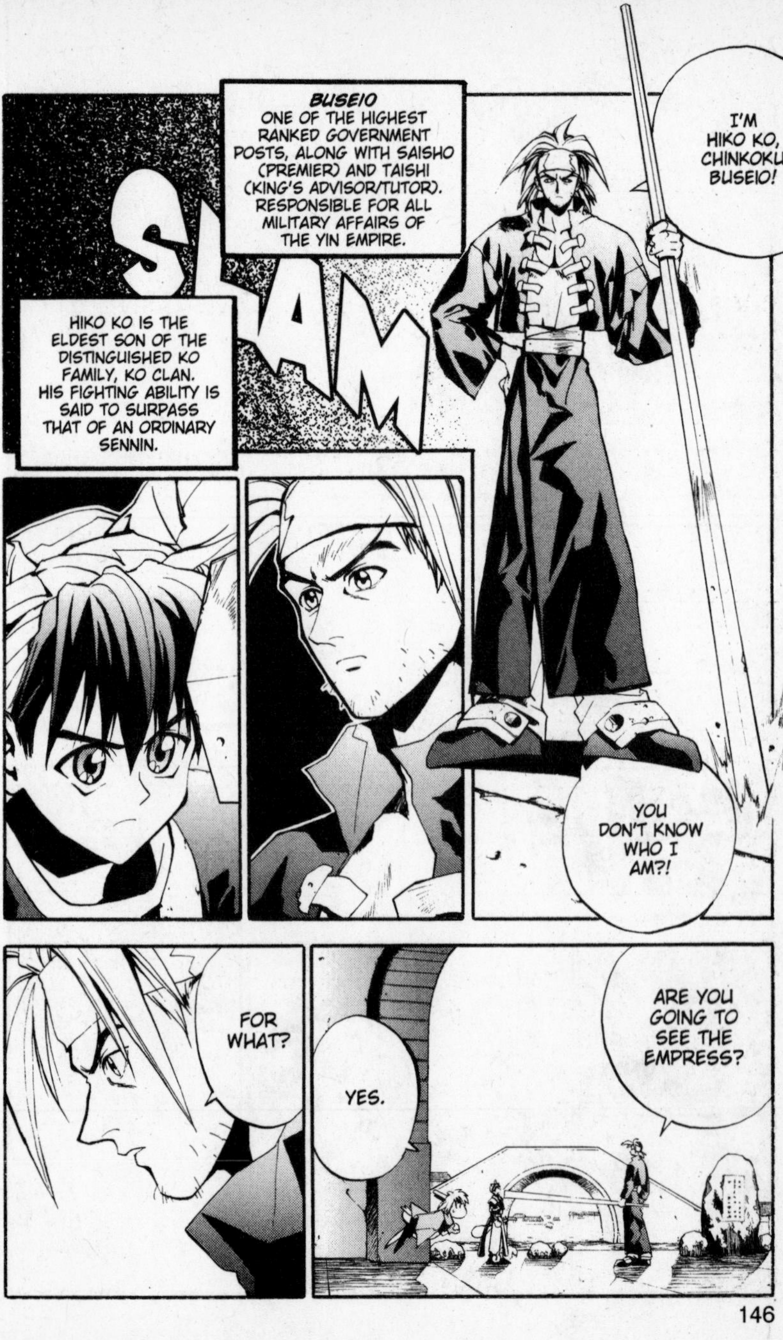
I'M HIKO KO, CHINKOKU BUSEIO!
YOU DON'T KNOW WHO I AM?!
SLAM
BUSEIO
ONE OF THE HIGHEST RANKED GOVERNMENT POSTS, ALONG WITH SAISHO (PREMIER) AND TAISHI (KING'S ADVISOR/TUTOR). RESPONSIBLE FOR ALL MILITARY AFFAIRS OF THE YIN EMPIRE.
HIKO KO IS THE ELDEST SON OF THE DISTINGUISHED KO FAMILY, KO CLAN. HIS FIGHTING ABILITY IS SAID TO SURPASS THAT OF AN ORDINARY SENNIN.
ARE YOU GOING TO SEE THE EMPRESS?
YES.
FOR WHAT?

READ THIS WAY

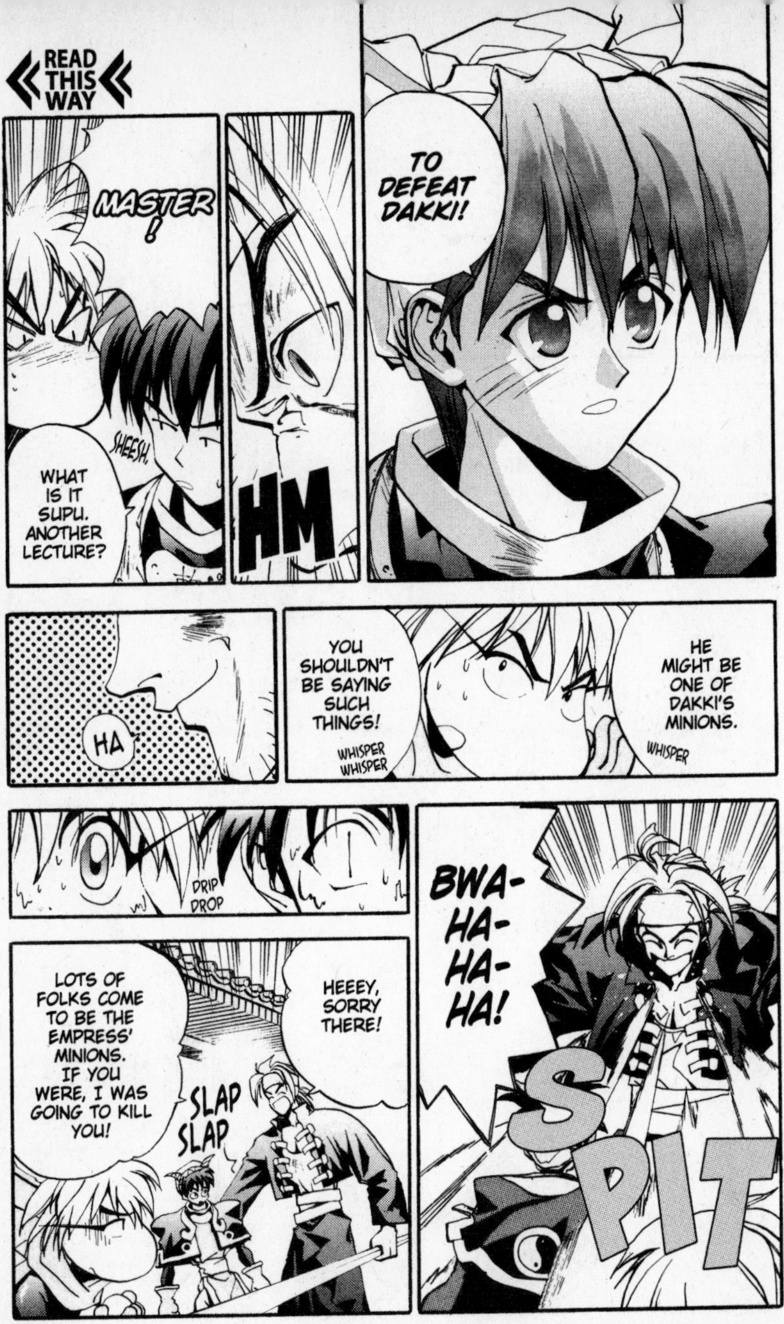
TO DEFEAT DAKKI!
HM
MASTER!
SHEESH.
WHAT IS IT SUPU. ANOTHER LECTURE?
HE MIGHT BE ONE OF DAKKI'S MINIONS.
WHISPER
YOU SHOULDN'T BE SAYING SUCH THINGS!
WHISPER WHISPER
HA
BWA-HA-HA-HA!
SPIT
DRIP DROP
HEEEY, SORRY THERE!
LOTS OF FOLKS COME TO BE THE EMPRESS' MINIONS. IF YOU WERE, I WAS GOING TO KILL YOU!
SLAP SLAP

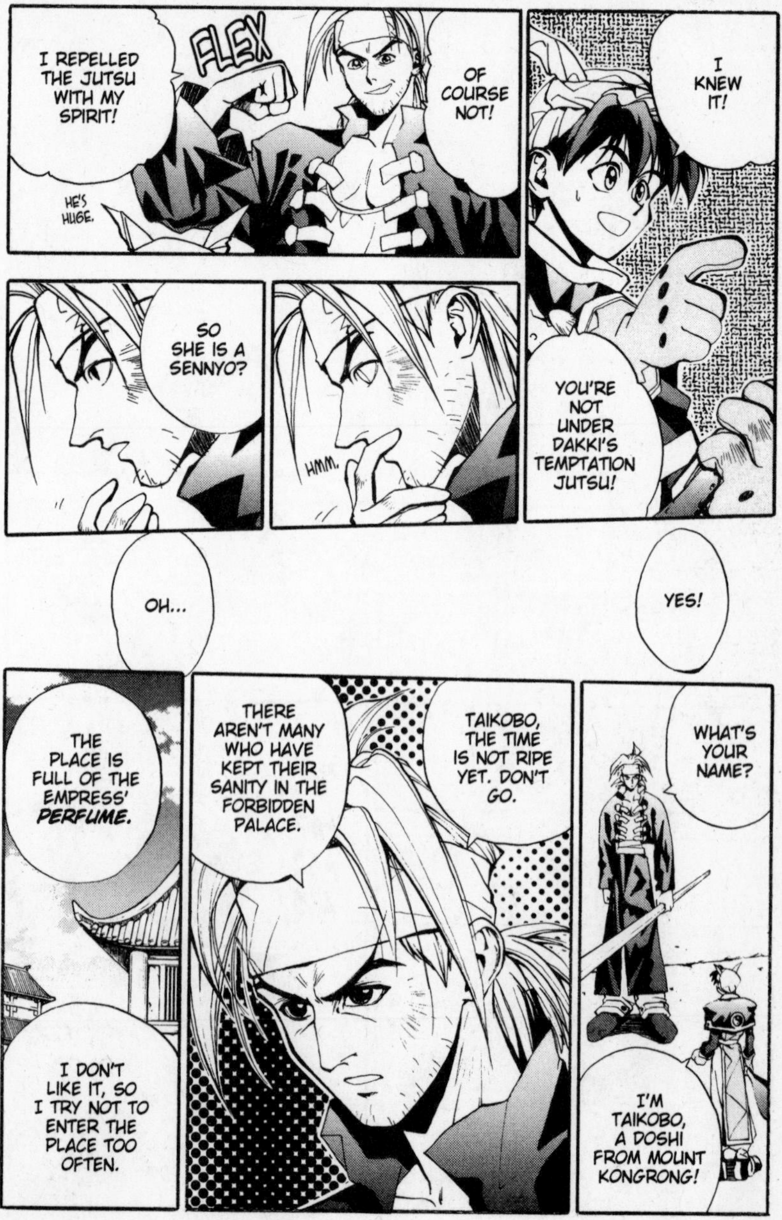
I KNEW IT!
YOU'RE NOT UNDER DAKKI'S TEMPTATION JUTSU!
OF COURSE NOT!
FLEX
I REPELLED THE JUTSU WITH MY SPIRIT!
HE'S HUGE.
HMM.
SO SHE IS A SENNYO?
YES!
OH...
WHAT'S YOUR NAME?
I'M TAIKOBO, A DOSHI FROM MOUNT KONGRONG!
TAIKOBO, THE TIME IS NOT RIPE YET. DON'T GO.
THERE AREN'T MANY WHO HAVE KEPT THEIR SANITY IN THE FORBIDDEN PALACE.
THE PLACE IS FULL OF THE EMPRESS' *PERFUME.*
I DON'T LIKE IT, SO I TRY NOT TO ENTER THE PLACE TOO OFTEN.

READ THIS WAY

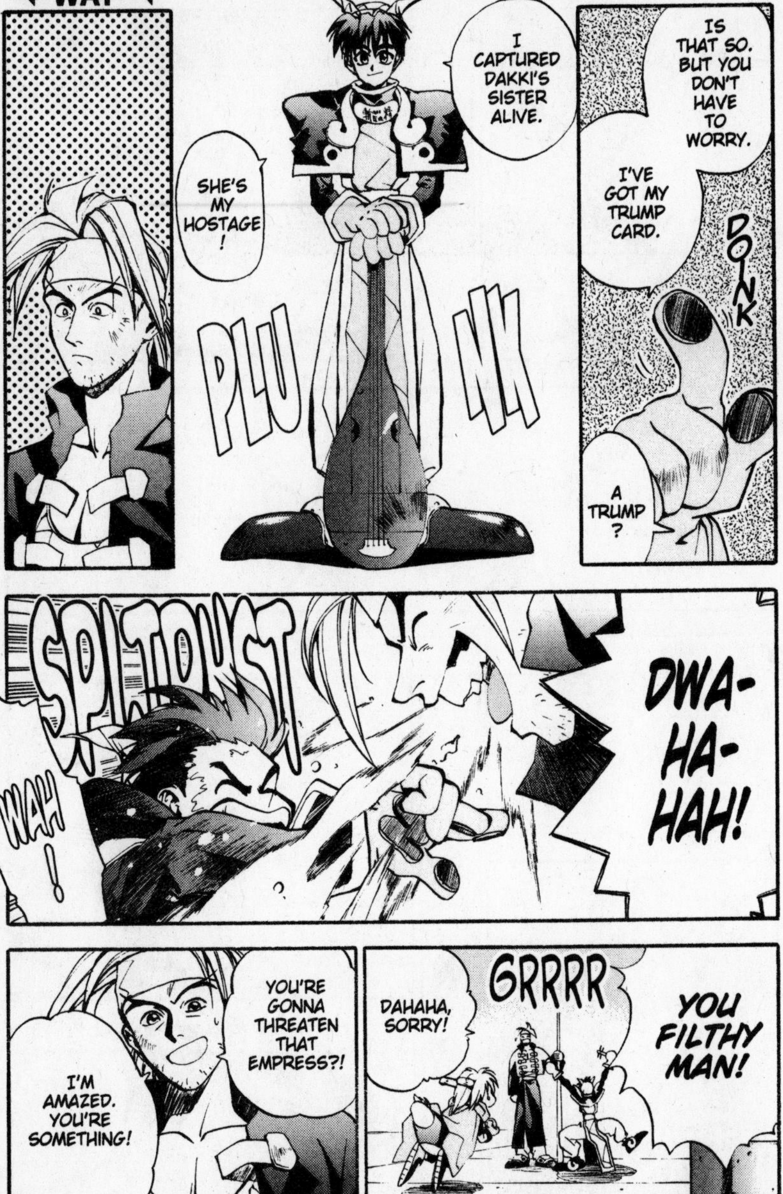
IS THAT SO. BUT YOU DON'T HAVE TO WORRY.
I'VE GOT MY TRUMP CARD.
DONK
A TRUMP?
I CAPTURED DAKKI'S SISTER ALIVE.
SHE'S MY HOSTAGE!
PLUNK
DWA-HA-HAH!
SPLTOWST
WAH!
YOU FILTHY MAN!
GRRRR
DAHAHA, SORRY!
YOU'RE GONNA THREATEN THAT EMPRESS?!
I'M AMAZED. YOU'RE SOMETHING!

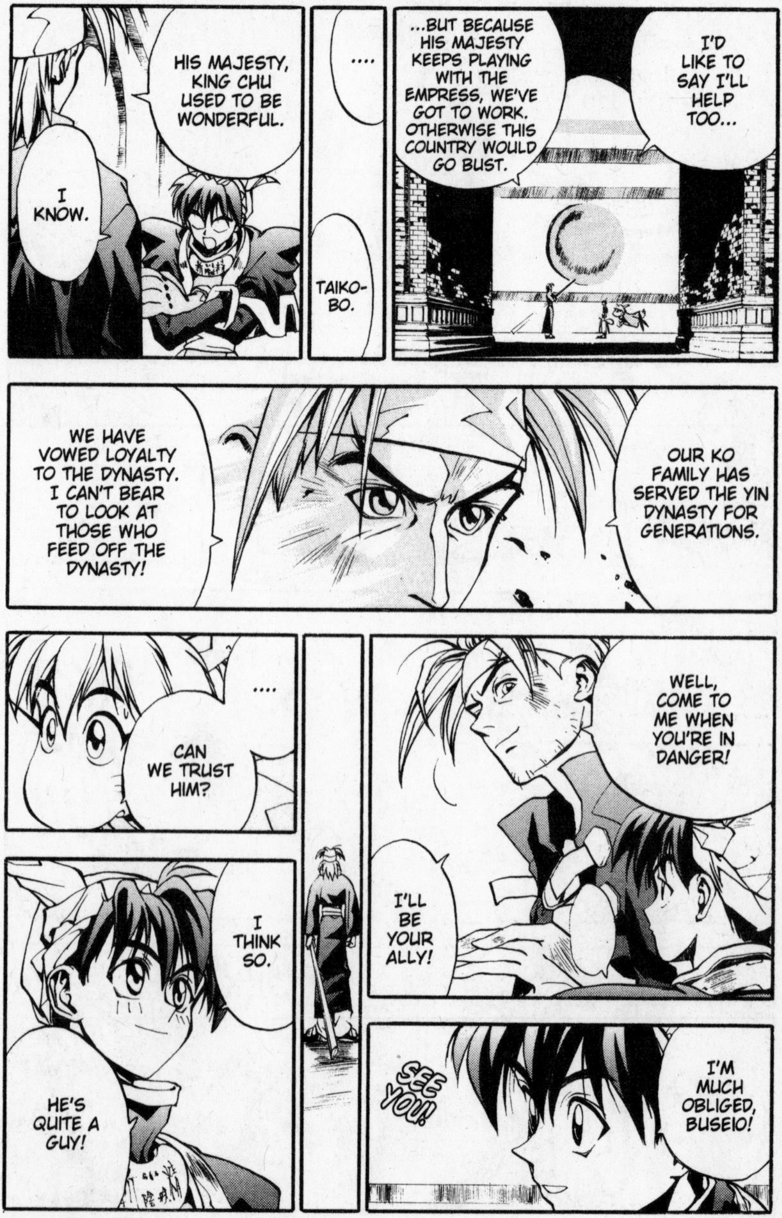
I'D LIKE TO SAY I'LL HELP TOO...
...BUT BECAUSE HIS MAJESTY KEEPS PLAYING WITH THE EMPRESS, WE'VE GOT TO WORK. OTHERWISE THIS COUNTRY WOULD GO BUST.
....
TAIKO-BO.
HIS MAJESTY, KING CHU USED TO BE WONDERFUL.
I KNOW.
OUR KO FAMILY HAS SERVED THE YIN DYNASTY FOR GENERATIONS.
WE HAVE VOWED LOYALTY TO THE DYNASTY. I CAN'T BEAR TO LOOK AT THOSE WHO FEED OFF THE DYNASTY!
WELL, COME TO ME WHEN YOU'RE IN DANGER!
I'LL BE YOUR ALLY!
I'M MUCH OBLIGED, BUSEIO!
SEE YOU!
....
CAN WE TRUST HIM?
I THINK SO.
HE'S QUITE A GUY!

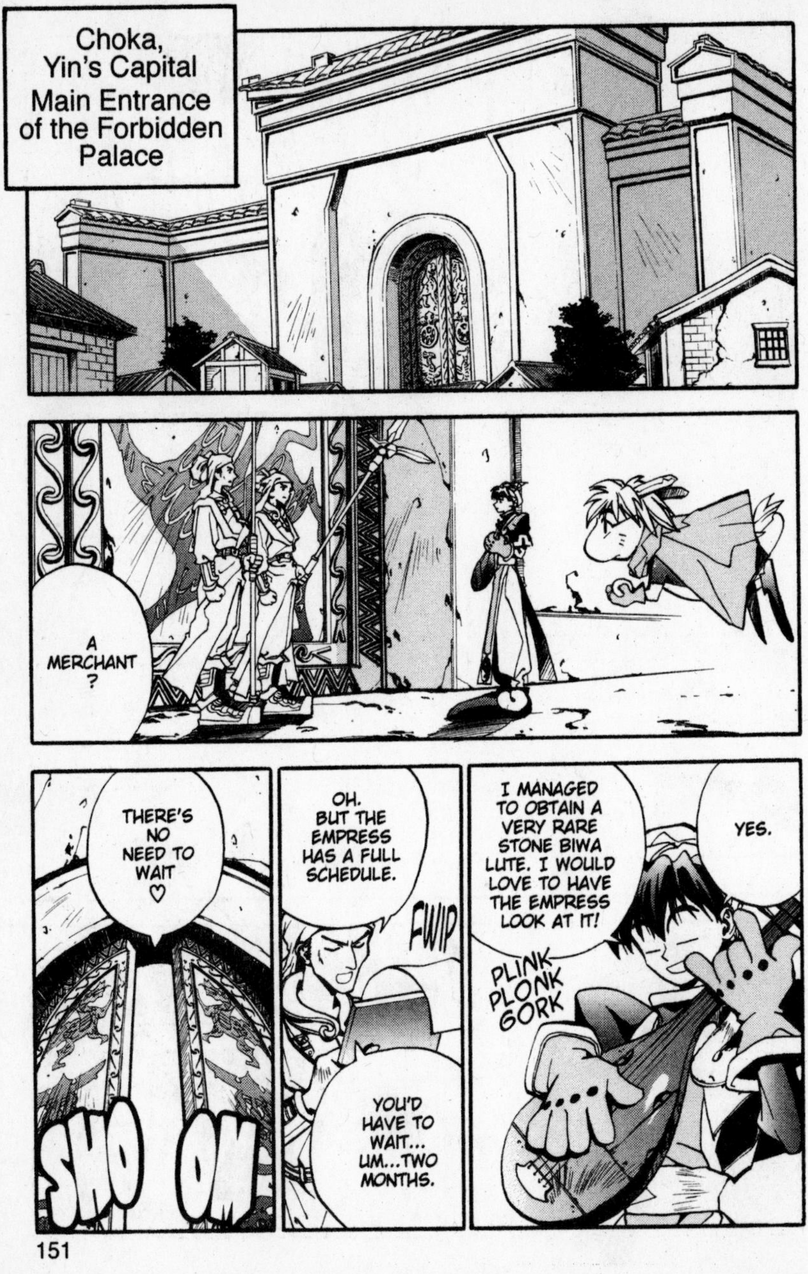
Choka, Yin's Capital Main Entrance of the Forbidden Palace
A MERCHANT ?
YES.
I MANAGED TO OBTAIN A VERY RARE STONE BIWA LUTE. I WOULD LOVE TO HAVE THE EMPRESS LOOK AT IT!
PLINK PLONK GORK
OH. BUT THE EMPRESS HAS A FULL SCHEDULE.
FWIP
YOU'D HAVE TO WAIT... UM...TWO MONTHS.
THERE'S NO NEED TO WAIT ♡
SHO OM

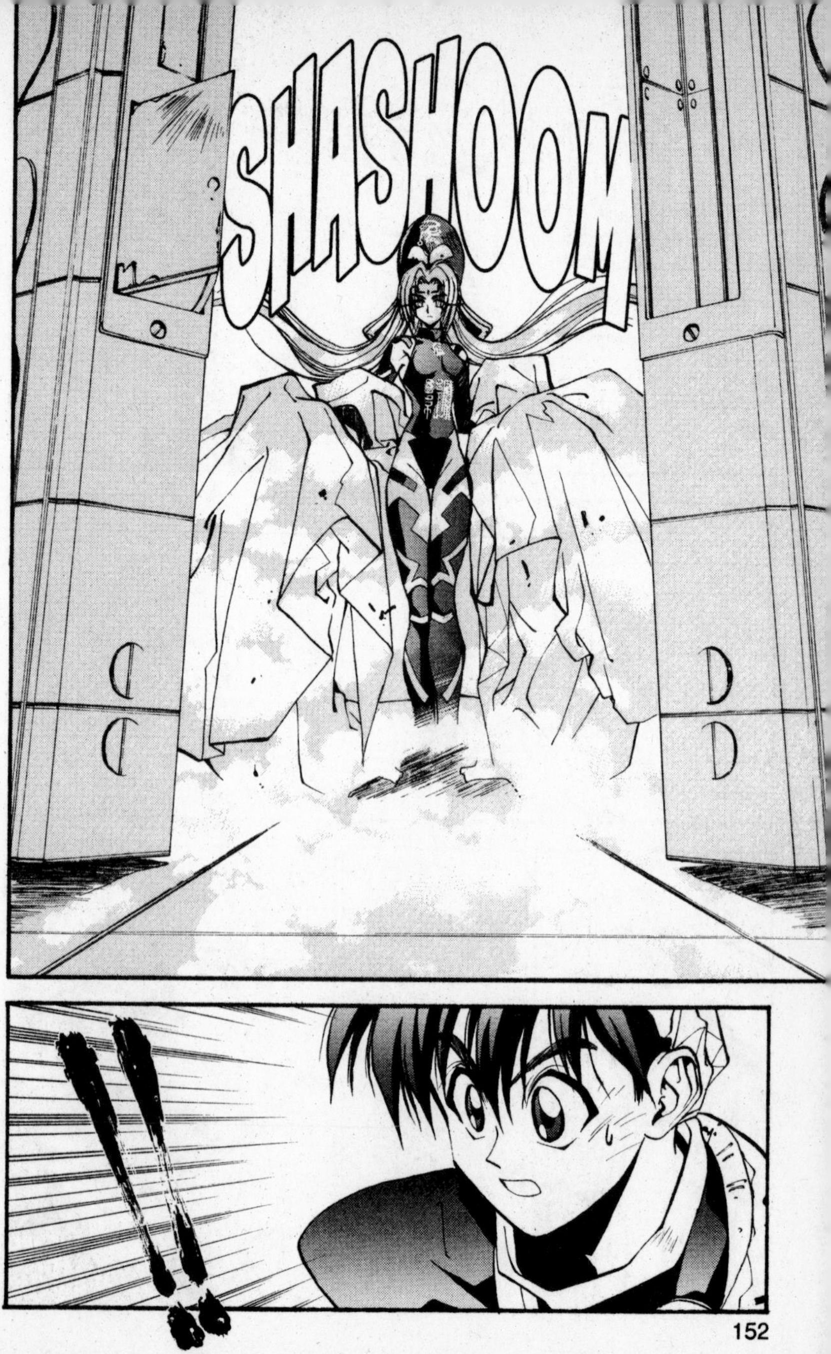
SHASHOOM

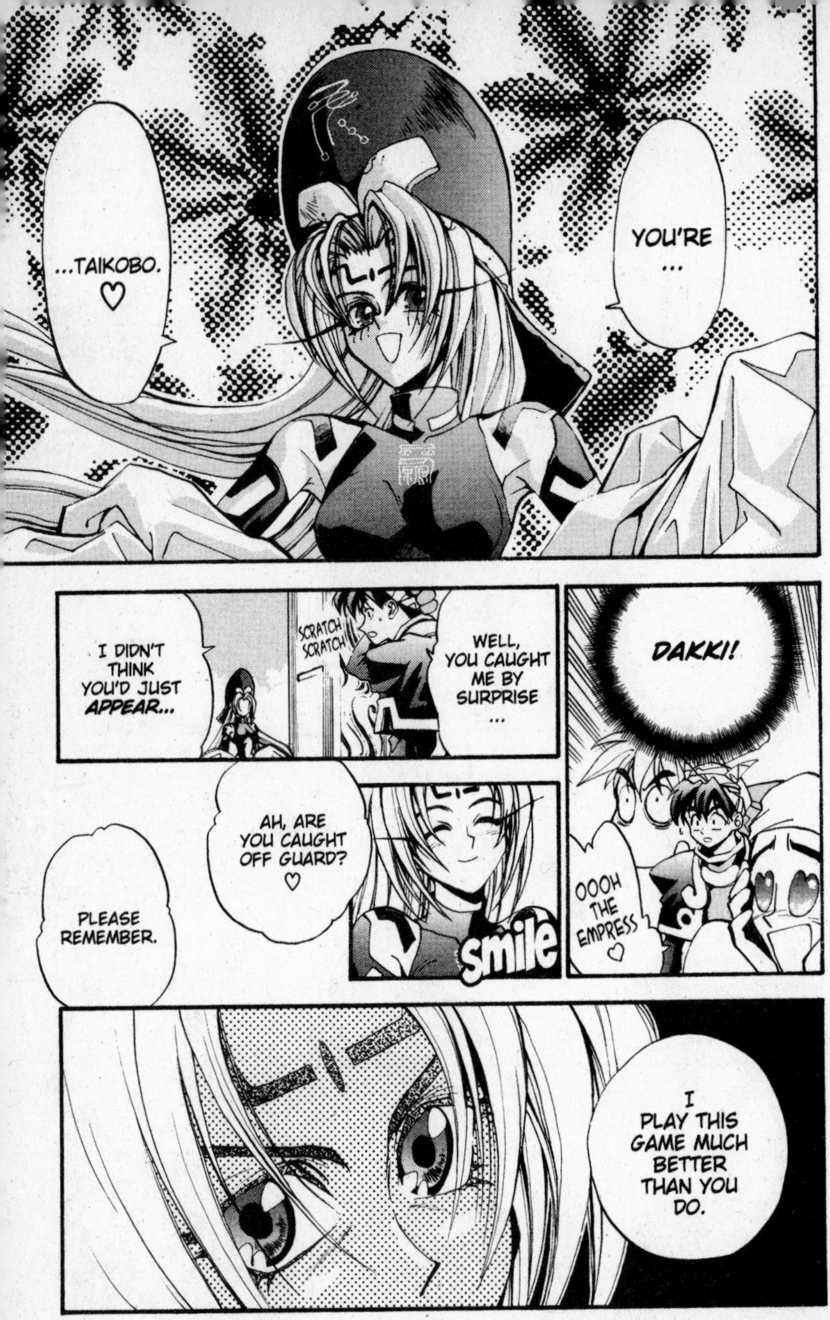
YOU'RE ...
...TAIKOBO. ♡
DAKKI!
OOOH THE EMPRESS ♡
WELL, YOU CAUGHT ME BY SURPRISE ...
SCRATCH SCRATCH
I DIDN'T THINK YOU'D JUST APPEAR...
AH, ARE YOU CAUGHT OFF GUARD? ♡
smile
PLEASE REMEMBER.
I PLAY THIS GAME MUCH BETTER THAN YOU DO.

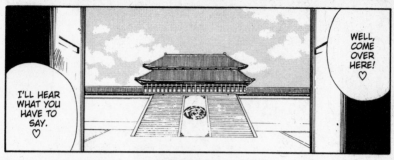

WELL, COME OVER HERE! ♡

I'LL HEAR WHAT YOU HAVE TO SAY. ♡

WHAT HAPPENED, SUPU?

HA.

BLUSH

NOTHING... I WAS THINKING SHE WAS MORE THAN WHAT WE EXPECTED.

YES! SHE'S TOUGHER THAN SHE'S RUMORED TO BE!

NO NO, HER BEAUTY! I'D WAKE UP, EVEN IF I'D BEEN ASLEEP FOR 100 THOUSAND YEARS!

REALLY? WASN'T OKIJIN LIKE THAT TOO?

TOTALLY DIFFERENT! SHEESH... I HATE OLD MEN WHOSE YOUTH IS LONG PAST!

154

READ THIS WAY

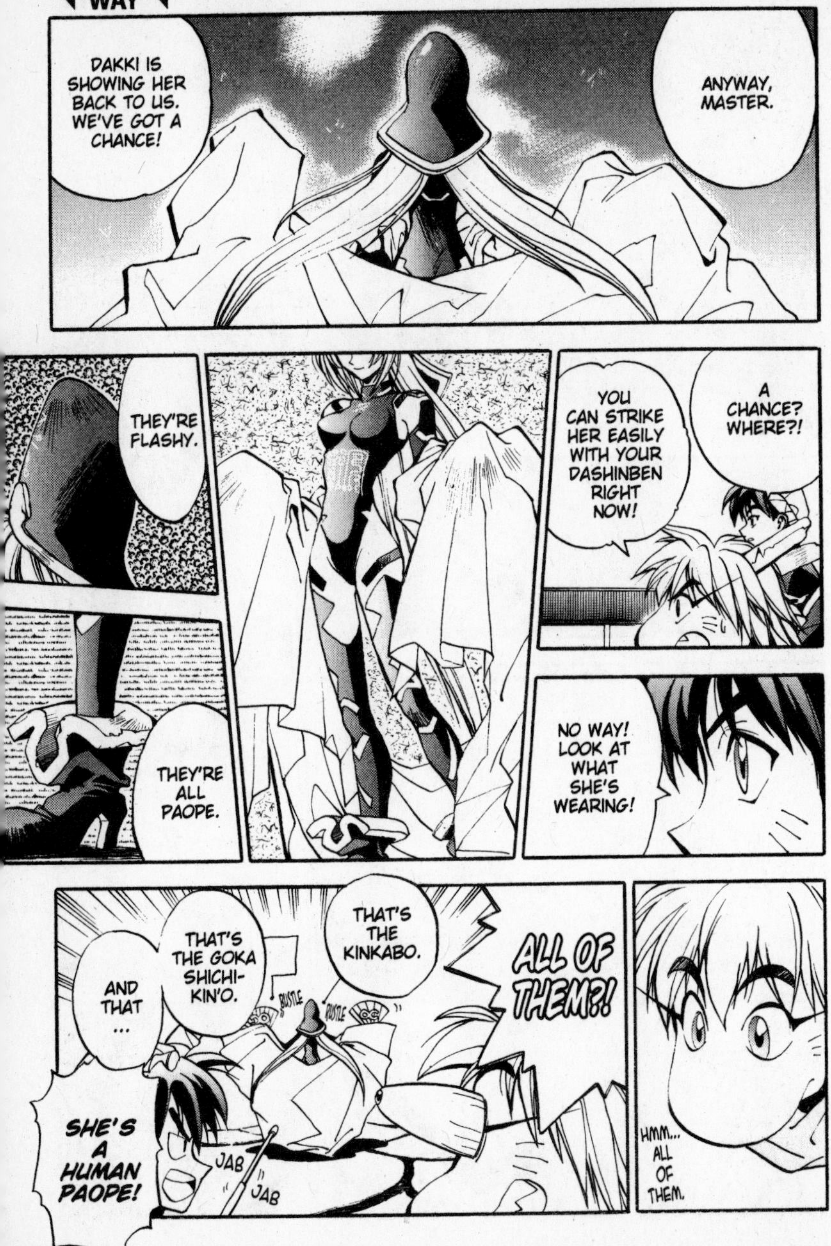
ANYWAY, MASTER.
DAKKI IS SHOWING HER BACK TO US. WE'VE GOT A CHANCE!
A CHANCE? WHERE?!
YOU CAN STRIKE HER EASILY WITH YOUR DASHINBEN RIGHT NOW!
NO WAY! LOOK AT WHAT SHE'S WEARING!
THEY'RE FLASHY.
THEY'RE ALL PAOPE.
HMM... ALL OF THEM.
ALL OF THEM?!
THAT'S THE KINKABO.
BUSTLE
BUSTLE
THAT'S THE GOKA SHICHI-KIN'O.
AND THAT ...
JAB
JAB
SHE'S A HUMAN PAOPE!

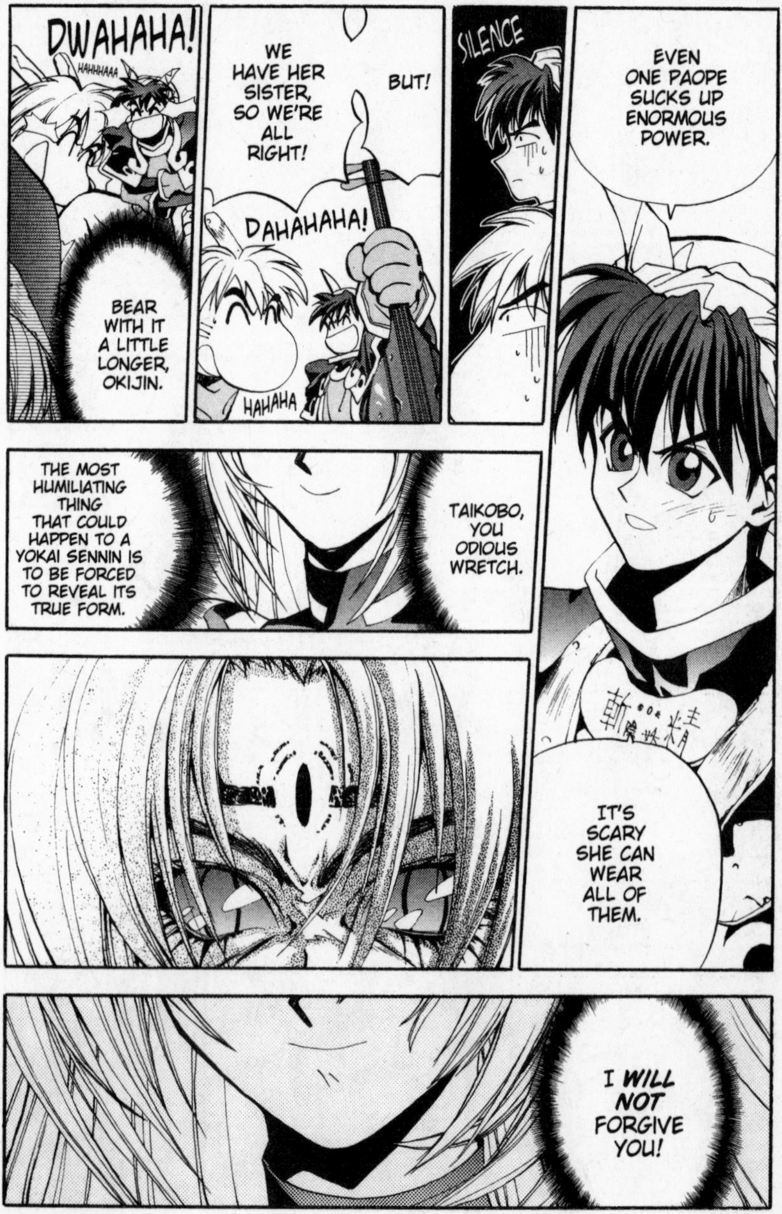
EVEN ONE PAOPE SUCKS UP ENORMOUS POWER.
IT'S SCARY SHE CAN WEAR ALL OF THEM.
SILENCE
BUT!
WE HAVE HER SISTER, SO WE'RE ALL RIGHT!
DAHAHAHA!
HAHAHA
DWAHAHA!
HAHHHAAA
BEAR WITH IT A LITTLE LONGER, OKIJIN.
TAIKOBO, YOU ODIOUS WRETCH.
THE MOST HUMILIATING THING THAT COULD HAPPEN TO A YOKAI SENNIN IS TO BE FORCED TO REVEAL ITS TRUE FORM.
I *WILL NOT* FORGIVE YOU!

READ THIS WAY

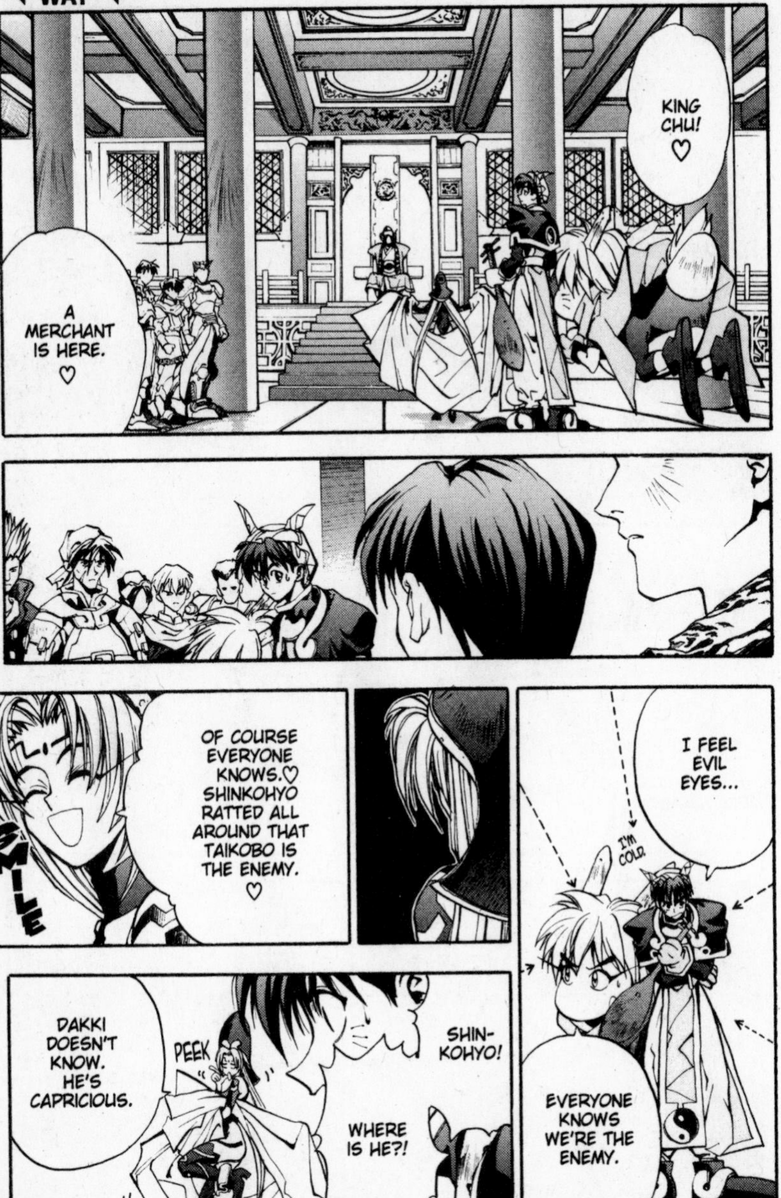

KING CHU! ♡
A MERCHANT IS HERE. ♡
I FEEL EVIL EYES...
I'M COLD.
EVERYONE KNOWS WE'RE THE ENEMY.
OF COURSE EVERYONE KNOWS.♡ SHINKOHYO RATTED ALL AROUND THAT TAIKOBO IS THE ENEMY. ♡
SMILE
SHIN-KOHYO!
WHERE IS HE?!
PEEK
DAKKI DOESN'T KNOW. HE'S CAPRICIOUS.

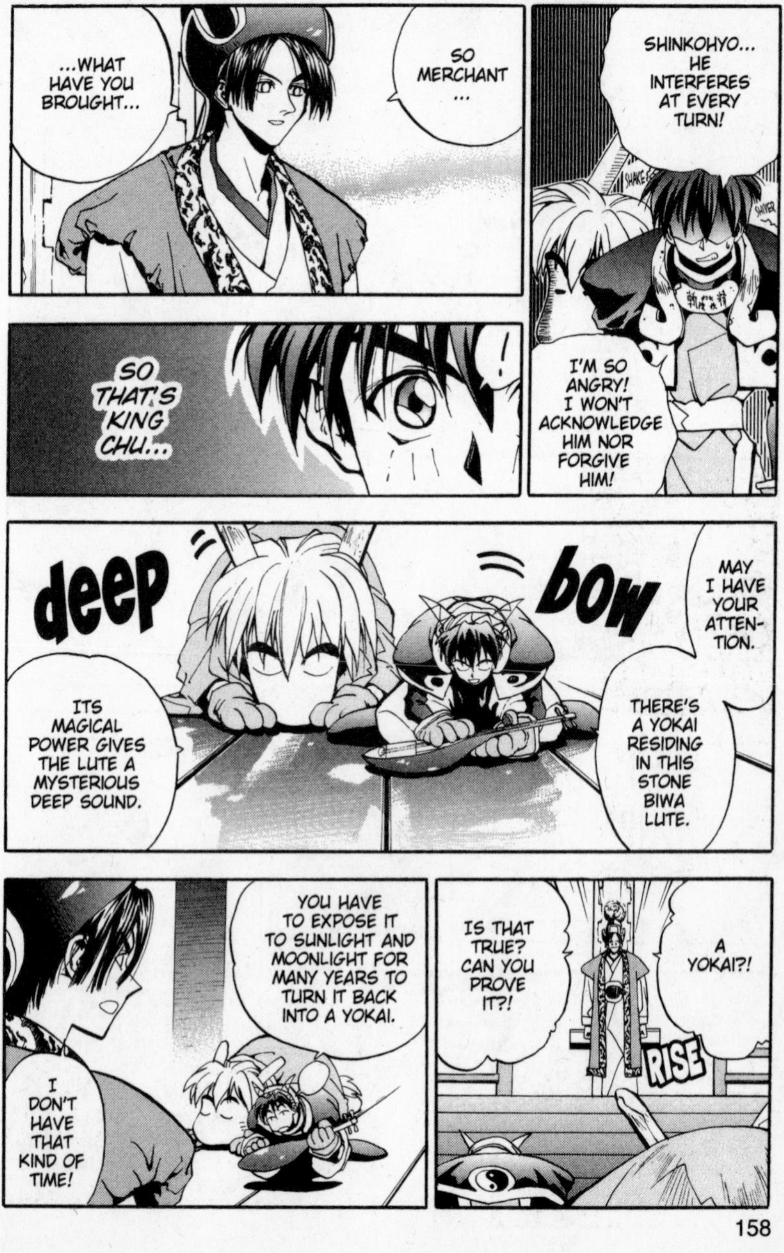
SHINKOHYO... HE INTERFERES AT EVERY TURN!
SHAKE
SHIVER
I'M SO ANGRY! I WON'T ACKNOWLEDGE HIM NOR FORGIVE HIM!
SO MERCHANT ...
...WHAT HAVE YOU BROUGHT...
!
SO THAT'S KING CHU...
MAY I HAVE YOUR ATTEN-TION.
THERE'S A YOKAI RESIDING IN THIS STONE BIWA LUTE.
deep bow
ITS MAGICAL POWER GIVES THE LUTE A MYSTERIOUS DEEP SOUND.
A YOKAI?!
IS THAT TRUE? CAN YOU PROVE IT?!
RISE
YOU HAVE TO EXPOSE IT TO SUNLIGHT AND MOONLIGHT FOR MANY YEARS TO TURN IT BACK INTO A YOKAI.
I DON'T HAVE THAT KIND OF TIME!

READ THIS WAY

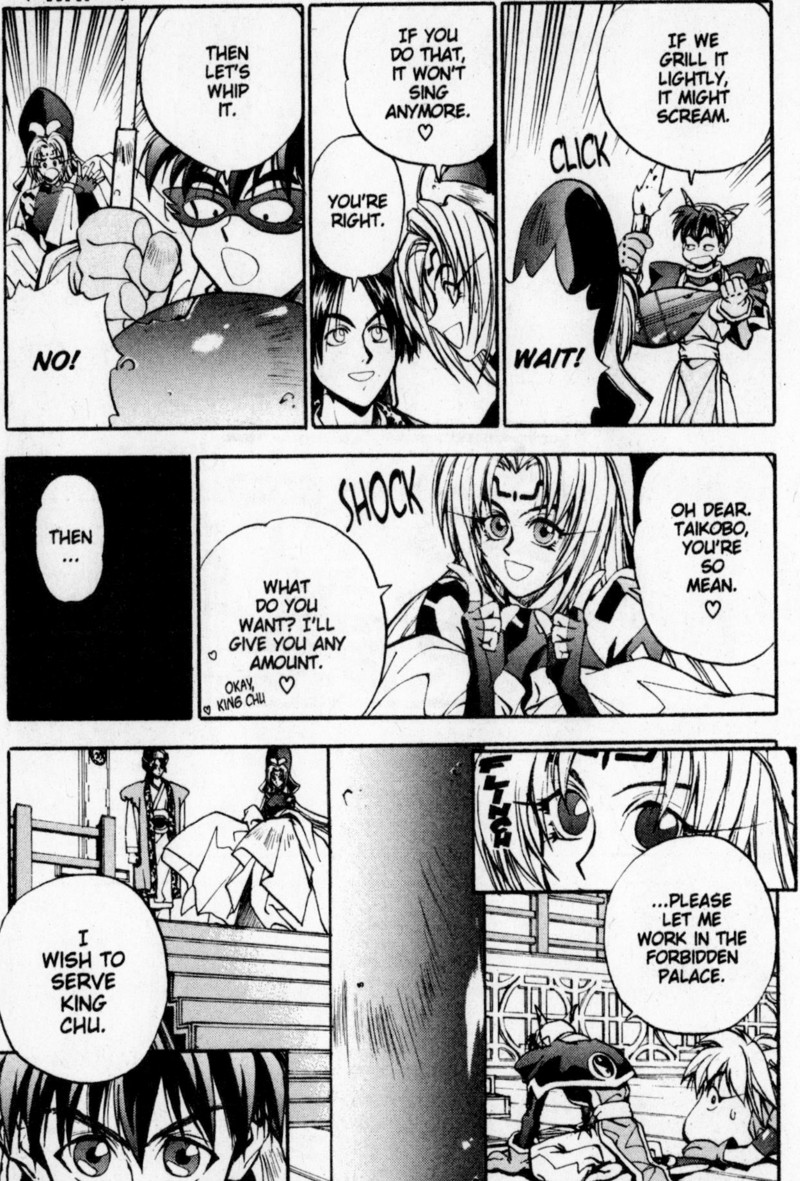
IF WE GRILL IT LIGHTLY, IT MIGHT SCREAM.
CLICK
WAIT!
IF YOU DO THAT, IT WON'T SING ANYMORE. ♡
YOU'RE RIGHT.
THEN LET'S WHIP IT.
NO!
OH DEAR. TAIKOBO, YOU'RE SO MEAN. ♡
SHOCK
WHAT DO YOU WANT? I'LL GIVE YOU ANY AMOUNT. ♡
♡ OKAY, KING CHU ♡
THEN...
FLINCH
...PLEASE LET ME WORK IN THE FORBIDDEN PALACE.
I WISH TO SERVE KING CHU.

封神演義

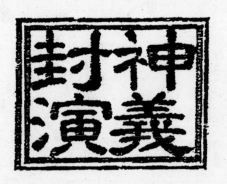

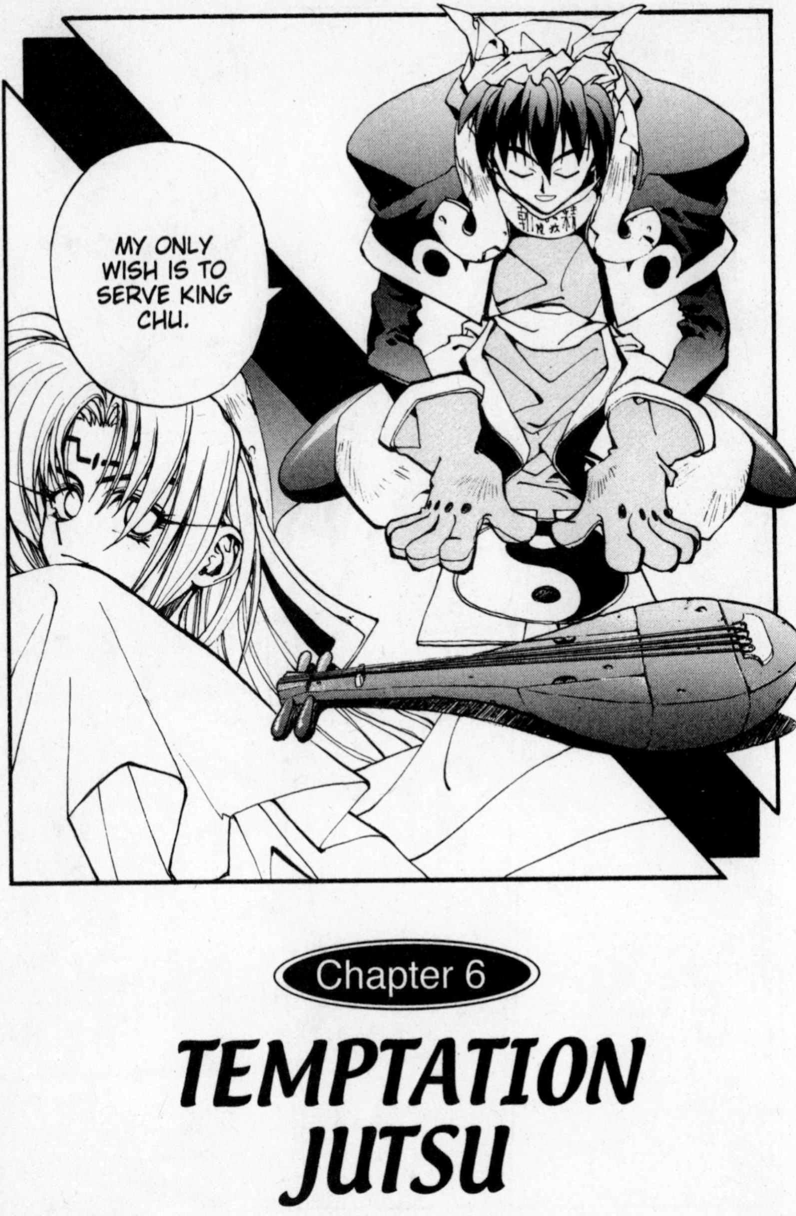
MY ONLY WISH IS TO SERVE KING CHU.

Chapter 6

TEMPTATION JUTSU

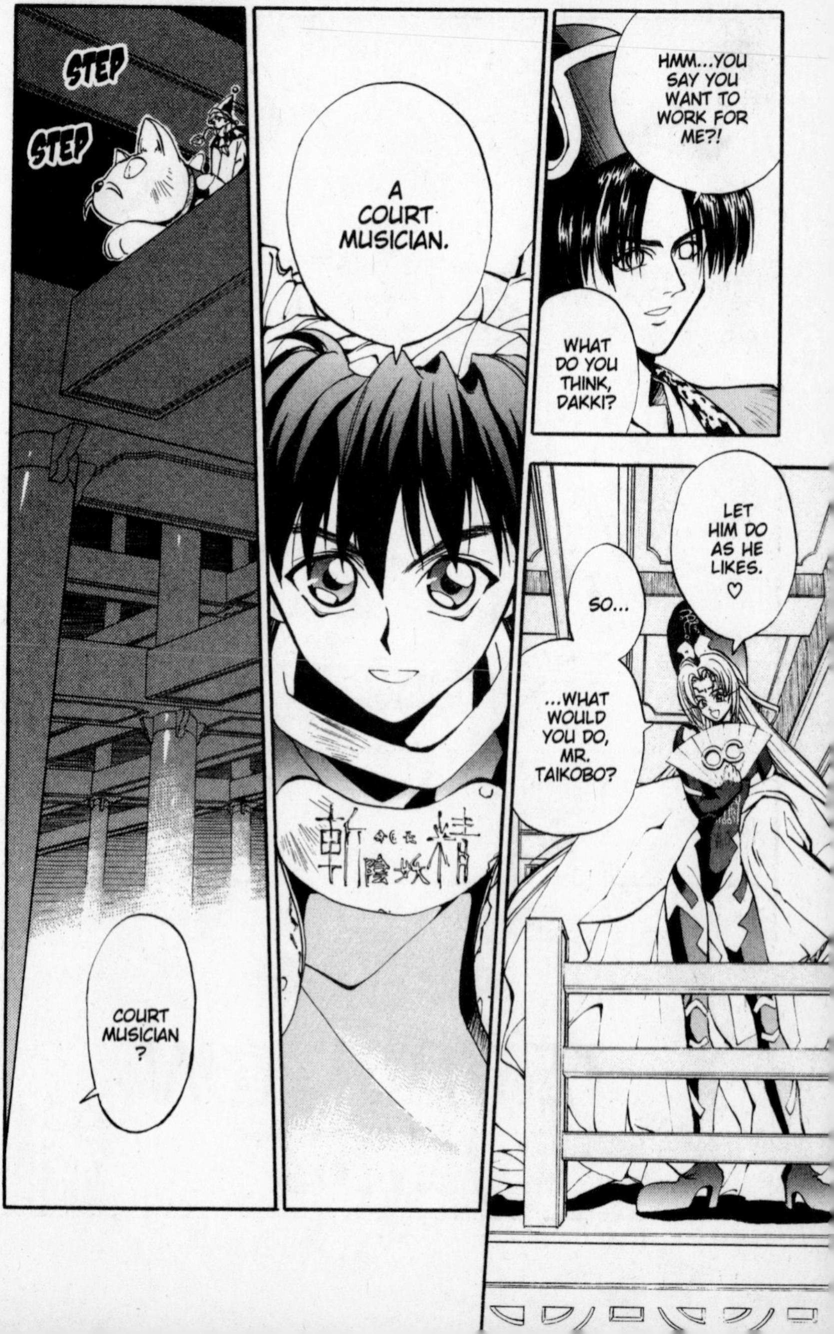
HMM...YOU SAY YOU WANT TO WORK FOR ME?!
WHAT DO YOU THINK, DAKKI?
LET HIM DO AS HE LIKES. ♡
SO...
...WHAT WOULD YOU DO, MR. TAIKOBO?
A COURT MUSICIAN.
STEP
STEP
COURT MUSICIAN?

READ THIS WAY

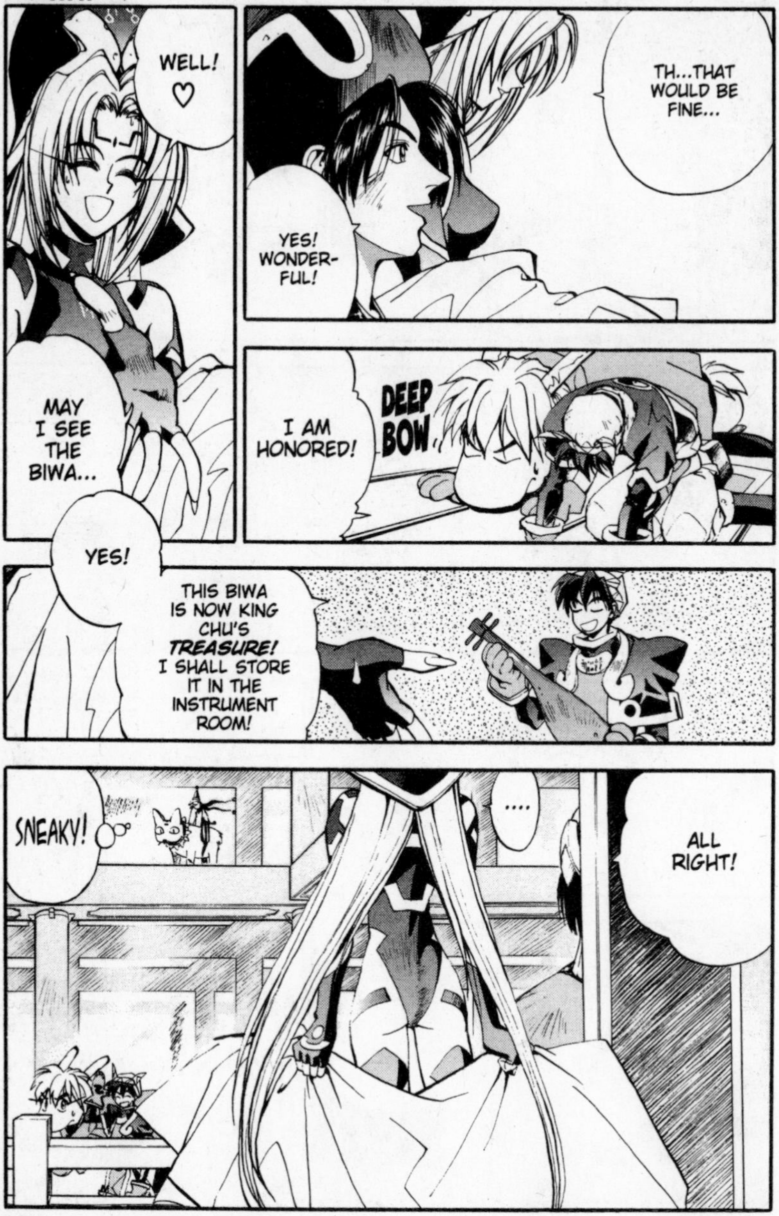
TH...THAT WOULD BE FINE...
YES! WONDERFUL!
DEEP BOW
I AM HONORED!
WELL! ♡
MAY I SEE THE BIWA...
YES!
THIS BIWA IS NOW KING CHU'S *TREASURE!* I SHALL STORE IT IN THE INSTRUMENT ROOM!
ALL RIGHT!
....
SNEAKY!

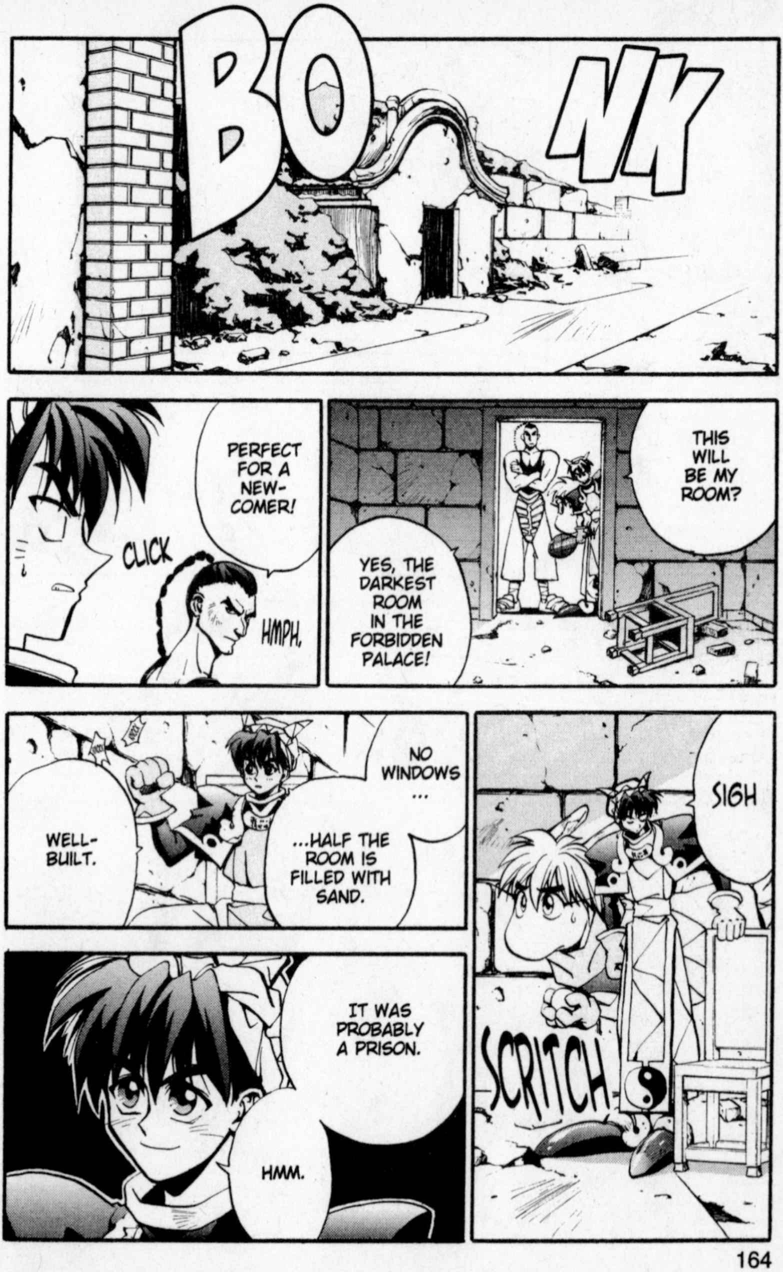
BONK
THIS WILL BE MY ROOM?
YES, THE DARKEST ROOM IN THE FORBIDDEN PALACE!
PERFECT FOR A NEW-COMER!
CLICK
HMPH.
SIGH
SCRITCH
NO WINDOWS ...
...HALF THE ROOM IS FILLED WITH SAND.
WELL-BUILT.
IT WAS PROBABLY A PRISON.
HMM.

READ THIS WAY

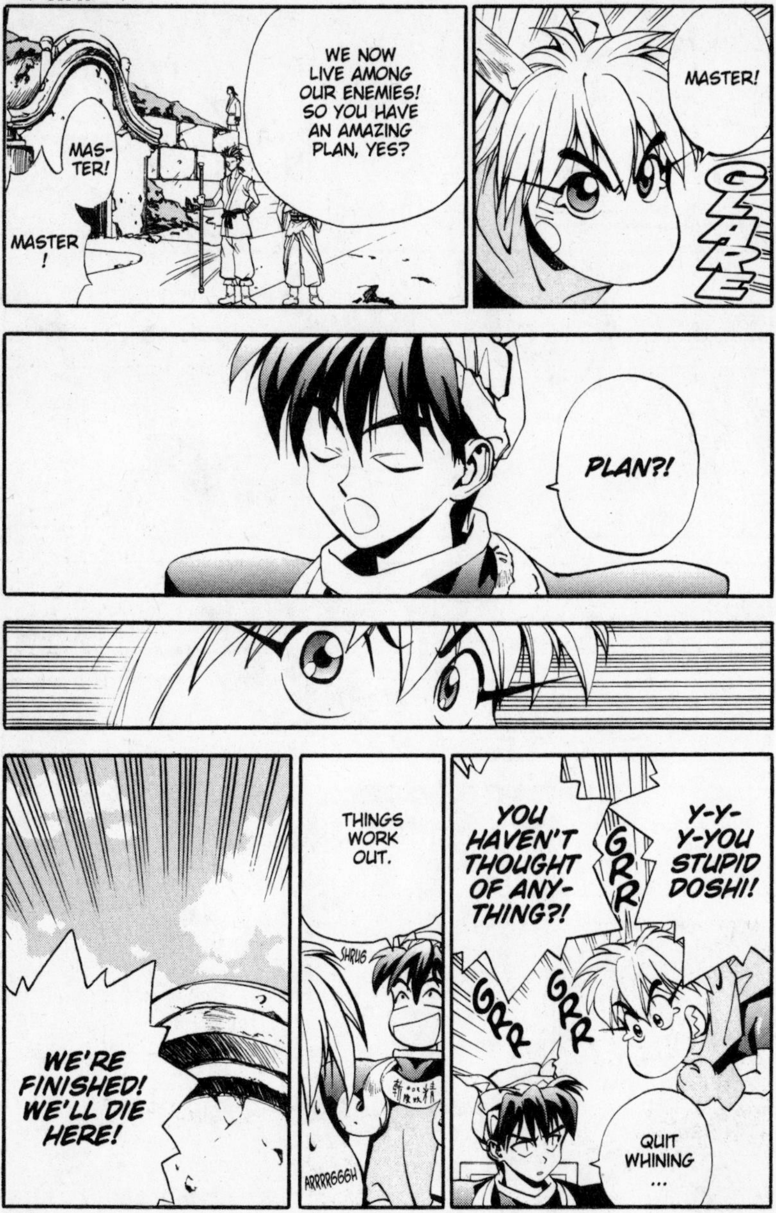
MASTER!
GLARE
WE NOW LIVE AMONG OUR ENEMIES! SO YOU HAVE AN AMAZING PLAN, YES?
MAS-TER!
MASTER !
PLAN?!
Y-Y-Y-YOU STUPID DOSHI!
GRR
YOU HAVEN'T THOUGHT OF ANY-THING?!
GRR
GRR
QUIT WHINING ...
THINGS WORK OUT.
SHRUG
ARRRRGGGH
WE'RE FINISHED! WE'LL DIE HERE!

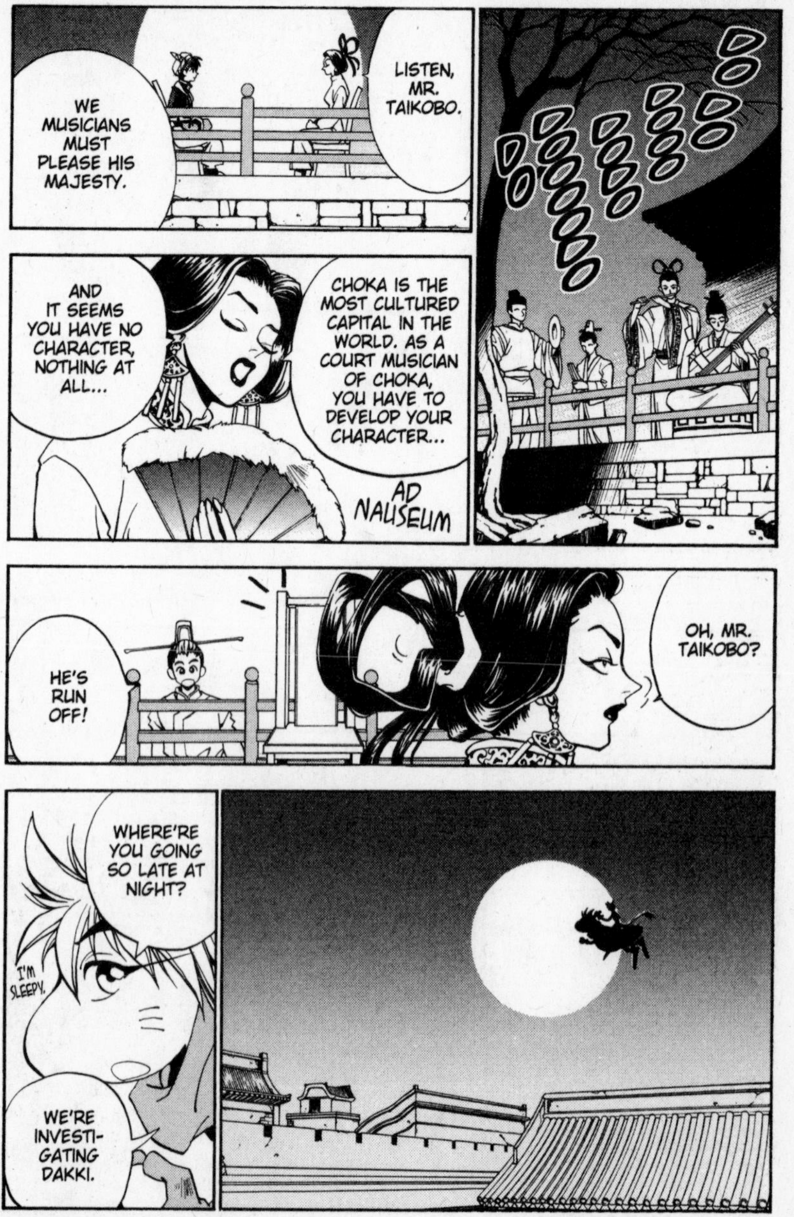
LISTEN, MR. TAIKOBO.
WE MUSICIANS MUST PLEASE HIS MAJESTY.
CHOKA IS THE MOST CULTURED CAPITAL IN THE WORLD. AS A COURT MUSICIAN OF CHOKA, YOU HAVE TO DEVELOP YOUR CHARACTER...
AD NAUSEUM
AND IT SEEMS YOU HAVE NO CHARACTER, NOTHING AT ALL...
OH, MR. TAIKOBO?
HE'S RUN OFF!
WHERE'RE YOU GOING SO LATE AT NIGHT?
I'M SLEEPY.
WE'RE INVESTIGATING DAKKI.

READ THIS WAY

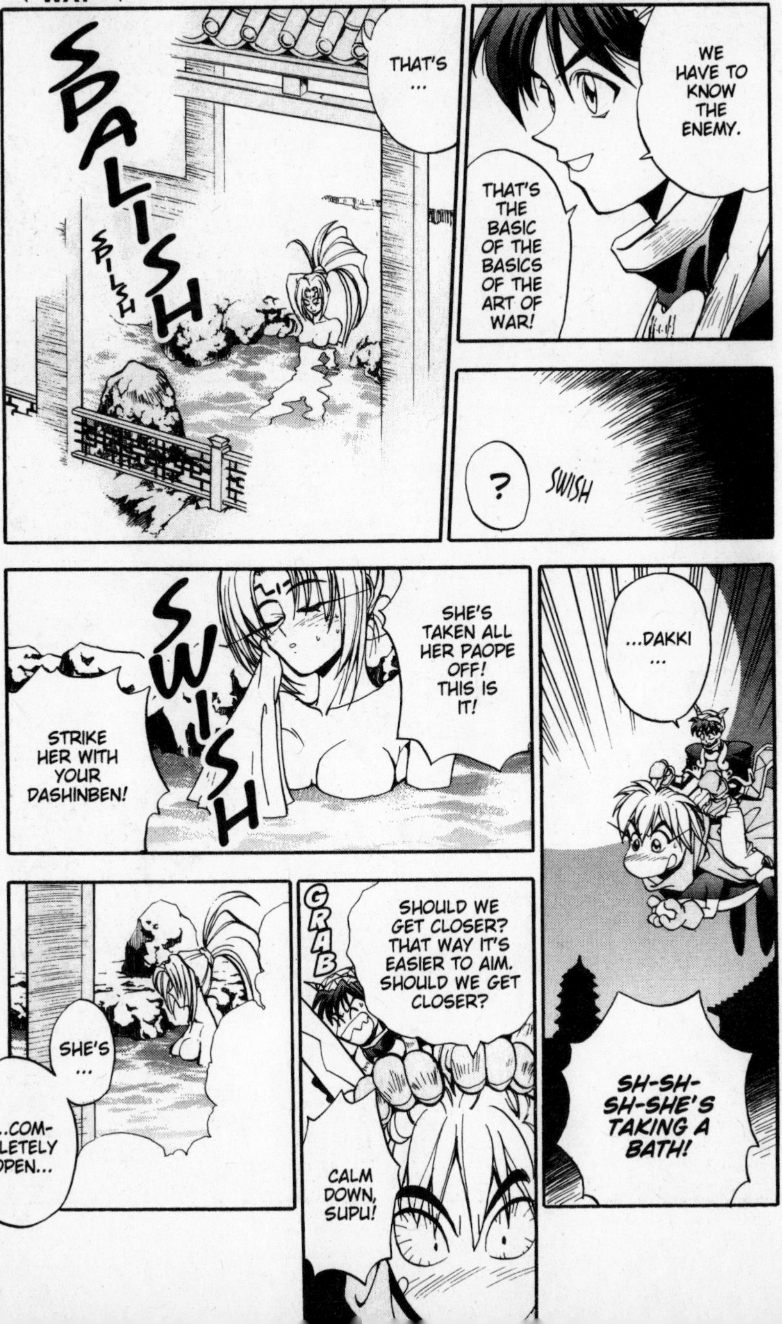
WE HAVE TO KNOW THE ENEMY.
THAT'S THE BASIC OF THE BASICS OF THE ART OF WAR!
?
SWISH
THAT'S ...
SPALISH
SPLISH
...DAKKI ...
SH-SH-SH-SHE'S TAKING A BATH!
SWISH
SHE'S TAKEN ALL HER PAOPE OFF! THIS IS IT!
STRIKE HER WITH YOUR DASHINBEN!
GRAB
SHOULD WE GET CLOSER? THAT WAY IT'S EASIER TO AIM. SHOULD WE GET CLOSER?
CALM DOWN, SUPU!
SHE'S ...
...COMPLETELY OPEN...

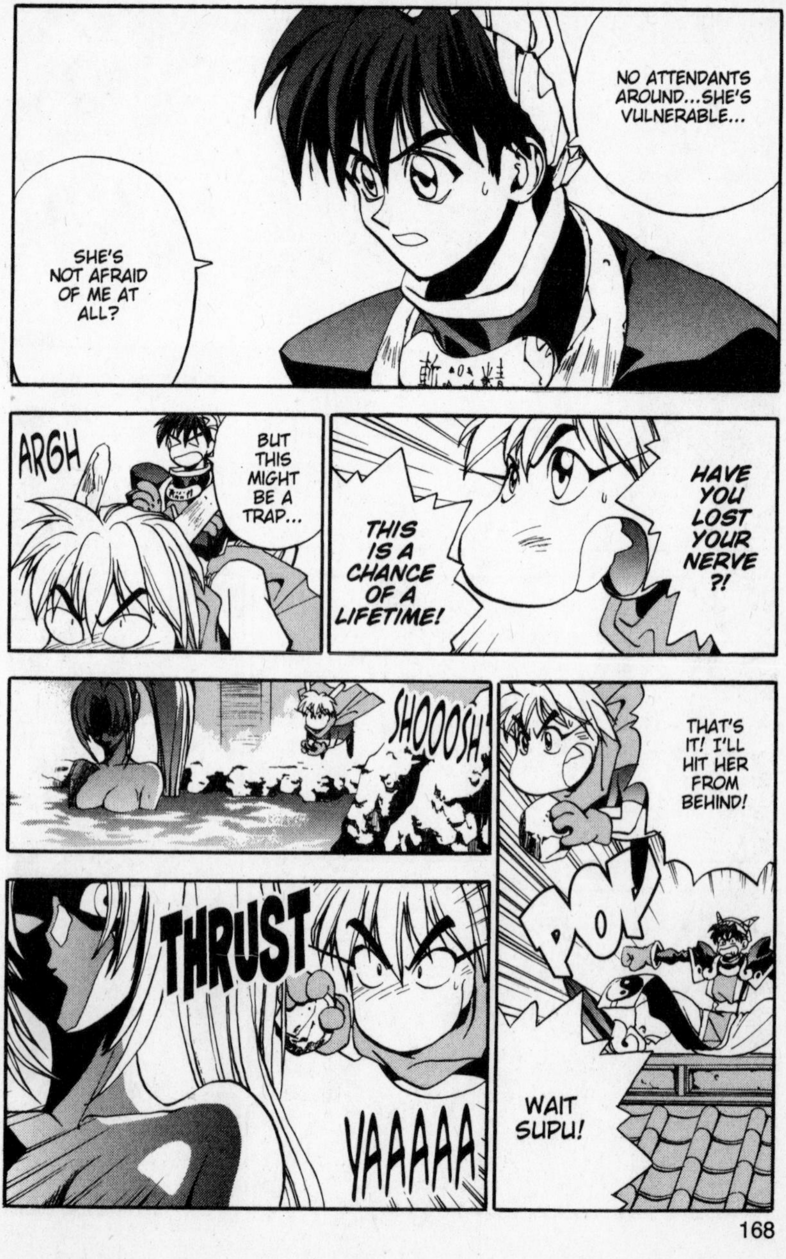
NO ATTENDANTS AROUND...SHE'S VULNERABLE...
SHE'S NOT AFRAID OF ME AT ALL?
HAVE YOU LOST YOUR NERVE?!
THIS IS A CHANCE OF A LIFETIME!
BUT THIS MIGHT BE A TRAP...
ARGH
THAT'S IT! I'LL HIT HER FROM BEHIND!
POP
WAIT SUPU!
SHOOOSH
THRUST
YAAAAA

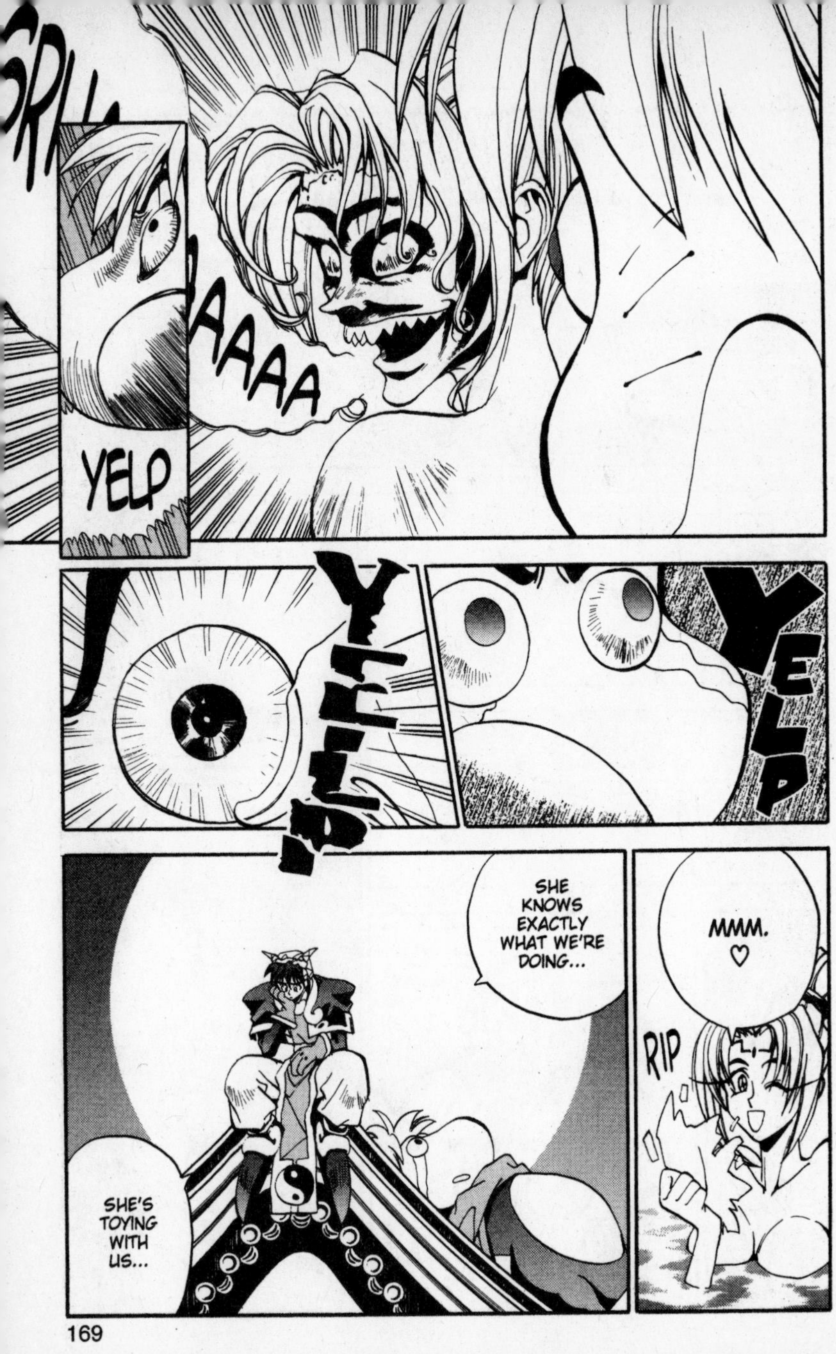
YELP
YELP
YELP!
MMM. ♡
RIP
SHE KNOWS EXACTLY WHAT WE'RE DOING...
SHE'S TOYING WITH US...

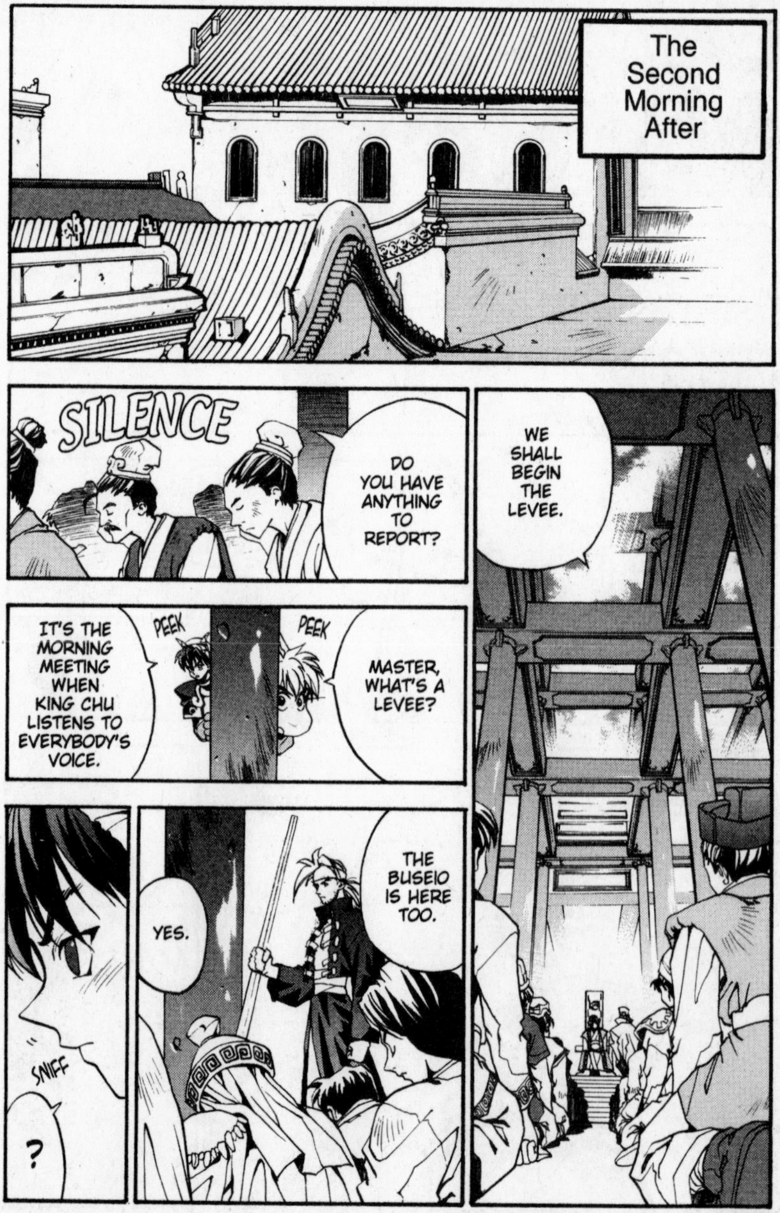
The Second Morning After
WE SHALL BEGIN THE LEVEE.
SILENCE
DO YOU HAVE ANYTHING TO REPORT?
PEEK
MASTER, WHAT'S A LEVEE?
PEEK
IT'S THE MORNING MEETING WHEN KING CHU LISTENS TO EVERYBODY'S VOICE.
THE BUSEIO IS HERE TOO.
YES.
SNIFF
?

READ THIS WAY

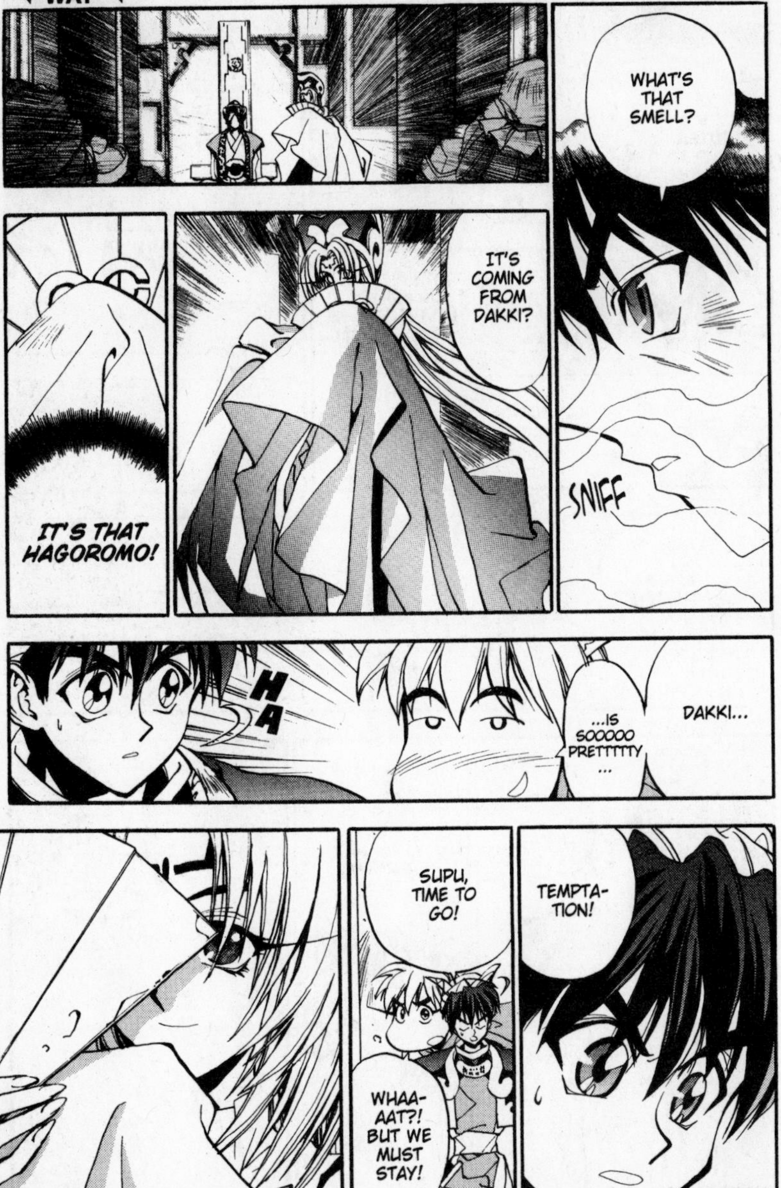
WHAT'S THAT SMELL?
SNIFF
IT'S COMING FROM DAKKI?
IT'S THAT HAGOROMO!
DAKKI...
...IS SOOOOO PRETTTTTTY ...
HA
TEMPTA-TION!
SUPU, TIME TO GO!
WHAA-AAT?! BUT WE MUST STAY!

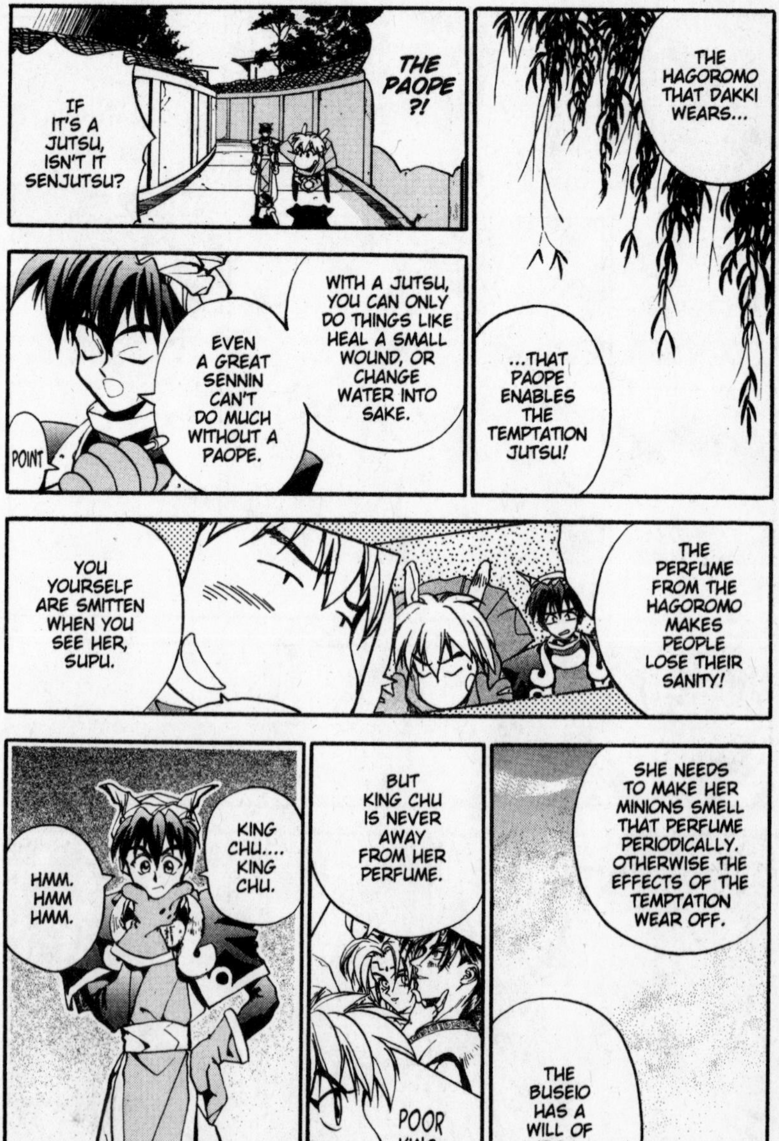
THE HAGOROMO THAT DAKKI WEARS...
...THAT PAOPE ENABLES THE TEMPTATION JUTSU!
THE PAOPE ?!
IF IT'S A JUTSU, ISN'T IT SENJUTSU?
WITH A JUTSU, YOU CAN ONLY DO THINGS LIKE HEAL A SMALL WOUND, OR CHANGE WATER INTO SAKE.
EVEN A GREAT SENNIN CAN'T DO MUCH WITHOUT A PAOPE.
POINT
THE PERFUME FROM THE HAGOROMO MAKES PEOPLE LOSE THEIR SANITY!
YOU YOURSELF ARE SMITTEN WHEN YOU SEE HER, SUPU.
SHE NEEDS TO MAKE HER MINIONS SMELL THAT PERFUME PERIODICALLY. OTHERWISE THE EFFECTS OF THE TEMPTATION WEAR OFF.
THE BUSEIO HAS A WILL OF IRON.
BUT KING CHU IS NEVER AWAY FROM HER PERFUME.
POOR KING.
KING CHU.... KING CHU.
HMM. HMM HMM.

READ THIS WAY

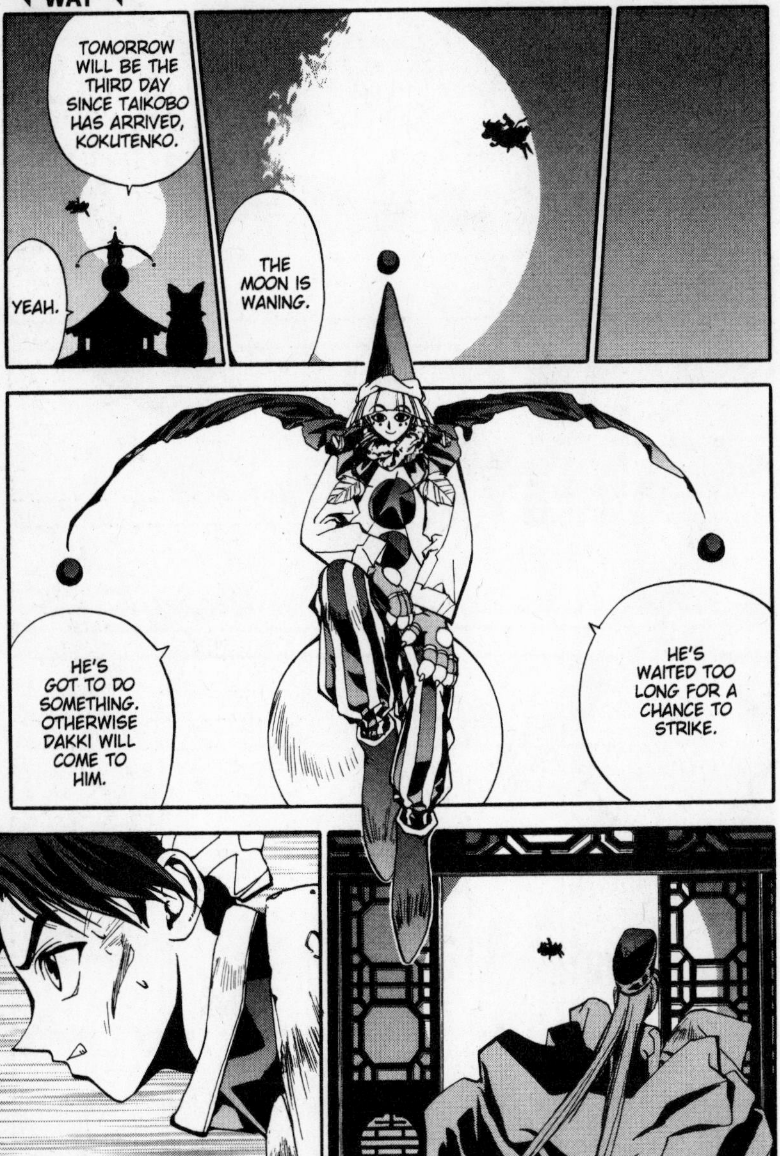
THE MOON IS WANING.
TOMORROW WILL BE THE THIRD DAY SINCE TAIKOBO HAS ARRIVED, KOKUTENKO.
YEAH.
HE'S WAITED TOO LONG FOR A CHANCE TO STRIKE.
HE'S GOT TO DO SOMETHING. OTHERWISE DAKKI WILL COME TO HIM.

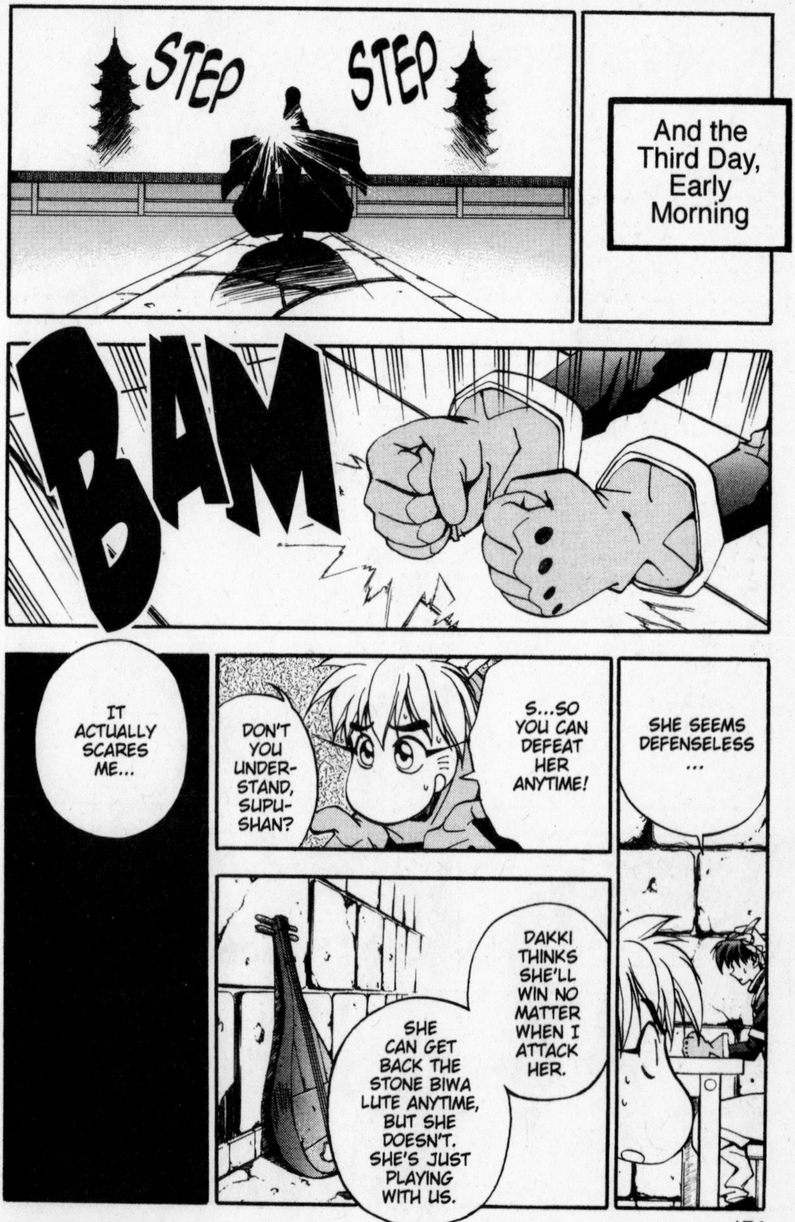
And the Third Day, Early Morning
STEP
STEP
BAM
SHE SEEMS DEFENSELESS...
S...SO YOU CAN DEFEAT HER ANYTIME!
DON'T YOU UNDER-STAND, SUPU-SHAN?
DAKKI THINKS SHE'LL WIN NO MATTER WHEN I ATTACK HER.
SHE CAN GET BACK THE STONE BIWA LUTE ANYTIME, BUT SHE DOESN'T. SHE'S JUST PLAYING WITH US.
IT ACTUALLY SCARES ME...

WHERE ARE YOU GOING, WITHOUT YOUR ATTENDANTS? IF ANYTHING HAPPENS WE'LL BE ...

I DON'T NEED ANY ATTENDANTS. ♡

TEMP TATION

DAKKI-SAMA!

...TIRED OF PLAYING WITH TAIKOBO. ♡

I'M...

STEP STEP

....

MASTER, I'M WORRIED.

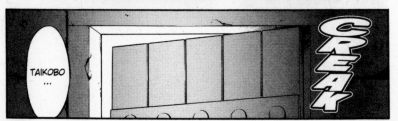

TAIKOBO ...

CREAK

175

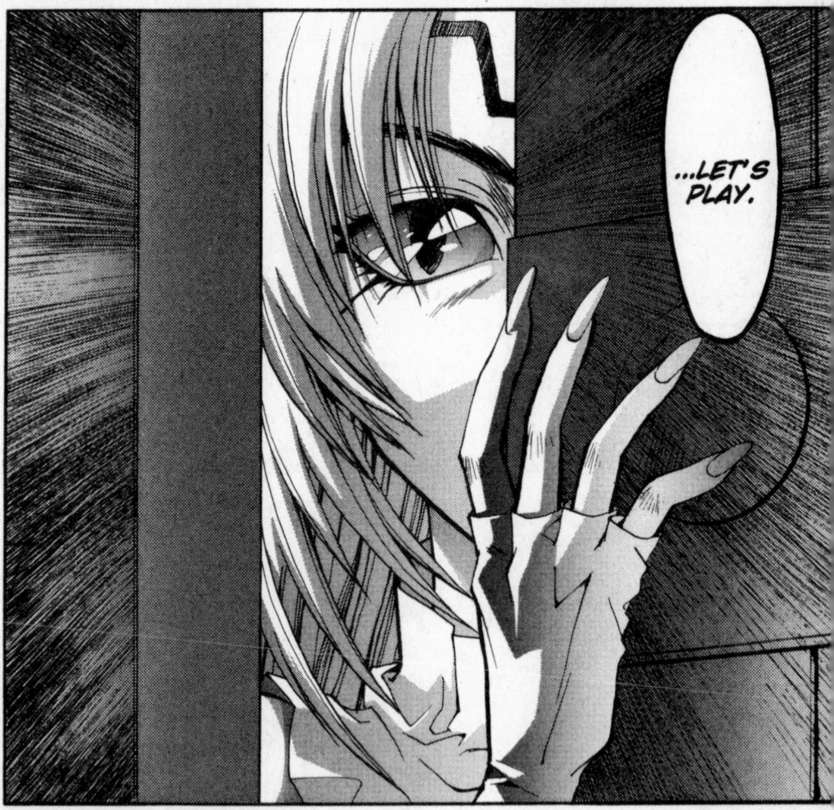
...LET'S PLAY.

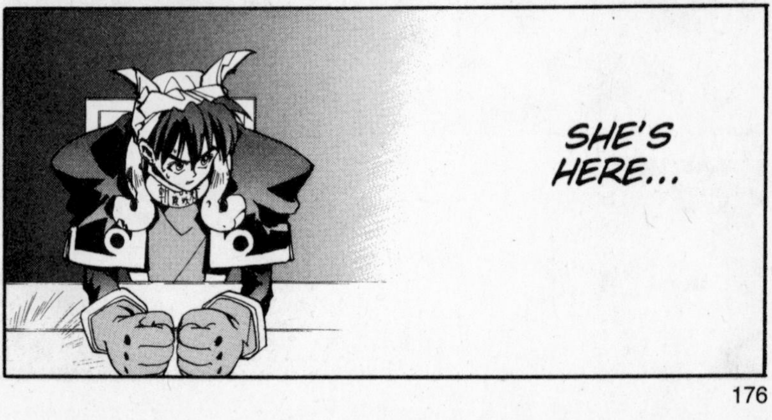
SHE'S HERE...

READ THIS WAY

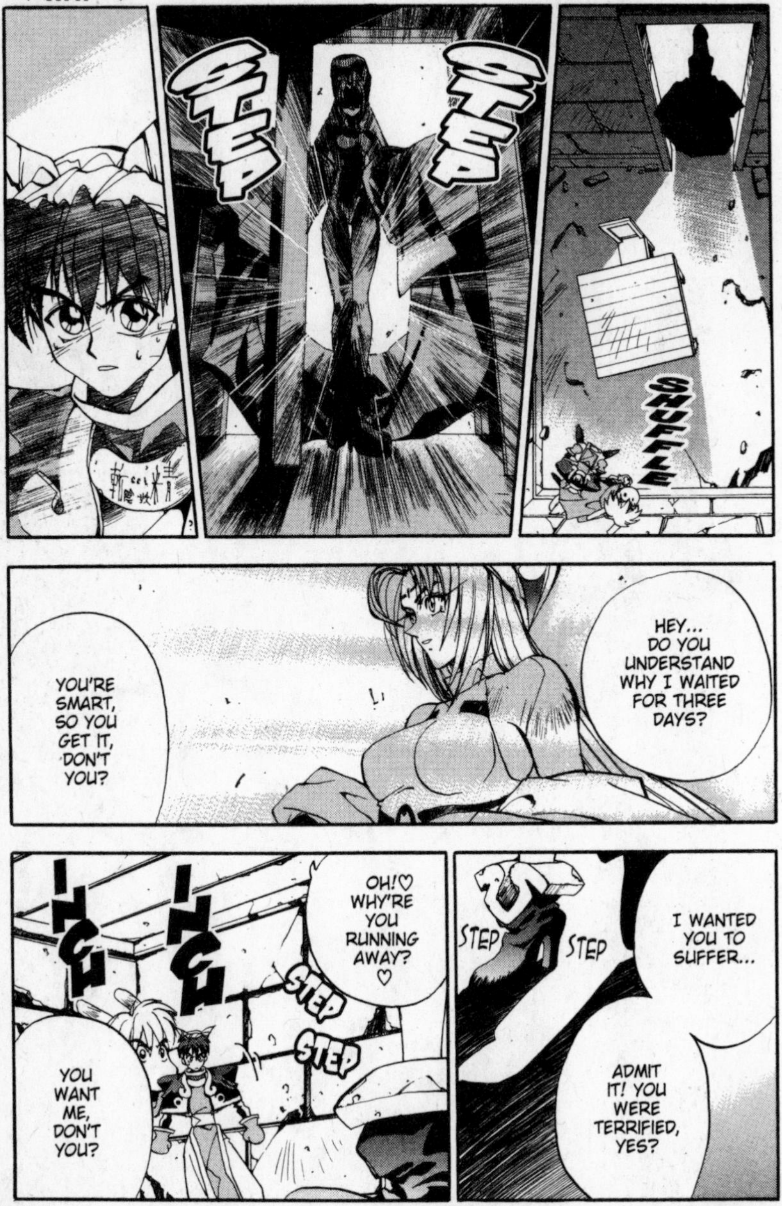
SHUFFLE
STEP
STEP
HEY... DO YOU UNDERSTAND WHY I WAITED FOR THREE DAYS?
YOU'RE SMART, SO YOU GET IT, DON'T YOU?
STEP
STEP
I WANTED YOU TO SUFFER...
ADMIT IT! YOU WERE TERRIFIED, YES?
OH!♡ WHY'RE YOU RUNNING AWAY?♡
INCH
INCH
STEP
STEP
YOU WANT ME, DON'T YOU?

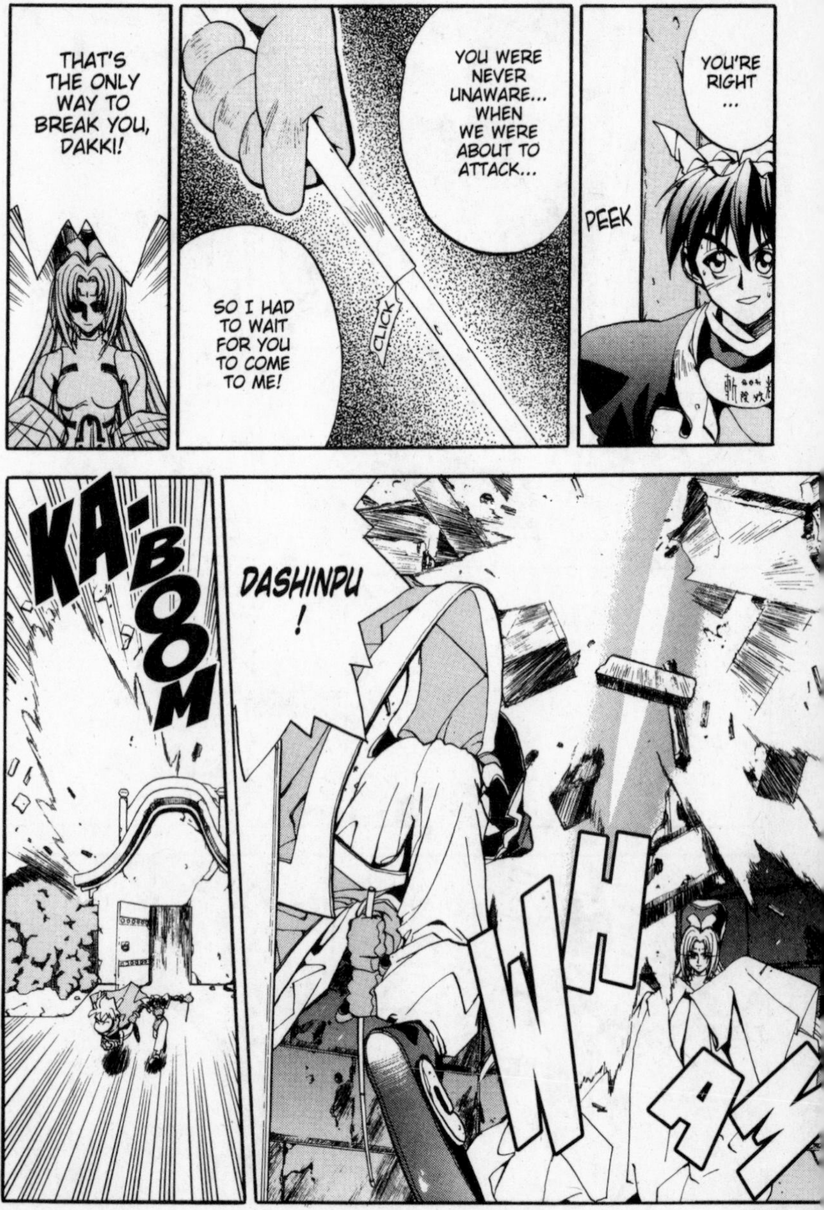
YOU'RE RIGHT ...
PEEK
YOU WERE NEVER UNAWARE... WHEN WE WERE ABOUT TO ATTACK...
CLICK
SO I HAD TO WAIT FOR YOU TO COME TO ME!
THAT'S THE ONLY WAY TO BREAK YOU, DAKKI!
DASHINPU!
WHAM
KA-BOOM

READ THIS WAY

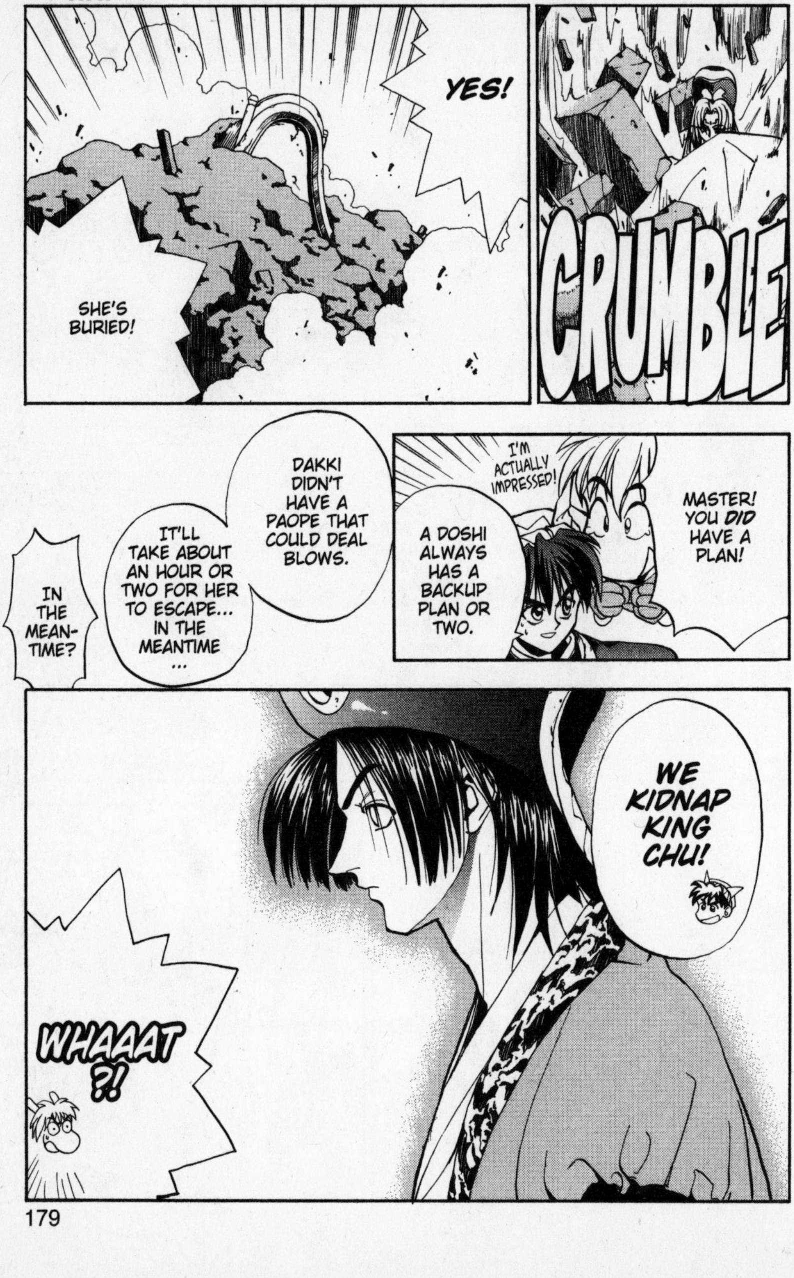
CRUMBLE
YES!
SHE'S BURIED!
MASTER! YOU DID HAVE A PLAN!
I'M ACTUALLY IMPRESSED!
A DOSHI ALWAYS HAS A BACKUP PLAN OR TWO.
DAKKI DIDN'T HAVE A PAOPE THAT COULD DEAL BLOWS.
IT'LL TAKE ABOUT AN HOUR OR TWO FOR HER TO ESCAPE... IN THE MEANTIME ...
IN THE MEAN-TIME?
WE KIDNAP KING CHU!
WHAAAT ?!

THE SHEER PRECIPICE, WHERE IS IT NOW?

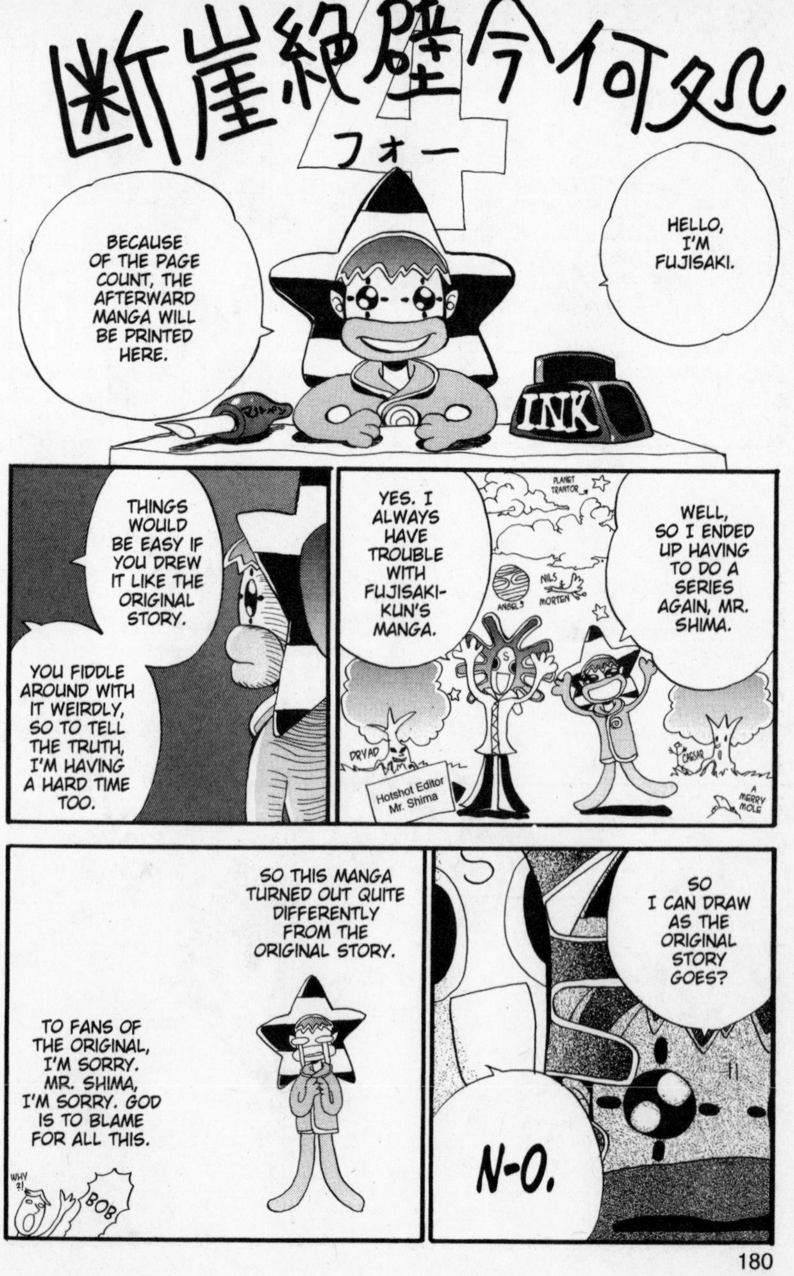
断崖絶壁今何処
4
フォー
HELLO, I'M FUJISAKI.
BECAUSE OF THE PAGE COUNT, THE AFTERWARD MANGA WILL BE PRINTED HERE.
INK
WELL, SO I ENDED UP HAVING TO DO A SERIES AGAIN, MR. SHIMA.
YES. I ALWAYS HAVE TROUBLE WITH FUJISAKI-KUN'S MANGA.
PLANET TRANTOR
NILS MORTEN
DRYAD
Hotshot Editor Mr. Shima
CAESAR
A MERRY MOLE
THINGS WOULD BE EASY IF YOU DREW IT LIKE THE ORIGINAL STORY.
YOU FIDDLE AROUND WITH IT WEIRDLY, SO TO TELL THE TRUTH, I'M HAVING A HARD TIME TOO.
SO I CAN DRAW AS THE ORIGINAL STORY GOES?
N-O.
SO THIS MANGA TURNED OUT QUITE DIFFERENTLY FROM THE ORIGINAL STORY.
TO FANS OF THE ORIGINAL, I'M SORRY. MR. SHIMA, I'M SORRY. GOD IS TO BLAME FOR ALL THIS.
WHY?!
BOB

CHAPTER 7: THE TAIBON

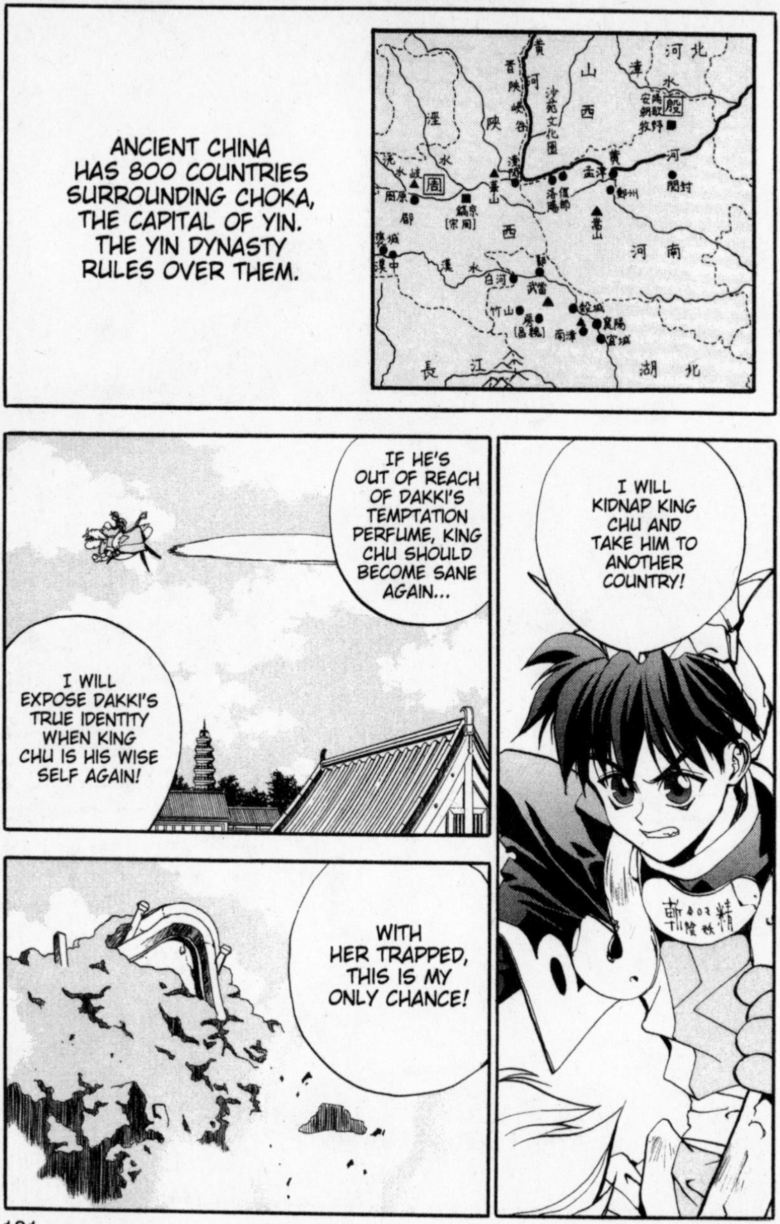
ANCIENT CHINA HAS 800 COUNTRIES SURROUNDING CHOKA, THE CAPITAL OF YIN. THE YIN DYNASTY RULES OVER THEM.
I WILL KIDNAP KING CHU AND TAKE HIM TO ANOTHER COUNTRY!
IF HE'S OUT OF REACH OF DAKKI'S TEMPTATION PERFUME, KING CHU SHOULD BECOME SANE AGAIN...
I WILL EXPOSE DAKKI'S TRUE IDENTITY WHEN KING CHU IS HIS WISE SELF AGAIN!
WITH HER TRAPPED, THIS IS MY ONLY CHANCE!

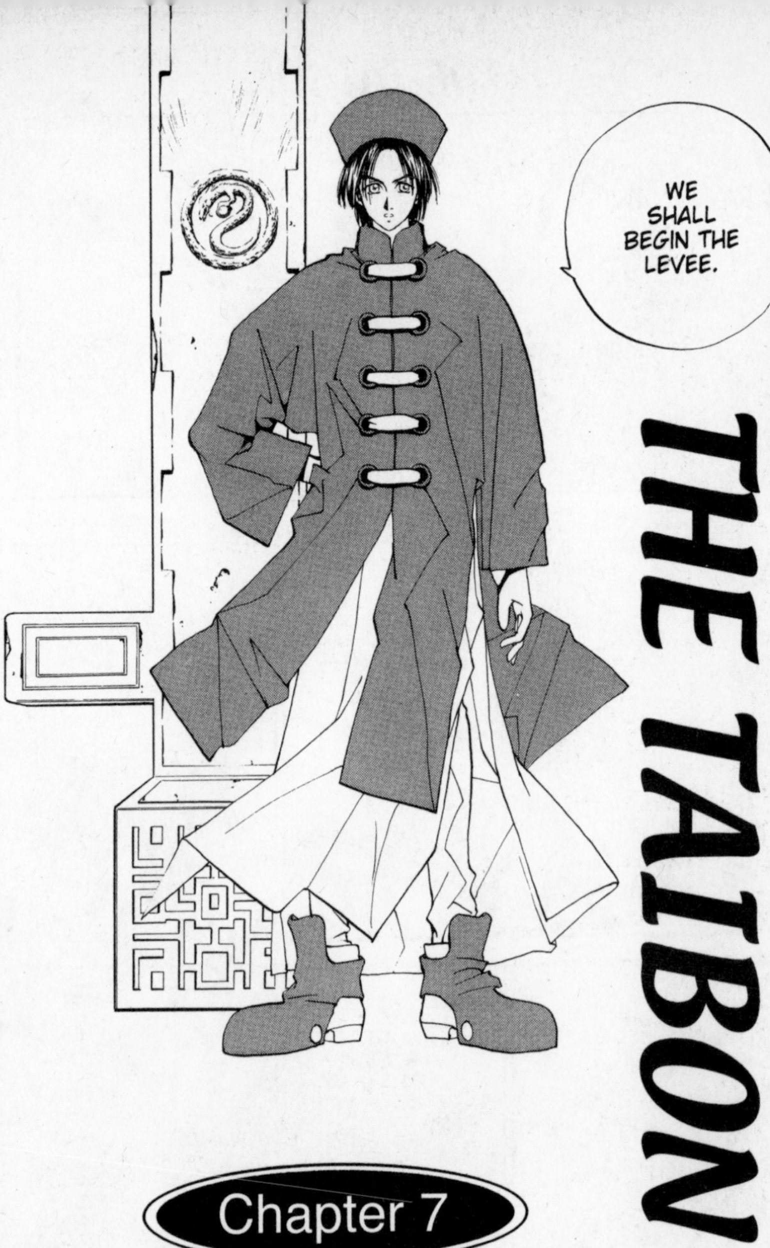
WE SHALL BEGIN THE LEVEE.
THE TAIBON
Chapter 7

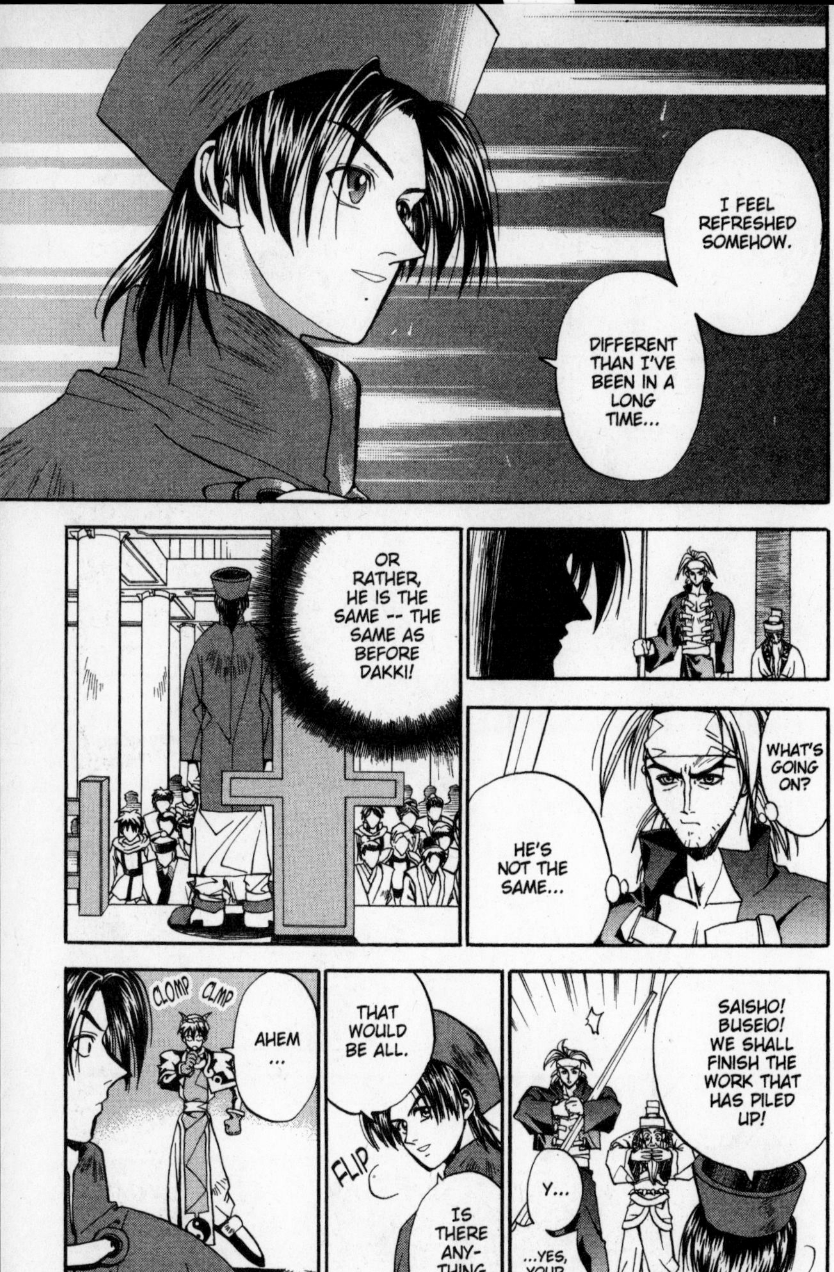
I FEEL REFRESHED SOMEHOW.
DIFFERENT THAN I'VE BEEN IN A LONG TIME...
WHAT'S GOING ON?
HE'S NOT THE SAME...
OR RATHER, HE IS THE SAME -- THE SAME AS BEFORE DAKKI!
SAISHO! BUSEIO! WE SHALL FINISH THE WORK THAT HAS PILED UP!
Y...
...YES, YOUR MAJESTY!
THAT WOULD BE ALL.
FLIP
IS THERE ANYTHING ELSE?
CLOMP CLMP
AHEM ...

YOU... THE BIWA MERCHANT?

DEEP BOW

HURRAH! HURRAH! *HURRAH!*

TAIKOBO!

TAIKOBO, THE COURT MUSICIAN, PRAYS FOR HIS MAJESTY'S LONGEVITY!

TOMORROW, THERE WILL BE A FANTASTIC GALA IN SHUGEN, THE CAPITAL OF THE WEST. THREE HUNDRED EXOTIC WOMEN WILL BE IN ATTENDANCE.

KING CHU!

YOU'RE LYING THROUGH YOUR TEETH...

YOU LECHER.

FLIP

WHAT? THREE HUNDRED EXOTIC WOMEN?! I SHALL ATTEND!

READ THIS WAY

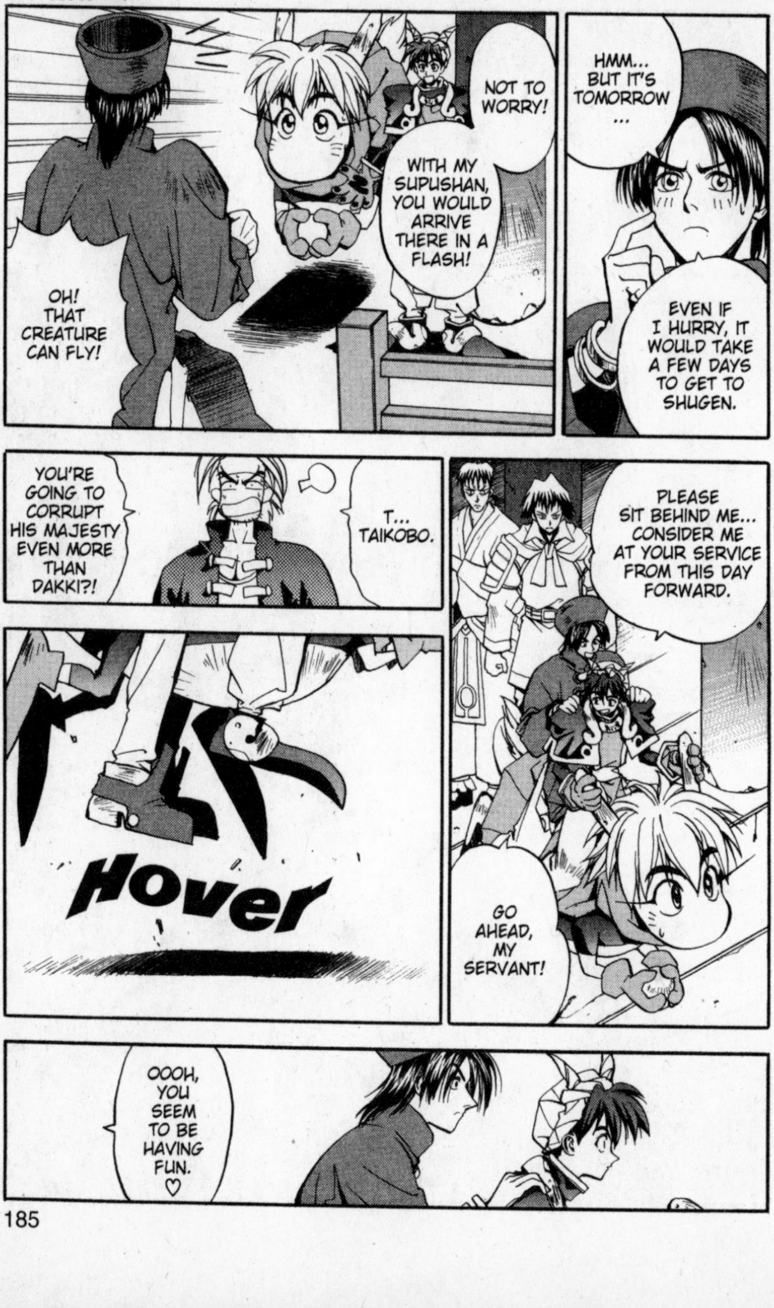
HMM... BUT IT'S TOMORROW ...
EVEN IF I HURRY, IT WOULD TAKE A FEW DAYS TO GET TO SHUGEN.
NOT TO WORRY!
WITH MY SUPUSHAN, YOU WOULD ARRIVE THERE IN A FLASH!
OH! THAT CREATURE CAN FLY!
PLEASE SIT BEHIND ME... CONSIDER ME AT YOUR SERVICE FROM THIS DAY FORWARD.
GO AHEAD, MY SERVANT!
T... TAIKOBO.
YOU'RE GOING TO CORRUPT HIS MAJESTY EVEN MORE THAN DAKKI?!
Hover
OOOH, YOU SEEM TO BE HAVING FUN. ♡

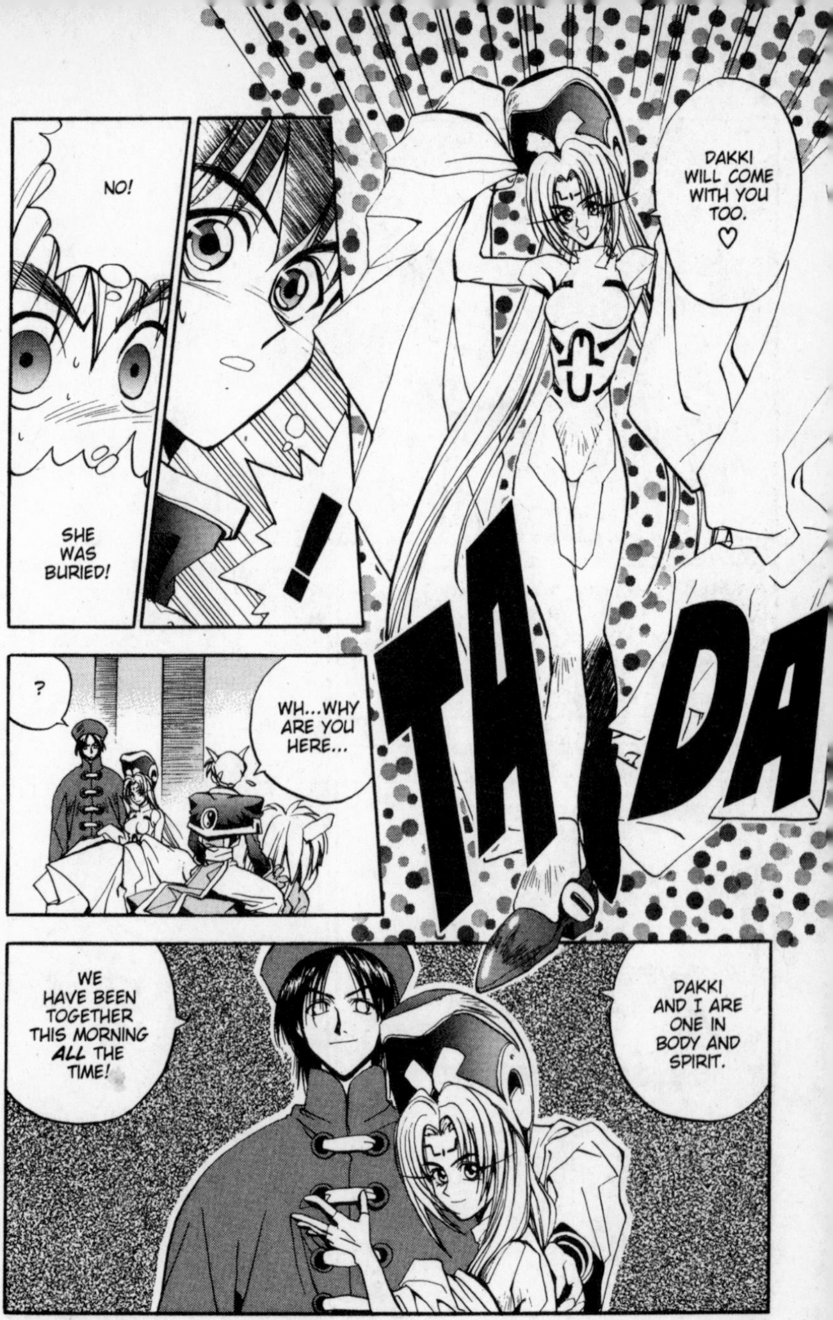
DAKKI WILL COME WITH YOU TOO. ♡
TA DA
!
NO!
SHE WAS BURIED!
WH...WHY ARE YOU HERE...
?
DAKKI AND I ARE ONE IN BODY AND SPIRIT.
WE HAVE BEEN TOGETHER THIS MORNING ALL THE TIME!

READ THIS WAY

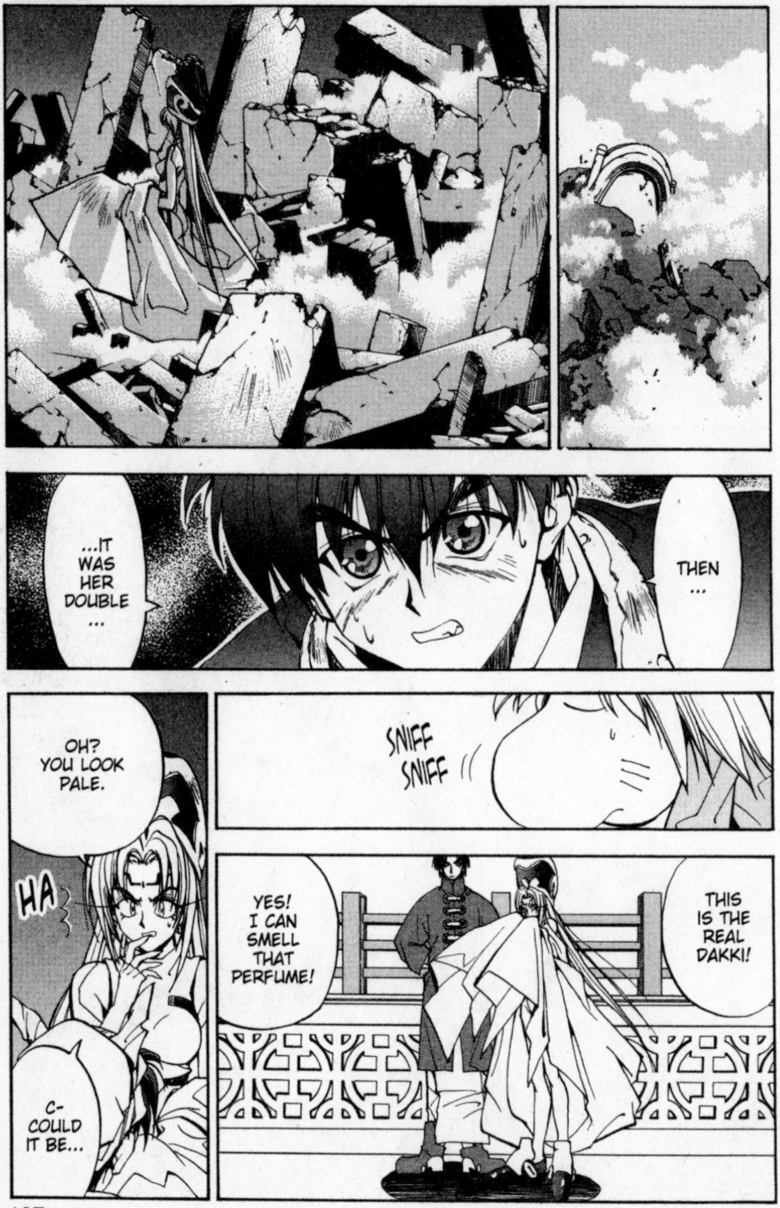
THEN ...
...IT WAS HER DOUBLE ...
SNIFF SNIFF
THIS IS THE REAL DAKKI!
YES! I CAN SMELL THAT PERFUME!
OH? YOU LOOK PALE.
HA
C-COULD IT BE...

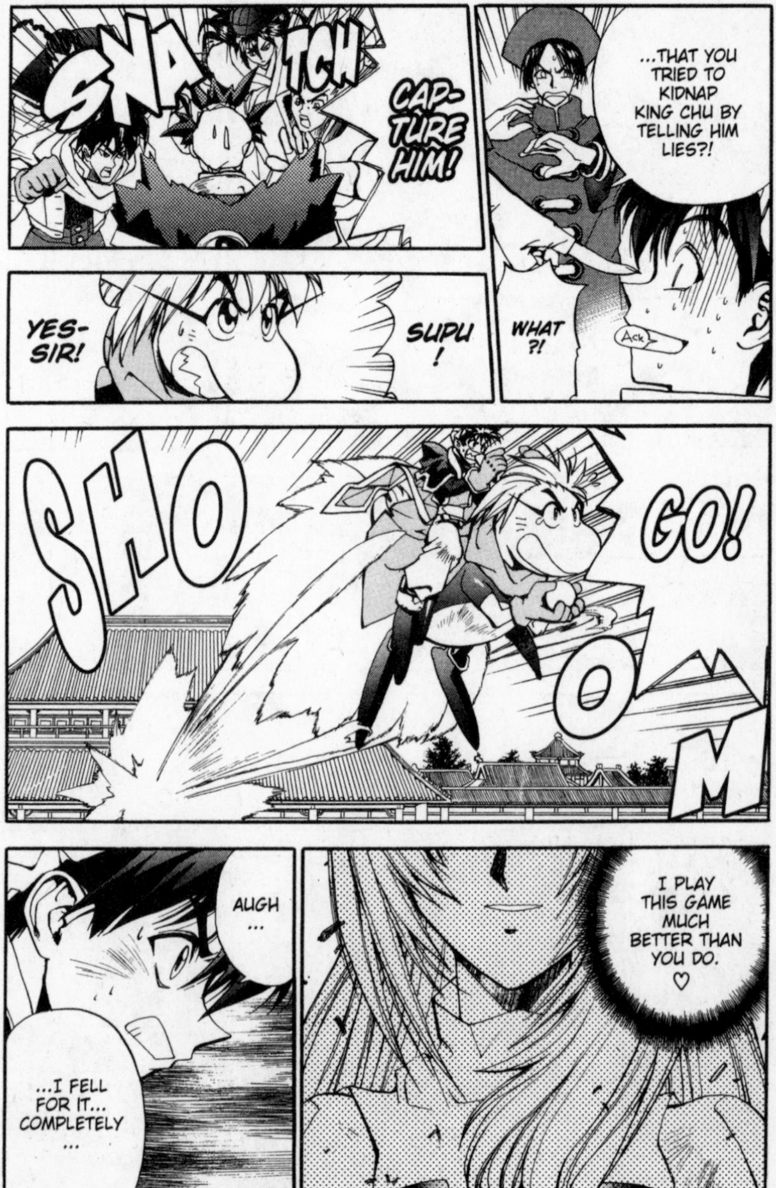
...THAT YOU TRIED TO KIDNAP KING CHU BY TELLING HIM LIES?!
Ack
WHAT?!
SNATCH
CAPTURE HIM!
SUPU!
YES-SIR!
GO!
SHOOOM
I PLAY THIS GAME MUCH BETTER THAN YOU DO. ♡
AUGH...
...I FELL FOR IT... COMPLETELY...

READ THIS WAY

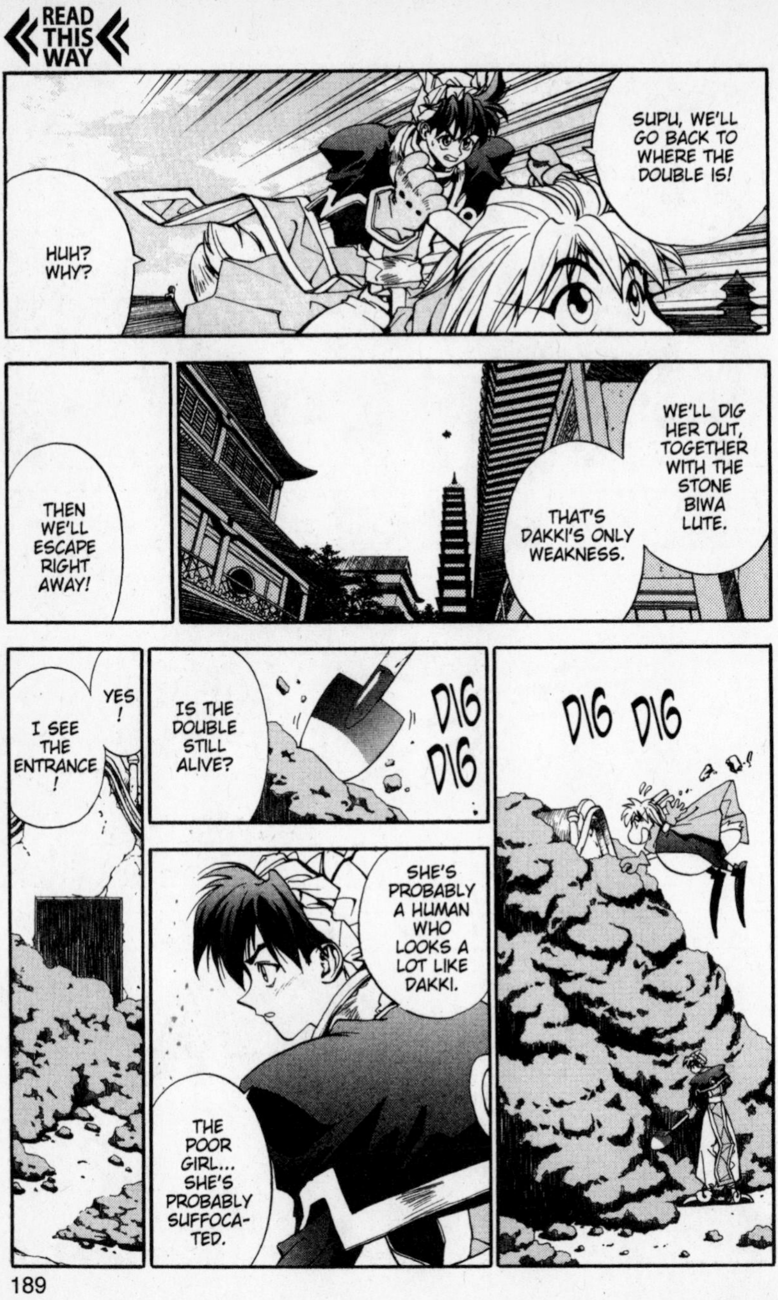
SUPU, WE'LL GO BACK TO WHERE THE DOUBLE IS!
HUH? WHY?
WE'LL DIG HER OUT, TOGETHER WITH THE STONE BIWA LUTE.
THAT'S DAKKI'S ONLY WEAKNESS.
THEN WE'LL ESCAPE RIGHT AWAY!
DIG DIG
DIG DIG
IS THE DOUBLE STILL ALIVE?
SHE'S PROBABLY A HUMAN WHO LOOKS A LOT LIKE DAKKI.
THE POOR GIRL... SHE'S PROBABLY SUFFOCATED.
YES! I SEE THE ENTRANCE!

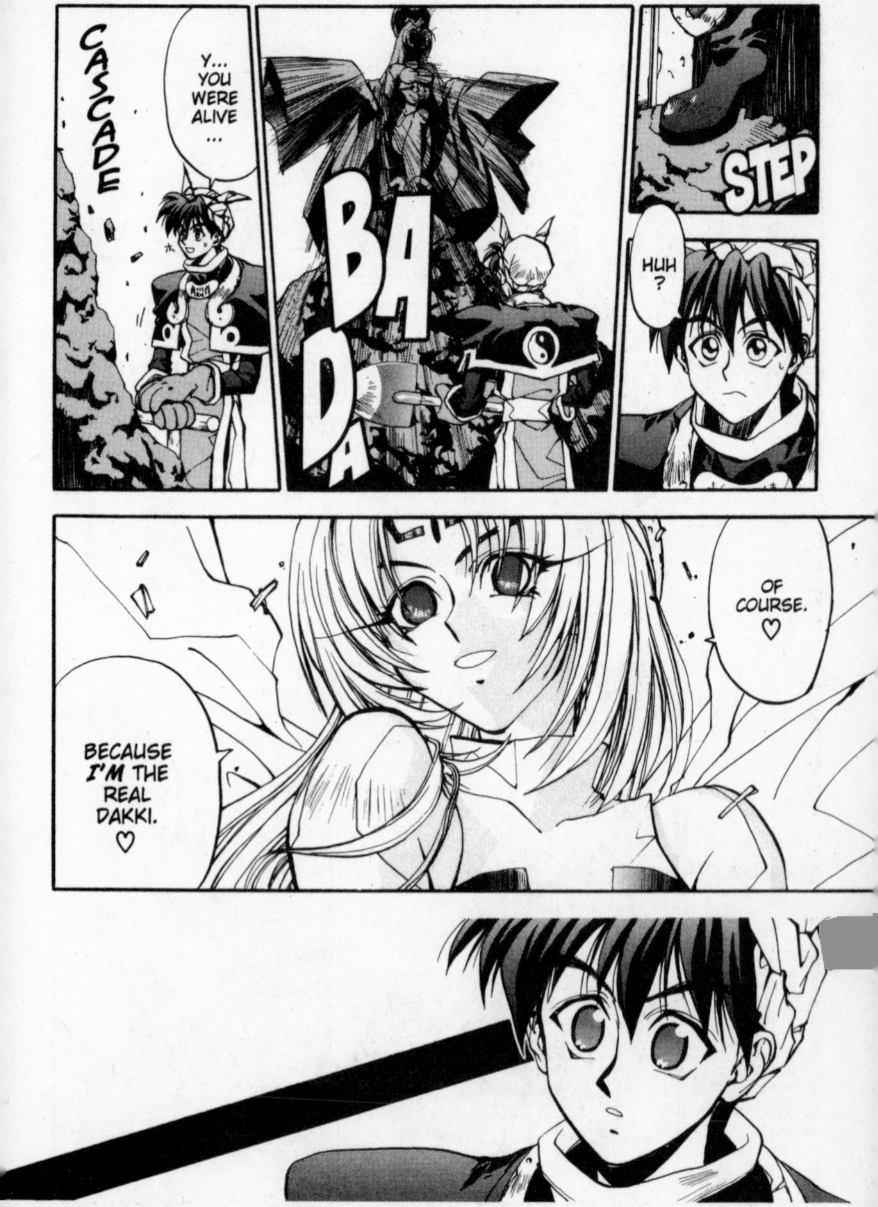
STEP
HUH?
BADA
CASCADE
Y... YOU WERE ALIVE...
OF COURSE. ♡
BECAUSE I'M THE REAL DAKKI. ♡

READ THIS WAY

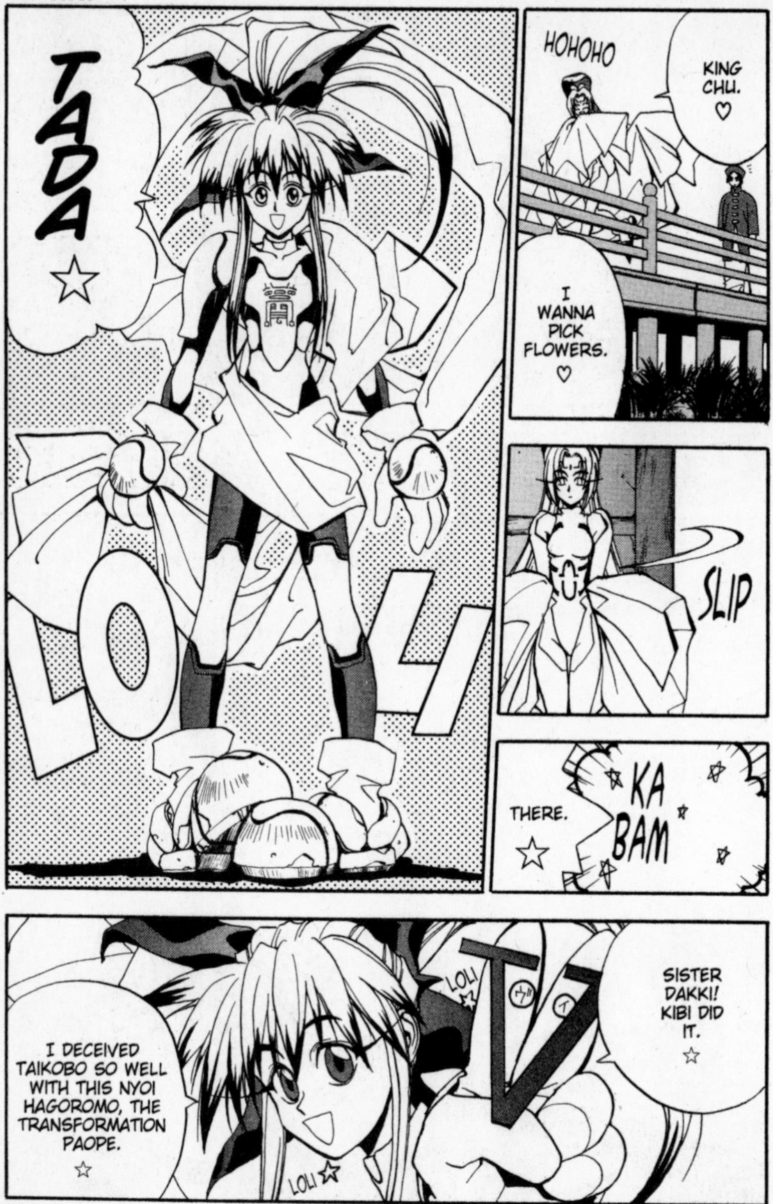
KING CHU. ♡
HOHOHO
I WANNA PICK FLOWERS. ♡
SLIP
KA BAM
THERE. ☆
TADA ☆
LOLI
SISTER DAKKI! KIBI DID IT. ☆
V
ヴ
イ
LOLI ☆
I DECEIVED TAIKOBO SO WELL WITH THIS NYOI HAGOROMO, THE TRANSFORMATION PAOPE. ☆
LOLI ☆

(The circles spell "V" in Katakana.)

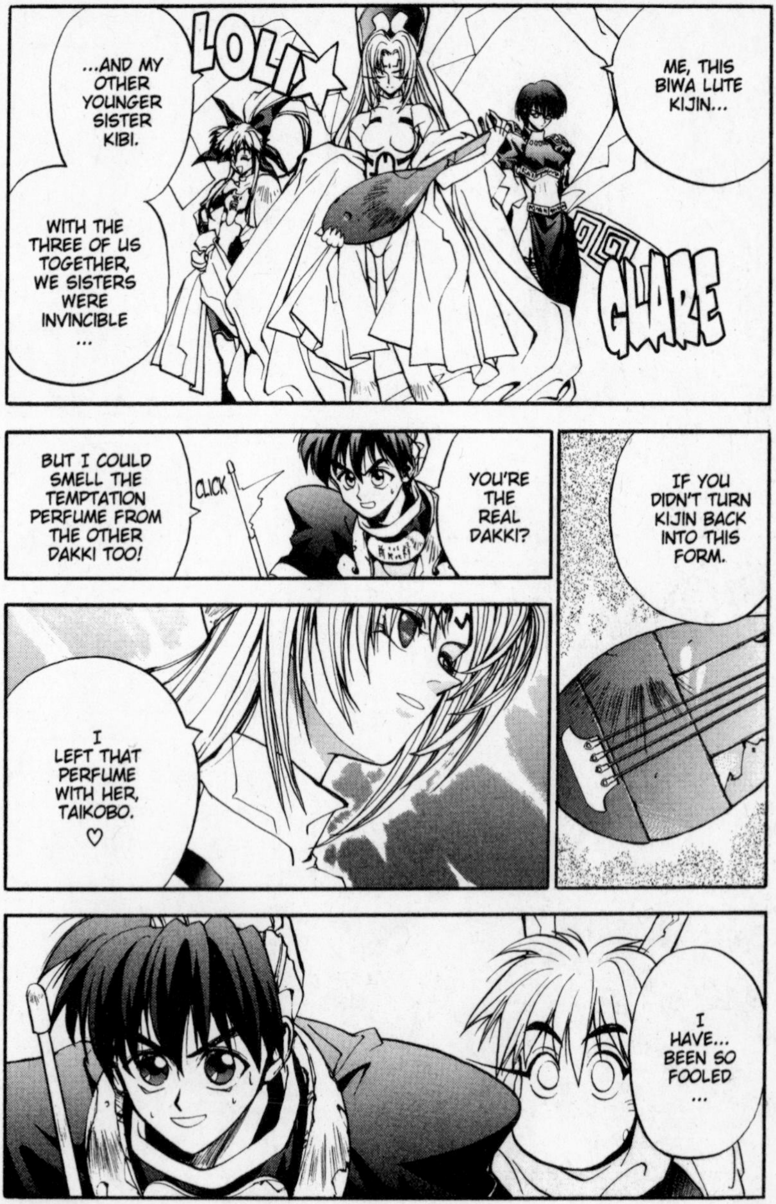
ME, THIS BIWA LUTE KIJIN...
LOLI
...AND MY OTHER YOUNGER SISTER KIBI.
WITH THE THREE OF US TOGETHER, WE SISTERS WERE INVINCIBLE ...
GLARE
IF YOU DIDN'T TURN KIJIN BACK INTO THIS FORM.
YOU'RE THE REAL DAKKI?
CLICK
BUT I COULD SMELL THE TEMPTATION PERFUME FROM THE OTHER DAKKI TOO!
I LEFT THAT PERFUME WITH HER, TAIKOBO. ♡
I HAVE... BEEN SO FOOLED ...

READ THIS WAY

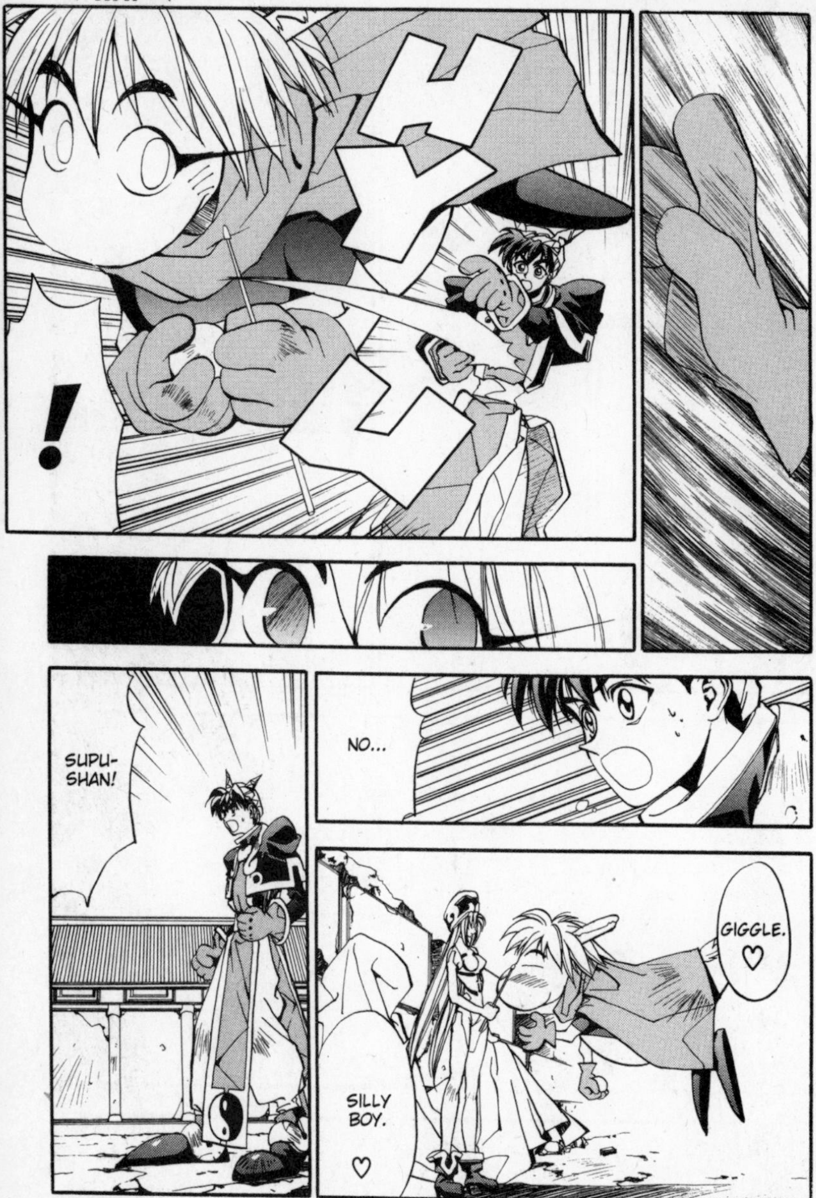
!
NO...
GIGGLE. ♡
SILLY BOY. ♡
SUPU-SHAN!

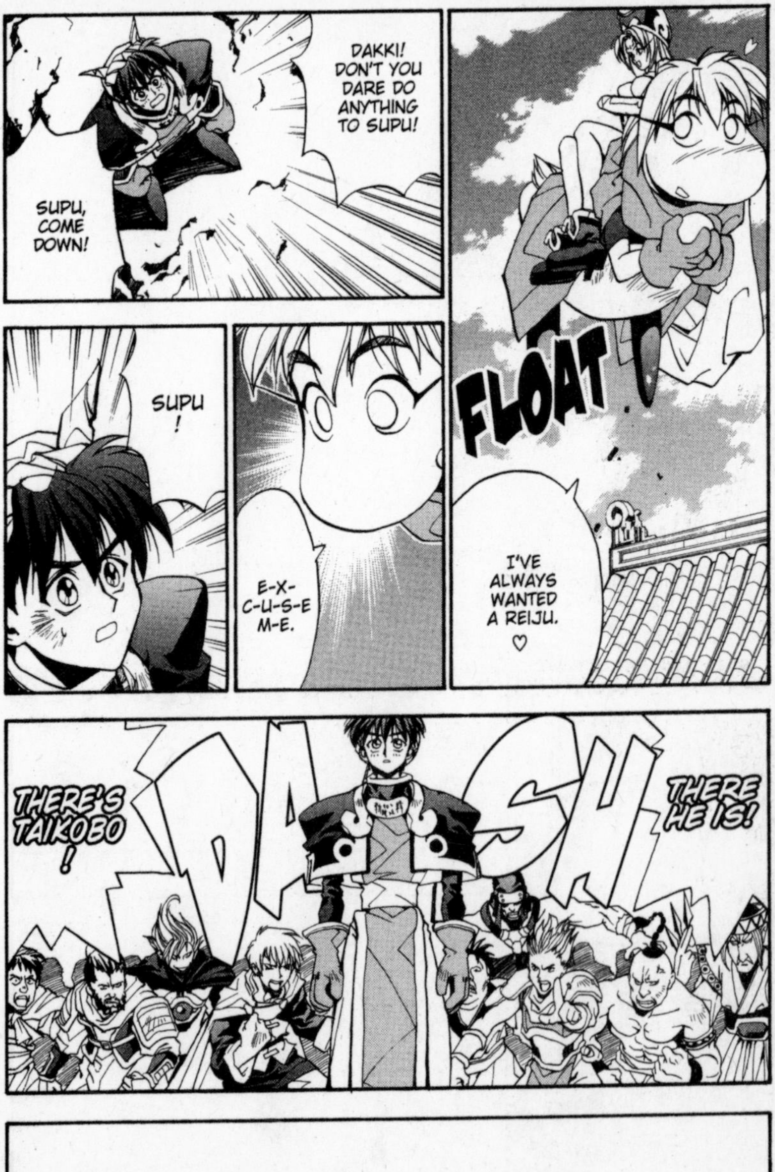
FLOAT
I'VE ALWAYS WANTED A REIJU. ♡
DAKKI! DON'T YOU DARE DO ANYTHING TO SUPU!
SUPU, COME DOWN!
E-X-C-U-S-E M-E.
SUPU!
THERE HE IS!
DASH
THERE'S TAIKOBO!

READ THIS WAY

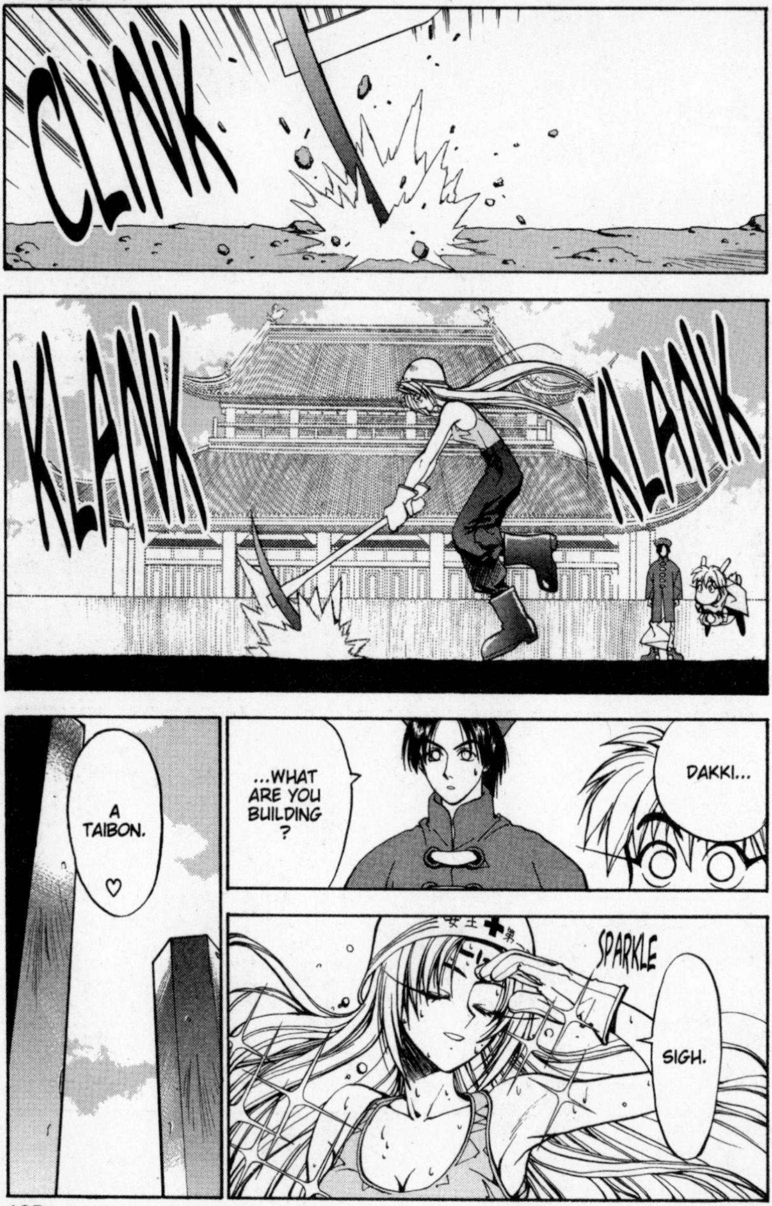
CLINK
KLANK
KLANK
DAKKI...
...WHAT ARE YOU BUILDING?
SPARKLE
SIGH.
A TAIBON. ♡

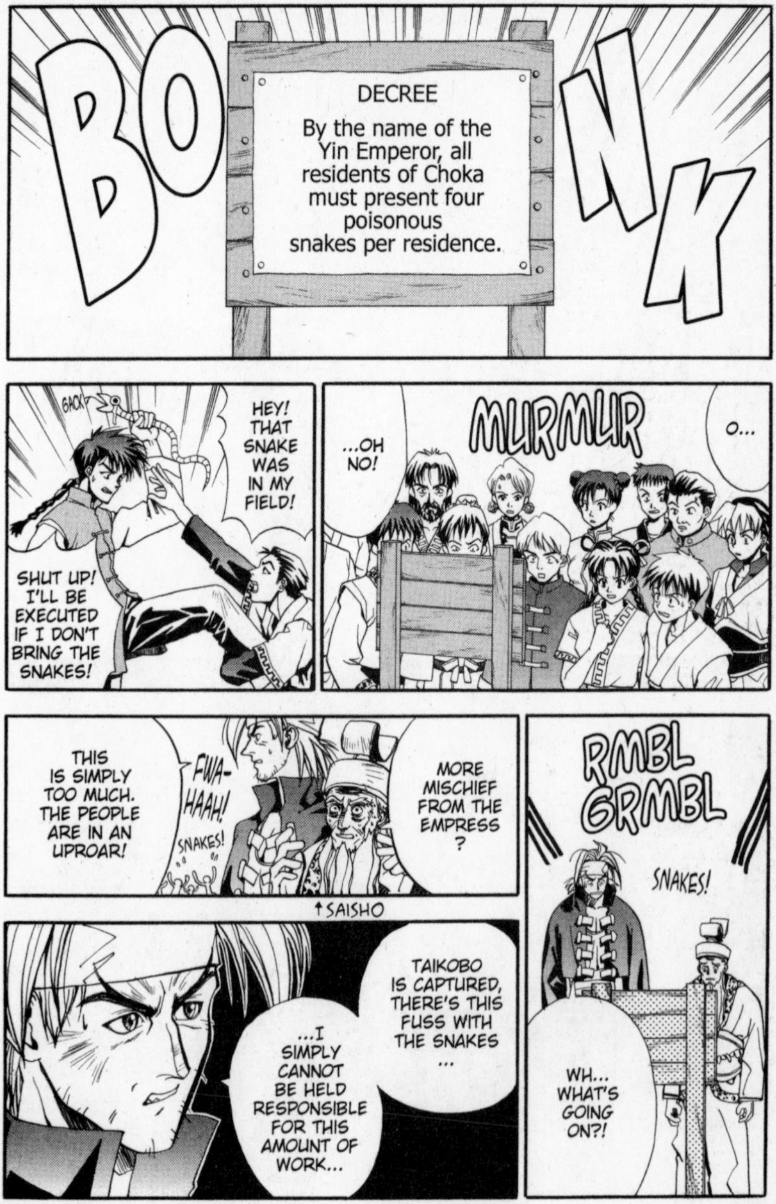
BONK
DECREE
By the name of the Yin Emperor, all residents of Choka must present four poisonous snakes per residence.
O...
MURMUR
...OH NO!
HEY! THAT SNAKE WAS IN MY FIELD!
GACK
SHUT UP! I'LL BE EXECUTED IF I DON'T BRING THE SNAKES!
RMBL GRMBL
SNAKES!
WH... WHAT'S GOING ON?!
MORE MISCHIEF FROM THE EMPRESS?
FWA-HAAH!
SNAKES!
THIS IS SIMPLY TOO MUCH. THE PEOPLE ARE IN AN UPROAR!
↑SAISHO
TAIKOBO IS CAPTURED, THERE'S THIS FUSS WITH THE SNAKES...
...I SIMPLY CANNOT BE HELD RESPONSIBLE FOR THIS AMOUNT OF WORK...

READ THIS WAY

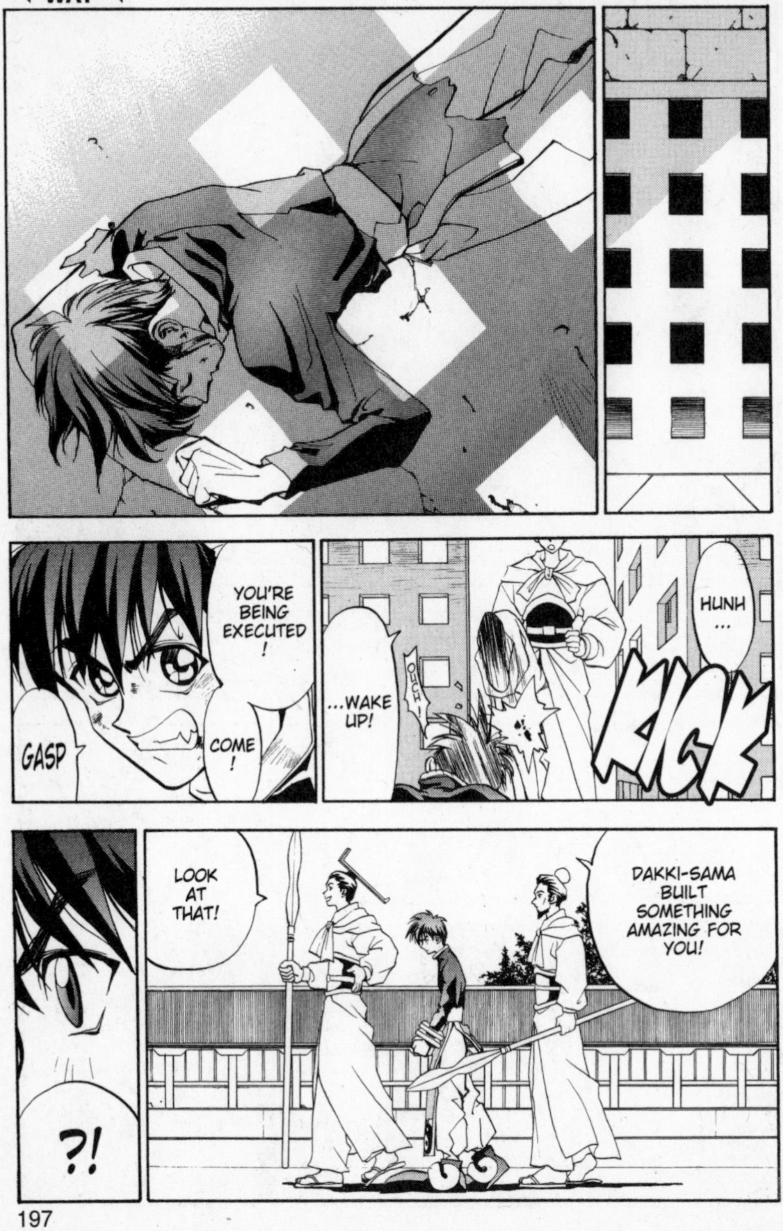
HUNH ...
KICK
OUCH!
...WAKE UP!
YOU'RE BEING EXECUTED!
COME!
GASP
DAKKI-SAMA BUILT SOMETHING AMAZING FOR YOU!
LOOK AT THAT!
?!

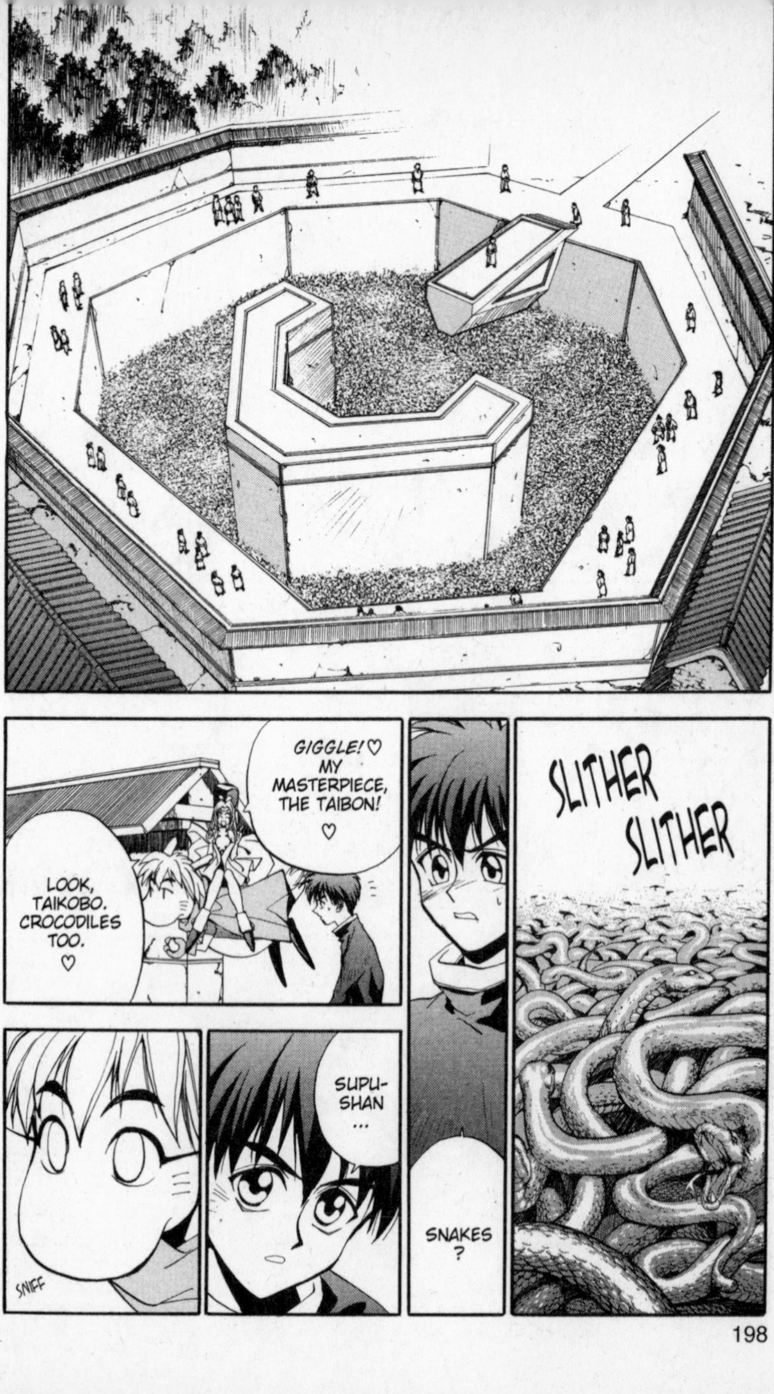
SLITHER SLITHER
SNAKES?
GIGGLE! ♡ MY MASTERPIECE, THE TAIBON! ♡
LOOK, TAIKOBO. CROCODILES TOO. ♡
SUPU-SHAN...
SNIFF

READ THIS WAY

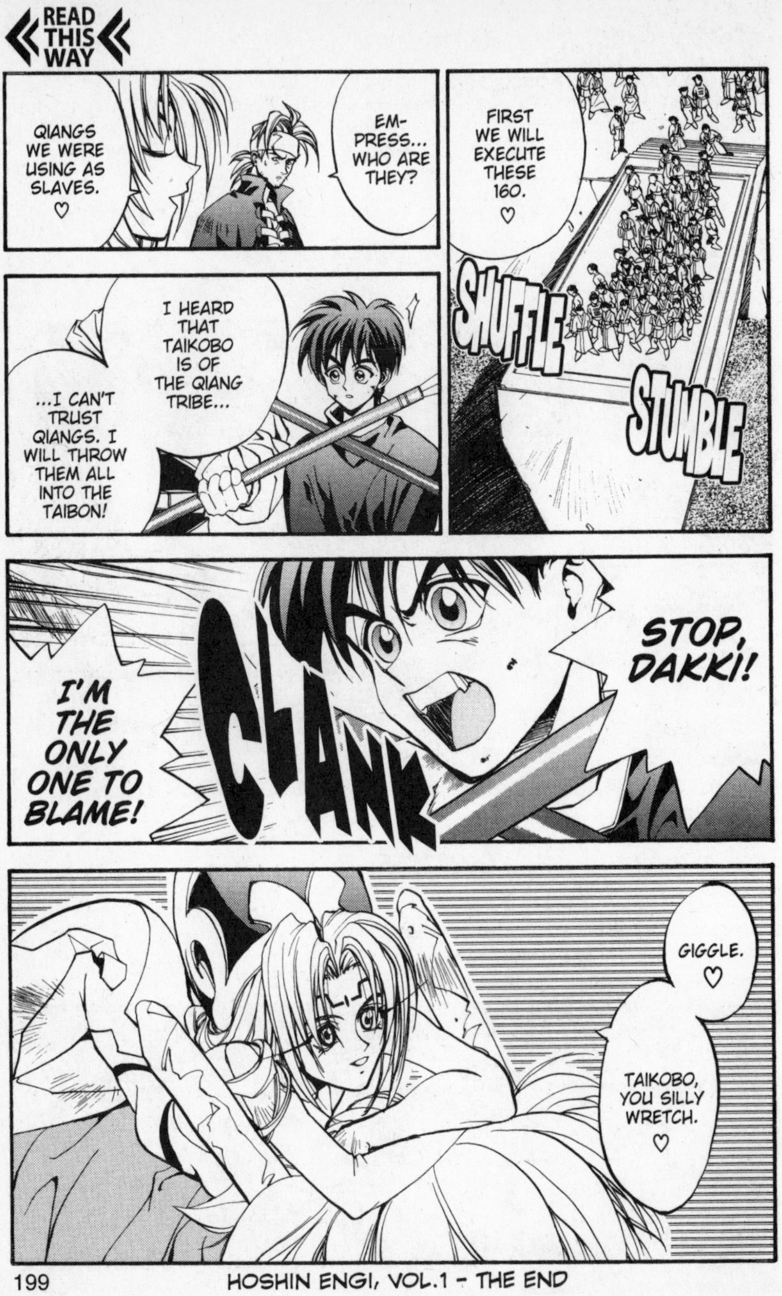
FIRST WE WILL EXECUTE THESE 160. ♡
SHUFFLE
STUMBLE
EM-PRESS... WHO ARE THEY?
QIANGS WE WERE USING AS SLAVES. ♡
I HEARD THAT TAIKOBO IS OF THE QIANG TRIBE...
...I CAN'T TRUST QIANGS. I WILL THROW THEM ALL INTO THE TAIBON!
STOP, DAKKI!
CLANK
I'M THE ONLY ONE TO BLAME!
GIGGLE. ♡
TAIKOBO, YOU SILLY WRETCH. ♡

Hoshin Engi: The Rank File!

You'll find as you read *Hoshin Engi* that there are titles and ranks that you are probably unfamiliar with. While it may seem confusing, there is an order to the madness that is pulled from Ancient Chinese mythology, Japanese culture, other manga, and, of course, the incredible mind of *Hoshin Engi* creator Ryu Fujisaki.

This glossary has been compiled by Viz as a guide for terms used in *Hoshin Engi*. It did not appear in the Japanese edition. Where we think it will help, we give you a hint in the margin on the page the name appears.

Japanese	Title	Job Description
武成王	Buseio	Chief commanding officer
大諸侯	Daishoko	Great feudal lord
軍師	Gunshi	Military tactician
北伯侯	Hokuhakuko	Lord of the north region
上大夫	Jotaifu	Court ranking similar to "Lord"
南伯侯	Nanhakuko	Lord of the south region
宰相	Saisho	Premier
西伯侯	Seihakuko	Lord of the west region
総兵官	Soheikan	A military rank, in command of soldiers at places like forts where armies are stationed
太師	Taishi	The king's advisor/tutor
東伯侯	Tohakuko	Lord of the east region

Hoshin Engi: The Immortal File

Also, you'll probably find the hierarchy of the Sennin, Sendo and Doshi somewhat complicated. Here, we spell it out the easiest way possible!

Japanese	Title	Description
道士	Doshi	Someone training to become Sennin
仙道	Sendo	Used to describe both Sennin and Doshi
仙人	Sennin	Those who have mastered the way. Once you "go Sennin" you are forever changed.
妖孽	Yogetsu	A Yosei who can transform into a human
妖怪仙人	Yokai Sennin	A Sennin whose original form is not human
妖精	Yosei	An animal or object exposed to moonlight and sunlight for more than 1000 years

Hoshin Engi: The Magical File

Paope (宝貝) are powerful magical items used by Sennin and Doshi. Sometimes they look like regular objects, like a veil or hat. These are just a few of the magical items, both paope and otherwise, that you'll encounter in *Hoshin Engi!*

Japanese	Magic	Description
打神鞭	Dashinben	Known as the God-Striking Whip. This is Taikobo's paope. Click! WHAM!
風火輪	Fukarin	Wind Fire Wheels that allow you to fly!
五火七 禽扇	Goka Shichikin'o	A fan made from the feathers of seven types of raptors that can discharge five types of flame.
火竜鏢	Karyuhyo	The Flame Boomerang
傾世元禳	Keisei Genjo	A veil that emits the "perfume of Temptation," protection against enemy attacks.
乾坤圏	Kenkonken	Shoots circles of copper at your target
金霞帽	Kinkabo	Keeps you sane! A golden hat that protects against psychological attacks.
混天綾	Kontenryo	The heaven silk can vibrate liquid quickly.
哮天犬	Kotenken	The Howling Dog can fly and be used as an attack paope.
九竜 神火罩	Kyuryu Shinkato	The Nine Dragon Basket of Fire is used to capture the enemy.
如意羽衣	Nyoi Hagoromo	Transformation veil
雷公鞭	Raikoben	The Thunder Whip
霊獣 / 霊珠	Reiju	There are different types of reiju, which basically means a "magical entity." For example, Taikobo's flying pal, Supu, is a reiju in the form of a flying beast. 霊獣 is kanji for spirit/soul + beast. Another type of reiju is the Soul Sphere, which can create a human paope out of an unborn child. 霊珠 is the kanji for spirit/soul + sphere.
三尖刀	Sansento	A three-pointed sword that can create shock waves.
紫綬羽衣	Shiju Hagoromo	Disguised as a purple veil, this paope allows the user to fly and emits a deadly poison.

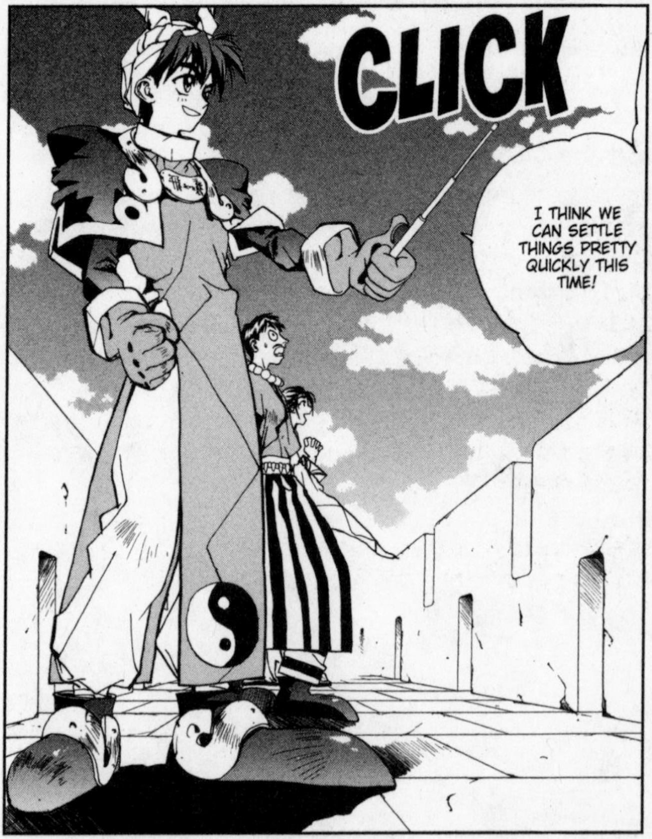
CLICK
I THINK WE CAN SETTLE THINGS PRETTY QUICKLY THIS TIME!

Coming Next Volume: Changes

Sparks fly when Taikobo meets a tough kid with an even tougher mission: revenge against his own family. And as he delves deeper into the Hoshin Project, Taikobo learns how little he really knows about his mission. What is his true destiny? He may find out sooner than he anticipated.

Available August 2007!

Read Any Good Books Lately?

Hoshin Engi is based on *Fengshen Yanji* (*The Creation of the Gods*, written in the 1500s by Xu Zhonglin) one of China's four classic fantastical novels of adventure, magic and mystery. The other three are *Saiyuki* (*Journey to the West* by Cheng'en Wu, late 1500s), *Sangokushi Engi* (*Romance of the Three Kingdoms* by Guanzhong Luo), and *Shui Hu Zhuan* (*Outlaws of the Marsh*, by Shi Nai'an, mid-1500s).

Want to read these books? You can! They're all still in print, more than 500 years later!

These books are North American in-print editions only.

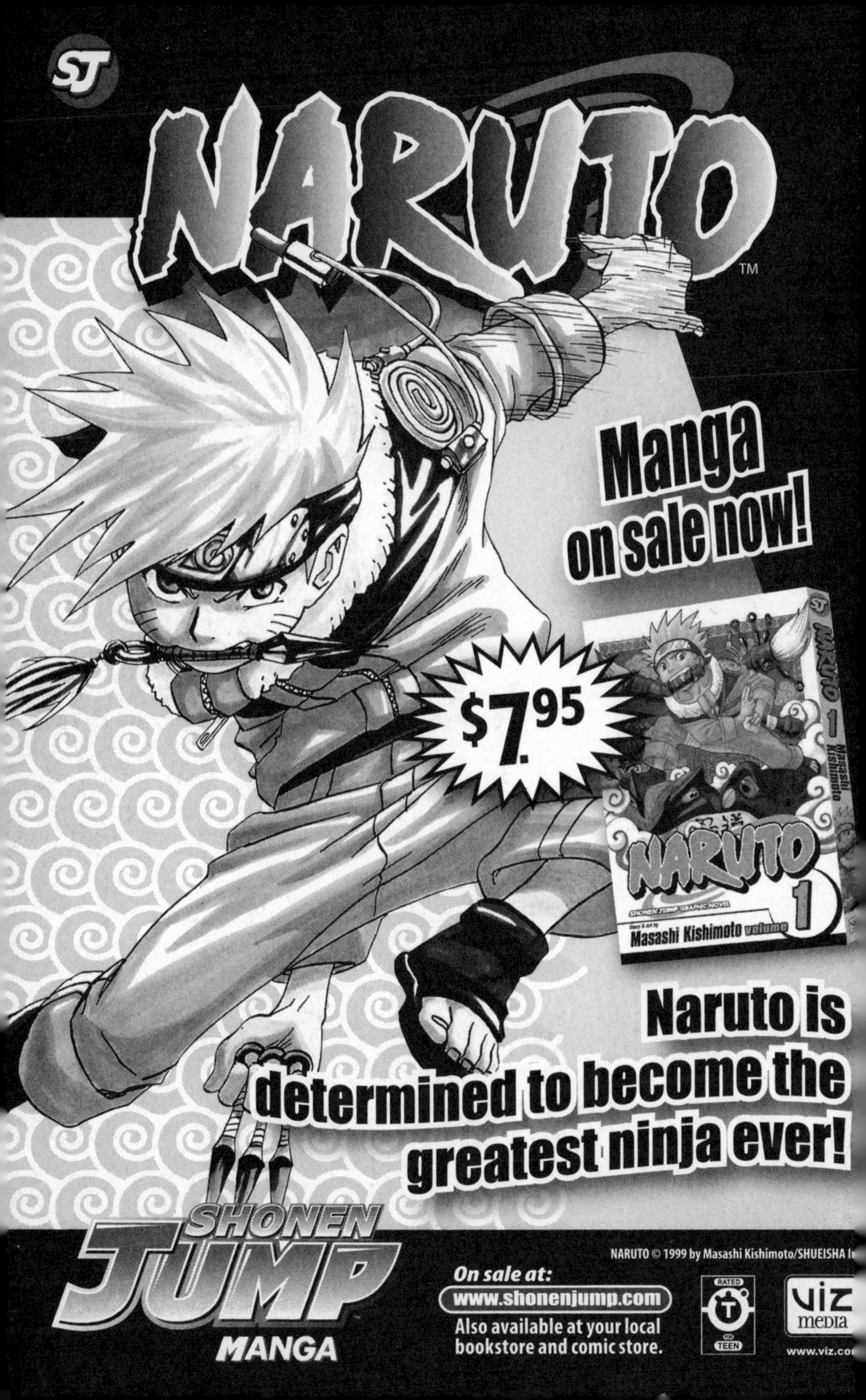
SJ
NARUTO™
Manga
on sale now!
$7.95
NARUTO 1
Masashi Kishimoto
SHONEN JUMP GRAPHIC NOVEL
Masashi Kishimoto volume 1
Naruto is
determined to become the
greatest ninja ever!
SHONEN JUMP MANGA
NARUTO © 1999 by Masashi Kishimoto/SHUEISHA I
On sale at:
www.shonenjump.com
Also available at your local
bookstore and comic store.
RATED T FOR TEEN
viz media
www.viz.co

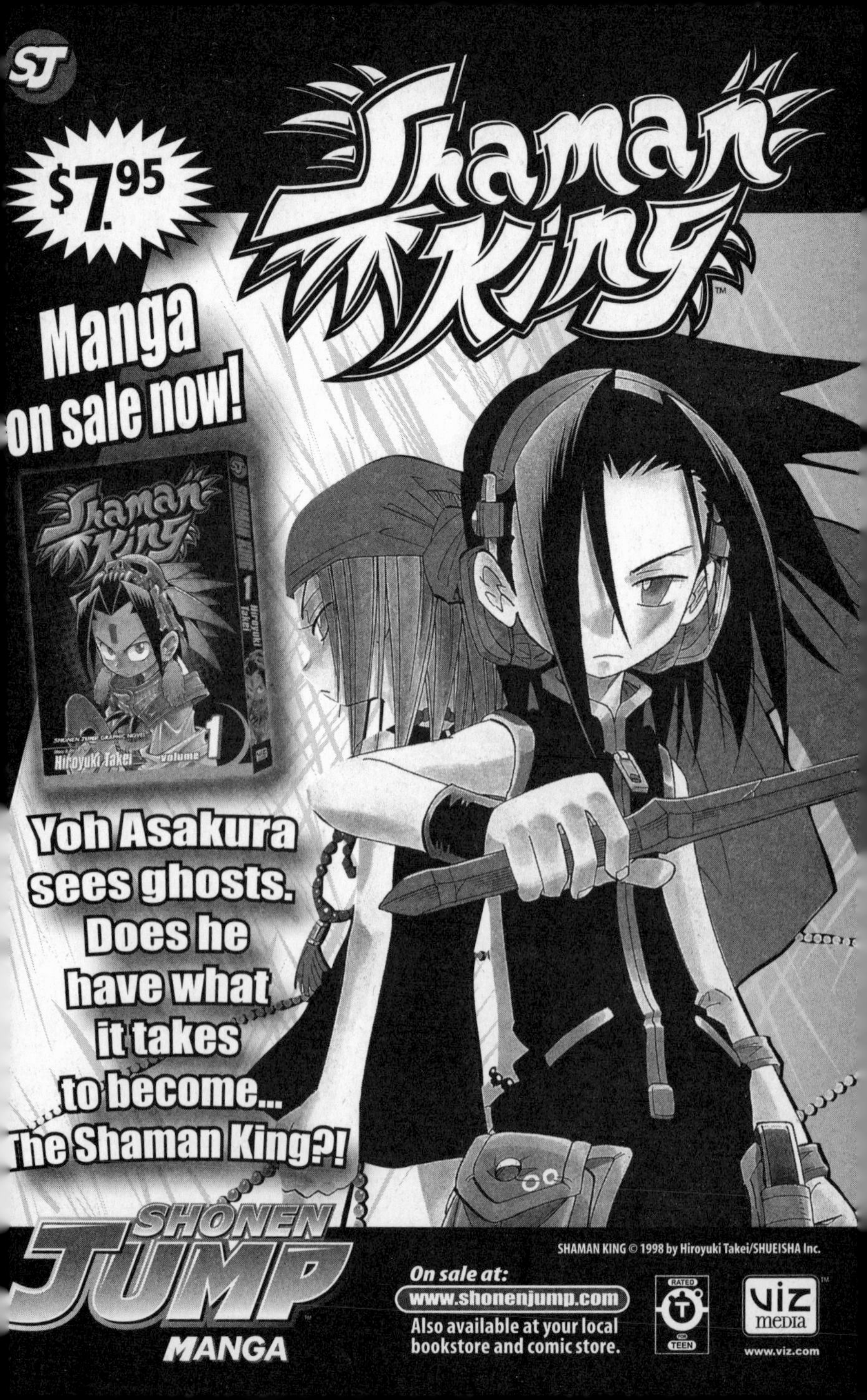
SJ
Shaman King
$7.95
Manga on sale now!
Shaman King
1
Hiroyuki Takei
volume 1
Yoh Asakura sees ghosts. Does he have what it takes to become... The Shaman King?!
SHONEN JUMP MANGA
SHAMAN KING © 1998 by Hiroyuki Takei/SHUEISHA Inc.
On sale at:
www.shonenjump.com
Also available at your local bookstore and comic store.
RATED T FOR TEEN
VIZ media
www.viz.com

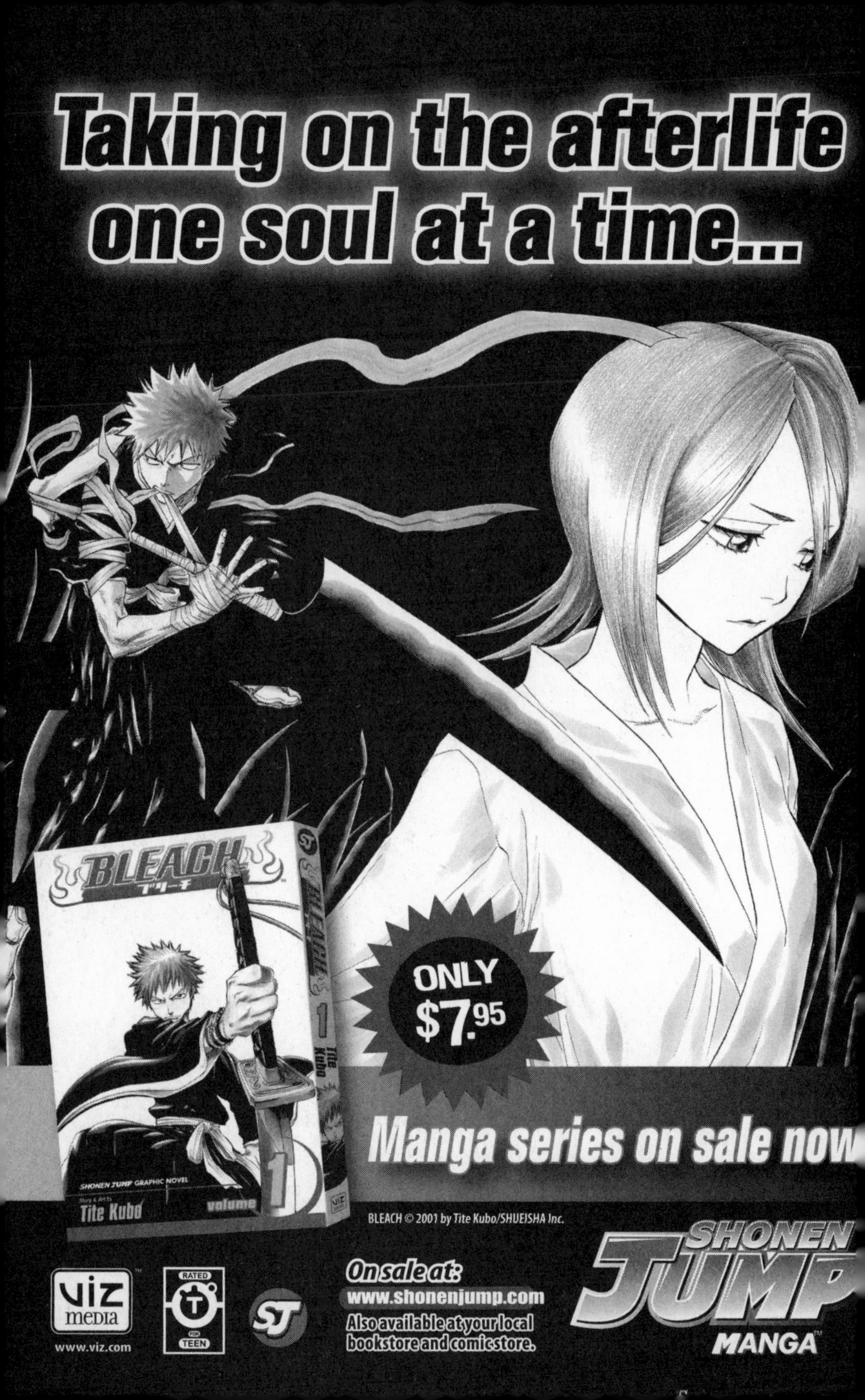

Taking on the afterlife one soul at a time...
BLEACH
ブリーチ
SHONEN JUMP GRAPHIC NOVEL
Story & Art by
Tite Kubo
volume 1
ONLY $7.95
Manga series on sale now
BLEACH © 2001 by Tite Kubo/SHUEISHA Inc.
viz media
www.viz.com
RATED T FOR TEEN
SJ
On sale at:
www.shonenjump.com
Also available at your local bookstore and comic store.
SHONEN JUMP MANGA

Check us out
on the web!

www.shonenjump.com